SAVING the SUN

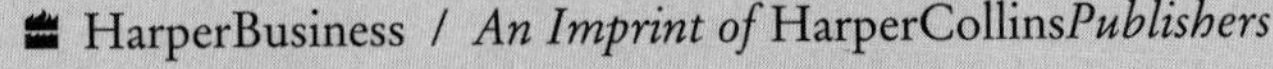
HarperBusiness / *An Imprint of* HarperCollins*Publishers*

How Wall Street Mavericks Shook Up Japan's Financial World and Made Billions

SAVING the SUN

GILLIAN TETT

 For information address HarperCollins Publishers Inc., 10 East 53rd Street, New York, New York 10022.

HarperCollins books may be purchased for educational, business, or sales promotional use. For information, please write Special Markets Department, HarperCollins Publishers Inc., 10 East 53rd Street, New York, New York 10022.

Book design by William Ruoto

All photographs courtesy of the author unless otherwise noted.

The Library of Congress has catalogued the hardcover edition as follows:

Tett, Gillian.
Saving the sun : how Wall Street mavericks shook up Japan's financial world and made billions / by Gillian Tett.
p. cm.
Includes bibliographical references and index.
ISBN 0-06-055424-X
1. Japan—Economic policy—1989– 2. Financial crises—Japan. 3. Bank failures—Japan. 4. Financial institutions—Japan. 5. Structural adjustment (Economic policy)—Japan. I. Title.

HC462.95.T48 2003
330.952'049—dc21
2003050933

ISBN 0-06-055425-8 (pbk.)

08 ❖/RRD 10 9 8 7 6 5 4 3

CONTENTS

Note to Reader vii

Foreword ix

Prologue xv

Chronology xxi

PART I 1

1. Samurai Bankers 3
2. Blocked Reform 18
3. Money Madness 29
4. The Trillion-Yen Man 44
5. The Bubble Bursts 54
6. Takahashi's Revenge 70
7. Onogi's Choice 81
8. The Swiss Gamble 97
9. Scapegoats and Seeds 113

PART II 127

10. An American Dream 129

11. "Cowboy" 146

12. Negotiations 166

PART III 183

13. Yashiro's Dream 185

14. Culture Clash 196

15. The Sogo Shock 208

16. Homma's Death 221

17. The Fight with the FSA 227

18. Stalemate 238

19. Success? 250

20. The Bad Loan Surprise 260

21. Saving the Sun? 274

Epilogue 281

Notes 295

Notes on Bad Loans 317

Sources and Bibliography 321

Acknowledgments 325

Index 331

NOTE TO READER

The guiding principle in this book has been to produce a narrative that makes the opaque world of Japanese banking relatively accessible to non-Japanese readers. So, in the interests of simplicity, the following approach has been taken:

- Japanese names have been written in the form that is most familiar to Americans (namely, with the surname second) rather than their usual Japanese usage.
- An approximate exchange rate of Y100 to the dollar has been used for most currency conversions. In practice, the rate has fluctuated dramatically in the last two decades, from Y150 to Y80, and at time of writing it stood around Y120 to the dollar. However, a rate of Y100 to the dollar gives a rough sense of value; the main exception in this narrative occurs in the immediate postwar years, when the rate was fixed at Y360 to the dollar.
- The book uses the American definition of trillion, i.e.: one thousand billion, and not the old European definition of trillion.
- The term "bad loan" has been used in a generic sense to refer to all non-performing loans; for a detailed discussion about terminology and ways of measuring bad loans see "Notes on Bad Loans," page 317.

FOREWORD

Exactly 150 years ago, in 1853, American warships forced their way into Japanese waters for the first time, ending the country's self-imposed seclusion. Their arrival left the Japanese impressed by American technology, but horrified by the destabilizing impact of the tall, hairy "outsiders." It also inspired mixed emotions in the interlopers: The first Americans spotted that Japan offered some exciting business opportunities, but also a baffling environment that lacked attributes they took for granted—a sense of individual identity and worship of the profit motive.

Many of these mutual impressions remain. Indeed, if anything, Japan's economy has become more, not less, baffling in recent years for Americans. A decade ago, the country seemed to have created an extraordinary economic miracle, rebuilding its economy with dazzling speed after the total destruction of World War II. Indeed, this "miracle" was *so* extraordinary that Americans feared that Japan was poised to overtake the U.S. and become the most powerful economy in the world. But then the miracle soured. Since 1990, the economy has stagnated, gross debt to GDP levels has risen toward 150 percent, deflation has taken hold to a degree not seen since the 1930s U.S. Depression, and the country's credit rating has been downgraded to the same level as Botswana's. Meanwhile, the Japanese banks have become engulfed in a tidal wave of bad loans, on a scale unprecedented in history.

The Japanese government estimates that this bad loan problem has topped one trillion dollars during the last decade, a sum the size of the entire British economy; private sector economists put the figure two or three times this. Either way, there is still no end in sight, which also puts Japan in a grim historical category of its own. Although plenty of other Western countries have experienced banking crises in the past, these have usually been resolved after a few years. Yet a full *thirteen years* after Japan's economy entered a downturn, the problem remains intractable: The total level of recognized bad loans keeps rising and the banks' capital resources have dwindled to a point where economists believe most large banks are now effectively insolvent. Thus far, Japan has managed to prevent a full-scale financial crisis by throwing money at the problem, but this is steadily becoming harder. With every year that passes, in other words, the risk rises that Japan's financial problems could explode, shaking markets across the world.

But why has this situation developed? Why does it drag on? And why has the Japanese government been so unwilling to do anything about it—even though it seems obvious to most Americans (and other outsiders) that something urgently needs to be done, to prevent a full-blown, potentially catastrophic crisis?

This book explores some of these questions, but from a slightly unusual point of view. In recent years there have been many admirable macroeconomic analyses of Japan's problems. But what most of these "top-down" discussions have lacked is any sense of the cultural context and political pressures that have played such a critical role in creating this mess. They tend to feel as if they have been written from 30,000 feet. And when they offer prescriptions for Japan's problems, these tend to ignore the issue of *incentives*—or, more specifically, the fact that the incentives driving Japanese behavior today are often different from what Americans might assume to be normal and universal.

This book tries to offer a different emphasis, by telling the banking tale from a deliberately "bottom-up" perspective. More specifically, this book tells the history of one specific bank that epitomizes both Japan's economic problems and the search for a solution to them—the Long Term Credit

Bank. This was once the ninth largest bank in the world, before it collapsed in 1998, with some $50 billion of bad loans (much of which had been concealed). The bank was then nationalized and sold to new owners—a group of American investors, who renamed it "Shinsei" and tried to introduce American management techniques as a bold new experiment in financial reform. In its own way, this experiment was as shocking for Japan's banking world as the arrival of the American warships 150 years ago: Until the sale of LTCB, no Americans had ever attempted to bash their way so deeply into Japan's financial world, let alone change the country's hallowed corporate ways. Shinsei, in other words, marks an extraordinary historical first.

The narrative falls into three parts: The first section tells the tale of LTCB and Katsunobu Onogi, its last president, which epitomizes the postwar Japanese economic system. Although some of this history may not seem directly relevant to the current Shinsei tale, I believe it is essential to look back at history to understand why this postwar system floundered and the incentives at work in Japan today. The second section is centered on Tim Collins, an American entrepreneur, who helped to organize a foreign investment consortium that acquired LTCB in 1999, and introduced a distinctly alien Wall Street philosophy into Japan. The last section is focused on Masamoto Yashiro, a Japanese businessman appointed to run the new bank, who has spent the past three years trying to carve out a new vision of reform, and blend the contrasting Japanese and American approaches to business. Each of these three men, in his own way, has been committed to trying to resolve Japan's woes; yet their approaches—and level of success—have varied wildly.

Two words of caution. First, I have deliberately focused the book on one particular bank, in an attempt to make the opaque world of Japanese finance seem a little more accessible. However, in describing the problems in LTCB before 1998, I do not mean to "pick on" Onogi or LTCB. On the contrary, it should be emphasized at the start that I believe Onogi to be a well-intentioned man, who has become a tragic casualty of a system he tried to defend. What makes the history of LTCB so desperately relevant to the situation today is that it epitomizes a pattern of behavior that was happening at all Japanese banks, including those that have survived, *and is still continuing to some degree*. LTCB is just a paradigm of a system.

Secondly, this book does not set out to present any comprehensive prescription for how to fix Japan's economic problems, let alone take a clear stand on the debate that obsesses many American economists: namely, whether a "solution" should focus first on supply issues (i.e., structural reform) or demand issues (i.e., monetary policy and/or devaluation and/or the savings surplus). Common sense would suggest that eventually some combination of both measures will be needed, but the demand issues are largely outside the scope of this book. However, what this LTCB-Shinsei saga does do is to offer a general moral about structural reform: namely, that if a country continually tries to avoid short-term pain by clinging to outworn institutions, and refusing to adapt to a changing world with some "creative destruction"—in Schumpeter's famous phrase—this can carry a terrible long-term cost, not just in terms of lost growth but also shattered lives. In a country with vast financial resources—like Japan—the price of procrastination can be concealed for a long time; but covering up the problems is likely to make the eventual cost of dealing with them even worse. Sooner or later, Japan's government needs to face up to the putrefying mess inside its banks, preferably as part of a broader, coordinated process of policy change. Above all else, Japan urgently needs to find a more flexible way of moving money around the economy, so that it can remove resources from outdated and unproductive companies and institutions, and channel them into more productive areas. If it does not, then Japan seems doomed to slow decline (at best) or a full-scale financial crisis (at worst); or, most perniciously a combination of the two. Either way it is a scenario that could be brutal, not only for Japan but for global investors.

In making this point, I do not mean to argue that Japan should blindly copy the Wall Street free-market approach to business. As recent corporate scandals indicate, the American system also contains flaws. And, as the tale of Shinsei shows, the Wall Street philosophy sits uneasily with many admirable Japanese values. Yet, copying the Wall Street model is not the only way for a country to fix a broken banking system or remove dead wood from the corporate world. Sweden, to name but one example, fixed its banking woes in the early 1990s partly by government intervention and it is possible to imagine that some variant of a more collectivist, state-driven reform model might be better suited to Japan. However, the essential moral of this book is this: *Whatever* system Japan uses to move capital around the economy—whether by bankers, bureaucrats, capital market investors, or some combination of these—it needs to find some method of doing this more effectively and flexibly, to let its economy *adapt* to changing circumstances and remove dead wood. The tragedy of Japan today is that it finds itself in a strange limbo position, where neither capital market investors nor banks nor bureaucrats are strong enough to force rapid change. As a result, the old mechanisms of corporate governance are breaking down, resulting in a debilitating paralysis.

Yet 150 years ago, Japan was mired in a similar mess, locked into economic stagnation and political paralysis. Back then, it was precisely the "shock" of the arrival of American warships—or the "black ships," as they are known—that prodded the Japanese government into dramatic policy change and built the foundations for the nation's extraordinarily successful economic revival in the late nineteenth century. It may be overoptimistic to hope that the same pattern will play out at Shinsei: namely, that the arrival of a small group of Wall Street adventurers will shock the whole banking system into reform. But if the history of LTCB shows what has gone wrong in Japan in the past, perhaps the saga of Shinsei might mark a step—albeit a tiny one—in a new direction.

In any case, it would be nice to hope so.

— Prologue —

THE KID FROM KENTUCKY

How did a kid from Kentucky end up buying one of the largest Japanese banks? It is a question that a lot of people might wonder.

—Tim Collins

Tim Collins eased into seat 1C on the ANA flight from New York to Tokyo next to a wizened Japanese man who had a distinguished air about him. Since the sixty-nine-year-old Japanese man was sitting in the first-class section where tickets cost more than $10,000 each, he was also clearly either rich or important—or both.

"Who's *that?*" Collins wondered.

It was a question that he often asked. For one of Collins's key talents in life was an ability to collect people's names and then use them later to his great advantage. It was a skill that had served him well in the forty-three years since he had been born in the South, to a family that had once run a tobacco farm in Kentucky. After an early career in a local auto plant he went to business school before winding up on Wall Street as an investment banker and then transforming himself into an expert on corporate restructuring. In 1995 he reinvented himself again as an entrepreneur. He created an investment firm called "Ripplewood," named after his family's old Kentucky tobacco farm, which made a living by buying distressed companies cheaply, restructuring them, and reselling them at a profit. Collins liked to describe this as a "private equity" or "restructuring" fund and he would claim—with solemn, evangelical zeal—that his business represented part of the genius of the American capitalist system. For what he maintained was that his fund cleaned out dead wood from the corporate world, in a process of "creative destruction," thus making the American economy more productive and efficient. "I believe in using capital as a catalyst for change," he liked to explain. To Collins's irritation, Ripplewood was sometimes also known as a "vulture fund," or a company that scavenged among corporations in distress.

Either way, Ripplewood rapidly expanded, gobbling up an auto parts company in Texas, an English-muffin maker in Ohio, and a refrigerator manufacturer in Illinois. Another acquisition was a frozen-pie company based in Hope, Arkansas. "And I have to say, we are the largest employer in Hope!" Collins liked to tell his investors, with a significant chuckle. "As in *Hope, Arkansas*." That was Collins's way of letting people know he had powerful friends in Washington, New York, and London. Hope, Arkansas. As in, the birthplace of Bill Clinton.

But, as Collins eased into seat 1C on the plane to Tokyo in September 1998, he was starting to think bigger than Arkansas—outrageously big, in fact. A few years earlier, when he had been trying to raise funds, Collins had approached Japan's mighty trading company, Mitsubishi Corporation. To his delight, Mitsubishi had taken a large stake in Ripplewood, and Collins had become curious about Japan. There was little in his background that made Tokyo a natural destination for Collins. He was a southern American boy—or a "kid from Kentucky," as he liked to say—who believed in the importance of the family, free markets, the Democratic Party and Baptist church. One of his favorite books was *Pilgrims in Their Own Land*, the story of how the Protestant ethic had infused American culture. Indeed, Collins had once considered becoming a minister, before he decided that his real talent in life was making money.

Though Japan was a very alien land, it fascinated Collins. From a distance, the place seemed bizarre. Back in the 1980s, like most Americans, Collins had been dazzled by Japan's power. But then everything had gone badly wrong and for an entire decade Japan's economy had stagnated. Since 1990, more than one *quadrillion* yen (Y1,000 trillion or $10 trillion) of Japan's wealth had been destroyed by the crash; the debt to GDP ratio had soared toward 150 percent, higher than anywhere else in the industrialized world, and the banks had become engulfed with more than Y100 trillion of bad loans. This was equivalent to a trillion dollars, a sum as large as the British economy. More baffling still—at least in Collins's eyes—was the way Japan's government had responded. It seemed self-evidently clear that Japan desperately needed restructuring. It had to remove the excess debt, get rid of its deadbeat companies, and revamp the business culture. In short, Japan urgently needed to do on a macro scale the type of "cleanup" process that Ripplewood performed whenever Collins purchased a company.

Such a plan may have seemed self-evident to Collins, yet the Japanese government had sat on its hands, year after year, seemingly unwilling or unable to tackle the situation. To Collins, that paralysis seemed not just foolish, but morally *wrong*. He believed—like most Americans—in the concept of action and individual responsibility. He also assumed that a key role of a government was to make its citizens as rich as possible.

Yet, Collins was also an optimist—and opportunist. He could see the great potential profits lurking in this strange situation in Japan. What was happening in Japan was not unique: Back in the 1970s, for example, American industry had also grown flabby, complacent and paralyzed, creating economic problems. The American private equity business had eventually emerged—and made private equity firms very rich—from the discovery of ways to reclaim exhausted and dilapidated companies. Although the concept of private equity was unknown in Japan and Tokyo had traditionally been hostile to foreign investors in general, Collins believed that Japan would become the next great theater for the drama of a business turnaround. No economy could stagger on in this type of self-destructive limbo forever, he reasoned. And when change came, this could create amazing opportunities for foreigners. A corporate shake-out was the only way that the economy could be truly saved from its current decline. Like generations of American pioneers before him, Collins believed it was time to head west.

The plane carrying Collins and his Japanese seatmate made its way slowly up over the Rocky Mountains, traveled high above the Alasksan waste, and began to crawl down over the ocean past the Aleution and Kurile Islands toward Japan. Half an hour before the flight landed in Tokyo, Collins caught the eye of the mysterious Japanese man. "So why are you going to Tokyo?" Collins asked, with the expansive friendliness of an American overseas. "What do you do?"

"I am retired," the Japanese man answered, in perfect English. Prodded, he explained in vague terms that he had once worked in banking and the oil industry—but now was living in London.

Collins's mind went into overdrive. A Japanese banker? Who worked in industry? With foreign connections? Who looked about sixty-nine? Suddenly it clicked and Collins could barely believe his luck.

"*You* must be Masamoto Yashiro!" he declared. The Japanese man nodded, surprised; he was not used to people recognizing him. "How do you know?"

Collins switched on the charm and reached for a file of papers. Before he had boarded the ANA plane in New York, Collins had asked his friends on Wall Street and in Washington if they knew of any Japanese businessmen who might be willing to help him bring the gospel of restructuring to Japan. Rick Bradock, the former head of Citibank—and another "friend" of Collins—had offered a particularly interesting name: Masamoto Yashiro, the former chairman of Citibank's own operations in Japan. The man sounded intriguing: Yashiro was a close friend of John Reed, the former chairman of Citibank, and had spent his whole life working for foreign firms, which meant that he was probably well versed with the concepts of restructuring and private equity, Collins reasoned. However, the elderly Japanese man was also connected to some of the most powerful politicians, businessmen, and bureaucrats in Japan. In fact, Yashiro was *so* well connected that Collins was unsure whether he would be able to persuade Yashiro to talk to him—an unknown American—at all.

But now Yashiro was sitting right next to him on the plane, in seat 1A. Fate—or God—seemed to be on Collins's side. "I have been looking for you, looking *everywhere!* You have this wonderful reputation!" Jubilantly, Collins waved his files at the Japanese man, pointing out Yashiro's CV.

Yashiro eyed the American man curiously. It was extremely odd, by Japanese standards, for a stranger to accost somebody on an airplane like this. Japan's culture is reserved and polite, everybody acts according to the twin guidelines of hierarchy and harmony. But Yashiro had spent decades of his life trying to bridge the vast cultural gulf that separated America and Japan and he knew Wall Street men were apt to do strange things.

"Why do you want to talk to me?" Yashiro asked.

Collins hastily made his pitch. He described what Ripplewood did and explained that he wanted to take its operations to Japan. After all, he pointed out, Japan urgently needed to reform its economy—and the country seemed to be opening up to new ideas and to the outside world.

Yashiro, like many men of his generation, was feeling rather downhearted about the state of his nation. As a child he had suffered the horrors of World War II and for the past five decades he had watched with immense pride as Japan had rebuilt itself after defeat. But now, in the 1990s, this miracle had lost its magic powers. Yashiro was convinced that the only way to fix these problems was to introduce radical reform into the corporate world by importing fresh ideas, vision, and energy. Indeed he believed that he had a duty to help promote this change. But Yashiro also knew that Japan was a consensus-based culture. And thus far change had been painfully, dishearteningly slow.

The arrival of some outsiders, like this chatty Mr. Collins, could possibly help to shake the country up. It was not such a strange idea. Yashiro knew that Americans had helped trigger change in Japan before. Most Japanese believed that the only reason why the country had embarked on its stunningly successful bout of industrialization in the nineteenth century, for example, was because American black warships had sailed across the Pacific and forced their way into Japanese waters, shocking the old shogun government with their military might. The arrival of the American soldiers in 1945 had acted as another "shock" that propelled the country toward its postwar economic miracle.

Moreover, Yashiro also knew that inside Japan itself there were some intriguing hints of change. Just before he had boarded the plane in New York, the newspapers had carried the news that Long Term Credit Bank, one of the country's most prestigious banks, was on the verge of collapse and the government was considering nationalizing the bank before selling it to new owners, perhaps even Americans. It seemed to be a shocking development. Yashiro knew LTCB—and its president Katsunobu Onogi—relatively well from his days at Citibank; he figured that the bank's history epitomized everything that had gone wrong with the Japanese corporate system in recent years. The bank was, after all, a cornerstone of the postwar financial world, once the ninth largest bank in the world. Just a few years earlier, it would have seemed inconceivable that the government should sell it.

"Will you have dinner with me?" Collins eagerly asked, as the plane finally landed at Narita airport in Tokyo, after its fourteen-hour journey. Collins desperately needed a Japanese ally to help him realize his dreams. Warily, Yashiro agreed to meet Collins again. He was far from sure that he wanted to work at Ripplewood. But he always loved discussing what was wrong with Japan's economy—and what could be done to fix it. *It's just a dinner; there is no commitment*, Yashiro thought.

It was only later that he realized that the plane ride was the starting point of one of the strangest financial experiments ever seen between Tokyo and Wall Street; a journey that would eventually pull Collins and Yashiro into the tangled history of LTCB and deep into the thorny question of what had gone wrong with Japan's banks—and what might be done to fix them.

CHRONOLOGY

1853: American warships force their way into Japanese waters triggering the Meiji Restoration.

1897: The Nippon Kangyo Bank is created by the Japanese government to help Japan's "catch up" with the West.

1941: Japan enters World War II.

1945: Japan is defeated by America and the U.S. military administration takes control.

1952: The United States hands power back to a Japanese government. The Ikeda council draws up a postwar financial plan, including the creation of the long-term credit bank system.

In December the Long Term Credit Bank is created out of part of Nippon Kangyo Bank.

1953: Japan's period of high economic growth—the "miracle"—starts.

1961: LTCB moves to a new headquarters in Otemachi; its business booms.

1968: Japan's economy grows so fast that its output of goods and services surpasses that of West Germany and every other capitalist country except America.

1973: The oil shock slows growth; LTCB steps up its overseas expansion.

1975: Japanese government starts to create a bond market in Japan, effectively undermining the old LTCB system.

1985: LTCB draws up a reform plan calling for the bank to move away from traditional lending to new investment banking businesses; it is blocked by vested interests.

The yen strengthens after the "Plaza accord." Japan's asset price "bubble" becomes entrenched.

1987: American stock markets crash; the Bank of Japan cuts rates, fueling Japan's bubble.

1989: The Nikkei 225 hits a peak of almost 40,000 and Japan's share of world GDP reaches 9 percent.

LTCB is ranked ninth largest in the world by asset size, with a market capitalization several times that of Citibank.

1990: The Nikkei plunges 40 percent after the Bank of Japan tightens interest rates at the end of 1989. The real estate market starts to slip. It is estimated that 80 percent of bank lending is directly or indirectly linked to real estate.

1993: LTCB finally moves to a lavish "bubble era" headquarters building.

The LDP temporarily loses power for the first time, amid popular unease with the end of the economic miracle; growth slows sharply.

1995: Government uses public money to rescue Tokyo Kyowa and Anzen, the first such step in Japan since World War II. The ensuing scandal forces the LTCB president to resign.

1996: MoF inspection of LTCB finds about Y4 trillion ($40 billion) of nonperforming loans (NPLs); this is covered up.

Ryutaro Hashimoto, Japan's prime minister, unveils the "Big Bang" reforms to make the Tokyo markets "free, fair, and global." The Japanese economy appears to be recovering.

Spring 1997: Japanese government tightens fiscal policy, pushing the economy back into recession; Nippon Credit Bank almost collapses but is rescued.

Summer 1997: Asian financial crisis starts.

Autumn 1997: The financial system experiences its first serious turmoil and Hokkaido Takushoku, Sanyo Securities, and Yamaichi collapse.

Spring 1998: The Japanese government creates its first rescue package for the banks, injecting around Y1.8 trillion ($18 billion) into the largest banks; it admits that NPLs have reached more than Y60 trillion ($600 billion); a new Financial Supervisory Agency is founded to oversee the banks.

Summer 1998: The Asian financial crisis intensifies; the Americans intervene to support the yen and ask the Japanese government to resolve the banking problems and bad loans.

Rumors about LTCB's problems trigger a share price collapse.

Autumn 1998: Americans intensify pressure for Japan to produce new banking measures; Japan finally produces a new Y60,000 billion safety net to support the banks. LTCB collapses and is nationalized, as a gesture of reform. NCB is nationalized soon after.

Winter 1998: The government appoints Goldman Sachs to find a new owner for LTCB.

Spring 1999: Renault effectively takes control of Nissan, the first deal of this size seen in Japan's corporate world.

Alliances accelerate between foreign and Japanese companies.

Summer 1999: IBJ, Fuji, and DKB announce that they are merging to create Mizuho, the world's largest bank by asset size. Subsequently, alliances are announced between Sumitomo and Mitsui (Sumitomo-Mitsui), Bank of Tokyo Mitsubishi and Mitsubishi Trust (MTFG), Tokai and Sanwa (UFJ). This creates four "megabanks."

Autumn 1999: Japanese government announces that LTCB is to be sold to the Ripplewood group, using the controversial "put."

Spring 2000: Ripplewood takes control of LTCB; Yashiro is appointed president. The Nikkei rises above 20,000; foreigner investors buy Y10,000 billion ($100 billion) Japanese shares in hopes of policy reform and economic recovery.

Summer 2000: The bank changes its name to Shinsei.

Sogo asks Shinsei for debt forgiveness; Shinsei gives the loans back to the government, leading to political uproar.

Autumn 2000: NCB is sold to a consortium of Japanese and foreign investors and renamed Aozora. Homma, its president, is found dead.

Spring 2001: Japan's economy starts to tip into a new recession, the third since 1990. Deflation becomes entrenched.

Junichiro Koizumi, a self-styled "reformer," unexpectedly becomes prime minister.

Shinsei embarks on a new attempt to clean up its loan book. This sparks bitter political controversy.

Summer 2001: Relations between the FSA and Shinsei become tense.

The FSA comes under growing international criticism for its failure to recognize the scale of banking problems.

Autumn 2001: Shinsei is reprimanded by the FSA. Yashiro is dragged into parliament yet again.

Spring 2002: The Nikkei tumbles below 10,000 as hopes fade of policy change. Fears of a new financial crisis mount, but the Japanese establishment props the markets up.

Summer 2002: Shinsei starts to make progress in cleaning up its loan book. It unveils net profits of Y60 billion ($600 million) in its second year of operations.

Autumn 2002: The Bank of Japan unexpectedly announces a plan to buy equities from the banks. The government appoints Heizo Takenaka as Financial Services minister and he launches a new bank reform plan.

Winter 2002: Takenaka's reforms trigger bitter opposition and are mostly emasculated.

Japan's debt to GDP rises to around 140 percent; its credit rating is downgraded to the same level as Botswana.

Spring 2003: The Nikkei 225 closes the fiscal year end below 8,000, its lowest level for twenty-one years, intensifying strains in the financial system. The four "megabanks" survive by issuing Y2 trillion ($20 billion) in new capital, but the dilution triggers a collapse in the banks' share prices, worsening their fundamental problems. The government creates the Industrial Revitalization Corporation, allegedly to "clean up" bad loans. Shinsei's "put" option runs out. The bank reveals that it has cut its bad loan ratio from 30 percent to 5 percent. It posts net profit of almost Y53 billion ($530 million), its third year of profitability.

Summer 2003: Mizuho posts Y2.4 trillion ($24 billion) loss for FY 2002, a record for Japan's corporate sector, due to falling share prices and bad loan writeoffs. The other "megabanks" also record large losses. There is little sign of any significant decline in the bad loan total.

Japan posts its fifth consecutive year of deflation; ten-year interest rates hit a record low of 0.5 percent. The Nikkei falls to new twenty-year lows, well below 8,000.

PART ONE

— *Chapter 1* —

SAMURAI BANKERS

After the war we had a system that was really a type of socialism under the disguise of capitalism. The bureaucrats directed everything, in a wise way, and we all accepted that and worked together very hard. The system worked well for a few decades.

—Yoshiyuki Fujisawa, former chairman of IBJ

In the evening of June 8, 1999, the Tokyo police telephoned Katsunobu Onogi at his house. "Tomorrow we are going to arrest you," the caller said politely, "please take care to be ready!" Staging the arrest so everything could be done in the proper fashion, the police asked Onogi to suggest a convenient location. Japan is clearly not a country that leaves room for surprises.

Nor was Onogi surprised. As he put down the telephone, part of him felt relieved. He was grateful that the police did not plan to drag him away in a disorderly fashion. At the age of sixty-three, Onogi had spent his entire life behaving with dignity and he had absolutely no intention of going to prison without being properly attired in the suit and tie that was the badge of a Japanese "salaryman." The possibility of such shame appalled him.

At the same time, Onogi was terrified, too. Even with the correct clothes—and with all the perfect etiquette—prison was a frightening place. Onogi had always been an intellectual and methodical man. He wore large, bookish glasses and an impassive expression on his square face, broken only by a tense half smile that turned down at the corners of his mouth. Whenever he faced a problem, he liked to scour history books for answers and in the weeks leading up to his arrest, Onogi had furtively peeked into bookstores to see if there was any guide to what a middle-aged man should do in prison.

Alas, there was no way to bone up on the ordeal ahead. Nor had Onogi's professional career given him any idea of what to expect in jail. Onogi could scarcely have imagined that he would share the fate of a common criminal. He had spent his whole life believing that he was a member of the *elite*, a respectable man who did things right, according to Japanese ideas of duty. He had slaved for forty years of his life in Long Term Credit Bank, one of Japan's most prestigious banks, where he had risen to become president. Normally, such service would have guaranteed Onogi a comfortable retirement. Holidays in Hawaii; rounds of golf; group trips with former colleagues to Japan's hot springs; the satisfaction of knowing that he had served his country well. That was how most sixty-three-year-old Japanese bankers lived.

But somehow it had gone horribly wrong for Onogi. LTCB had collapsed with almost $50 billion of bad loans, engulfing Onogi and his employees all in a shame that was too much for some of the most senior LTCB bankers to bear. A few weeks earlier, fifty-nine-year-old Takashi Uehara—the man who was expected to succeed Onogi as LTCB president—also received a telephone call from the police warning that his arrest was imminent: Uehara and the other LTCB managers were accused of hiding the bank's bad loans. Uehara decided to commit suicide. Once the Japanese believed that the correct way to kill oneself was to slash the stomach open with four precise strokes of a sword, letting the guts spill out, a method known as *seppuku*. Nowadays, that was deemed "selfish," since it created a bloody mess that needed to be cleaned up. Consequently, when executives committed suicide in the 1990s, they usually hung themselves in an anonymous hotel—to spare their family "shock." Uehara had always been a stickler for etiquette: He checked himself into a little suburban hotel and hanged himself, leaving a note on the table for Onogi and the other LTCB bankers. It said: "I am so sorry."

Onogi, however, did not want to kill himself. He considered it his duty to suffer his shame alive—to "endure the unendurable," as the Japanese emperor had described the American conquest after World War II. So, he fixed his mind on cheerful things. He reflected on an Italian film he had just seen on television about a concentration camp in World War II, called *Life Is Beautiful*. Onogi liked the title, and he desperately tried to convince himself that life could be beautiful. "Life is beautiful!" he told himself. "Life *is* beautiful."

He also resorted to his favorite mental survival trick: He imagined that he was looking down at himself from far outside his own body, as if he were an academic writing one of the sweeping pieces of history that he loved to read. Onogi had always found that trick comforting. It seemed to put life into perspective; to give a broader dimension to his own, little fate; to give a meaning to the terrible events that had engulfed LTCB. It was, he sometimes admitted with a dry chuckle, a very *strange* tale—not just for him, but for Japan.

And it seemed to be getting stranger, with every year that passed.

For Onogi, the LTCB story had started almost exactly four decades earlier, on April 1, 1959, a time when the pink cherry blossoms were blooming in Tokyo. On that day he turned up at the bank, as a fresh young graduate for his first day at work. "Onogi Katsunobu here!" he declared to an official, with a bow, using his surname first in the Japanese manner. He was wearing a suit and tie back then as well. But it was an ill-fitting, cheap, dark blue outfit, identical to the suits that all the other new graduate trainees wore. Fourteen years earlier Japan's economy had been smashed to pieces in World War II. So the bank had assumed that the new trainees would be too poor to afford to buy their own suits, since these cost Y30,000 ($84) each, or three months' average wages, so they doled out matching outfits to the graduates for free.

Onogi could have worn his own suit for his first day at work, if he had wanted. His ancestors had been "samurai"—literally, "those who serve," or a privileged warrior class with a strong code of honor—who served Lord Maeda in the Kanazawa region of northwest Japan. During Japan's bloody revolution of the mid-nineteenth century, when the country's traditional shogun system was overturned and the samurai disbanded, some of his relatives had fought on the losing side and later committed suicide by *seppuku*. But Onogi's father and grandfather had come to Tokyo, and, like thousands of other ex-samurai, laid down their swords and turned themselves into civil servants. Onogi's father rose to a senior position in the local Tokyo government and bought a plot of land in the Aoyama area, later one of the most chic sections of Tokyo, where Onogi was born.

During World War II, the family home burned to the ground when American B-29 bombers created a firestorm in Tokyo by dropping incendiary bombs from low level. Onogi, a terrified nine-year-old child, watched the destruction. He never forgot the horror of that night. The family survived and after the war they retained enough wealth to send him to school and the elite Tokyo University, where Onogi chose to study agricultural economics. "I was interested in history and before the industrial revolution in Japan, agriculture was the economy," Onogi later explained. He spent much of his time playing tennis at the university's prestigious *Akamon* ("Red Door") club, named after the traditional Japanese gate on campus. Onogi vaguely presumed that after graduation he would work in the government bureaucracy, like his father. But the elder Onogi happened to have a former classmate who was the president of LTCB, who suggested that Onogi come to the bank instead. Onogi knew little about banks. Indeed, like much of Japan's elite, he had always considered commerce rather distasteful: The old culture of the samurai respected pure, ascetic lives. "At that time the Japanese economy was very stagnant and there were not many jobs around," Onogi said. "Banks were one of the few places hiring graduates." Onogi reasoned that bankers and bureaucrats had similar jobs, since both seemed destined to serve the nation as it recovered from the war. "I was attracted to LTCB," he said, "because it was helping to rebuild industry."

Jobs may have been scarce but the Onogis were still better off than most. Just before Onogi started work, his proud father took him to the tailor to buy a smart new suit.

Yet for his first day of work Onogi wore his nasty company uniform anyway. Japan was not a country where anybody ever wanted to stick out. Before World War II Japan had been a country riddled with social hierarchy, with the divine emperor at the peak. But when the Americans had taken charge, they had tried to impose new concepts of democracy and equality. Now everybody wished to appear middle class. So Onogi arrived at the shabby building next to Tokyo station where the bank was located, and filed obediently into a hall with the other, identically dressed new recruits, to listen to their president, Iwane Hamaguchi, address them. If they had been born a decade earlier, the men would have been conscripted into an army, wearing a uniform with imperial symbols; instead, they were "salarymen," dressed identically to fight for Japan's economic power.

"Welcome!" Hamaguchi declared, in a brief speech that explained that the new bank was now dedicated to support the industrial growth of Japan. "*Gambatte*—work hard and overcome!"

"We understand! We will work hard!" the graduates declared, with a deep bow, standing in a neat line. Onogi felt rather excited.

LTCB was considered a prestigious institution, a pillar of the economic system. The bank traced its origins back to the Meiji era of the late nineteenth century—a period when Japan's government had decided to end its previous, self-imposed isolation from the rest of the world—and was frantically scrambling to industrialize its economy, to "catch up" with the West. In the Meiji era, as in the post–World War II era, the government embarked on this task with the same "catch-up" tactics: It sent young bureaucrats overseas to study the foreigners' systems, copy the best ideas, and then bring them back to Japan. One of these emissaries, Masayoshi Matsukata, a government bureaucrat, visited Europe and was very impressed by the "Crédit Foncier" idea in France, whereby specialized banks provided credit to agriculture and industry. When Matsukata was appointed finance minister in the 1890s, he established the "Nippon Kangyo Bank" to act as a Japanese version of these "Crédit Fonciers." The bank would raise funds by issuing bonds, and then use these funds to make cheap loans to agriculture and small business ventures. The idea spread, and soon afterward two more banks were created with similar structures: Industrial Bank of Japan, and Hokkaido Takushoku, a smaller regional group.

For four decades, these banks quietly flourished. They survived the financial turmoil that battered Japan in the 1920s and the global depression of the 1930s. Later, when Japan started building an Asian empire, Industrial

Bank of Japan played a key role in financing the military industrial complex. Nippon Kangyo Bank developed a large lending presence in the Japanese colony that is now modern Taiwan. But after Japan lost the war in 1945, IBJ shriveled and Nippon Kangyo Bank was reduced to financing a hotchpotch of state initiatives, such as providing a Y30 million ($80,000) loan to create brothels to serve the incoming American troops. Many observers presumed that IBJ and NKB would eventually be dissolved, since all the banks' reputations had been so tarnished by their role in World War II.

In 1952, IBJ and NKB were suddenly given a reprieve. As the American military administration was leaving Japan, Hayato Ikeda, the new finance minister, declared in parliament one day: "We need to consider new ways of financing our economy!" More specifically, Ikeda called for a council to discuss a crucial question: What type of financial sector should a newly independent Japan use to rebuild its country? One based around stocks, bonds, banks—or something else?

The choice was not obvious. Until the 1930s, the Japanese financial system looked similar to the systems in use in the United Kingdom and United States at the time. Companies raised part of their finance from banks, but also tapped the capital markets by issuing bonds and equities, and investors and other free-market forces played a powerful role in the financial world. Down in Osaka—historically the commercial center of Japan—there had been a long history of market trading. Then, with the rise of a Japanese military government in the 1930s, the army decreed that most of Japan's financial flows should pass through banks, which were easier to control than anonymous markets, and the freewheeling market culture of Japan's commercial class wilted in the face of heavy state control.

With the defeat and discrediting of the militarists in World War II, some U.S. officials initially wanted to rip apart the bank-centered financial system. Their rationale was simple: The banks had supported the rise of the military government and shared some of the blame for the war. These reformers had hoped that free capital markets would, in turn, support the development of democracy in Japan. However, by the time that Ikeda's financial policy council convened in 1952, the Americans' initial burst of enthusiasm for free markets and democracy had been replaced by hard-nosed strategic concerns. With the United States preoccupied by its cold war with the USSR—not to mention the heated fighting in nearby Korea—the American planners shifted their attention from reforming the financial and political culture of Japan to insuring a reliable source of industrial supplies from a stable Japanese economy. And Ikeda's government believed that the best way to achieve this was to retain most of the wartime financial controls. Capital was extremely scarce in the '50s and Ikeda believed that it was essential to channel Japan's scarce financial resources to the industries that could quickly rebuild the economy again. Relying on stock and equity markets seemed risky, Ikeda argued, since the government might have different priorities from individual investors; it would be better to use the banks to push money around the economy, since this could be *controlled*.

Thus, in the summer of 1952, the Ikeda council decreed—with America's tacit support—that banks, not capital markets, would henceforth be the main source of finance in the economy. The government did not abolish the idea of capital markets entirely: The Tokyo Stock Exchange was reopened. But, in Japan, there was a unique function for shares. They were not usually considered speculative or investment instruments, but as means for companies to solidify their ties to each other through a system of interlocking ownership known as "cross shareholding." And these ties linked groups of companies into specific corporate "families" or "tribes" that were commonly known as *"keiretsu."*

Into this system, Ikeda's government also mixed the old Meiji era idea of "specialized" banks—overlaid with legislation similar to the Glass-Steagall act in America that separated financial functions into different corporate entities. Instead of allowing each bank to offer a range of financial services, separate categories of financial institutions were allotted different tasks. Brokers were given the task of handling the equity markets; "city" banks served consumers, and made short-term loans to large companies; "trust" banks focused on asset management services; and "regional" banks served small customers. Meanwhile, Ikeda also created a brand-new category of bank as his pet idea to help revitalize Japan, called "long-term credit banks." These banks were authorized to provide long-term investment loans to "special priority" industrial sectors, such as steel or shipping. In prewar America and Japan companies usually raised these funds by issuing bonds to investors. However, Ikeda's theory was that a "long-term credit bank" should issue bonds *itself* to raise funds and then lend this money to companies, like the old Nippon Kangyo Bank—eliminating the need for corporate bond markets.

So, in 1952 each of the banks in Japan was told to choose what type of bank they would become. Hokkaido Takushoku became a "city" bank and Nippon Kangyo Bank split into two. Half its staff created a "city" bank, eventually known as Dai-Ichi Kangyo Bank; the rest formed one of Ikeda's specialized banks, with his close support. Unimaginatively, Ikeda's pet was christened the "Long Term Credit Bank." IBJ, too, opted to become a long-term credit bank and a third bank of this type, Nippon Credit Bank (NCB), was created a few years later. Long Term Credit Bank was given some office space in a library annex of the Bank of Japan—the best accommodation available at the time in bomb-flattened Tokyo—and started operations with a few dozen staff just as the new year of 1953 got under way. It was the first full year of independence from the American administration—and later known as "Year One of the Japanese Economic Miracle."

Onogi spent the first year of his career feeling like a human photocopier. The fresh young graduates were usually assigned to a loan department, where they sat in rows quietly shuffling the paperwork necessary to lend money. Onogi's department was called "lending section number three," which served companies making electrical appliances and transport equipment—items in high demand due to the Korean War. The main role of the new recruits was to copy loan documents by hand. In America, the task was usually performed with carbon paper; however, Japan was too poor to waste funds on these luxuries. So the bankers sat in rows frantically writing. In winter, they huddled next to oil stoves or sat under futons because the bank could not afford central heating. In summer, they sweltered in temperatures of 100 degrees. LTCB, ever the paternal organization, provided light summer suits, but these fitted as badly as the winter attire—and itched.

Nevertheless, the young LTCB bankers had little time to complain; LTCB was a cog in a complex financial machine, which effectively converted short-term deposits by Japanese savers into long-term loans for industry—at a subsidized rate. Throughout the year, the three long-term credit banks (LTCB, IBJ, and NCB) would issue "debentures" or a five-year bond. Then, armed with this cash, the banks would extend cheap long-term loans to favored industrial companies. They rarely had any trouble in selling these debentures. The long-term credit banks were the only banks that enjoyed the privilege of issuing these five-year bonds and these securities were considered to be effectively government-backed. Moreover, when other banks bought debentures, the long-term credit banks usually later extended some of this money to the banks' related companies—creating, in effect, a financial merry-go-round. The idea was that the long-term credit banks provided *long-term* funds, supplementing short-term finance from other banks.

This meant that LTCB occupied a slightly unusual position within Japan's corporate structure. Before World War II, this corporate world had been very tribal in nature, dominated by large industrial conglomerates known as *zaibatsu* with names such as Mitsui, Mitsubishi, and Sumitomo. After the war, the Americans had briefly tried to break up some of these conglomerates. However, most of the old *zaibatsu* had reassembled themselves as corporate "families"—*keiretsu*—assembled around a bank and operated as tight-knit groups: Mitsubishi companies, for example, would always deal with other Mitsubishi names, and borrowed money from Mitsubishi Bank. But LTCB was one of the few institutions that straddled the different *keiretsu*, partly because it had no *keiretsu* of its own. It bought shares and lent money to different *keiretsu* and dozens of regional banks. Thus, by the time that Onogi started at the bank, LTCB was developing tentacles across the entire system—which could not be easily detached.

After his year as a human photocopier, Onogi moved a notch up the career ladder and became an assistant loan officer, covering a few small shipping companies. It made him a popular man. Week after week, a stream of company officials would visit Onogi and his colleagues at the bank and beg for loans. The lending officers would sift through the applications and work out which companies would receive funds—and which not.

Their lending decisions depended on two things. First, the bankers knew that they were supposed to be channeling their loans into companies of "national importance," which were initially defined by the government to be shipbuilders, power companies, steel, and coal mining. Later, other manufacturers, such as car companies, joined this list. Second, the bankers knew they should only give money to companies that were "viable." Unlike later generations of American bankers, Japanese bankers did not try to assess what was "viable" by looking at the financial returns a specific business *project* would produce. Nor did they look at the cost of money over time. Instead, they assumed that when they lent to a company, they created a relationship that would last for a long period. Thus, they tended to measure whether a loan was sensible by looking at the *entire* company, and its future prospects. And they considered that a company's prospects depended not simply on corporate statistics, but also on social contacts: companies with a web of reliable *keiretsu* allies would usually survive in the Japanese system, but companies without allies could easily die.

Thus, when the Japanese bankers looked at their money, they did not change the interest rate to reflect the risk of different customers, since it was the government that set the price of money. Asking weak customers to pay more for their money than strong customers was considered distasteful. And the concept of trying to use money to make *more* money, purely for its own sake, was also considered rather disloyal to the national interest. Money was seen as a means to an end, not an end in itself—and the end was the revival of Japan.

By the early 1960s, LTCB's business was growing so fast that it moved into a proper head office, in Otemachi, the financial district in central Tokyo near the hallowed Imperial Palace. It was a controversial choice of location. The site was next to a shrine dedicated to Taira no Masakado, a Japanese warrior who staged a failed rebellion in 940 and had his head chopped off. The head had supposedly then flown to Tokyo and was buried on that spot, beneath a statue of stone toads, and there were rumors that the site was haunted. Indeed, many Japanese were so terrified of Masakado's vengeful spirit that the Ministry of Finance had deliberately relocated its building away from the site in 1923—and when American occupation troops subsequently tried to build a car park on the spot, they were forced to drop their plans. LTCB did not appear to be entirely immune from the legend either. Soon after the move to Otemachi, several senior officials died—and local staff promptly blamed the bank leaders for failing to honor Masakado. In subsequent years, LTCB always took care to perform the proper rituals in front of the stone toads. Still, some bankers remained uneasy. "There is a *tatari*—curse—on our bank," they muttered, whenever any trouble hit.

As far as Onogi could initially see, however, LTCB was going from strength to strength. Japan's industrial "army" was booming on a diet of  cheap bank finance, import barriers, and artificially weak yen, that had been fixed by the outgoing American administration at a mere Y360 to the dollar. The economy was growing at a dizzy ten percent a year. By 1963 LTCB alone had poured several hundred billions of yen worth of funds into domestic manufacturing companies such as Toyota, Toray, Kawasaki Steel, Tokyo Electric Power, Bridgestone, and Toshiba—names that would soon become corporate giants. Better still, LTCB was starting to help some of these companies to look out, overseas. At the start of the 1960s, for example, Toyota approached LTCB asking for the bank's help. The carmaker wanted to purchase an American automatic assembly line, since the best equipment in the world for making cars at that time was found in the United States. Toyota did not have access to dollars because the government had imposed capital controls—and although the company had asked American banks for a loan, the foreigners had haughtily brushed off the request. Most American businessmen considered that Japan was too underdeveloped to make cars and too poor not to be considered a credit risk. LTCB—with the Ministry of Finance support—backed a loan application for Toyota with the American Exim Bank, the first of this kind. Toyota eventually got its assembly line, and started producing a new model of car, dubbed the "Publica," because it was intended to be a car for the "public," and American-sounding names were considered chic. For years afterward, when LTCB bankers saw a model pottering along, they would proudly declare: "That's one of *our* cars! It's made with *American* technology!"

Shortly after this success with Toyota, a senior manager wandered across to Onogi's desk and asked: "Do you want to go to a university to learn English?" The senior LTCB managers had realized that if their clients were looking overseas, the bank needed men who spoke languages and who understood how *gaijin*—foreigners—worked. Onogi jumped at the chance. Back in the late nineteenth century and early twentieth century, elite Japanese had often traveled overseas to absorb foreign ideas: Onogi's own grandfather, for example, had studied at the University of Michigan. However, between the early 1930s and late 1950s, this door had been shut.

Onogi was keen to prize it open again, since—like many men of his generation—he had a vague hope that the horrors of World War II could be wiped away with a newly "international" stance. He eagerly agreed to learn English at university in Tokyo and then was sent on a training course at Midland Bank, a British institution, in London. The idea was for Onogi to learn the strange ways of foreign bankers and bring their skills back to Japan—just as Matsukata, the finance minister of the 1880s, had tried to pinch *gaijin* ideas in the Meiji era. Other young LTCB bankers were also being sent off with similar magpie missions to learn financial skills in America, France, and Germany—just as Japanese manufacturers, like Toyota, were trying to copy foreign technical practices.

Onogi adored England. Though the swinging 1960s were not an entirely easy time to be Japanese in London. Some Japanese bankers were warned not to visit the northern town of Newcastle because many local men had died at the hands of Japanese in World War II, and it was feared that the local population might try to take revenge. Luckily Onogi lived in the southern county of Surrey, and spent his free time visiting concert halls, always rushing out before the *finale* to catch the last train home from London. He liked the culture of British merchant banking. In some ways, the City of London felt strangely comfortable to him—or more comfortable than the aggressive world of Wall Street he later saw. British banking was a small, cliquey club, dominated by men with aristocratic backgrounds, who considered it most distasteful to talk in public about money and—as in Japan—valued politeness, understatement, and tea.

Onogi followed his training course at Midland Bank with an internship at MHL, a British merchant bank owned by the American bank Manufacturers Hanover. There, he earned himself the nickname "Nobby," since Katsunobu was far too difficult for the British to remember. Onogi badly wanted to fit in. "I was very nervous, since like any young man I wanted to be accepted by the club," Onogi recalled. "But the members of MHL were very kind. It was perhaps the most exciting experience of my youth."

Then, LTCB decided to establish a branch office in London, and appointed Onogi to work in that. Tactfully, some of his colleagues hinted that it was time for him to find a wife—so Onogi, ever dutiful, rushed to comply. Elite families in Japan traditionally had arranged marriages, so Onogi was introduced to a woman who would make a suitable banker's wife: Yasuko. The courtship did not go entirely to plan. Onogi had presumed that he could wrap everything up with Yasuko in a few days, but she—like many women in postwar Japan—was not quite as conformist as her future husband. Her generation had watched Hollywood films and read American books, and had developed distinctly "modern" ideas about romance. Yasuko insisted on meeting Onogi several times to check him out. Onogi was taken aback by her need to get acquainted because it was delaying the process. As a young "salaryman" serving his bank, he reckoned that he had little time to waste. Eventually the young couple married and settled in a smart flat in Chelsea, a location that Onogi had identified—from careful research—as the part of London where bankers were *supposed* to live.

As always, Onogi wanted to make sure that he followed all the social rules quite correctly.

Years later, Onogi concluded that his stay in Chelsea had been the happiest time of his life. The young Onogis forged a happy marriage and quickly had two daughters. They went out of their way to cultivate British friends, reveling in their freedom from the LTCB headquarters and the rigid hierarchy of the corporate culture in Japan. Back in Tokyo, bankers were expected to dedicate their lives to the bank. They arrived early in the morning, left late at night, and spent most evenings and weekends socializing with their colleagues. Wives saw their husbands only rarely—and even at home, the hierarchies of the office often intruded. Many of the unmarried young LTCB bankers in Tokyo lived in communal dormitories owned by the bank. The company provided special flats for families as well, like army barracks. There the women interacted intensively, according to their husbands' different statuses. Some women loved this warm "family" feeling. Indeed, many of the wives had worked for LTCB as well, since large companies in Japan deliberately hired secretaries who would make suitable wives for their "salarymen," and senior officials arranged marriages for junior colleagues. However, for anybody who stepped out of line, the atmosphere could be oppressive.

But London was different. There the Onogis lived apart from their colleagues. They socialized as a couple, since in England wives were not expected to stay meekly hidden. Yasuko, who had a bubbly character, quickly learned to speak better English than her husband and started voicing opinions in public. She was delighted that her husband was not forced to spend every evening playing mahjong and drinking *sake* with his colleagues. Onogi also had plenty of free time to indulge his hobbies. Unusually for a Japanese man, he learned to cook some European dishes. He also feverishly read books, often in English. Indeed, back in university his professors had suggested that he become an academic, since he seemed more of a thinker than a doer. In London, Onogi happily roamed around secondhand bookshops, devouring European and American works by Weber, the German political scientist, John Milton, the English author, and Charles Lamb, the English essayist who had written about the dangers of financial speculation and asset bubbles back in nineteenth-century London.

Work also seemed exciting. Onogi's main job at the London branch was lending money to Japanese trading and shipping companies, who were starting to expand enthusiastically overseas. Onogi's second mandate was to develop ties with local bankers. Back in the mid-1960s, when Onogi had first arrived in London, most of the European and American banks had been utterly patronizing toward LTCB. Japan was considered to be backward and impoverished, and its financial system was isolated from the outside world by postwar capital controls. By the mid-1970s, American and European bankers had slowly realized that something extraordinary was unfolding in Japan: Companies like Toyota were exporting their cars; the economy was booming; Japan was no longer an impoverished state. On the contrary, some of the companies and banks seemed almost rich. Suddenly, names like LTCB not only commanded interest, but also a modicum of respect.

"We felt so excited about what we had achieved!" Onogi recalled, two decades later. "We all felt very proud." Just three decades after its terrible defeat, Japan was back on the world stage, together with its samurai bankers.

— Chapter 2 —

BLOCKED REFORM

It is true that all the main reasons for creating the long-term credit banks have disappeared . . . but we have resources which we think should be used to help the economy.

—Mamoru Sakai, LTCB president, in 1985

In the late 1970s, Onogi was sent back to Tokyo. First he was given a job as a general manager in the international section. Soon after, he moved to the corporate planning department, a distinct honor, since corporate planning was usually the most powerful department in Japanese companies. "Young Onogi-san looks as if he is heading to the top!" some of his colleagues began to say with a mix of admiration and envy. Japanese society placed harmony and consensus at the peak of its pantheon of virtues. But that didn't eliminate the universal human tendency toward gossip, resentment, and competition.

Onogi himself was not without his own inner strife. Privately he harbored twinges of unease about the state of LTCB. Soon after he arrived back at the bank, he was asked to produce a new memo for the senior management outlining the correct strategy for LTCB's international operations. In some ways, the bank seemed to be in a stronger position than ever before. The bank was awash with cash. Customers were scrambling to purchase the bank's debentures, and its loan book was at record levels, generating a rising level of interest income. All around the bank, the Japanese economy as a whole was booming. Between 1953 and 1970 the country had more than *tripled* its level of GDP per worker from $3,600 to $11,500—the fastest pace of growth that a major economy had ever seen. It was as if Japan had leapt from the 1990 economic level of India to 1990 South Korea, in just a decade or so's time. Better still, growth had continued, albeit at a slightly slower rate, through the 1970s. By the end of the 1970s, Japan's GDP per capita had reached 66 percent of America's; in 1955 it had been 21 percent. And Japan was beginning to aspire to American living standards as well: Japanese households were filled with shiny new televisions, refrigerators and tape players. LTCB's industrial clients were becoming corporate giants, churning out products at a dazzling speed, and selling them to the rest of the world. The little "publica" car Toyota had built with LTCB support now seemed passé and cheap. Toyota was not only using American machinery to build cars for Japan, it was also starting to selling cars *into America itself.* The pupil was challenging the master at its own game.

Yet, this very success also contained a dangerous risk for LTCB. During the 1960s and 1970s, bank lending in Japan had surged by about 11 percent a year, slightly higher than the pace of GDP growth, a trend that was not likely to continue, especially when companies like Toyota were making such big profits by the late 1970s that they were cash rich—meaning that they no longer needed to borrow as much money from the bank. Japanese companies were also becoming strong enough to contemplate—for the first time—raising money overseas, in international capital markets. This meant that they no longer needed the financial bottle-feeding of the old, self-enclosed Ikeda system.

At the same time, the internal mechanism of the system that had initially supported LTCB—and the other long-term credit banks—was starting to crumble. The price of money, in the first few years after World War II, had always been carefully controlled under a rigid plan set by the bureaucrats, not the markets. The anchor for this system was the Bank of Japan's discount rate. The banks lent money at a prime lending rate, fixed at a precise gap above the Bank of Japan interest rate. And the long-term credit banks sold their debentures to the retail and regional banks at an interest rate that was *always* 90 basis points lower than long-term prime lending rate—regardless of how many buyers wanted bonds. Depositors who placed money with banks were paid an interest rate set a little lower than the lending rate. It was such a precise pattern, the bankers often called it the "four-and-a-half-*tatami*-mats" system *(yo-jo-han-taike)*. In a Japanese house, rooms came in a variety of sizes, but none were smaller than four and a half tatamis, referring to the *tatami* rush mats used on floors. The metaphor was meant to convey the tiny margins between borrowing and lending, especially since the rush mats were always a regular size and laid out in a precise pattern on the floor.

Though rigidly enclosed and tightly controlled, the system worked relatively smoothly, like a well-calibrated engine. With interest rates determined politically and not by the laws of supply and demand, the system ensured the bank a profitable spread on any lending.

But what would happen, Onogi wondered, if lending stopped growing? Or the price of money was no longer fixed?

In the middle of the 1970s the Japanese government took the first steps toward creating a bond market. Starting in 1975, the Ministry of Finance began issuing Japanese government bonds to fund the national deficit. With this the Ministry allowed the interest rates in the secondary market to float and be set by investor demand. Later still in the late 1970s, the government grew even more comfortable with the rule of financial markets and began to permit more Japanese companies to issue bonds and removed a few more interest rate controls. Suddenly part of the system for pricing money was *not* fixed: a small, dissonant element had been introduced into the system, like a piece of grit in a machine. Japanese bankers discovered that the lines on the tatami mat could move. And although this "free-market" element was still very small, it threatened to wear away at the balance in the system, undermining the banks' spreads. Worse, if companies could meet their long-term financing needs by issuing bonds, they wouldn't need traditional banks. LTCB, like the other long-term credit banks, was becoming redundant. "You know, I think we are rather an artificial bank," Onogi started to tell to some of his friends. "I am really not sure how long we can continue like this."

It never occurred to Onogi that it might be sensible to abolish the bank. Banks and bureaucracies were considered sacred in Japan and the concept of voluntarily letting an institution die—or allowing free market competition to kill it off—was an alien one. Instead, Onogi looked for ways that LTCB could change its role and he searched for new ideas overseas. During his London years, Onogi had seen that companies often raised money by issuing bonds, rather than just borrowing from banks. Merchant banks—such as the MHL, where the young "Nobby" had done an internship—usually organized the issue and trade of these bonds. What had really caught Onogi's attention, though, was that these merchant banks had not always dealt in bonds: A few decades earlier they had provided loans for British trade and industry, like LTCB. But as the markets developed—and the British economy matured—the merchant banks had changed. Following their clients, the banks carved out a new niche, gradually moving from traditional lending into capital markets. It seemed obvious that LTCB should do the same thing. Indeed, it seemed compelling to Onogi that all Japanese banks should be moving from state-protected lending to market-based banking.

The Ikeda financial system had worked very well for three decades after the war, but now the country had outgrown this developmental model. It needed to move forward—and the banks needed to *adapt* with the economy, moving into the capital markets. "I think we ought to become like a merchant bank," Onogi declared to his colleagues. "We should be a Japanese version of a British merchant bank!"

Onogi was by no means the only banker expressing desire for change. Many of the other young salarymen at LTCB, particularly those who had also traveled overseas, could also see that Japan was outgrowing the old Ikeda system. "Everyone was aware that there was a structural change under way in corporate financing, from long-term bank loans to the capital markets," Onogi later recalled. Similar sentiments were being voiced even inside the mighty Industrial Bank of Japan—a bank that considered itself the "older brother" of the long-term credit banks, since it was the largest and most prestigious of the three. Nobody ever stood up and shouted in public that something was going wrong. But like thousands of droplets of moisture stealthily forming a cloud, a consensus was forming in corners of LTCB.

So, as the 1980s got under way, the bank threw itself into the task of changing its business strategy. Just like the Meiji government, LTCB started by sending young bankers abroad on missions to study how American and European banks had come to be in their contemporary form. Onogi liked the British merchant bank model; other young LTCB bankers preferred to look at American examples. J. P. Morgan was one bank that triggered interest, since it had also had a commercial banking background with strong government links, but managed to turn itself into an investment bank. Bankers Trust was another fascinating model, since it had started life in custody services but later become a powerhouse in derivatives and other capital markets products.

Intrigued by its research, LTCB started looking for ways to move into the capital markets, by trading bonds or providing structured finance. The Ministry of Finance did not permit the bank to get involved in bond or equity business *inside* Japan; however, there were fewer restrictions outside Japan. So LTCB drew up plans to create a small "merchant banking group" charged with developing some new business lines, such as bond trading, advisory work, and structured finance. It started to copy the business of currency swaps that was being developed by groups such as Salomon Brothers and Bankers Trust over on Wall Street. Getting involved in something like currency swaps demanded a huge intellectual leap in strategic thinking and daily management. LTCB bankers had grown up with the idea that the price of money was neatly set along precise lines—and the bank's business *inside* Japan was still based on that concept. The business of swaps was based on the concept that the price of money was completely fluid, and set exclusively by investor demand. It seemed difficult to imagine how the inexperienced LTCB bankers were going to reconcile these two different systems. But the bankers who became involved in the trading business skirted over the contradictions of their education of experience, and diligently set about trying to learn about swaps. They presumed that if Japanese manufacturers like Toyota were able to copy American technology, reproduce it effectively—and then challenge the Americans at their own game—Japanese bankers should try to perform the same trick with financial techniques the Americans had pioneered.

Trading forays were just the beginning. By 1984, LTCB was ready to pursue the biggest reform initiative it had ever conceived. In that year, the senior management decided to draw up a new strategic plan for the bank, and appointed a young banker called Mario Mizukami to head the team.

Mizukami was just two years older than Onogi and the two men knew each other well. They were both keen tennis players and their mothers had been college friends. But that's where the similarities ended. Mizukami was a very different man. Indeed, his personality was a sharp contrast to most Japanese bankers: He had the rare ability to be a maverick—or, to put it more accurately, an *in*ability to accept the consensus.

Mizukami blamed this "trait" on his childhood. He came from a relatively prosperous family, who left Japan to live in Latin America during the 1930s. His family did not stay long in Latin America, returning to Japan at the start of World War II. Nonetheless, Mizukami was born in Brazil, and his pioneering parents decided not to give their son a traditional Japanese name but the local, Portuguese name of "Mario" instead.

This always made him stand out. The Japanese write their first names with Chinese characters called *kanji,* with specific pictograms designated for every indigenous word. "Mario," however, did not have any characters that naturally matched his own name, since it was not traditionally Japanese. Although he used kanji to spell the name phonetically as "Ma"-"Ri"-"O," it looked odd to Japanese eyes—and his sense of isolation and defiance was reinforced when he was evacuated as a young boy from Tokyo during World War II, and sent to live alone among strangers.

Despite this "handicap," Mizukami was bright—and rich—enough to attend a prestigious high school and Tokyo University. And after he joined LTCB in 1956, he quickly rose through the ranks. His keen intelligence was harnessed to a burning ambition—not to mention the patronage of Binsuke Sugiura, the man who ruled LTCB during most of the 1970s and early 1980s with an iron fist. By chance, Sugiura and Mizukami had attended the same high school in Tokyo, several decades apart—a bond that was extremely important in corporate Japan. And Sugiura saw echoes of his own character in Mizukami. The president was an overbearing, strong character, who had had the good fortune to build his career during the chaos of the postwar decade, when—for a brief period—strong-minded characters thrived in Japan. Admiring Mizukami's strength of personality, Sugiura was convinced that Mizukami should become president of LTCB one day.

Not everyone shared this optimism: Mizukami became controversial as his career flourished. He wore stylish ties to work. He was outspoken. Most shocking of all, in Japanese eyes, Mizukami would not cater to the consensus. "The Japanese think that *wa* is very important. I don't necessarily disagree, at least if *wa* means discussing things with people—and acknowledging that there can be different points of view. But some people think that *wa* means that you can never rock the boat and that you must always silently accept the consensus view to maintain a peace. I don't agree with that idea of *wa* at all!" From time to time, Mizukami's friends would quietly suggest he keep a lower profile. "Have respect for harmony!" they would say.

Onogi was considered a perfect example of how a noble Japanese banker *should* behave. Gentle with his colleagues, unfailingly courteous and humble, Onogi never displayed his emotions in public. He always tried to maintain consensus and harmony. Most of the LTCB bankers considered that the popular Onogi—not Mizukami—seemed the perfect man to become a future president.

Even with their differences in personalities, both Mizukami and Onogi were in broad agreement on the bank's strategic direction, away from traditional banking—and toward the capital markets. Any corporate plan produced by Mizukami was likely to be a clarion call for reform. And when Mizukami did finally release a corporate strategy plan in the spring of 1985, it did not disappoint. It had not actually been written by him: Instead, much of the legwork had been done by Takashi Uehara, an aloof but forceful character who was renowned for his extremely hard work, helped by Koji Hirao, another young reformer. Other young bankers were also seconded to help, from numerous departments, in the interest of creating "consensus." But with Mizukami in charge, the plan had taken on an unexpectedly radical tint. It bluntly declared that the financial climate and economy in Japan had become dangerously distorted. The pace of economic growth in the 1960s and 1970s had been so dramatic that the financial system had never caught up. It was still stuck in systems designed for the capital-starved 1950s. "There is [now] a chronic savings surplus in the private sector," coupled with a "chronic current account surplus" and "growing public sector budget deficit," the LTCB plan said.

This meant the role of banks had to change. Instead of simply channeling consumer savings to industry through simple loans, banks needed to offer more advanced financial products. "In the old fixed interest rate system, a bank made more profits by being as big as possible—and a large size meant that the management was judged well," it said. "But during the process of deregulation and internationalization, we can no longer assume that just being big will mean receiving more profit . . . and when the process of deregulation is over, profitability, not size, will be the important measure of performance." Thus the bank should move away "from a focus on maintaining market share to increasing income by meeting our clients' new financing needs—and an aggressive approach to entering new high growth markets." Specifically, the bank needed to develop a corporate finance arm, project finance, derivatives, and securities operations. It also needed to change its employment culture. "In the future personnel will be evaluated based on achievement. We will move from developing generalists to specialists and there will be a radical change in compensation which will reflect individual achievement and a flatter management structure."

Mizukami knew these ideas were revolutionary. LTCB had entirely the wrong staff to run an investment bank, and by social convention, the bank was not allowed to sack its staff. Like all Japanese companies, men at LTCB were ranked according to what year they had joined, not their skills. Nevertheless, Mizukami insisted that LTCB needed to try to embrace this bold vision of radical change—otherwise it would lose its raison d'être. "We have no time to waste," he insisted.

The plan quickly came under attack. Although other banks were discussing similar ideas, none had presented reform in such a bold, stark way and as 1985 wore on, voices inside LTCB started to complain that Mizukami's reform ideas were simply *too* radical to be tolerated. There was consensus that LTCB needed to carve out a new business niche. But it was ridiculous, some of the LTCB bankers objected, to expect LTCB to abandon traditional lending overnight. The critics rarely confronted Mizukami directly, since that would have been considered too un-Japanese. Instead, gossip swirled around the bank stealthily shaping the group consensus into a new direction—and whenever Mizukami tried to confront the criticism, it melted away in a mist of polite apology. He felt like one of the ancient samurai, lunging at his enemy, only to see the foe vanish into thin air, over and over again. "I always think it is important to have a debate when people disagree," Mizukami later fumed. "But what used to annoy me at LTCB was that nobody would criticize me to my face—always just behind my back."

As the tension rose, a rift developed within the bank. When LTCB had been founded in the 1950s, the employees had seemed as homogeneous as an army. But when the bank had expanded overseas in the 1960s and 1970s, LTCB became divided into two distinct camps. One was the "internationalists," which included men such as Hirao, Uehara, and Onogi, who had worked overseas, studied the principles of Anglo-Saxon corporate finance, and believed that Japan's banking system needed to catch up with the rest of the world. The other was the "domestic" tribe, or men who had forged their whole career inside Japan, making loans to Japanese companies in the traditional way—over endless cups of green tea, building complex relationships of trust, recording it all on piles of handwritten paper, and occasionally skirmishing with the *yakuza*, Japan's ubiquitous groups of gangsters. The brightest of the young LTCB staff were often internationalists, since working overseas had been popular for top recruits, but it was the traditionalists who dominated the top levels of management. The "internationalists" often felt frustrated with their domestic colleagues, whom they considered hopelessly out of date. The domestic wing of the bank was equally irritated with the "internationalists," whom they considered "frivolous." "They have gone American!" the traditionalists mocked. "They're not really Japanese anymore!"

The traditionalists seemed to have the Ministry of Finance on their side. The Ministry was staffed with men who were generally bright in an academic sense—and thus could see that reform was needed. They knew as well as Mizukami that imbalances were developing in the Japanese economy and financial system, and that banks like LTCB were losing their core business. Moreover, from the early 1980s onward, the American government had been badgering the Japanese to start deregulating its financial system—to give greater freedom for Wall Street firms. Yet the Ministry was unwilling to reform in a hurry. The bureaucrats derived much of their power from their ability to manipulate the financial flows in the Japanese economy, and they did not particularly want to alienate their own power. The mandarins could see that radical reform was likely to prove highly controversial—and Japanese bureaucrats hated public controversy. Though the bankers were lobbying for change, brokers like Nomura and Yamaichi were lobbying to block the banks from the capital markets. The brokers had strong backing from politicians, partly because politicians supplemented their income by receiving stock tips and bribes from the brokers. These vested financial interests meant that many senior officials in the ruling Liberal Democratic Party strongly opposed any measure which would damage the brokers—and the Ministry concluded that it could not reform the banking system without unleashing full-scale civil war in the financial world.

So the Ministry's compromise was to introduce reform—but at a snail's pace. In the early 1980s the bureaucrats promised to deregulate the interest rate regime (to placate the Americans) and let the banks move into the capital markets *overseas* (to placate the banks). But it blocked the banks' requests to move into the capital markets at home or implement any rapid or radical financial reform (to placate the brokers).

For a while, the reformers at LTCB tried to ignore these constraints, pressing ahead with their investment banking plans. Onogi was appointed to run a new "merchant banking group." Hirao, the coauthor of the reform plan, was sent to New York, where he threw himself into developing the capital markets capabilities of LTCB. He oversaw the purchase of a stake in Peer's, an American mergers and acquisitions house, and then bought Greenwich Capital, a primary bond dealer. Onogi's dream was that these operations would act as a platform for the bank to learn how the capital markets worked overseas. Then these skills could eventually be easily imported back into Japan. "We could not create many profits because of all the regulations," Onogi admitted. "However, we were convinced that we had lots of capable staff—and so that when we were given a chance to use these skills in Japan, we would have a good start."

In reality, the momentum behind Mizukami's dream was rapidly dissipating largely because of the Finance Ministry's curbs and politicians' resistance to change. "Since the Ministry regulation still separated banking and securities business," Onogi explained later, "the future of investment banking still lay very much in the Ministry's hands, rather than anything LTCB could do." And this played directly into the hands of traditionalists at the bank, who pointed out as time passed, that it was impossible to make money from investment banking.

More importantly, they claimed that there was a much more profitable new niche developing in Japan: real estate. By late 1985, a striking shift was taking place in the Japanese economy. Across the country the price of real estate and stock market shares was starting to spiral upward toward a classic asset price bubble. As this occurred, a new category of real estate borrower appeared who was positively *eager* for cash—and seemed more than willing to replace the old industrial companies that had been LTCB's bread-and-butter clients.

Suddenly real estate seemed like the answer to all the bank's problems.

— *Chapter 3* —

MONEY MADNESS

Back around 1986 and 1987, practically everyone in Japan was convinced that the economy would continue heading up and up indefinitely. This was a period that saw many people so intoxicated by the economic bubble that they lost their powers of rational judgment.

—Masamoto Yashiro

In the late 1980s, Koji Hirao was working in LTCB's office in New York when a Japanese businessman called to see him. The man introduced himself as the head of a small company called EIE and announced that he wanted to build a hotel. His name was Harunori Takahashi.

"It will be the best hotel that New York has ever seen!" Takahashi said with ebullience. "The very best!"

Hirao knew that he was supposed to feel thrilled to have someone walk into his office asking for a big loan. Three decades earlier, the Japanese economy had been reeling from its World War II defeat. But by 1986, or when Hirao was posted to work in New York—after helping to draft the controversial 1985 reform plan—Japan was quickly becoming recognized as the new global economic king. Now American bookstores were filled with titles like *Japan as Number One*, or *Yen: Japan's New Financial Empire!* that predicted that the comparatively tiny island nation would soon overtake the United States as the world's economic engine. In that time, too,

LTCB had been awarded the highest possible recognition from America's financial community. The bank had received a "triple-A" rating from both Standard and Poor's and Moody's, the two main American rating agencies. "We are a six-A bank!" LTCB staff liked to tell each other with outsized pride. Better still, the bank was starting to make its mark beyond Japan with a significant presence on Wall Street: It was drawing up plans to acquire Greenwich Capital, the bond dealer, and was earning a reputation for being one of the more sophisticated capital market players among Japanese banks.

Moreover, closing a deal with EIE could be a great coup for the New York office, boosting its reputation even higher. EIE was one of LTCB's favorite business customers. Although it had been almost entirely unknown a few years earlier, the company had ridden on the back of Japan's real estate boom, gobbling up properties across the world, to build a hotel and leisure empire. Stretching from Tokyo through Hong Kong, Sydney and Milan to Los Angeles and across to Fiji, Takahashi's empire had an enormous appetite for borrowed cash. It was a prized client. Which meant that LTCB was happily scrambling for EIE business—and bankers would win accolades for any new deals.

Yet something about Takahashi made Hirao uneasy. The man did not *look* odd. He wore neat, discreet clothes and had a slight physique, topped by a bland, inscrutable face and weak chin. Takahashi's nondescript appearance was matched by an airy demeanor when it came to details. He was very vague about his plans for his New York hotel. He said that he wanted to borrow about $350 million. The only other information he would give was that he had already selected the site in central Manhattan, between Park and Madison Avenues on prestigious 57th Street—a place New Yorkers would eventually know as the location of the Four Seasons hotel.

"Have you got a project manager for your hotel?" LTCB staff asked. "An accountant?"

Takahashi ignored the question. "I have got an architect!" he said triumphantly. And it was a triumph. Takahashi had hired I. M. Pei, one of the most prestigious architects of the day, who had just finished working on an extension for the Louvre. But this was little comfort to Hirao, nor was the fact that Pei was already drawing up extravagant plans for the 57th Street hotel, including a design that called for the edifice to be clad in a rare limestone that was particularly pricey. With the appearance of an obelisk, Takahashi's hotel would be a monument to himself and his company.

"But what about a project manager?" bankers persisted, trying to get the elder man to discuss the financial controls on his audacious vision. Takahashi shrugged.

Knowing Takahashi's importance to the bank, Hirao closed the meeting and handed Takahashi's sketchy ideas to his junior staff for further investigation. During his time in New York, Hirao had seen that American finance worked on different principles from Japanese banking. American bankers used a rigorous system of credit analysis to decide when to make loans—and when not. Hirao had deliberately built a project finance team that would employ the same tools by hiring a group of Americans with the relevant experience, and using these to train some promising young LTCB staff who had studied at business schools in America. Armed with its phalanx of analysts, LTCB had even been bold enough to turn down a loan request from Donald Trump, the hotel, condominium, and gambling magnate, because the Americans thought that Trump's business projections were not profitable enough.

Unfortunately, the EIE numbers looked far odder than Trump's. Takahashi had said that he wanted to build a hotel with about 400 rooms at a cost of $350 million. The junior LTCB staff in the New York office calculated that the maximum viable investment in a hotel that size on that site would only be $150 million. "Perhaps we have got the project mixed up with something else?" suggested some of the young LTCB bankers.

They checked: No, they were told. Takahashi *was* planning to spend $350 million. The bankers in New York puzzled over the figures again. Then they heard that the LTCB headquarters had approved Takahashi's plans, ignoring their cash flow analysis. "This is crazy," one of the bankers declared, as he took the long flight back to Japan. "We have to tell Tokyo that this project cannot pay."

When he arrived, the banker found the Tokyo headquarters of LTCB was quite insistent: "Give Takahashi as much money as he wants!" It was ridiculous to worry about cash flows or rates of return, the bank's executives told him. That was the type of thing that *Americans* did! And now, the

LTCB bankers in Tokyo pointed out, Americans were writing books saying that the Japanese way of doing business was now the best in the world!

Peeved, Hirao and his New York colleagues put some LTCB bankers onto the project to oversee costs. "Those crazy EIE men are ordering expensive limousines to travel just a block!" he carped. But his complaining had little effect. As the project was announced, Takahashi swept into town again, trailing limousines, and threw a lavish party for the press at the Rainbow Room, on the fifty-sixth floor of Rockefeller Center in New York. The location of the party was symbolic. Rockefeller Center had recently fallen under the control of Mitsubishi Real Estate, in a blatant new display of Japan's rising economic power. As the hotel rose, so did the costs. By 1989 the 57th Street hotel was projected to cost considerably more than $400 million. It was the most expensive hotel New York had ever seen. Having worked on Mizukami's strategic plan for LTCB—and joined the bank at a time when banks faced a capital *shortage* and dispensed their money with care—the sight of the spendthrift Takahashi's celebrations was particularly galling. Hirao had learned much from America's emphasis on analysis and investigation and the hotel magnate seemed too suspicious to trust. But he was powerless to keep it under control. Hirao sat meekly in the audience at the Rainbow Room, while champagne flowed, and nervously wondered what was going on.

If Hirao had known anything about Takahashi's background, he would have been even more concerned. For EIE had partly sprung from a side of Japan that was very different from the official, stuffy world of LTCB. Hirao had grown up imbued with the ideas of the "samurai" bankers—a place where men diligently sacrificed their lives to rebuild the country from the war, cooperating with each other in an orderly financial system. *That* harmonious world of hardworking salarymen at large companies, however, had only ever represented a small part of the postwar system. Underneath this orderly surface was a more brutal demimonde of small-time entrepreneurs, naked capitalist competition, and gangster violence. The Japanese government did everything it could to avoid showing this second world to outsiders, since it contradicted the country's official image. Nonetheless, these two sides of Japan were both authentically Japanese and, as much as they tried to gloss over it, their coexistence was no coincidence. The story of EIE, which partly sprung from this second side, shows this clearly.

The origins of Electronics and Industrial Enterprises, as the company was originally known, went back to 1947. During the chaos of those early postwar years, a powerful Japanese family called Goh apparently decided to create EIE to import cassette tapes from the American market. Using the Goh family's powerful political connections, EIE won a license to distribute the tapes in Japan from 3M, the American conglomerate. A tiny operation, the business initially had just five employees, apparently lead by Yuriko Goh, a wealthy Japanese woman who made frequent trips to the United States. In the 1960s, the Goh family gave its blessing to a maverick inventor called Yoshiro Nakamatsu, who took control of the company and turned EIE into a large import business. Nakamatsu increased the staff to 350, won distribution contracts with U.S. companies, such as Grand Magnetics, and floated the company on the second section of the Tokyo Stock Exchange. Nakamatsu also started importing video equipment from America and became acquainted with a man the EIE staff always referred to as "the older Takahashi"—who was working at a television station at the time.

In the middle of the 1970s, almost out of the blue, the older Takahashi launched a hostile takeover of EIE. In theory, this type of takeover bid was not supposed to happen in Japan. The postwar financial system presumed that the main role of equities was to enable members of the *keiretsu* and banks to hold large stakes in each other's enterprise. It was unheard of for large companies to launch hostile attacks on each other. Yet beneath the bank-based web of large companies—the *keiretsu*—there was a ruthlessly competitive world of small companies vying for a leg up in the system. Foreigners only saw the polite, tidy world of corporate life, but Japanese contended with a host of scrappy operators with little respect for the law. Thus, though most shares on the Tokyo Stock Exchange were locked up in the hands of passive banks with *keiretsu* ties or other dependent companies, a group of small-time companies and speculators existed who regarded equity as a tool for gambling or extortion—or both. Unable to curb the instinct of ruthless, free competition, the government had inadvertently pushed it to the margins of society. The tightly entwined political and gangster worlds had an edge over the law in the stock market.

Nakamatsu tried to stop the hostile raid on EIE—and a court eventually ruled that the takeover was illegal—but he quickly gave up the fight. Some EIE staff believed that Takahashi's funds came from a well-known stock market speculator, whom they referred to as "the strange Iwasawa-san." "Takahashi was a bad man—a very, very bad man," Nakamatsu concluded. "They robbed me of my company and I didn't have a chance."

If the story ended there, the speculation might have amounted to little more than bitterness and frustration. But then events took an even murkier turn. The older Takahashi died and Iwasawa completely vanished. Iwasawa's family initially claimed that Iwasawa was dead as well. Yet, in the early 1990s—or a full fifteen years after his supposed death—Iwasawa's family unexpectedly staged a funeral for him, attended by some leading politicians. Local journalists suspected that Iwasawa had been hiding from his creditors during the intervening years.

The only thing that was crystal clear was that EIE was controlled by Harunori Takahashi, son of the "older Takahashi"—and, by a happy coincidence, also the son-in-law of the mysterious Iwasawa. Taking charge at the start of the 1980s, the younger Takahashi, then in his late thirties, set up operations in a small office in the Ginza, the entertainment and shopping center of Tokyo. There was no elevator to his office and guests who wanted to visit him had to climb up four narrow flights of stairs, to find a tiny, poky room, where a few staff worked on cheap, gunmetal gray desks. During the day, the sound of children shrieking could be heard in the office through an open window that overlooked a school. At night, the district became a neon jungle, surrounded by sushi restaurants, geisha bars, yakuza haunts, and sex clubs.

During this period, Takahashi liked to describe EIE as an import business specializing in electronics products—and it seemed to be doing well. With the yen rising in strength against the dollar throughout the late 1970s and early 1980s, the cost of American imports was drastically reduced. "I got very lucky at EIE," Takahashi liked to tell journalists years later. "I took over the business when the yen was one level, and within a few months it had strengthened sharply and so our profits were going through the roof. What was the secret of my success? Luck—like anywhere in business. Not ability! Luck, luck, luck!"

His frankness didn't mean Takahashi was humble. He clearly felt destined for greater things. Regardless of the unusual history of EIE, Takahashi had access to some of the inner citadels of the Japanese establishment. While he was a child, Takahashi's family had managed to send him to the prestigious Keio primary school, an elite establishment beloved by Japan's leading political and industrial families. He got expelled from Keio in his teens for adolescent pranks, but somehow won a place to the elite Keio University, from which he graduated in 1964. For the following decade he worked at Japan Airlines (JAL), a company filled with the sons of aristocrats and politicians and a traditional grooming ground for high office in Japan. At JAL he earned the nickname *warunori,* or joker, before leaving the company in the late 1970s, apparently to work at EIE.

This background had given Takahashi a veneer of respectability. It also gave him plenty of powerful friends. One of these was Shintaro Abe, a senior politician in the ruling Liberal Democratic Party, nicknamed "the kingmaker" because of his legendary ability to control events behind the scenes. Another friend was Ichiro Ozawa, a man who would later become a leader of the LDP and be hailed as a "reformer" by the American government. Toshio Yamaguchi, a future labor minister, was also a good friend. Another acquaintance was Seichi Ota, a man who would still be serving in the senior echelons of the ruling Liberal Democratic Party in 2003.

By the early 1980s, Takahashi had decided to act on his ambitions and expand the business of EIE. He harbored dreams of becoming an entrepreneur and a business tycoon, like the Tsutsumi brothers, who controlled a hotel, retail, and transport empire. Takahashi realized that he could not do that by simply focusing on electronic imports—and real estate seemed a much more lucrative business. So, in the middle of the 1980s, Takahashi declared that he was going to turn EIE into a real estate group and announced that he would give up drinking alcohol—a most unusual move in Japan—to concentrate on becoming a successful entrepreneur. "I cannot let alcohol cloud my mind!" he told his friends. "If you are a samurai warrior about to face his enemies, you would not drink sake the night before!"

Takahashi's timing was impeccable. Just as he was looking to spread his wings in the mid-1980s, Japan was embarking on an extraordinary real estate boom. Precisely what triggered this mania remains an issue of some dispute among economists. Nonetheless, it was a symptom of the same underlying problem that dogged LTCB: namely, government failure to accept the need for structural change. By the 1980s three decades of high-speed growth had left Japanese consumers and industry extremely rich. To a layman's eye, this tidal wave of wealth initially seemed like a dream come true. But too much wealth can be a double-edged sword. A nation's money only has value for future generations if the current generation can find a way to invest it *productively,* either at home or overseas. In Japan's case, this was becoming increasingly difficult to do. The 1952 financial system was designed to fund domestic industry. However, after three decades of rapid economic growth, the country was already awash with factories and industrial investment projects and—as the banks knew to their cost—Japan's traditional manufacturing companies had limited need for cash *inside* Japan.

Textbook economics would suggest that one solution to this problem would be to take the money outside Japan. This happened to a certain extent. Life insurance companies and banks bought foreign instruments, such as U.S. Treasury bonds, helping to finance the massive U.S. deficit. However, ordinary Japanese savers could not export their cash so freely, due to foreign exchange controls. And there was little incentive for them to keep pouring all their funds into the banks, since the banks paid a pitifully low rate of interest—also due to the postwar controls. So, as time passed, consumers and companies started to look for other places to put their cash; two obvious outlets were the stock market and real estate sector. From 1981 onward, the price of land started to creep up. Then, as investors concluded that these rising prices in the real estate markets made land a good investment, they poured more money into the sector, pushing prices even higher—and attracting more funds.

A similar pattern was at work in the stock market. As the Nikkei 225 rose, it became ludicrously cheap for companies to issue shares, so they did that on a massive scale. Then, since they could not find anywhere to invest the cash, they, too, poured it into real estate. And since real estate prices were rising, this appeared to increase the value of these companies, which pushed shares even higher in a self-reinforcing spiral.

Government policy fanned the flames. In September 1985 policy leaders of the Group of Seven industrialized countries gathered in the Plaza Hotel in New York and agreed that the yen should be strengthened against the dollar. After the Plaza meeting, the currency surged from Y240 to the dollar to Y150, effectively doubling Japan's spending power in international terms, and creating the impression that there was even *more* excess money in Japan. Then the Bank of Japan added to the frenzy: under strong pressure from the Americans, it cut interest rates repeatedly in an attempt to boost domestic demand in Japan and offset the potential damage of a weak yen. It was like pouring kerosene onto a fire. Suddenly real estate prices were spiraling higher and higher. And thousands of companies were rushing to join the party, flush with cheap cash.

It was in this overheated atmosphere that Takahashi started searching for ways to realize his real estate ambitions. He knew that he could not work alone. So he recruited a couple of additional allies. One of these was Bungo Ishizaki, a jovial Japanese in his forties, who had previously worked as a university professor. Ishizaki met Takahashi through LDP politicians and agreed to become a consultant to EIE. The other new employee was Iwao Nomoto, a small, nerdy-looking man in his twenties. Nomoto had been a medical student in the early 1980s, but had dropped out of his training when he realized that he could not stand the sight of blood. Again, it was LDP politicians who introduced Nomoto to EIE.

Neither Ishizaki, Nomoto, nor Takahashi knew anything about the real estate business. Indeed, when Nomoto first arrived at EIE he was unsure how to operate a calculator. Still they were hardly worried: By 1985, there were thousands of other small companies springing up to take advantage of the nascent property bubble and most of these knew as little about real estate as EIE. Takahashi appointed Ishizaki, who had grown up in America and spoke fluent English, as his main international "fixer" for future real estate deals. Nomoto was told to look after the accounts. "The idea was that Takahashi would pick properties, Ishizaki would negotiate, and I would do the logistics," Nomoto later explained.

Then Takahashi hunted for some deals. Though he was keen to buy property in Japan, he had a hunch that since he was outside the Japanese mainstream corporate world, it might first be easier to break into the market overseas. Through friends of friends, he heard that a Hyatt hotel was for sale in the U.S.-run Pacific protectorate of Saipan. It is usual in the hotel industry for the owners of a hotel to be entirely separate from the company that actually runs it on a day-to-day basis. In this case, the hotel was managed by the Hyatt group but the real estate was owned by a group of Chinese—and the Chinese wanted to sell. Takahashi got in touch with Hong Kong and Shanghai Banking Corp. (HSBC), the Hong Kong–based bank that had been appointed to manage the sale, and indicated that he was interested in bidding. Then he made contact with LTCB, and asked them if they would fund the project.

LTCB was keen. The bank knew Takahashi slightly since it had lent Y100 million ($1 million) to EIE in the early 1980s to finance the import business. The traditional bankers at LTCB were eager to get involved in real estate deals and Takahashi also had one feature that made him very attractive to the LTCB bankers: In comparison to most of the upstart real estate investors that were emerging in Japan, he looked fairly respectable. Takahashi had studied at Keio. He was not overly ostentatious. He also had a very distant family link to Binsuke Sugiura, the former LTCB president. Most important of all, Takahashi had close ties to powerful politicians. "LTCB was dying to get into real estate and they loved Takahashi because he seemed posh," Ishizaki later said. "They couldn't wait to sink their fangs into him."

Perhaps more surprisingly, HSBC also seemed interested in Takahashi. The Saipan project fell into the orbit of a man called John Bond, then a senior figure in HSBC's Asian investment banking operations (but who would later rise to become executive chairman of the entire bank). Bond and the other HSBC bankers did not know very much about EIE, but with such a potential gold mine in fees awaiting anyone who did business with these cash-rich Asian entrepreneurs, they did not wish to ask too many questions. "John Bond of HSBC was always very helpful, and very friendly to us," Ishizaki recalled later. "But then, so was everybody else."

EIE quickly bought the Saipan hotel for Y30 billion ($300 million), with funds from LTCB and HSBC. Takahashi was thrilled—and promptly decided to change the name of the company to EIE International. "We thought people might get confused with our old name," Ishizaki later explained. "They might wonder why we were buying hotels." Then Takahashi and Ishizaki started looking for more hotels, via the Hyatt network. The hotel managers were eager to help. They discovered that the jovial ex-professor shared a taste with some of the Hyatt managers for visiting Asian sex bars. Ishizaki was soon bonding with the Hyatt men over joyful, drunken evenings and enthusiastically comparing notes on the girls—and potential real estate deals.

Eventually, the Hyatt managers told EIE that there was another Hyatt hotel for sale down in Sydney. Takahashi and Ishizaki flew to Australia and the Hyatt managers arranged for local prostitutes to visit their room that night as a "welcome" gift from the hotel. To Ishizaki's disappointment, however, Takahashi sent the girls away. "Takahashi was never a terribly horny man," Ishizaki concluded later. "Of course, he had girlfriends, and he used to look after them, but not many. He was too ambitious and serious about his business."

The next day Takahashi asked to be taken on a tour of Sydney. As they were cruising along the waterfront, Takahashi stopped the limousine. "Look!" He pointed his finger at a magnificent skyscraper facing the sparkling blue waters of the Sydney harbor and the city's futuristic opera house. "Look at that hotel!" The tower bore the large, impressive logo: The Regent Hotel. "We should buy *that* hotel. It is much better! It has a much better location than the Hyatt," Takahashi declared.

Ishizaki peered at it. "But you have never been to Sydney, so how do you know? We don't even know if it is for sale, or what type of hotel it is!"

"Ishi!" Takahashi reproached him. "*Everything* is for sale, somehow, Ishi. It is a great hotel. Go and find out who owns it."

Ishizaki wandered into the lobby and asked a bellboy who owned the hotel, and whether he could buy it. The bellboy looked blank. But Ishizaki ascertained that the managers of the hotel were the Regent Hotel Group, based up in Hong Kong, while the owners were a consortium of Chinese entrepreneurs. The Chinese owners indicated that they were willing to sell the hotel—at a very high price. Ishizaki was unsure whether the bank would agree. However, when he asked LTCB for a new loan, the bankers barely blinked. Instead, the LTCB bankers demanded that this time *they* should be the main lender to EIE on the deal, since they did not want to let

HSBC grab too much business. They were more interested in winning the deal, in other words, than worrying about the price.

LTCB's attitude reflected some peculiarities about the way Japanese banks did business. In most countries today, when banks lend money for corporate investment they pay close attention to the likely *cash flow* of a project. What banks want to know is whether a company will be able to pay the loan back out of a future stream of earnings. In Japan during the 1980s, however, the banks only ever cared about one thing: collateral, or the asset that a company could sell to repay a loan, if it ever faced a crunch. And the only collateral that mattered—at least in the eyes of bankers—was land. For by 1985, banks like LTCB had come to the conclusion that land was an almost fail-safe store of wealth; its value could only ever *increase*. Land had always been a highly valued commodity in Japanese culture, because most of the population had traditionally been employed in agriculture and the supply of good farming land was severely limited by the mountainous terrain. Moreover, most Japanese had only ever known a world where land prices always rose. Property prices had risen every single year since World War II, except in 1973, the year of the oil shock. Given this, the bankers reasoned that there was little risk in lending to real estate projects, as long as these were usually backed by property as collateral. If a client ever ran into trouble, the bank could simply sell the land at a high profit to repay the loan.

A few Japanese bankers suspected that this equation might not work overseas. They knew that in places such as Saipan or Sydney, property prices had actually gone up and down in recent years, rather than always increasing. Yet most Japanese bankers looked at the rest of the world through the prism of their Japanese experience, and presumed that the Japanese reverence for prestigious real estate was a universal affair. Thus, as long as a developer had some real estate to offer, the banks were willing to lend. Indeed, to the Japanese, it seemed positively crazy *not* to act. As the yen rose in value, the price of overseas real estate was dropping dramatically in yen terms. It was as if Europe, Asia, and America were holding a half-price sale. Suddenly, Japanese investors could purchase a large house in

Hawaii, a flat in London, or a golf course in America, for a sum of money that could barely buy an apartment in Tokyo.

Takahashi loved his new Sydney hotel. The Regent brand was lavish, glamorous—and oozed international prestige. Japan was becoming obsessed with brand names, and to Takahashi, owning a "Regent" hotel now seemed to be far more exciting than owning a mere "Hyatt" or "Hilton." Indeed, it was so exciting that Takahashi decided he wanted more: He asked Ishizaki to find out if EIE could buy *all* the Regent hotels in the world.

By a happy coincidence, the man who had created the Regent hotel group lived in Hong Kong—and was more than willing to talk. He was an American called Bob Burns, who was blessed with gentle blue eyes and the affable manner of the perfect host. He had come to the Pacific region two decades earlier as the general manager of the Kahala Hilton in Hawaii. There, he had displayed an early flair for public relations by offering free lodging to Yasunari Kawabata, the Japanese Nobel Prize–winning author. The move immediately sucked in a wave of Japanese tourists to the Hilton hotel, dramatically boosting hotel revenues, and Burns's reputation in the region. In 1970 Burns left the Hilton group and formed a joint venture with Tokyu, a Japanese railway and hotel company. But Burns found it frustrating to work for a Japanese group. "The bureaucracy was just awful," he remembers. He split with Tokyu, and created his own "Regent" hotel management company, whose flagship hotel was in the heart of Hong Kong. The group won prestigious management contracts across the world, and in 1984 Burns bought the revered Dorchester Hotel in London, backed by a loan from HSBC.

By 1986, Burns was looking for new investors for his Regent group, since he had quarreled with two of his original partners. By another happy coincidence, HSBC's John Bond knew Burns well. Indeed, Bond sat on the board of Regent, since the bank owned a 5 percent stake. When Bond heard that Burns was looking for more investors for the Regent group, the name EIE cropped up.

It seemed to be a match made in heaven. Takahashi—and LTCB—were keen to buy into a prestigious hotel group. Burns, for his part, was thrilled by the prospect of dealing with a partner with plenty of cash. In most corners of the hotel industry, a natural tension exists between the companies that own the hotels and the managers who run them on a day-to-day basis. Owners always want to limit costs; managers hope to create the most fabulous environment possible by spending the owner's money. Burns was a man who adored luxury, and he spotted that LTCB and EIE did not seem to worry about mundane details such as short-term profits.

Burns also liked Takahashi personally. He found it difficult to communicate with him, since Takahashi spoke very limited English, but what Burns could see, seemed charming. "Ishizaki was a bit wild. Takahashi was a real gentleman," Burns concluded. "There didn't seem to be a single dishonest bone in his body!" Best of all, since EIE knew relatively little about hotels or real estate, Burns reckoned that Takahashi was likely to accept his advice about which hotels should be built—and which not.

So, in 1987 Takahashi took a 30 percent stake in the Regent hotel management group. Burns did not want to sell the entire Regent group to EIE, because he still considered it his "baby," thus he retained a 65 percent stake in the management group, with HSBC holding the remaining 5 percent. However, Burns agreed that he would help EIE to acquire more hotels to be owned by Takahashi—but run by Regent. It seemed a perfect deal.

On a glorious sunny day in the autumn of 1987, when the skies were cobalt blue and the leaves vivid red, Burns took Takahashi to visit New York. The Japanese man had never been to New York. So Burns accompanied Takahashi to the top of a building on 57th Street, where they gazed down on Manhattan. "That's Fifth Avenue! That's the Empire State Building! That's Park Avenue!" Burns explained, pointing out the key landmarks.

"So what can we do here, Burns-san?" Takahashi asked. "I want a hotel."

"Well, you have to think about this like the Ginza!" Burns cautioned. "It is going to be very expensive!"

Burns knew that a friend of his, Bill Zeckendorf, a prominent American real estate developer, had assembled 25,000 square feet of vacant property on 57th Street between Madison and Park Avenues. Burns also knew that when Zeckendorf saw EIE coming, he would raise the price. By 1987

American real estate owners had realized that the Japanese were so keen to buy overseas properties that they could get away with adding 10 percent—or even 50 percent—to a deal. Burns also passionately believed that the site could produce an extraordinary hotel. He had spoken about the site to the architect I. M. Pei, and Pei had suggested building a tall, limestone tower. Takahashi might sometimes be vague on the details of his projects, but Burns knew *exactly* what Regent was doing. Burns created his hotels with armies of project managers. Every lampshade, showerhead, bedcover, and cutlery set was planned with military precision. The hotels he created were pricey; but luxury did not come cheap. And the hotel Burns was planning for Manhattan would be truly lavish; a legendary masterpiece.

"Don't worry about it being expensive, Burns-san!" Takahashi said. "I am sure the banks will help. They always help."

Burns believed him.

— Chapter 4 —

THE TRILLION-YEN MAN

Despite all the praise and all the criticism, Takahashi was a person who symbolized his era.

—Toshio Yamaguchi, labor minister and friend of Takahashi's

By the late 1980s, the LTCB bankers were feeling so self-confident that they had decided it was time to erect a new monument to their own prestige. Back in the 1960s, when LTCB had built its first headquarters in Otemachi, a plain, seven-story building had seemed respectable. By the 1980s, however, the LTCB management started to feel the Otemachi building too shabby for an internationally prestigious bank. So, in the late 1980s the LTCB managers started planning to create a lavish new, twenty-story tower, over in a prestigious spot near the Imperial Palace. It was designed as an architectural jewel, complete with a costly 100-foot-high glass atrium, high-ceilinged meeting halls, and white marble in the reception. Indeed, the price tag was projected to be Y50 billion or more ($500 million). Nobody objected, or even considered the plans odd.

Yet, as Onogi watched Japan's wild real estate party get even wilder, he sometimes felt uneasy. This was *not* because he feared an imminent crash. Onogi, like almost everybody else in Japan, assumed that real estate values would continue to rise indefinitely and along with them the economy would continue to expand. No. Onogi's problem was that he had little taste for the nouveau riche culture the real estate bubble engendered. His generation had grown up with a sober, ascetic work ethic. Not for him was the new Tokyo of designer clothes, jewelry shops, and restaurants that could charge as much as $500 a head for dinner or sprinkled gold leaf on their sushi. Onogi liked to think of himself as a child of the Meiji Restoration, an elite intellectual who made it his mission in life to embrace international ideas and place his country on the world stage through its intellect and technological skill. He dreamed of a Japan that could hold its own in international finance, an equal to the blue-chip Wall Street names or snooty British merchant banks. Instead of gawping at the riches of Tokyo, or acknowledging the existence of Japan's swamp of corruption, he threw himself into the task of developing LTCB's operations in London and New York.

Yet, by the late 1980s it was becoming harder for Onogi to entirely ignore what was going on inside Japan. He had been appointed a managing director of the bank, in the summer of 1987, and given the post of head of corporate planning, replacing the maverick Mizukami. The highly prestigious post meant that it was Onogi who had the difficult task of drawing up the next strategic plan outlining the bank's future direction together with a team of other LTCB bankers. But Onogi was torn over what that plan should say. Part of his conundrum was that the 1985 plan had clearly stated that it made no sense for LTCB to keep expanding its traditional loan business. Yet, between 1985 and 1988 the bank's assets had grown from Y18.4 trillion to Y22.6 trillion ($184 billion to $226 billion), largely due to a massive increase in real estate–related loans. If Onogi stuck to his original reform ideas, he would have to call on the bankers to *cut* the loan book. Or he could take notice of the expansion of real estate lending and perform a complete U-turn in the next strategy paper by endorsing it.

Personally, Onogi still firmly believed in reform and the principles of the 1985 plan. Intellectually he knew that in the long term, LTCB had to find a new business as an investment bank, rather than just relying on traditional lending. But Onogi was also haunted by his respect for *wa,* or group harmony. As land prices rose ever higher, all the Japanese banks were becoming obsessed with real estate. Moreover, the real estate business appeared to be delivering high profits—while investment banking was losing money, because it was hobbled by the Ministry of Finance's rules. Onogi was not the type of man to defy the consensus by suggesting that LTCB stop real estate lending.

So, Onogi decided to back the *wa*. In 1989, when the bank finally published the sixth strategic plan, this declared that LTCB should develop investment banking in the long term, but focus on corporate lending as its main business in the short term. It also called on the bank to develop a new focus on making small- and medium-sized company loans, and take advantage of new opportunities in real estate.

In later years, Onogi vehemently denied that this sixth plan was a reversal. He preferred to call it an *amplification* of the original plan. "We were still so constrained in the investment banking business that we simply could not rely on that to generate enough profits straightaway," Onogi later explained. "And until the investment banking became stronger, we had to create profits another way, because we were losing our large traditional corporate borrowers." But though Onogi may have been satisfied with that face-saving logic, the "domestic tribe" at the bank sensed victory. Real estate was now deemed more important than reform. And the emboldened "domestic tribe" moved to press its advantage: LTCB restructured its loan departments and, for the first time, placed the credit control officers under the authority of the loan promotion business. The move, which was being made at many other banks as well, removed checks from the system. In the old days, if a junior officer had wanted to make a loan to an industrial client, he had to first get his plans vetted by a different, credit control department. Now, if a loan officer wanted to supply cash to a real estate developer, he could simply rubber-stamp the loan himself. As long as a customer had some property—or simply plans to buy property—LTCB was ready to lend. So was every other Japanese bank.

Years later, Nomoto at EIE sometimes tried to work out how much money EIE borrowed during this heady period. He reckoned that he had *personally* handled about $4 billion in deals between 1986 and 1990. But he stressed that was only a rough estimate, and just covered the international operations, which were about half the group. "We were doing deals so fast," Nomoto explained. "We hardly had time to add them up." To make it easier to find hotels, Takahashi bought a Falcon jet so that he could travel around the world quickly. Then, he decided that a Falcon was too modest, so he added a Boeing 727 to his collection as well. Burns, who often accompanied Takahashi on these shopping trips, disliked the plane. "It was a strange thing," he grumbled later. "It leaked petrol. Once we almost got stranded in Burma because it ran out of fuel." So eventually Takahashi leased a third, more reliable plane: a Boeing 737.

As they careered around the world, Takahashi jumped on whatever real estate he liked. He snapped up the Regent Beverly Wilshire in Los Angeles, the Regent hotels in Bangkok, Bali, and Milan, a Hyatt hotel in Guam, a floating hotel in the Australian Barrier Reef, the luxury Sanctuary Cove resort in Queensland, Australia, and the Landmark Hotel in London. To this he also added two more Hyatt hotels in Australia, three Tahiti hotels run by the Beach-comber group, and an entire island in Fiji. "We took all the cabinet members in the Fiji government for a ride in our planes and showed them a *really* good time!" Ishizaki later chuckled, pleased to have become a Malcolm Forbes–like plutocrat. "I think that was why we got the island . . . the planes were very useful like that. We considered the planes a capitalist tool."

Sated on hotel and luxury properties, Takahashi decided to diversify. Down in Sydney, Takahashi met Alan Bond, the Australian developer, who persuaded EIE to invest in a private Australian university that Alan Bond was founding for his own grandiose purposes, called "Bond University." As a bonus, EIE also purchased a stake in the Bond Center, a large Hong Kong shopping and office complex. Lacking the steadfast support of a Japanese bank, Bond went bankrupt in the late 1980s and was eventually jailed for fraud in Australia. Loyal or opportunistic, Takahashi obligingly took over the entire shopping center and university.

Oil was EIE's next interest. In 1988 Takahashi and Ishizaki flew across to Vietnam, where some lucrative new oil fields had recently been discovered. The local Vietnamese officials had never seen a private corporate jet before and were so thrilled by Takahashi's arrival that they insisted on coming aboard to stamp the passports. As they lounged in the jet's leather seats, Takahashi plied them with Château Lafite wine and Dom Pérignon champagne. "That went down very well because Vietnam had been a French colony, so they had a taste for French labels," Ishizaki later explained. "It was Takahashi's idea to do that . . . he was a genius at that type of thing."

Impressed, the local governor invited Takahashi and Ishizaki for dinner, where Takahashi presented him with an entire case of Dom Pérignon champagne and tactfully posed his question: Would the Vietnamese sell him the concession rights to an oil field?

The Vietnamese governor looked doubtful. The world's largest American, European, and Japanese oil companies were already scrambling to buy a stake in that oil field. "What we really need is a five-star hotel," the governor hedged. "We need that before we sell the oil rights."

"Fine. We will provide a five-star hotel in six months," Takahashi replied. "If we do that, will you sell us the oil concession?" The Vietnamese laughed. "Do you clowns really think we are dumb—you cannot do a five-star hotel in six months!" the governor declared. "But if you can, you get the oil."

What the Vietnamese hadn't considered was that among Takahashi's hotel treasures acquired over the years of his shopping spree was a giant barge decked out as a floating five-star hotel moored on the Australian Barrier Reef not too far from Vietnam. Back in Australia, Takahashi's lawyers pointed out that the floating hotel was collateral to a bank loan and that sailing his collateral out of Australian waters was illegal and would nullify the loan. With so much to gain from delivering the promised five-star hotel, Takahashi simply ignored his lawyers. Soon after the ship moored in Vietnamese waters, the Vietnamese granted EIE the rights to develop a group of oil fields.

As the deals piled up, the LTCB bankers became increasingly excited. Ever since the bank had been founded in 1952, the staff had suffered an inferiority complex with respect to Industrial Bank of Japan. IBJ was the so-called "big brother" of LTCB, and tended to grab all the best and most prestigious industrial clients. Traditionally, if there were an international oil deal to back it would be IBJ that financed it. Now, LTCB reveled in evening the score. And pride of place went beyond simply taking a piece of IBJ's pie; the LTCB bankers started to ooze with national self-confidence, fired up with the belief that the banks were now carrying the message of Japan's industrial might out into the wider world. They remembered only too clearly that four decades earlier their nation had been defeated by America; now Japanese were gobbling up trophy sites across the world, even in America. It felt very sweet.

Flush with the heady excitement of this new "mission," it seemed almost churlish for a bank to worry about dull issues such as the rates of return. The bankers had never worried about returns when they were engaged in their national mission of rebuilding Japanese industry; why should they do so now that they were projecting Japan's power on the world stage? "The banks never really questioned our hotel plans," recalled Nomoto, who had the task of submitting written projections whenever EIE asked for a new loan from LTCB. "Half the time they would just take our plans," Ishizaki said with a laugh, "rip the cover off, photocopy it, and pass it around as their plan. They were just so eager to give us cash, they didn't care."

The other Japanese banks were no different. These banks usually preferred to operate as a team, since it reinforced the sense of community. The New York hotel on 57th Street, for example, was backed not only by LTCB, but also by Mitsubishi Trust, Mitsui Trust, Ashikaga Bank, and Sumitomo Trust. However, none of those banks ever challenged EIE's numbers either. Instead, their main concern was to find out whether EIE had *more* deals that they could finance. "The bankers would ask me things like: 'Are you sure you only want to borrow $100 million? How about $125 million?' " Nomoto said. " 'What about building some hotels in Africa?' "

And as the spending grew wilder, prices became crazier by the day. At the beginning of the decade, the value of real estate in Japan was about the same as land in America. By the end of the decade it had become four times larger than the value of U.S. land—even though Japan's population was only half the size of the United States. Brokers reckoned that the plot of land under the Imperial Palace in Tokyo alone had the same value as the whole of California. Or Canada. Meanwhile, outside Japan, some American brokers estimated that Japanese companies had acquired about two-thirds of the value of real estate in Manhattan. Mitsui Real Estate had spent $610 million to buy the Exxon building in New York, even though the building was initially valued at just $375 million. Mitsubishi Real Estate bought Rockefeller Center in New York for $850 million, at its time a record deal in New York. Japanese companies were also spending lavishly on other trophies: Sony acquired Columbia Pictures for $3.4 billion. Matsushita paid $6.6 billion for MCA. Yasuda Fire and Marine paid $39 million for a single Van Gogh painting.

As Burns scurried around looking for more Regent hotels to develop with EIE, the American hotelier sometimes reflected that this bank behavior was a little odd. When hard-nosed Chinese bankers had financed his Regent hotels in the past, they quibbled about every penny. The Japanese, by contrast, offered a stream of blank checks. "I thought the Japanese banks were just taking a long-term perspective on things," Burns later said, explaining why he never wasted much time pondering the Japanese motives. "There were all these American business books saying that the Japanese businessmen were very long term in their views, and people thought that was a *good* thing." However, Burns comforted himself with the thought that Takahashi was not at all unusual: There were hundreds of other companies such as EIE. And Burns himself was not the only foreigner drinking from this strange financial well: With the same sharp eye for a deal that had driven American traders to Japan in the nineteenth century, foreign investment bankers were falling over themselves to find ways to exploit this new Japanese trend. Lines of Americans, decked out in expensive suits, were flying out to Tokyo and then climbing the four flights of stairs to reach EIE's shabby office in the Ginza. They battled with each other to gain a seat on the EIE plane, to show Takahashi new projects. They pitched ever more exotic ideas, aware that the Japanese were willing to snap up properties without any of the usual hard-nosed bargaining so common in America.

Morgan Stanley, for example, often worked with Burns. The head of its Japanese real estate team in Japan, an American called Bill Kahane, had had the luck—or extraordinary wisdom—to get involved in real estate in the early 1980s, and by the late 1980s had established himself as a key wheeler and dealer in this world, cutting lucrative deals with companies such as EIE. "Sometimes you are just in the right place at the right time," Kahane said in retrospect. "It was crazy—the market was so frothy. Once EIE got involved in bidding for this piece of dirt in Hawaii. It was a working cattle ranch, about 1,100 acres, but Takahashi wanted to build a hotel. It was appraised at $20 million, but in the end Takahashi bought it for $150 million—and there were two other Japanese bids at that level. Everyone [at Morgan Stanley] thought I was a genius."

Occasionally, Kahane would wonder who was exploiting whom. "The problem with the Japanese was that they were so unseasoned," Kahane said. "They were *juvenile.*" He comforted himself with the knowledge that Japan's financial and political establishment clearly knew what was going on. "These companies like EIE were like surrogates. I am convinced that they were created because the banks wanted to get into real estate and the banks knew that they could not control the big *keiretsu* companies. In that sense, EIE was just an invention of the system. I knew two dozen companies like EIE and the one unifying factor was that none of them knew anything about real estate."

And Takahashi's own lifestyle illustrated this broader Japanese support. Between his hotel-hunting trips, Takahashi sometimes invited Burns or Kahane to dinner in Tokyo to "display" him to his powerful friends. He would arrange an evening meal in his favorite *ryotei*—traditional Japanese restaurant—in the Tokyo district of Akasaka. Geisha girls would entertain the guests as they sat on the tatami floors eating Japanese delicacies with their chopsticks. Then Takahashi would urge Burns—via Ishizaki, the translator—to describe his hotels to the other diners, who were usually bankers, senior politicians, and bureaucrats. "Go on, Burns-san! Tell them about our hotels! Tell them about our wonderful projects in New York! The hotel in Milan! Fiji! Bali! Prague!"

On one of these nights, Burns was thrilled to be sitting on the tatami mat next to Shintaro Abe, the "kingmaker" of Japanese politics. Abe spoke reasonable English, and offered to write out Burns's name in Japanese calligraphy. "You know, Burns-san, young Takahashi is a great man!" Abe confided to Burns. "One of these days I would really like to see him become the transport minister of Japan."

In addition to the *ryotei* restaurant in Akasaka, Takahashi sometimes entertained politicians at a nightclub that he owned in Ginza, called the "Chat Blanc." He took politicians and bankers on trips in his jets to sunny locations, where he arranged for them to stay in resorts, with girls and golf thrown in for free. Sometimes bureaucrats from Japan's mighty Ministry of Finance joined these trips, too, but Takahashi cannily recognized that he was not in their league. The Ministry of Finance bureaucrats considered themselves the crème de la crème of Japanese society, and most of them were wary about accepting hospitality from total strangers, like Takahashi. Instead, EIE hired an establishment insider, as a consultant, and asked him to build "contacts" with his old friends and colleagues, by entertaining them at restaurants, golf courses, and sex bars.

"The secret of [his] success was that he looked so completely harmless," Ishizaki later recalled. "He would invite the bureaucrats to a karaoke bar. They would never go with someone they were unsure of. And because there would be pretty young things around, they would accept. . . . Once you broke the ice with them, they'd go out with you, they'd go drinking with you, they'd go fucking with you, they'd do anything with you . . . there's a sugar daddy around who picks up the tab—no quid pro quo. Do this for a year, build up their confidence, then start dropping hints that you want a favor. These guys would consider small favors harmless, and so it begins."

One of the favorite spots for entertaining these bureaucrats was a *no-pan shabu shabu* in Akasaka, an establishment where waitresses traditionally wore no panties (or "*no-pan*" in Japanese English), while serving the traditional Japanese dish of *shabu shabu*, or meat cooked in a boiling broth. The *no-pan* waitresses stood next to tiny fans, which the diners could activate with electronic buttons as the women reached up to pour drinks from high, bar bottles. For added titillation, the diner could also point remote controlled video cameras up the waitresses' skirts, using the latest high-tech gadgetry to beam the pictures of the women onto the dinner table between bottles of soy sauce as they ate their dinner. The bureaucrats loved it.

Sometimes, when Takahashi was flying around the world with his friend Ishizaki in search of hotel deals, he would get reflective. The two men would board the company Boeing on the way to a new hotel deal, stretch out in the leather seats and start to chat. Ishizaki liked to drink champagne on these journeys. However, Takahashi had strikingly simple tastes, even at the height of his power: His favorite dish was "curry rice," a type of cheap Japanese junk food.

"Ishi," Takahashi would say as he lounged in his seat eating his curry rice. "How long can this all continue?"

Ishizaki knew better than to answer the rhetorical question. He saw absolutely no reason why the Japanese banks should ever stop lending money to real estate companies, and thus no reason for EIE to curb its plans. But he would usually hold his counsel and let his boss talk. And Takahashi's musings usually reached the same conclusion: "Someday, someday it will end," he would say. "But while it lasts, we should make our company as large as we can, and then tidy it up. While the spigot is open, we must borrow!"

— *Chapter 5* —

THE BUBBLE BURSTS

They say that the problem with Japanese banks is that it is all smoke and mirrors with the accounts. I think it is even worse than that. I fear they don't even know what the problems are themselves.

—Gary Brinson, former head of Brinson asset management and alliance partner of LTCB

One of the first signs that the climate was changing occurred on Christmas Day, 1989. Initially the incident seemed almost innocuous. But that is often the way with bubbles: One minute the euphoria seems unstoppable; then a small unexpected jolt occurs and the house of cards starts tumbling down. During the latter part of the 1980s, the Bank of Japan had maintained a very loose monetary policy to offset the rising yen. But this policy also fueled a soaring stock market and property market. By December 1989 the Nikkei 225 had reached 39,000, four times its level in 1980. The numbers were impressive, but like the price of real estate, Japanese stocks had lost touch with their underlying reality. To put it in perspective, in 1989 Japanese shares accounted for more than half of the world's entire stock capitalization. If that weren't enough, some market analysts dared to predict the Nikkei 225 could touch 60,000.

In late 1989, the Bank was becoming nervous. It was time, officials decided, to "cool" the bubble a little. So, to the market's surprise, the Bank announced a sudden sharp interest rate rise on Christmas Day, 1989. The Bank economists hoped this would slow the rise in stock and land prices. It never occurred to anybody in the government that a rate rise could really damage the economy. However, the Nikkei 225 immediately tumbled toward 34,000.

Inside EIE—and every other real estate company in Japan—the rate rise also came as a very unpleasant shock. In the heady optimism of late 1989 the company had moved out of its scruffy, fourth-floor office in Ginza into new headquarters in Akasaka, a district with hotels, restaurants, and many foreign banks. The new building was airy, with plush carpets, state-of-the-art air-conditioning, and plenty of wall space to hang EIE's growing collection of expensive paintings. Takahashi was very fond of art and particularly keen on buying pieces by Chagall and Picasso. As with his other fine tastes, Takahashi bankrolled his collection using money borrowed from LTCB.

Ishizaki, ever the fixer, would arrange the art deals with the help of a female French friend who was a retired prostitute. "She had grown too old to be a hooker," Ishizaki said, "she had a few too many wrinkles, so she decided to become a freelance art dealer." Though she had switched careers, the Frenchwoman had not lost her accommodating ways. "I'd ask her to draw up a valuation certificate for, say, ten million dollars," Ishizaki later explained, "and then the bankers would come and look at this painting. The bankers didn't know a Cezanne from a Monet, but they'd nod and say, 'Yes, this is worth ten million, so we'll lend you eight million against it.' Then my French friend would sell us the painting, probably under a different name, and take a commission on the deal."

The source of so much easy money had ultimately been the Bank of Japan's loose monetary policy. But if interest rates rose, it was not clear EIE would be able to keep up with the payments on its art loans—let alone its real estate portfolio. Before 1990, nobody in EIE or LTCB had ever tried to calculate what higher interest rates do. Money was plentiful and cheap, costing a mere 2 or 3 percent a year in nominal terms (and far less in real terms). The bankers' borrowers had presumed it would stay that way indefinitely. And both EIE and LTCB had also presumed that if the company did ever need to raise a great deal of cash in a hurry, it could simply sell one of its buildings, at a large profit to pay off the debt. "In retrospect, I do realize that was a mistake," Ishizaki later admitted. "We probably ought to have created a debt servicing plan." Unfortunately, the men at EIE spent more time creating flight plans for their Boeings.

If interest rates started to head up, however, EIE's business model could quickly fall apart. By 1990, its total level of bank borrowing had risen to around Y700 billion ($7 billion). Thus a 1 percent increase in interest rates would force the company to find an additional Y7 billion (or $70 million) a year in profits from its operations to cover the increased debt service. EIE's businesses were not that easy to milk for extra profits or increased revenue. And Y7 billion was a lot of money. The only way that EIE could pay higher debt servicing costs was to borrow *more* money or sell its buildings—presuming of course that it could find a willing supply of buyers.

In the spring of 1990 Takahashi quietly approached some of his old friends at the bank. As always, he presented a bullish attitude. EIE was running into temporary shortages of funds, Takahashi said, after running through the long list of current projects and acquisitions. Citing the squeeze on his cash flow, the hotel magnate asked the bank to hold off on its rate increase and even issue an additional loan to cover the shortfall. Takahashi exuded confidence in his prospects: "It will just be temporary."

The request was discussed by Tetsuya Horie, then president of Long Term Credit Bank, and other officials who were in charge of loan business. Horie decided to accept Takahashi's request, and the job of executing this was delegated to Suzuki. A short man, Suzuki had joined LTCB in 1962. He had spent his career dealing with the domestic business. During the 1980s he had worked in the loan promotion department, spending endless evenings with the bank's corporate clients, eating at traditional Japanese restaurants, often playing the traditional Japanese board game *go*. He spoke no English and had little experience overseas. When he once traveled to New York to stay in the EIE hotel on 57th Street, he had to ask LTCB colleagues for help in turning on the American television.

Behind the scenes, "Katsu-chan"—as he was known to his intimates—wielded enormous power. Indeed, he epitomized the way that Japanese bankers did their domestic business, away from the eyes of the outside world. Unusually tough and decisive for a banker, he was blessed with an awesome memory for numbers. "He is a typical Edo man," colleagues would sometimes say, referring to the fact that men from Edo, as Tokyo had traditionally been called, were reputed to be resolute characters. This numerical skill and tough character made him a fearsome problem "fixer"—particularly when dealing with domestic loans. "He was like a robot, or the perfect bureaucrat," one colleague recalled. "When you gave him a problem, he solved it."

More surprisingly, "Katsu-chan" was also a close ally of Onogi. Back in the 1980s, the ever astute Onogi had become uneasy about the gulf that was developing between the "internationalists" and "domestic" wing at LTCB. He had deliberately tried to breach it in his own personal career, by telling his superiors that he would like to have a domestic banker appointed as his deputy. That, he argued, could help promote the type of "consensus" that Onogi considered to be so important. More pragmatically, it would also boost his career, since men who were perceived to be too exclusively "international" rarely made it to the very top. One of these "domestic" men who worked closely with Onogi was Suzuki. Although the two men were very different in character, they forged an unexpectedly close bond. Onogi recognized that "Katsu-chan" was a skilled and ruthless organizer; Suzuki admired the slightly older Onogi for his vision, public speaking skills, and international flair. "Suzuki was a natural deputy—like the small shark who swims with a whale," Ryuji Konishi, an LTCB banker, later explained. Another colleague added, more charitably: "Onogi was a thinker; Suzuki a doer."

It did not take Suzuki long to decide what to do with Takahashi's request. His career inside LTCB had flourished on the back of the real estate boom, and though Suzuki was not particularly close to Takahashi, Suzuki's power base had grown as the EIE account rose in value to the bank. Indeed, by 1990, EIE had become one of the bank's ten largest customers, and the bank was estimated to have more than Y300 billion ($3 billion) loans to EIE. Suzuki also knew that this pattern could work in reverse. If Takahashi became a public liability, this could trigger recriminations, leaving the domestic loan department losing "face"—and power.

In April, Suzuki and another senior manager quietly authorized another "temporary" Y6 billion ($60 million) loan to plug the financing gap. This flew in the face of all prudent banking theory, or macroeconomic logic. When a "bubble" bursts, it makes most sense in macroeconomic terms for a country to *remove* resources from sectors of the economy that have become overheated, or simply unproductive, rather than pour more money into the problem. By giving Takahashi more loans, the bank was simply increasing its own risk. Worse still, the LTCB bankers did not ask for additional collateral from EIE or initiate fresh credit checks. The only condition attached to the loan was a tacit promise that Takahashi would halt his plans to buy a lavish new Paris hotel. Yet the LTCB bankers hoped that a new loan would be a quick fix, to stop the "embarrassing" situation coming to light, and they reasoned that Y6 billion was a trifling amount compared with the loans the bank had already made to EIE. "Asking for another credit check seemed unnecessary," one of Suzuki's colleagues explained, years later. "We all knew Takahashi so well." The LTCB bankers had taken the first step onto a slippery slope.

LTCB tried to brush the incident off. In midsummer the bank published its annual report for the financial year to March 1990, which highlighted a string of prestigious international investment banking deals that the bank had done, boosting its reputation on the world stage. This also proudly revealed Y64 billion ($640 million) in net profits, slightly lower than the previous year but still the second highest level ever recorded. In passing, the bank noted that its loan book had risen by 16.1 percent during the previous year alone largely due to a sharp increase in "loans to small and medium-sized companies." This had left total assets at Y30,000 billion ($300 billion), almost *twice* the level just five years earlier. However, LTCB did not explain what caused this or express any unease.

Despite this silence, the pressure was building. The Bank of Japan raised interest rates for a third time in August 1990, taking them to 6 percent, compared with 2.5 percent fifteen months earlier. Stocks fell again and by October 1, the Nikkei 225 was trading around 21,000, 48 percent lower than at the start of the year. Three hundred *trillion* yen ($3 trillion) of paper wealth had been destroyed in nine months. Meanwhile, Takahashi was returning to the LTCB bankers to ask for more "temporary" injections of cash. And he was not the only one. Across Japan, thousands of other companies were in exactly the same position. Outwardly, there was still relatively little sign of trouble. Very few companies had gone bankrupt, because the banks were still propping them up. Meanwhile, the official government statistics suggested that property prices were still static. But this was only because the property market was completely frozen. Nobody wanted to buy land because they guessed that the market was going to fall. The logic that had underpinned the banks' loans was falling apart.

Behind the scenes, some of the officials in Suzuki's team furtively started to discuss what it should do about EIE—and all the other companies. In America, there was a well-worn formula for dealing with companies that were unable to repay their loans. When default occurred, a bank was usually expected to acknowledge the problem, quickly work out the scale of damage, write off the losses, and recoup whatever value it could, either by imposing a bankruptcy or even forcing the company into liquidation. American banks did not always live up to these ideals. But if their clients kept bleeding cash without any prospect of recovery or liquidation, they would usually write the loan off and walk away.

That approach would have undermined the foundations of postwar Japanese finance. The corporate system created in the early 1950s was based on the concept of mutual support and perpetual growth. No bank had *ever* dared to force a client into bankruptcy or abandoned a closely related company, because they never believed they needed to. Instead, if a company fell into difficulties, the main bank usually sent in some of its own staff to monitor a gentle restructuring program, carried out in the most polite manner possible, with additional infusions of cash if necessary. If a bank ever hesitated in this duty, the mighty Ministry of Finance would sometimes orchestrate a "friendly," cooperative workout, since the bureaucrats were as opposed as anybody else to the idea of a bank "abandoning" its clients. At all costs, the banks were supposed to avoid an embarrassing public mess.

On January 4, 1991, two dozen LTCB bankers turned up at the EIE office in Akasaka. They carried name cards reading "LTCB—special projects" and declared that they were now effectively moving into the building, to oversee the company and find a way of repaying some of the debt.

"We are here to *help* you," a senior LTCB banker explained to Takahashi, as the EIE staff rushed around to find desks and chairs for the new arrivals. The bankers explained that their goal was to sell about Y250 billion ($2.5 billion) of EIE's stated assets of Y690 billion ($6.9 billion). "The developer is not thought of as a problem company," the bank explained to journalists. "We think EIE's core business of resort development is very strong. The difficulty is that higher interest rates have caused problems for their cash flow."

Nomoto was blown away. During 1990, Takahashi had seemed confident that the bank would keep supplying funds to keep EIE afloat without any questions. After all, he had spent hours—and millions of yen—cultivating his political and banker "friends." However, it was now clear that LTCB believed that it was running EIE, even though no legal action had ever been taken. The LTCB bankers started shuffling through the company files, and peppering the EIE team with questions. "How do you do all of this travel?" one asked. "How do you get to your hotels so fast?" "I use one of the jets," Ishizaki replied.

"Doesn't your company have a travel form?" the banker went on. "Don't you have to get it signed by a superior when you travel?" Ishizaki replied that he just telephoned the pilots of the jet whenever he wanted to travel. Sometimes it took a while, he added, since the planes were usually parked in the Pacific island of Guam.

"Aah—that's the problem," the bankers declared. "From now on, you must get your travel approved in advance with a form. We are going to create some forms for you to complete."

"Do you have a system to control the photocopying?" The bankers continued looking for cost savings. Nomoto explained that the EIE staff just used the copy machine whenever they needed to. Since he was the person in charge of most of the logistics, much of the copying was done by him. "You need another form for that, too! This is completely out of control."

Then, the LTCB bankers started drawing up a plan to sell off some of the EIE assets to raise cash. "I know somebody who would buy one of the jets for three million dollars or so," Ishizaki said. The LTCB bankers responded that their orders from headquarters were to sell the salable items themselves. "But if you sell it, you won't get nearly as much money! You will only get one million or so!" Ishizaki protested. The bankers brushed him off. It was, they explained, more important to obey the commands of their superiors correctly than worry about saving $2 million.

The bankers then turned their attention to the Regent hotels. A couple of LTCB officials took up residence in a brownstone building in New York, next to where the Regent officials were overseeing the construction of the Four Seasons on 57th Street, and started to pepper Burns with questions. "Do you need to clad the whole of the hotel in limestone? It will cost millions of dollars! Why not put the limestone just at the bottom?"

Burns pointed out that the limestone finish had been part of I. M. Pei's design from the start, when it was planned back in 1987. The idea was that the inside of the hotel would be lined with limestone, like a giant Egyptian temple, while the outside would soar up midtown Manhattan. Wouldn't it look rather silly, Burns argued, if the tower changed color halfway up? That would ruin the whole obelisk effect.

"What about the furniture?" A junior LTCB banker pointed out that the lavish plans for the hotel would require vast quantities of solid wood. "Why do you have to have solid wood desks? Why not just a wood veneer?" Irritated, Burns argued that solid wood desks lasted longer than veneers. "Veneers look tacky!" Burns declared. "How can you have guests paying hundreds of dollars a night to stay in a hotel with *veneers* on the desks?"

As the questions gathered pace, Burns grew baffled. Since he was deemed an "outsider"—and an American at that—nobody from LTCB bothered to formally explain to him exactly how power had changed at EIE. As far as Burns could see, Takahashi was still the official chairman of EIE, since there had been no declaration of bankruptcy or *legal* change of ownership. Yet now LTCB was dictating the spending plans—and doing so in a way that seemed completely irrational to Burns. In his long career as a hotel manager, he had had plenty of experience with bankers getting fussy about costs. Hard-nosed Hong Kong Chinese investors had always tried to trim his spending. But the Chinese had quibbled about his plans *in advance*. The Japanese had done a U-turn midstream: First they gave Takahashi leeway to do anything he wanted; now they had "put him under house arrest," as Burns joked. He could understand why LTCB might be feeling worried about the scale of its international exposure. But he believed that the bank's behavior was going to make it harder to recoup value; if they wanted to get their money back, Burns wondered why they did not just sell the hotel?

Yet, whenever Burns spoke to LTCB, he found it difficult to get the Japanese bankers to talk about long-term strategy. The bankers either denied that any problems existed, or tried to offer a few short-term fixes. To Burns and Kahane, the broker at Morgan Stanley, it seemed as "juvenile" as the way that the Japanese had rushed overseas and snapped up properties in the 1980s. "Don't these bankers understand how money works?" Kahane wondered.

The economic news became steadily worse. By 1991 Japan was not yet in a recession—or not as it was usually defined in America or Europe—since the economy was still posting growth of almost 1 percent a year. But 1 percent was dramatically slower than anything seen in the 1980s, and by the summer of 1991 the Nikkei was trading under 20,000, less than half its level eighteen months before. Meanwhile, there were signs that real estate prices were also starting to slip further as real estate brokers estimated that Y50 trillion ($500 billion) worth of property was waiting to be sold. Just as the real estate market and stock market had ratcheted up in tandem during the 1980s, now they were both threatening to drag each other down.

This was extremely bad news for the LTCB, and all the other banks. During the 1980s bubble, lending by the Japanese had doubled, creating an additional Y260 trillion ($2.6 trillion) of credit. Most of these new loans had been extended to real estate companies, or offered to individuals and non-manufacturing companies for property investment. Indeed, by the early 1990s, 25 percent of the banks' loan portfolio (or Y116 trillion—$1.16 trillion) was *directly* extended to the property and construction sectors, while another 55 percent was believed to be indirectly linked to land. Yet the banks had a mere Y3 trillion ($30 billion) of reserves on their books, to protect them if property prices fell. In theory, the banks still had a very large pool of capital they could use to plug any gap. But Japanese banks—in contrast to American groups—had traditionally held a great deal of their capital in the form of equities, which the decline in the stock market had badly eroded. Meanwhile, in a move that had added to the pressure, the Bank for International Settlements (BIS) had recently moved to tighten global international capital adequacy standards, which made it even harder for the banks to issue stock. Worse still, the banks' core operating profits were suffering. In 1985, the government had finally embarked on the interest rate deregulation that it had promised to introduce—under American pressure—which had slashed the banks' lending margins. The banks were thus losing their revenues just when they needed them most.

LTCB continued its internal debate over what could be done to get out of the hole. It was becoming clear to the bankers that the problems at companies like EIE could not be fixed by simply selling a few buildings, or planes. It was also clear that the government did not want LTCB and the other banks to walk away from all the troubled real estate borrowers. Indeed, the government had not admitted in public that there was any real "problem" lurking in the banks at all. The official rhetoric coming from the Ministry of Finance and LDP was that the downturn in land prices and the stock market was simply a *temporary* phenomenon and the economy would soon be forging ahead. "Nobody thought that land prices would keep falling," explained Tetsuro Nishizaki, an adviser to the Ministry at the time. "We all kept expecting the Japanese economy to recover very shortly after the collapse of the bubble."

The LTCB bankers decided that the most sensible thing they could do was play for time. And as they waited for land prices to rise again, the bankers also decided that it made the most sense to keep the existing problems under wraps. After all, the Ministry did not want any bank to do anything that might hurt market confidence. Falling confidence could delay a recovery. So, as 1991 wore on, the bank quietly started to develop schemes to ensure that its problems remained under wraps.

Subterfuge was by no means a new tactic in Japan. Japanese culture has traditionally assumed that a distinction exists between "public" or "official" reality (known as *tatemae*) and "private" truth (known as *honne*). It was accepted that companies would want to keep "embarrassing" secrets out of public view and LTCB itself had done this before. When the Bank of Japan announced that it was conducting an inspection of LTCB's operations in the early 1990s, for example, the most junior bankers were ordered to pack any "embarrassing" files into boxes and carry them down to a "B3" base-

ment, three floors beneath the bank building, before the inspectors arrived. There they were hidden away in a concrete manhole. "It was an absolute pain," one of the young bankers later recalled. "We went up and down, carrying these heavy boxes, to put them in this manhole thing—and then when it was all over we had to do it again!"

As far as the young bankers could tell, there had never been anything desperately illegal in these boxes: Most of them simply related to minor infractions of laws. Nor was the hiding place particularly foolproof: If the bank inspectors had wanted to take a peek at the basement, they could have. Yet, the presumption was that if the boxes were not staring the inspectors in the face, they could ignore them with a clean conscience; and if the LTCB bankers were not asked difficult questions by the inspectors, they would never need to lie. Hiding the problem thus ensured that everyone could save public face and maintain "harmony."

Exactly the same principles were applied to accounting. In Japan companies were only required to reveal what was happening in their subsidiaries if they owned a significant stake in them. In the case of LTCB—and most banks—there were dozens of subsidiaries and affiliates that were effectively controlled by the bank, but below the radar screen since the legal relationship was small. Thus, it was relatively easy for a bank to park problems in these subsidiaries for a period, hidden from outside eyes. Subsidiaries could act as the accounting equivalent of a concrete manhole to hide embarrassing secrets.

As the problems mounted up, LTCB started to take advantage of this principle. In December 1991, the bankers created a company called "NR," which was designed to act as a warehouse for some of the nonperforming loans. Starting in late 1991, the bank started to "sell" its assets to NR at book value, together with the risk attached to these loans. This did not, of course, really remove the problem in the long term. Companies like NR were only able to purchase these risky loans *because LTCB itself lent it the cash*. Thus LTCB had simply replaced one set of bad loans with another. However, NR was such a tiny, obscure group that nobody outside the bank noticed the scheme. Better still, the bank was allowed to classify its loans to NR as "healthy," since NR was considered to have the support of LTCB and the risk inside NR did not need to be reported on LTCB's balance sheet.

The problem seemed to have been magically removed. So, as time passed, more subsidiaries appeared. A couple of years after creating NR, the bank established another satellite called Hibiya Sogo Kaihatsu—or "Hibiya General Development Group"—and started to furtively "sell" some assets to this group, again at inflated prices. Then the bankers realized that they might attract attention if they loaded too many assets into just one or two groups, and so they created a dozen more companies with names such as Yurakucho Sogo Kaihatsu and Shimbashi Sogo Kaihatsu. Some of the LTCB bankers drolly referred to these as the "seven sisters." Then the bank created some subsidiaries of these subsidiaries, so firmly off any balance sheet that many LTCB staff barely knew they existed. It also started to shuffle loans into some of the existing subsidiaries with bona fide business, such as Japan Lease, a leasing affiliate that had been created in the 1970s, NED, a group that was designed to support venture capital, and Nippon Landic, a designated real estate group. These affiliates not only took over loans, but stock and real estate. In a classic type of deal, Nippon Landic agreed to "buy" LTCB's headquarters building in Otemachi in 1991. Until that point, the "value" of the property had been recorded at Y2 billion ($20 million) on the LTCB books, since that was the amount the building and land had cost back in the 1960s. When the building was sold, Nippon Landic arbitrarily decided that the "real" price was Y100 billion ($1 billion)—creating an instant Y98 billion ($980 million) "profit" in the LTCB accounts.

These tricks relied on the cooperation of friendly subsidiaries—and the assumption that the staff of these subsidiaries would be willing to "buy" assets at inflated prices. But that did not present a problem. It was usual practice in Japan's banking world for the chairmen and president of a bank subsidiary to have started their careers at the bank, and in the case of the major LTCB subsidiaries the presidents were a particularly privileged group of bankers. Most of them had been in the first class of new graduates that joined the bank back in its founding year of 1952, or Showa 28. They were a tightly knit bunch who wielded great power inside LTCB, and were more than ready to perform their "duty" for LTCB.

Then LTCB discovered more exotic games. In 1992, Bob Burns of the Regent hotel group finally decided to retire and sell his 65 percent stake in the business. The American appointed Morgan Stanley to manage the sale and hoped to cut a deal with Wharf, a Hong Kong–based company, with whom he had friendly ties. Wharf offered about $200 million for Burns's stake and a deal seemed almost done. But in the middle of the negotiations some Credit Suisse First Boston bankers secretly proposed a different deal. CSFB—like many of the other investment banks—had earned healthy profits during the 1980s by helping the Japanese banks acquire property overseas. When this game ended in the early 1990s, these same investment banks spotted a new niche: namely devising schemes that would allow Japanese banks to disguise losses on their assets and prevent the fall in property prices from hurting their balance sheets. The scheme for the Regent hotels was a classic of this kind. CSFB knew that a second hotel group, Four Seasons, was desperate to acquire the Regent management group—indeed, so eager it would be willing to use an unusual accounting structure to get the deal done. So CSFB proposed that instead of letting Burns sell his stake in Regent to Wharf, LTCB itself would acquire the whole of Regent and then sell the entire company to Four Seasons in a way that would temporarily disguise some of the losses, in a legal manner, via a new off-balance sheet paper company called the Hotel Investment Corp. (HIC). The Four Seasons group was happy because, in exchange for helping LTCB to do this, it took control of Regent at a fire sale price.

When Burns found out about the CSFB plans, he was utterly livid. He regarded the Regent as his "baby," and though he was willing to sell it to his friends at Wharf, he absolutely did not want to let his hotel group fall into the hands of his arch rival, the Four Seasons group. "If I had had the faintest idea of what was going to happen," Burns later wailed, "I would never have sold out at all!" Nonetheless, Burns could not stop the deal, since under the terms of EIE's original investment in Regent the Japanese had first option to buy if Burns wished to sell. In the summer of 1992, the Regent hotels were sold to the Four Seasons, using the "HIC" structure. To the LTCB bankers delight another swath of problems had been hidden from public view, at least for while.

Foreign investment bankers offered help in other ways. In the early 1990s, CSFB salesmen started to aggressively market financial products to help the Japanese banks to "temporarily" improve their accounts. These were based around a type of investment trust, which exploited accounting loopholes to flatter the banks' results. Just like corporate subsidiaries, these trusts, known as *tokkin*, were considered to be off the core balance sheet under Japanese accounting laws—meaning that the detailed activities of a *tokkin* fund did not need to be displayed. So what the CSFB salesmen typically did was to take some money from a Japanese client for a five-year period and invest this in a manner that could allow the client to book an immediate, up-front profit by using structured financial products like derivatives. If the scheme actually produced a loss, not a profit, at the end of this period, the money was simply rolled over again, concealing the loss.

The Ministry of Finance did not appear to have any objection to Japanese banks using these schemes. So, from the early 1990s a host of American and European banks, such as Morgan Stanley, Merrill Lynch, Deutsche Bank, UBS, and Paribas, started to sell these services to the Japanese. But CSFB was generally considered the real expert at the game, partly because it had an unusually freewheeling, aggressive culture. In the early 1990s, a pugnacious Wall Street banker called Allen Wheat had joined CSFB from Bankers Trust, bringing with him a host of other BT bankers, such as Chris Goekjian. Wheat and Goekjian had risen to power from a background in derivatives and had a sharp eye for profits. They were willing to do whatever business appeared to offer quick returns, and to them, Japan offered low-hanging fruit.

In the spring of 1993, the Ministry of Finance finally decided to make a token effort to tighten up the banks' reporting standards. Rumors were starting to trickle into the markets about losses in real estate companies, and the bureaucrats wanted to calm investors. So, for the first time ever, the government insisted that all the banks should file data on their bad loans according to a standardized system, instead of simply leaving this to the discretion of each bank, as the government had done in the past. Defining a "bad loan" is a fiendishly difficult issue in any country, since it effectively involves not simply measuring the past, but also guessing whether a company will be able to repay money in the future, which in turn relies on predictions about the economy. Consequently, when banks produce information about "bad loans" in the Western world, they usually present this as a spectrum: At one end are the clearly bad loans made to companies that have *already* collapsed and cannot repay loans; at the other end lie loans to companies that are still operating, but appear unlikely to repay the loan in full if economic conditions deteriorate. The words "bad loans" can thus have a host of different meanings at any one time, depending on whether an observer just looks at the past—or future dangers as well. Not fully prepared to grasp the difficulties of real reform, the Japanese government decided to take a relatively lenient stance. "Bad loans" were defined as loans to bankrupt enterprises or companies that had not been able to make interest payments during the past six months.

The results from even this lenient classification made uncomfortable reading. According to the Ministry, the level of bad loans for the twenty-one major banks in March 1993 was Y11.7 trillion ($120 billion)—or about 2 percent of the total—against which the banks had made reserves of Y3.4 trillion ($34 billion). This was a far bigger problem than the Ministry had previously admitted. And yet this data did not cover the losses sitting in the subsidiaries of the banks. Nor did it even cover the risky loans—or loans to companies that were still managing to cobble together just enough money to pay interest, but secretly sitting on huge real estate losses. Just how many more of those loans would turn bad in the future was anybody's guess, but it seemed dangerous to ignore them. Land prices were still falling sharply and the losses were spreading far beyond the real estate developers. The state of the *jusen*, for example, was attracting particular concern. These were small financial companies that had been created in the early 1970s as independent mortgage lenders, but had then diversified in the late 1980s to invest heavily in some of the riskiest real estate projects. The banks were closely linked to the *jusen* and one of these—Dai-Ichi Housing—was effectively an affiliate of LTCB. The Ministry had known since 1991 that a third of the Y12 trillion-odd ($120 billion) *jusen* loans were nonperforming, but chose to ignore this in its official bad loan data.

Indeed, in the case of LTCB, the gap between the public and private numbers was becoming bigger by the day. As far back as 1991, the Bank of Japan had noted during an inspection that there were some Y1,628 billion ($16.28 billion) of loans sitting on the bank's balance sheet that could be potentially risky. This roughly tallied with internal data secretly collected by Suzuki's team, although the official level of bad loans reported by LTCB was just Y21.5 billion ($215 million). The Ministry of Finance conducted an inspection a year later, which separately calculated that risky and bad loans were Y1.3 trillion ($13 billion). However, officials decided that there was no point in publicly revealing this data, or forcing LTCB to change its figures. After all, they reasoned, most of the risky loans had not turned bad—and might never do so if the economy recovered. And when the Bank of Japan returned for its next inspection in December 1994, it saw little reason to change this stance. The Bank concluded in a confidential report that LTCB's bad and potentially risky loans had now ballooned to Y3.4 trillion ($34 billion), or about a fifth of all its loans. The Bank passed the results on to the Ministry of Finance and warned the LTCB managers that it was not a good idea for a bank to have so many subsidiaries. That was it. The Ministry and Bank did not offer any specific reprimands, or any guidance about what exactly LTCB should do about its bad loans. Nor did they suggest that LTCB should change the way it reported its bad loan figures.

Elsewhere, such official forbearance might have been considered shocking. Sweden, for example, had also suffered an asset price bubble in the 1980s and in the early 1990s—or about the same time as Japan. This bubble burst, creating a wave of bad loans at Swedish banks. Within a few years, the Swedish government started drawing up plans to nationalize some banks, forcing the banks to reveal their bad loans and take measures to write them off. But over in Japan, the bureaucrats—and bankers—blithely insisted that such radical action was not only unnecessary, but would needlessly make the problems worse. "We didn't want to create panic in the financial markets or among consumers. We wanted to deal with the problems slowly and calmly," Tetsuro Nishizaki, head of the Ministry of Finance's financial advisory committee in the mid-1990s, later explained. "Anyway, absolutely everybody believed that land prices would rise in the future, and would cure the problems. Most of the other banks were doing exactly the same thing as LTCB."

— *Chapter 6* —

TAKAHASHI'S REVENGE

Freezing bad loans at a time when land prices are declining is like putting rotten meat in a freezer. Rotten meat does not return to its previous condition.

—Anzai investigation report

The first serious knock to LTCB's house of cards occurred in the spring of 1995. And it came from a most unlikely source: a corruption scandal that pushed Takahashi back into the limelight, along with some of Japan's infamous sex bars—and catapulted Onogi into power. "My fate has been a strange one," Onogi once joked. "When I look back on my life I sometimes feel as if I have been like a small boat on a river, swept along by a current. For years I tried to paddle hard, and avoid being swept over the edge. But the current took me anyway."

The rumblings of the scandal started in the autumn of 1994 with revelations in the local tabloid newspapers that Takahashi had been offering some lavish entertainment to bureaucrats, politicians, and bankers—including golf tournaments, holidays, and wild evenings at establishments such as the *no-pan shabu shabu* restaurants. Initially, the Japanese establishment paid relatively little attention. The newspaper industry—like so much else in Japan's corporate world—was polarized into two, symbiotic extremes. At one extreme lay the "respectable" papers, such as the *Nikkei, Yomiuri,* and *Asahi,* which received privileged access to the government via special press cartels—known as *kisha* clubs—but practiced a strict self-censorship in exchange for this access. They rarely wrote anything the government did not want them to reveal, let alone anything raunchy. At the other extreme was the tabloid industry, which was as wild as the seamier side of the stock market. These tabloids had little respect for press controls or libel laws and dotted their pages with pornography and lurid gossip that was often deliberately planted by politicians, businessmen, or even *yakuza* to discredit rivals or manipulate markets. Yet the tabloids also produced brilliantly hard-hitting investigations of political and financial matters, tucked between pictures of undressed schoolgirls. Indeed, many of articles were actually written by journalists who worked for the "respectable" press: Working under pseudonyms, they used the tabloids to write the stories that would be censored by the official papers.

The Takahashi scandal—as it became known—was a classic illustration of this split. Journalists had been aware of the sleaze surrounding EIE and the banks for several years; however, none of the official press had dared to write about it, since Takahashi had friends in the mighty Ministry of Finance. But in the autumn of 1994 the political climate started to shift, and some tabloid journalists became willing to take a closer look at what was happening at EIE, egged on by opposition party politicians. And what they found was a distinctly embarrassing saga, not just for the Ministry but also for LTCB.

By 1994, LTCB's official line on EIE was that it had stopped bailing Takahashi out. The previous year it had finally judged that EIE's problems were so serious—and the company sufficiently isolated from any *keiretsu*—that it could afford to display a rare burst of ruthlessness. In July 1993 it abruptly issued a statement declaring that it was cutting ties with EIE and admitted that it had Y190 billion ($1.9 billion) of outstanding loans to EIE, of which half were bad. "We could not agree with EIE on the restructuring [of its company] so we have decided to end our support. We just could not go on providing funds the way things were going. We want to show that we are financially sound," the bank declared. "We don't want to be called the main creditor bank for EIE International anymore," Tsuneo Suzuki, head of the project loan division, pithily explained to a Japanese journalist. "We are not EIE's main bank."

At the time, the news left Japan's corporate world swimming. By some measures, the announcement marked the first time that a major bank had *ever* abandoned one of its ten largest clients. Western analysts were equally startled, but thrilled by the sight of a Japanese bank that appeared to have accepted economic logic. Almost overnight LTCB earned itself a reputation among foreigners for being one of the more "innovative" of the Japanese banks, and some foreign banking analysts started to recommend its shares to their clients. As time passed, however, LTCB's announcement began to seem a little odd—not least because Takahashi himself seemed unruffled by the news. "I am going off to play golf!" local journalists quoted him as saying when he heard that the banks were pulling the loans. Indeed, it seemed that the "shock" of bankruptcy had barely harmed Takahashi. He retained control over various luxury mansions and talked about embarking on new projects. He was still spotted with bureaucrats and bankers, staging golf tournaments at the Hill Crest Club in Tochigi and picking up the bill in the best Tokyo restaurants and most pricey sex bars.

The reason for this lay in a little-noticed detail of the EIE empire that was typical of Japan's corporate world. In addition to his web of luxurious hotels, resorts, and golf courses, Takahashi also controlled a couple of obscure "credit unions." These were a type of miniature bank that usually provided local financing for small businesses, rural families, farmers, and entrepreneurs in Japan, similar to the Savings and Loan groups in America. One of these credit unions was called Tokyo Kyowa, which had been initially established by a group of Chinese restaurant owners in Japan, before Takahashi took control in the 1980s. The second went under the grossly inappropriate name "Anzen"—"safety." Under Japanese banking law, credit unions were not supposed to lend to companies controlled by their directors. Nor were they allowed to lend more than 20 percent of their capital to any one single client. However, the credit unions in Japan were regulated even more lightly than banks, partly because local governments shared regulatory responsibility for the unions with the Ministry of Finance. Consequently, Takahashi flouted the rules cheerily. After LTCB started to cut off finance to EIE, the two credit unions poured money into companies linked to Takahashi, pushing their overall level of lending from Y40 billion ($400 million) to Y300 billion ($3 billion). Some money was channeled to EIE directly. Most of the funds went to Takahashi's network of EIE subsidiaries, or Takahashi's friends, such as Toshio Yamaguchi, the former labor minister. When this looked too suspicious, the credit unions then lent money to *friends* of Takahashi's friends: In 1993, Yamaguchi's siblings borrowed another Y34 billion ($340 million) from the credit unions and their affiliates.

The breaches were so blatant that by 1993 even the officials at the Tokyo Metropolitan Government—which was supposed to be monitoring the two unions—found them hard to ignore. Quietly, they asked the Ministry of Finance if it might be time to shut the unions down. But the Ministry bureaucrats insisted that there was no need to worry. Back in 1990, LTCB had taken a Y1.5 billion ($15 million) equity stake in Tokyo Kyowa and placed one of its bankers in the credit union. This was not mentioned in the bank's annual report and few LTCB employees were aware of the link, because information about different loans and customers were segregated among different departments. In the eyes of the Ministry of Finance, this connection meant that LTCB had a moral obligation to support the credit unions and to all intents and purposes, it seemed that LTCB was respecting this duty. "Anyone who believes that the LTCB really just walked away from Takahashi [in 1993] is pretty naive," Ishizaki later said. "They walked out through the front door but then they supported Takahashi through the back door. That's why there wasn't a single complaint from the Ministry of Finance, the Bank of Japan, or EIE's other backers . . . that's why nobody was fired, why the bills kept getting paid. There was a secret agreement, and the focal point of it was the Tokyo Kyowa Credit Union—the LTCB supported Takahashi through that."

For a while, this backdoor scheme allowed LTCB to stave off any showdown with Takahashi. But land prices continued to fall. By the autumn of 1994, the Tokyo Metropolitan Government bureaucrats calculated that well over half of the Y300 billion outstanding loans at Tokyo Kyowa and Anzen were bad. They approached the Ministry of Finance again and nervously asked—for the second time—if it was time to shut the credit unions down.

The Ministry of Finance was unsure. No financial institution had ever failed in Japan since World War II. Instead, the postwar financial system had been founded on the "convoy system" principle, or the assumption that the government would always protect depositors and creditors if a bank ran into problems, by persuading other banks to "voluntarily" rescue a weak group. So the bureaucrats asked LTCB to rescue Tokyo Kyowa and Anzen with a new injection of funds. However, LTCB was starting to get cold feet. The LTCB bankers knew that their bank was in no shape to spend another Y300 billion on Takahashi—and they had a sense that his political power was beginning to ebb. So the bureaucrats then attempted to organize a "collective" solution. In late 1994, the Bank and Ministry announced plans to "rescue" the two credit unions by merging them into a new bank, called Tokyo Kyodo, and indicated that the central bank itself would pour Y20 billion ($200 million) of its own funds into the scheme. The Tokyo Metropolitan Government agreed to contribute Y30 billion ($300 million) more. Then the Bank of Japan summoned the private banks and ordered them to contribute capital to this new bank, as it had done in earlier "rescues" of troubled financial groups. The process was dubbed *hougachou,* the word that was usually used to describe the practice of "encouraging" village families to contribute funds for a Japanese village temple at festivals.

This marked a policy watershed. Until then, the idea of using public funds to help the banks had been considered taboo in Japan. Indeed, it had not been done since 1927. The Ministry of Finance had cheerfully kept denying that there was any real banking problem. Using public funds to help Tokyo Kyowa and Anzen was thus tantamount to the government's first admission that something was going wrong. But the bureaucrats did not expect to face too much scrutiny—or opposition—to this policy shift. The Ministry had been overseeing the banks like a puppet master for decades, and the government officials considered that their job was to maintain the all-important sense of harmony in the financial world—without any need to explain themselves to anyone else.

However, outside the Ministry, the climate was subtly shifting. By late 1994, some new hints of rebellion were starting to bubble in the heart of Japan's corporate and political world. Banks were becoming increasingly irritated by the Ministry's assumption that they would always be willing to contribute to *hougachou* collections to help weak banks. More importantly, the Japanese public was becoming more cynical and critical of bureaucrats.

During previous decades, the population had been willing to tolerate political corruption and bureaucratic rule because the Japanese system had been delivering so much economic success. Thus there had been relatively little public criticism of the Ministry of Finance. By the 1990s ordinary voters could sense that the economic miracle had turned sour. Consequently, Japan's leaders were losing their air of infallibility and the public was becoming less tolerant of the steady stream of scandals. The LDP had even been briefly kicked out of office in national elections in the summer of 1993. Although the LDP had quickly grabbed power back again, the episode had left parliament fractious and the opposition parties feeling newly emboldened, and seeking weapons with which they could discredit the status quo.

Tabloid journalists—aided by disgruntled politicians—started to look into the two credit unions and their links with Takahashi, LTCB, and the Ministry of Finance. Breathlessly, the newspapers described how LTCB had poured money into EIE in recent years. Then they outlined, in sordid detail, the antics of "bubble gentlemen"—or *"baburu shinshi"*—and the parties that Takahashi had funded for bankers and bureaucrats in various bars and sex clubs. "These parties were often held in expensive Japanese restaurants in Gion or Nanzeni in Kyoto. They had geisha dancing or playing Japanese instruments during dinner. But the attraction for the bureaucrats was not the performance by geisha but the drinking place afterward in nightclubs [where] bureaucrats would pick up women and as time passed, get more intimate. The women would lean on the men and say things like 'You are wonderful!' and physically touch the man's body. Then the man would stop talking," went a typical article in the *Shukan Gendai* tabloid. "Many people also saw the participants at a bar in the Kyoto Brighten hotel," the tabloid continued, noting the guests at that party included a "man who must have been a *yakuza* gangster."

The main recipients of this entertainment, journalists explained, were politicians such as Toshio Yamaguchi, the former labor minister, and Keisuke Nakanishi, the former defense minister. Other favored "guests" of EIE included two senior bureaucrats at the Ministry of Finance, who had received cash payments, apartments, and other gifts from EIE. The evidence damned not only the LDP, but the opposition parties as well. It emerged, for example, that Takahashi had "lent" Y6 billion ($60 million) to Ichiro Ozawa, a former LDP leader who had defected in 1993 to form the main opposition party. That revelation was distinctly embarrassing since Ozawa had hitherto campaigned on a "clean hands" platform—and declared that he wanted to dedicate himself to *removing* corruption from Japanese politics, much to the delight of the American government and other foreigners.

In mid-March of 1995, as the scandal spiraled, Tetsuya Horie, the cherubic-faced LTCB president, was summoned to testify at the Japanese *diet*, or parliament. It was an imposing gray building, designed in joyless Teutonic style. By then, the revelations in the tabloid newspapers had forced the Ministry to sack two of its top bureaucrats, the finance minister to cut his pay as a gesture of "repentance," and Yamaguchi and Nakanishi to resign from political life. Now, the politicians wanted to know how LTCB had become involved. Did LTCB give the loans to Tokyo Kyowa to bail Takahashi out? Had Horie known that Tokyo Kyowa was lending most of its funds to EIE?

Since television cameras were screening the parliamentary proceedings to the nation, the LTCB staff furtively huddled around a few TVs in the bank to watch the events unfold. For many of them, the sight of Horie's face on television was a distinct shock. The LTCB bankers had spent their entire careers believing that bankers were deeply revered by the nation. Now Horie was in parliament, being questioned like a common criminal.

He attempted to retain what dignity he could. "We had no knowledge of what Takahashi was doing at the credit unions!" he solemnly declared. "LTCB is not responsible."

The politicians looked unimpressed: Didn't LTCB, they asked, control the two credit unions? Hadn't Takahashi once been one of LTCB's biggest clients? Surely the bank must have known what was happening?

"No! We had no knowledge of what was happening," Horie smoothly declared. He had little fear that this statement would ever be challenged. After all, by 1995 the financial world was cocooned in so many lies that most bankers and bureaucrats had little idea what the underlying "truth" in the banking world was anyway.

Horie reckoned without Takahashi. A few hours later, the former head of EIE also appeared in parliament. Underneath his impassive features, the "trillion-yen man" was feeling extremely bitter. In the past, Takahashi had never tried to hide the entertainment that he had offered politicians, bankers, and bureaucrats; he reasoned that such entertainment was totally normal in the Japanese system. And back in the 1980s politicians, bankers, and bureaucrats had competed with each other to get a place at the EIE table. Now, however, the Japanese establishment had lashed out. Takahashi suspected that the real reason he was being criticized was not because he had offered the entertainment—but because he had not offered *enough* entertainment to the most powerful people. Although Takahashi's political friends such as Yamaguchi were important, they did not control the government. The bureaucrats he had cultivated were not at the very top rung of the Ministry. His influence with LTCB was considerable, but the bank did not regard him as a longtime ally. Takahashi was thus still outside the core establishment of Japan—and he could be usefully blamed for everything that had gone wrong. "I am a scapegoat for everything," Takahashi fumed to friends. "It is completely unfair!"

Given that, Takahashi calculated that he had little reason to protect LTCB anymore. So, as the cameras rolled in parliament, he flatly contradicted Horie's version of events. Far from being a victim of the 1980s bubble, he argued, LTCB was a perpetrator—and the revered Horie a liar. "I think it is strange that public funds should be used [to rescue the credit unions]," Takahashi told parliament. "It's natural that LTCB, which is deeply involved [in the bad loans] pay the bill to rescue the credit unions." In chilling detail, Takahashi then explained that LTCB had known everything that was occurring at the two credit unions. Furthermore, he added, LTCB had directed much of the EIE lending in the late 1980s and had actively encouraged EIE to get involved in projects with leading politicians. On one occasion, LTCB even ordered EIE to build a golf course with a former finance minister who enjoyed close ties with the bank. "It is LTCB which is to blame for this," he added. "They were most irresponsible."

The startling betrayal was not enough to save Takahashi. A few weeks later he was arrested by the Tokyo prosecutors, and eventually charged with illegal corporate behavior at the credit union. Yamaguchi, the former labor minister, was arrested as well. Two years later both men were convicted of business fraud and given suspended sentences, which they promptly appealed.

However, Takahashi did have some revenge. A few days after he gave his testimony, the venerable Horie was dragged back into parliament—and onto the television screens. There, the politicians peppered him with more questions: Had the bank helped the credit unions? What exactly was LTCB's relationship with EIE? Had Horie been lying to the nation?

Horie knew that he was defeated. He was by no means the first company president to have become ensnared in a scandal in Japan. Since World War II scandals had erupted with monotonous regularity in the corporate and political world. Indeed, the pattern was *so* regular and ritualistic that sociologists sometimes speculated that scandals were a type of pressure valve for Japanese society, allowing conflict and stress to be regularly expressed and released—but in a manner that did not threaten the fundamentals of society or the underlying sense of harmony and hierarchy. LTCB had never quite expected to become caught up in that pattern. But now that it had happened, Horie—the diligent bureaucrat—knew how to play his part, according to the normal rules of etiquette.

"In some respects, you could say that LTCB was involved [in Tokyo Kyowa]," he quietly admitted to parliament, contradicting his earlier testimony. He bowed his head as he spoke. "I must now consider how to take responsibility." Shortly afterward, Horie resigned.

Over at LTCB headquarters, the senior managers squirmed in humiliation and wondered how to restore their honor. According to Japanese corporate tradition, it was assumed that the next president must come from *within* the organization, selected by the "consensus" of senior management—and Horie himself even though he had resigned. The concept of bringing in a manager from outside the bank—or the "family"—was almost unknown. There appeared to be two potential candidates inside LTCB, each of whom presented distinctly different choices for the bank. One of these was Mario Mizukami, the Brazilian-born maverick who had drawn up the controversial 1985 reform plan. The other was Katsunobu Onogi, the diligent banker who had been quietly rising through the ranks during the previous decade to become a deputy president. Some of the bankers considered Mizukami the most obvious successor. He was an able man with excellent relations with senior politicians and bureaucrats in Japan. Traditionally it had been considered critically important for a senior banker to have these types of relationships, to ensure that a Japanese bank could act as an interface between the political and corporate worlds. Moreover, Mizukami had always been a protégé of Sugiura, the former president of LTCB, who still wielded considerable power at the bank even though he had formally resigned in 1989. Sugiura blatantly wanted Mizukami to be the next president.

But in the months before Horie's sudden departure, Mizukami's candidacy had suffered a setback. One reason was that Sugiura's power was slipping at the bank. Indeed, in private many senior LTCB bankers deeply resented the autocratic former president—and perceived that one way to lash out at Sugiura might be to stop the candidacy of Mizukami. Many LTCB bankers disliked Mizukami's forceful style. They disliked his "reform" views even more. Since 1991, Mizukami had been muttering that the bank should become more transparent about the bad loans and clean up the problem, rather than moving them into subsidiaries. He had been particularly vocal about the need to take action on the *jusen*. This had made him a hero among some internationally minded younger managers, who had never forgotten that Mizukami had played a critical role in drawing up the first reform plan for the bank in the 1980s. However, Mizukami's "radical" comments had irritated men such as Yoshiharu Suzuki, the man who controlled the domestic loan book, and the Ministry itself. On several occasions the head of the banking bureau at the Ministry had bluntly warned Mizukami of severe repercussions if he failed to toe the line on the *jusen* issue.

By contrast, the second potential candidate to become president—Onogi—seemed a much safer pair of hands. Unlike Mizukami, Onogi was not particularly skilled at implementing difficult tasks. Nor did he have the all-important personal ties to senior politicians and bureaucrats, or good information about the domestic lending business. During the 1980s and early 1990s, Onogi had tried to keep as far away from the sleazy business of real estate as he could. Yet Onogi did have the strong support of a man who *did* have a tight grip on the domestic business—the older Suzuki. Most important of all, Onogi had made remarkably few enemies during his career. On the contrary, he prided himself for his ability to maintain *wa*. To the senior LTCB bankers, that seemed the most desirable trait of all, particularly since Onogi also projected the image of an intellectual gentleman who could keep company with foreigners—an image that could potentially counteract the sordid memory of Takahashi.

For a few weeks the debate about succession rumbled on inside LTCB. Then Takao Masuzawa, the bank chairman, declared that the "consensus" of middle managers had rejected Mizukami as president. In normal circumstances in a Japanese bank, that would imply that Mizukami would be appointed chairman instead as a consolation prize. However, Masuzawa cannily managed to hang on to that post himself and the maverick Mizukami was sent to run the LTCB research institute, well away from the center of power. "I guess my ideas just made people too uncomfortable—what I was saying would have challenged the *wa* too much," Mizukami later chuckled. Then Horie and Masuzawa announced the "consensus" choice for successor—Katsunobu Onogi. Faced with a choice between the path of radical reform and maintaining the consensus, LTCB had—yet again—taken the softer option in the name of harmony.

— *Chapter 7* —

ONOGI'S CHOICE

Was there any way to save LTCB except through the measures I took? I have been repeatedly asking myself this question, but I have not yet come to any conclusion.

—Onogi in June 2000

In mid-April 1995, with Horie's disastrous parliamentary testimony still ringing in their ears, one hundred of the bank's general managers gathered in the cavernous, glass-walled meeting room on the bank's twentieth floor to listen to the first speech by their new president, Onogi. Morale was low. The problem was not simply that LTCB had been humiliated on television before the nation. Rumors were also bubbling in the markets about LTCB's rising tide of bad loans, a new scandal was developing about the losses in the *jusen*—and there was *still* no sign of the long-awaited rise in land prices.

Worse, some of the younger bankers were distinctly unsure that Onogi's team could find a solution to these woes. In addition to Onogi, two new deputy presidents had also been appointed—Yasuhiro Kobayashi and Koji Hirao, the man who had once drawn up the 1985 reform plan. Both were popular, decent men, who had risen through the international operations of the bank, and thus were able to present a clean, sophisticated "face" to the outside world. However, neither man knew much about domestic banking. Most bankers thus suspected the *real* powerbroker in the bank was not Onogi at all, but his long-standing, ally—Yoshiharu Suzuki, the king of domestic lending and the man who had been so adept at overseeing schemes to keep the bad loans out of public view. It was common in Japan's political and business life for hidden backroom "fixers" to exercise the real power in an organization, rather than the official "front" leader. With Suzuki pulling the strings, it seemed unlikely that there would be radical reform.

When Onogi stood up to deliver his speech, however, his words were a surprise. Instead of offering the usual bland apologies, he insisted that he *did* want to change the bank. "We must frankly acknowledge that public trust in LTCB has been shaken," he declared with unexpected passion. "We must also reflect on the fact that there has been a lack of leadership in the organization, we have had a low level of risk management, and we have been excessively optimistic about our projections for the economy. We need to learn a lesson from [this scandal]."

Onogi went on to argue that the bank had spent too many years acting as if it was mentally sheltering behind the walls of a citadel. In the past, that "heads down" attitude had been enough to ensure LTCB's survival; however, Onogi argued that the bank could not expect a miracle to save them anymore. "The Japanese economy is now facing pressure to implement unprecedented structural reform, in politics and economics; we need a change on a scale to the change that occurred after World War Two . . . so as a bank, we now have to go out into the field and create new businesses!"

Onogi was talking from the heart. For so many years his generation of bankers had labored hard, helping to rebuild Japan. Yet now Onogi could see that somehow it had gone wrong. He had few illusions about how difficult it might be to put the problem right. Yet it had never occurred to him to refuse the promotion. Beneath his restrained mannerisms, Onogi had an ambitious streak—and he suspected that if anybody in LTCB could find an exit from the mess, he was the man to do it. Some colleagues dubbed this attitude elitism. "Onogi was always very sure of his intellectual abilities," Ryuji Konishi, one senior LTCB banker later recalled. Onogi's friends attributed this to an overwhelming sense of duty and service. Either way, at long last, Onogi was finally in a position to implement this "eternal vision" of merchant banking. He believed that becoming president was his fate. Running away from a job, however hard, was not something that a samurai did.

As summer wore on, the senior management at LTCB embarked on its first full-fledged debate about how to resolve the bank's woes. The litany of problems was chilling. At the end of March 1995, the bank had finally—belatedly—made some effort to sort out its loan book. It announced that its bad loan total had reached Y784 billion ($7.84 billion) and used its entire yearly profits to write off almost half of these loans. Outwardly, the bank claimed that this had resolved the problem. Inwardly, the bankers knew there were still many more problems left. The *jusen* housing loan corporations were on the verge of collapse, which threatened to create a new wave of losses for LTCB. Core LTCB clients, such as Sogo, a retailer, were already effectively bankrupt. Meanwhile, some LTCB affiliates, such as Japan Lease, were staying alive only because LTCB kept furtively pumping more and more funds into them. Thus, as the 1990s wore on, LTCB's exposure to the risky companies was actually *rising*—not falling—contrary to every concept of prudent banking. Instead of removing resources from ailing parts of the economy, the Japanese banks were effectively pouring more and more funds into these decaying sectors, making the problems even worse. By 1995 LTCB's business promotion team estimated that the "real" level of bad loans, never mind the mildly risky loans, had risen above Y2 trillion ($20 billion).

Moreover, LTCB—like every other bank in Japan—was running out of capital resources to write off these bad loans. Back in 1989 the bank had had more than Y3.8 trillion ($38 billion) of "hidden gains" on its equity portfolio. Even in March 1991 the size of this war chest was estimated to be Y2.3 trillion ($23 billion), or considerably more than the bad loans. By March 1995, however, these had plunged to just Y438 billion ($4.38 billion), since share prices had fallen and LTCB had already dipped into its equity resources to write off bad loans. At the same time, profits were dwindling. In the early 1990s, when the Bank of Japan had sharply raised interest rates, the bank had issued five-year debentures that had committed the bank to paying investors a fixed rate of 8 percent or more. Since then, interest rates in the rest of the financial market had fallen and the resulting mismatch had created a heavy financial burden for the bank. And LTCB's core business franchise was shrinking because companies had less and less demand for long-term loans—just as Onogi had often predicted back in the 1980s. Uneasily, the LTCB bankers mulled their options.

One of the LTCB men who was feeling alarmed was Takashi Uehara, a banker just a few years younger than Onogi and a rising star. A short, impish-faced man, Uehara had been born in Tokyo in 1940, and then studied at Tokyo University, where he devoted most of his time to running the university's baseball team. In 1964 he joined LTCB and quickly rose through the ranks, earning a reputation for being internationally minded and highly intelligent. Indeed, it had been Uehara who had provided much of the intellectual inspiration and strategic thinking behind Mizukami's controversial 1985 reform plan. Then in 1989 he moved to America, where he ran LTCB's New York operation for six years with considerable success.

Critics sometimes complained that Uehara was arrogant, since he rarely mingled with junior colleagues. His friends insisted that Uehara's aloof air reflected a shy, intellectual nature. The one thing that everybody agreed was that Uehara always took himself extremely seriously and liked to do everything correctly. When he spoke English, Uehara took pride in using *exactly* the right grammar, even when this sounded bookish. "I was always saying to Uehara-san: 'You must relax!' But he couldn't," one of his close friends later recalled. "Uehara was a man who always had tight shoulders."

In the spring of 1994, Onogi pulled Uehara back to Tokyo and placed him in charge of the powerful corporate planning department—an appointment that implied that Onogi was grooming Uehara to become the next president. It was an assumption that Uehara himself initially shared. But when Uehara arrived back in Tokyo, he quickly became alarmed—and depressed. During the years that he had been working in New York, Uehara had not been privy to the details of LTCB's Japanese loan book. Indeed, very few people outside the Suzuki team knew the scale of the asset problems or the tricks being used to "temporarily" disguise them. Even when Uehara returned to Tokyo he found it extremely difficult to prize much information from Suzuki. But the incomplete data that he saw horrified him, not simply in terms of the scale of the problem but also the way it was being handled. Over in New York, men such as Hirao and Uehara had taken pride in the fact that LTCB was running its banking operations according to international standards, using modern techniques of credit analysis; in Japan, the bank still seemed to be stuck in prehistoric times. But what was the point, Uehara fumed, of burying all the problems? Shouldn't LTCB and the other Japanese banks start writing bad debts off or restructuring some of the troubled borrowers?

At the back of Uehara's mind was his own experience in America. When he started running the LTCB business on Wall Street, America's banking world was struggling with its own bad loan problem, partly created by the collapse of America's Savings and Loans. The problems had been so severe that groups such as Citibank and Bank of America had appeared to be close to collapse. Yet by 1995—or just four years after their crisis—these two banks had recovered. They had done this by resolutely admitting the scale of the problem, writing off the bad loans, sacking their workers involved in creating the problems, and then raising more finance in the markets.

Uehara had been deeply impressed by that saga and other American corporate restructuring stories. In a particularly ironic twist, LTCB *itself* had helped to finance some of this restructuring, by supplying funds for leveraged buyouts in America. In the early 1990s, for example, LTCB helped to fund the restructuring of Morningstar, a debt-laden American dairy products group, which had once been on the verge of collapse. To Uehara's delight, the Morningstar deal was considered such a success that Harvard Business School used it as a case study to show how a company could emerge from the burden of excess debt—complete with admiring words about LTCB's role in the process.

If LTCB could help to perform that type of restructuring alchemy in America, Uehara asked, why couldn't it import the lesson into Japan? After all, companies such as the retailer Sogo did not look very different from Morningstar: They were both saddled with excess debt and urgently in need of restructuring. When Uehara raised these ideas, he quickly found—like Mizukami before him—this made him unpopular. So did anybody else who tried to discuss American-style reform. "In the early summer of 1995 I had breakfast with executives from Bank of America and asked them how they had managed to revive their bank after the crisis caused by a bubble," Kozo Tabayashi, the head of LTCB's Singapore operations later explained. The BOA executives were startled, but presented Tabayashi with a long list of measures: improve credit control, recognize the scale of the problem; remove the officials who had created the bad loans; and, above all, write off bad loans and cut credit to hopeless companies. "I thought that LTCB could learn from that experience and so I reported it to my seniors when I came back to Japan. But their answer was 'BOA could do that because it was in the United States. We cannot do that same thing in Japan!' The rejection was so clear-cut that I couldn't pursue it."

Frustrated, some of the young reformers tried to take their arguments directly to Onogi, hoping that he could see the logic behind them. After all, they reasoned, Onogi himself had worked overseas for years. To their surprise, however, Onogi also seemed wary of radical change. Intellectually, he could see perfectly well that restructuring had transformed America. But while Onogi wanted change, he wanted a gentle, *Japanese* type of change. "I may look radical but basically I am a very conservative person," he sometimes admitted. "I don't like revolutions. I prefer evolution.

"Or, I suppose what I really like is the idea of revolutionary evolution, if it is possible to have that."

When Onogi tried to explain why he—like the vast majority of Japanese bankers and bureaucrats—preferred evolution to revolution, he would sometimes reach for a pencil and paper. For at the heart of Onogi's worldview was a belief that the postwar financial system in Japan was fundamentally different from America, and thus required a different set of policies to fix its bad loans.

To illustrate his point, he would sketch out three different patterns. Under the word "America" he drew a square box with the word "shareholders," connected to two boxes labeled "banks" and "corporations." The idea was that America was fundamentally an economy based on capital markets, in which investors (shareholders and bond-owners) owned the banks and their clients. Thus, if a problem emerged in the system it was up to these investors to force pressure for change, since they had responsibility for corporate governance.

Under the word "Japan," Onogi drew a diagram labeled the "main bank" system, which looked like a pyramid of cascading boxes. At the top stood the Ministry of Finance, which exerted its control over the entire system through the practice of "administrative guidance." Below that was the "main bank," which was linked to clients through the lending relationships and cross shareholding. Thus, in Japan investors played only a limited role—at least, according to how Onogi saw the system. Instead, the real responsibility for corporate governance in Japan was balanced between the banks, their clients, and the Ministry of Finance. The only exception was when a company had fallen into such deep distress that its main bank had effectively taken control of the operations; in that situation, the bank was assumed to be the "parent" of the group, entirely responsible for corporate governance. To illustrate that, Onogi drew two boxes, with the arrows of power pointing from the bank to its subsidiaries.

Lastly, on another sheet of paper, Onogi drew the most important diagram of all: three boxes labeled "Bank A," "Bank B," and "Bank C," and three companies labeled A, B, and C as well. Although company A was the "child" of "Bank A," it also had lending relations with Bank B and Bank C; similarly, the B and C companies were also linked to the other banks. The entire system existed as a complex lattice of dotted lines that connected everybody to everybody else, and it hung together because it was assumed that a parent bank would always support its child. When Bank A lent to company B, for example, it was not doing so because it had confidence in the strength of company B, *but because it had confidence in Bank B playing its role*. The system worked only if everybody fulfilled their duty. But if any bank failed to play its correct part, the trust that underpinned the entire matrix would shatter. "The banks lend against the de facto guarantee of the main bank, which assumes that it has full responsibility to sustain its main client," Onogi wrote in the margins of his diagram. "If a parent bank abandons its responsibility the bank becomes an outsider in the network. For example, if Bank A lets its subsidiary A collapse, no other banks will keep their lending stance for the other subsidiaries."

Of course, Onogi reasoned, if *everybody* in the system agreed that the system should change, the banks would be free to change their behavior. Yet he saw no evidence that the government *did* want a revolution. The politicians were still vehemently opposed to using taxpayers' funds to create a proper banking safety net—and without that type of safety net, no government could afford to embark on a violent shakeout. Consequently, although the Ministry liked to talk in public about moving away from the "convoy" model, in private bureaucrats acted as if there was no alternative to dealing with the bad loan problem in the traditional manner. The official line was that the bad loan problem was over—and the bankers were ordered to echo this rhetoric. "The Ministry's policy was that for the safety of the Japanese financial system it was considered important to maintain this network," Onogi later explained. "The Ministry guidance was that banks should give programmed financial aid to their wounded subsidiaries for recovery."

Thus, Onogi believed, it was impossible for a Japanese bank to simply copy the solutions developed for Wall Street. If LTCB stuck out its neck and acted like Citibank or Bank of America, cutting off troubled borrowers, it could destabilize the entire system. That in turn would leave that bank dangerously isolated, bereft of all the traditional support systems. And if one bank or bank affiliate collapsed, that could set off a chain reaction. "It is very easy to say the words 'radical change,' but if you try to change rapidly and radically you risk sacrificing balance," Onogi later explained. "LTCB had a staff of 3,000 and we had 20,000 or 30,000 clients. So there were a lot of people to think about. A policy of simple, radical revolution just was not feasible."

In practice, this "revolutionary evolution" crystallized into a two-pronged policy. By the autumn of 1995, the senior LTCB managers had come to the conclusion that Suzuki's team were the best people to deal with the bad loans. They knew the loan book better than anybody else. More practically, Onogi had no desire to handle the task himself. He had never been directly involved in the expansion of real estate lending during the 1980s, or the accounting games in the early 1990s. He did not know exactly where all the skeletons were buried and he did not *want* to know either. Onogi preferred to let bankers like Suzuki handle those messy details, in whatever way he could. "In some ways Suzuki was the perfect bureaucrat," Konishi, a senior LTCB banker later observed. "Suzuki did whatever was asked of him. He was very loyal to Onogi. He could make sure that things always looked sufficiently pretty on the surface."

Then, with his eyes averted from the loan book, Onogi turned his mind to the issue that *did* interest him and where his talents lay—pondering the bank's future business strategy. By 1995 it was clear that even the healthy loans at LTCB were earning virtually no profit. Inside Japan the bank was still barred from many capital markets and outside Japan, LTCB had little hope of competing with the largest American or European banks. Moreover, the web of Ministry regulations meant that LTCB could not freely expand into new sectors with other groups: It was not allowed to merge with a domestic bank or securities house, and the Ministry had traditionally frowned on alliances with foreign partners in the domestic market. To all intents and purposes, LTCB seemed to be trapped.

Nonetheless, Onogi had never quite given up his twenty-year-old dream of turning LTCB into a merchant bank, and in his eyes, chasing this merchant bank vision was a far more exciting task than cleaning up the balance sheet. *That* was the type of "reform" that Onogi wanted to be remembered for; not cutting off deadbeat borrowers. It was a mission that would win LTCB prestige on the world stage. After all, Onogi reasoned, if the bank could find a way to boost its earnings, then it could use that money to write off the bad loans in a gentle fashion, and the asset problems would simply melt away. Or so he hoped.

In late 1996, Onogi received an unexpected boost to his plans. On an afternoon in mid-November Ryutaro Hashimoto, the Japanese prime minister, summoned his finance minister to his room and handed his minister a dull-looking document entitled *Structural Reform of the Japanese Financial Market; towards the Revival of the Tokyo Market by the Year 2001*. This contained proposals to deregulate Japan's banking system with the self-declared intention of making Tokyo's markets "free, fair and global." The program was called "Big Bang"—or *Bigu Ban* in Japanized English—after the financial deregulation reform that had transformed the British markets back in the 1980s.

By Japanese standards, the program seemed almost revolutionary. In theory, the Japanese government had been deregulating its financial markets since the middle of the 1970s. However, these reforms had occurred at a snail's pace, without any clear goal. *Bigu Ban,* by contrast, offered an intellectual road map for these reforms and moved with un-Japanese haste. By

2001, the government pledged to rip apart the barriers segregating brokers and banks, letting banks enter the capital markets on equal terms. Responsibility for regulating the financial markets would be removed from the Ministry of Finance and placed in a new agency. Foreign competitors would be encouraged to enter the system and the remaining foreign exchange controls would be abolished, allowing savers to take their funds overseas if they wanted. The last point had particular significance, since it was the Ministry's control over access to foreign exchange that had allowed it to regulate interest rates so tightly in the past—and keep the Japanese banks as an enclosed financial ecosystem. For the first time in history, the Ministry seemed to be de-emphasizing the role of banks in the Japanese economy and giving greater priority to capital markets. It was a startling repudiation of the 1952 Ikeda philosophy.

Just why Hashimoto had suddenly announced this policy U-turn was a subject of endless speculation. The official reason was that the government wanted to boost the international standing of Tokyo's financial markets and find a way for the country to use its savings more effectively, to offset the aging of its population. But when bureaucrats discussed the reforms, they often referred to a third goal, which was to make Japanese banks more healthy and competitive on the world stage. In practice, this last aim seemed to contradict the goal of introducing more competition into the system, since Japanese banks were ill-equipped to compete suddenly with foreign groups in deregulated markets. But, when the bureaucrats and politicians had drawn up their reform plans, they had believed their own rhetoric that the bad loan issue was over. The Japanese government was not prepared for the practical implications of a world where bureaucrats might lose some of their power—or Japanese banks might become weaker, not stronger, in a free market.

Despite these contradictions, the announcement of Big Bang thrilled foreign bankers. For years, foreign banks had been locked out of most of Japan's financial world by a myriad of regulations; now, the government suddenly appeared to have thrown down the welcome mat. And for Onogi the announcement of Big Bang was also a godsend. By late 1996, Onogi had reluctantly come to realize that LTCB was in absolutely no position to turn itself into a merchant bank using its own resources. The bank had entirely the wrong type of staff to be an investment bank. Ten years earlier, when LTCB was capital rich, it could have dealt with that handicap by throwing money at the problem and hiring foreign bankers or acquiring an entire American or Japanese bank. But now LTCB could no longer sustain its existing international network. Facing a capital crunch it had been forced to sell the U.S. bond dealer Greenwich Capital. Far from gobbling up others, LTCB badly needed another infusion of capital itself.

Onogi had another—far bolder—idea. LTCB was in no position to buy another bank; but there was nothing to stop it concluding an alliance or merger to get the skills that it needed, he argued. If LTCB entered into an alliance it could not only expand its business operations, but it might also get a new injection of capital. One way to do that would be to merge with a *foreign* bank. If LTCB linked up with a foreign group, it could get the global investment banking skills that it needed at a stroke. That would then allow LTCB to expand into new areas of business, raise its revenues, and then use the cash to write off its bad loans. "The investment banking capabilities of Japanese banks were so far below the level of first-class global banks by then, that we would have needed an enormous amount of time and money to fill that gap. In fact, I don't think we could have done it," Onogi later explained. "But an alliance with a foreign bank . . . could shorten the lead time to cope with the Big Bang and allow us to improve the financial services to our customers. The idea was to keep our traditional customers, but cut the overall loan book . . . and offer the traditional customers investment banking services instead."

There was one huge flaw in this argument, as far as LTCB bankers were concerned: Nobody had ever tried to ally with a foreign partner before in that way. Back in the 1980s Japanese banks had purchased stakes in European and American financial companies. The Japanese banks had always clearly held the upper hand in these deals and the deal had occurred outside the Japanese market. No Japanese institution had ever before voluntarily sold a stake in itself to foreigners inside the Japanese market. It flouted the first law of Japanese corporate ethics; namely, that Japanese companies should always stick together, for defense, in the face of outsiders.

But though Onogi had always bowed to the consensus view in most areas of his life, international strategy was one area where he was confident to take a bold gamble, and step outside the normally accepted wisdom. The great reformers of the nineteenth-century Meiji era whom Onogi so deeply admired had been willing to open their doors to the *gaijin* in the interests of advancing the nation. So why, Onogi asked, was it so shocking for LTCB to extend its eyes beyond the tight Japanese corporate world, and seek a foreign partner—at least, for a period? After all, if LTCB could learn the tricks of international investment banking, it could eventually catch up with the foreigners again, just as Japanese manufacturers had once done. Better still, Onogi argued, he had a potential partner close to hand. He had fond memories of the gentlemanly bankers he had known back in London in the 1970s, and he had particularly warm feelings toward one particular bank—Swiss Bank Corporation. In 1995 the SBC had bought SG Warburgs, a British merchant bank, and Onogi happened to know Hans de Gier, the SBC chairman, quite well since the two had met as young bankers in London. Onogi had already raised the idea of an alliance with de Gier and the response seemed hopeful. If he was going to do an alliance, Onogi privately suspected that a European group might present a cultural better fit for Japan than Americans. Better still, Onogi believed that SBC—unlike many other European banks—had a long-term commitment to investment banking. Furtively he contacted AT Kearney, the American consulting firm, and asked it to arrange a formal meeting with SBC.

On May 28, 1997, a team of LTCB bankers flew down in deepest secrecy to Sentossa, the holiday island, in Singapore. Waiting for them were senior bankers from Swiss Bank Corporation and consultants from AT Kearney. "I guess AT Kearney is here to do the *omiai* [the traditional marriage introductions]," joked one of the LTCB bankers. The location had been chosen to guarantee secrecy. Even though the two sides had already had preliminary chats in more convenient locations, they wanted the main discussions to take place far from the eyes of Tokyo's banking world.

A few feet from the beaches bathed in brilliant tropical sunshine, the SBC and LTCB bankers huddled in a dark hotel room concealed in the basement. On the Japanese side, Onogi had sent some of his most senior aides. On the Swiss side there were two key figures: Luqman Arnold, the suave Asia chairman of SBC, and Vittorio Volpi, a voluble Italian who was chairman of SBC's Tokyo branch. The two SBC men were distinctly different personalities. Volpi had spent a large part of his career in Tokyo, and had a deep affinity for Japan, perhaps because Japan's political culture was often similar to his native Italy. He had been friendly with LTCB men for twenty years, dating from the 1970s, when Volpi had once arranged a loan to Gabon that was jointly financed by an Italian bank and LTCB. "I always thought that Onogi and the other people at LTCB were high quality!" Volpi used to say, in his singsong Italian accent. "Onogi was most charming! Most charming!"

Arnold, for his part, exuded the type of deadpan polish and dry wit often found among British-educated elite. He was half Bangladeshi and half English and had been educated at a British boarding school. In his career before being appointed to the Asian SBC job, Arnold had scrambled up the corporate ladder in Paribas and Credit Suisse with dazzling speed and sleek efficiency. Behind his back, his colleagues called him "Lucky Luqman," but nobody doubted that he was ferociously ambitious, beneath his suave charm and keen intelligence.

And it was ambition that drove Arnold to talk to LTCB. He had been appointed to his job just a few months earlier, and like any new appointee knew that the fastest way to get ahead was to produce a big deal. On paper, he could see that linking up with LTCB could potentially be a brilliant move. Until that point, SBC's operation in Tokyo had been fairly modest, since the Swiss bank—like almost every other foreign bank—had found it difficult to get access to Japanese companies. Most of these companies were utterly loyal to the Japanese banks and brokers they had known for years. Yet, these Japanese banks and brokers lacked many of the products and financial skills that banks such as SBC could offer, such as mergers and acquisitions advice, advanced financial structured products, or even access to global distribution. Consequently, if a Japanese bank's relationships could ever be blended with a foreign banks' product base that would produce a winning formula.

Indeed, when Arnold looked at LTCB, he believed that the deal could not only help SBC inside Japan, but potentially transform its global business as well. On the world stage, the Swiss bank was lagging behind the largest, so-called bulge-bracket American banks, such as Goldman Sachs or

Morgan Stanley. Though it had a strong base in Europe, SBC had never managed to make much headway in America and seemed unlikely to be able to boost its operations there on its own. Arnold reasoned that a deal with LTCB might create a backdoor route for SBC to steal a march on its U.S. rivals on the world stage, by turning SBC into the first foreign bank fully operational in Japan. "We could see that Japan was the second largest economy in the world and an alliance with LTCB could give us a tremendous position in the Japanese market," Arnold later explained. "SBC needed to catch up and this was a chance to take a tremendous leap."

The LTCB bankers, for their part, were equally keen to talk. In the spring of 1997, the Japanese financial markets had experienced the most serious bout of jitters since the bubble's bursting. Rumors were abroad that Nippon Credit Bank—the so-called "younger brother" to LTCB—was effectively bankrupt. For a few nervous days, banks cut their credit lines to NCB until the Bank of Japan and Ministry of Finance stopped a crisis by forcing the rest of the industry to rescue the bank through a traditional pattern of "voluntary donations" (or *hougachou*) leaving an impression of calm. The rescue did not entirely soothe the markets; it was clear that the other financial institutions were very reluctant to help NCB. In the aftermath, the LTCB share price had collapsed to below Y400 ($4), or half its level the previous year, leaving Onogi desperate to find something that could push the share price back up.

In the hotel basement, the LTCB and SBC bankers exchanged ideas. Onogi had initially envisaged a sweeping deal in which each side would buy a significant stake in each other, or even a full-fledged merger, since the market capitalization of SBC was only about 20 percent larger than LTCB at the time. Arnold was wary; Volpi had warned him that LTCB's finances were not strong, and SBC had no desire to become entangled in LTCB's low-earning corporate lending business. Carefully, the two sides felt their way toward a compromise. At every new twist, Arnold and Volpi dashed out of the room to telephone de Gier back in Europe for approval, and the Japanese bankers relayed the discussions back to the LTCB headquarters in Tokyo. By the end of two days, a rough deal had been hammered out. SBC and LTCB tentatively agreed to take a stake of about 3 percent in each other, as a sign of their mutual commitment. LTCB clearly needed additional capital, so SBC also promised to help LTCB raise about $2 billion more funds through equity and bond issues, and it pledged to purchase about $1 billion of these shares, which it would not sell before 2001. Lastly—and most importantly in strategic terms—the two sides agreed to form a set of joint ventures to create three lines of business in Japan. One of these would be a Japanese investment banking operation that would link SBC's Japanese operations with the securities subsidiary of LTCB; the second a business specializing in asset management that would combine SBC's fund management business in Japan with LIMCO, LTCB's own subsidiary; and the third would create the first full-fledged private bank in Japan.

Two months later, SBC and LTCB unveiled their path-breaking move. Looking dignified, Onogi greeted the press with Hans de Gier, the SBC chairman, whom he presented as an "old friend." Then Onogi explained—in English—that SBC and LTCB planned to take a 3 percent stake in each other, as a "token" sign of their commitment. They would also create three joint ventures in investment banking, asset management, and private banking. Lastly, Onogi explained that LTCB planned to raise another Y200 billion ($2 billion) of capital, by issuing Y130 billion preferred shares and Y70 billion subordinated bonds. SBC would buy almost half of the preferred stock, meaning that the Swiss could invest about $850 million in the deal to become the second largest shareholder in LTCB and give Onogi the capital he so desperately needed. "This strategy realizes one objective—to take Japan to the world and bring the world to Japan," Onogi declared, beaming from ear to ear. "Our alliance with SBC is the perfect response to the opportunities provided by Big Bang. We want to transform LTCB into a completely new entity based on global standards. The alliance is part of that."

The night before the declaration, some LTCB bankers had felt so nervous they barely slept. No Japanese bank had ever formed an alliance with a foreigner in this way before and the LTCB bankers knew that the deal might provoke criticism that Onogi had "betrayed" the Japanese system. In the event, the market reaction was better than even Onogi had dared to hope. As investors digested the news, the share price of LTCB rose from Y427 to Y507. Almost overnight LTCB had cemented its reputation for being one of the most innovative of the Japanese banks; after all, the foreign banks had been urging the Japanese to produce a strategic plan to tackle their weakness for years. Now LTCB appeared to have finally done just that. Suddenly the bank had become a poster child for Big Bang—and the darling of foreign analysts.

Onogi was thrilled. For so many years he had been living with the terrible knowledge that bad loans were piling up inside the bank; now he believed that he had found a way out of this hole. If the alliance could yield a new stream of profits, that would allow the bank to slowly write off its bad loans, without the need for any of the painful measures that Onogi abhorred. "Onogi looked happier in those days than he had looked for a long time," one of his aides later recalled. "He laughed a lot and his face really relaxed. I think he finally thought that everything was going to be OK."

— Chapter 8 —

THE SWISS GAMBLE

There is only so far that honorable people can go, before the system traps them in Japan. The Japanese have this bad habit of protecting the tribe at all costs. Things that we might consider quite criminal in Italy or America just are not considered wrong in Japan if they are done to protect the group.

—Vittorio Volpi, former head of UBS Tokyo

As summer wore on, the Swiss bankers started to explore an issue that had been hanging over LTCB and the other Japanese banks for seven long years, but that most Japanese bankers resolutely kept ignoring: Just how big was the total level of bad loans in a bank such as LTCB?

Such due diligence was a routine part of any type of corporate alliance, before two parties signed a binding deal. And Volpi and Arnold were not unduly concerned about what they might uncover. During the process of negotiation between the two sides, SBC had heard rumors that large losses might be sitting in the subsidiaries of LTCB. Some of the Japanese staff at SBC had also tried to highlight these issues. Volpi and Arnold had reasoned that the risks in LTCB were probably manageable—or manageable enough to proceed with the deal, given its potential to deliver some fabulous benefits. "We knew there were some risks, particularly cultural and credit risks," Arnold later said. "But the prize justified taking risks." After all, the two men pointed out, SBC was not trying to buy the whole bank, but simply form an alliance. Moreover, LTCB was not just any old bank; it sat at the core of Tokyo's financial establishment, with close links to the Japanese government. Just a few years earlier LTCB had had a "triple-A" credit rating and the published accounts still looked moderately healthy, with a large—but manageable—level of bad loans. Surely a bank as prestigious as that wouldn't tell bald-faced lies about its accounts, Arnold argued. Surely the Japanese government wouldn't *let* LTCB get away with that scale of deception.

Unknown to SBC, however, some of the LTCB bankers were feeling distinctly uneasy. In the period since Onogi had become president, and delegated handling of the bad loan issue to Suzuki's team, this group had made several furtive attempts to measure the true scale of LTCB's bad loans. A highly secret internal document drawn up by the business promotion department in 1996 suggested that the subsidiaries had Y2.8 trillion ($28 billion) of bad loans, *in addition* to what was sitting on the main balance sheet of the bank. The business promotion department gloomily concluded that this meant the subsidiaries' liabilities now exceeded the assets—meaning they were bankrupt. Then, in the summer of 1996, the Ministry of Finance had done its own inspection of the bank—without inspecting the subsidiaries in detail—which concluded that the level of risky loans had tripled since 1992 to Y3.6 trillion ($36 billion), almost a quarter of the loan book. The Ministry inspectors suggested that a third of these risky loans were actually bad. The senior executives of LTCB agreed with the Ministry bureaucrats that it would not be in anybody's interests to reveal the full scale of the problems. Instead, the bank drew up a plan—with MoF approval—that envisaged that the bank would write off Y200 billion ($2 billion) of bad loans a year. On the basis of this, LTCB declared in the spring of 1997 that it had Y840 billion ($8.4 billion) of risky loans, of which Y350 billion ($3.5 billion) were seriously bad. But which number, the LTCB bankers wondered, should they give to SBC to explain their "bad loan" position? The Y350 billion *official* figure for bad loans? The Y840 billion figure for risky loans? Or the Y3.6 trillion ($36 billion) estimate for potentially problematic loans that had been produced by the Ministry's inspection—and then promptly covered up?

The LTCB bankers mulled the issue for a few days. They knew that if they gave the Swiss bankers the full Ministry data, this could invite political repercussions for the bank. After all, the Ministry was loudly telling the outside world that it was on the verge of resolving the bad loan problems—and according to the published Ministry data, the total level of bad loans among *all* the major twenty-one banks was supposed to be a mere Y18 trillion ($180 billion). If LTCB ever publicly revealed that just *one* bank was sitting on Y3.6 trillion of problem loans, that would expose the Ministry's figure as an utter sham. Yet, the LTCB bankers also knew that they could not fob off the Swiss with the official data. So eventually, the LTCB staff decided to dodge responsibility: They provided SBC with a list of the bank's top 400 borrowers, together with the level of the provisions that the bank had made for the outstanding loans, and let the foreigners draw their own conclusions.

The SBC staff combed through the numbers. Many of LTCB's top corporate borrowers were listed on the first or second sections of the Tokyo Stock Exchange and some had even been clients of SBC in the past, meaning that the Swiss already had extensive information about them. From this, the Swiss bankers concluded that LTCB had about Y1.4 trillion ($14 billion) loans to potentially risky corporate clients, and needed to make additional provisions worth perhaps Y400 billion ($4 billion) to offset this risk. That seemed manageable given the size of the bank. But as the Swiss staff peered closer, they noticed the bank had made absolutely no provisions at all for almost two dozen of their largest borrowers, such as Japan Lease, Nippon Landic, and NED. These were subsidiaries of LTCB, about which SBC knew relatively little. "Can we have more information?" the Swiss asked the LTCB staff. "Why haven't you made provisions?"

The LTCB staff explained that they could only offer basic data on profits and losses, because these were unlisted companies. There was no need to worry, they cheerfully added. The subsidiaries were considered risk-free under Japanese accounting law, since it was assumed that LTCB would always support its subsidiaries. It was a tautology—but Japanese bankers and bureaucrats believed it made sense in a world where each institution always propped everybody else up.

Volpi and Arnold were stunned. Some of these subsidiaries appeared to be in deep trouble and the SBC staff estimated that there could easily be another Y1 trillion or Y2 trillion worth of bad loans there. Ten to twenty billion dollars of risk with no provisions. "Instead of worrying about the parent company and seeing the affiliates as a footnote, we realized that it was the parent company that was the footnote and the affiliates the issue," Arnold said. "They were neither distanced enough to leave the parent company with no liability, nor close enough to be transparent." If even a fraction of those loans to the affiliates turned sour, in other words, they could take down the whole of LTCB. They might potentially take down SBC as well, if the Swiss bank let itself become too exposed.

Volpi and Arnold asked for an appointment with Eisuke Sakakibara, the voluble vice minister for international affairs at the Ministry of Finance. The implications of what SBC had uncovered were horrifying, not just for LTCB, but Japan's entire financial system. During the course of 1996 and early 1997, many economists had assumed that Japan was making encouraging progress tackling its mountain of bad loans. The data at LTCB blew that assumption apart. If the pattern at LTCB was typical, there were literally trillions and trillions of unseen bad loans sitting in the Japanese financial system. Far from coming to the end of the bad loan problem, it seemed that Japan had barely started. Arnold and Volpi wondered what they were getting themselves into. To get a straight answer—or straight enough for Japan—they went directly to Sakakibara. The vice minister was considered to be a good friend to foreign bankers, since he had worked in America for several years and acted as a self-appointed spokesman for Japan's government on the international stage. Moreover, Sakakibara had enthusiastically cheered on the alliance between SBC and LTCB behind the scenes, telling anybody who would listen that the deal was precisely the type of reform catalyst that Japan needed.

Arriving at Sakakibara's scruffy room on the second floor of the Ministry, which housed souvenirs of global financial meetings and memorabilia linked to one of Sakakibara's favorite hobbies—drinking expensive French wines—Volpi and Arnold immediately unburdened themselves. They sketched out what they had discovered at the Japanese bank, and then asked the crucial questions: Why hadn't LTCB made any provisions for its subsidiaries? Did the Ministry know what was going on?

Sakakibara airily shrugged. In Japan, he explained, banks sometimes made provisions for these affiliates, but sometimes they did not. It was their choice. He did not think that LTCB was so unusual.

Volpi and Arnold pointed out that this attitude created a huge risk for SBC. How could the Japanese government expect foreigners to invest in their banks if it was impossible to measure the size of the black hole? Wasn't the government itself worried by the implications of all this?

Sakakibara made a few reassuring noises, and then suggested that if the Swiss wanted to get tough with their Japanese partners, the Ministry of Finance would have no objections. Volpi and Arnold wondered what that meant. Were they being given a carte blanche to make LTCB bankrupt? Nervously, they asked the Ministry to write a letter that explicitly stated that the Swiss would not be considered responsible for rescuing LTCB if problems ever emerged. The Ministry obliged.

Volpi and Arnold then asked for a meeting with Onogi. Unusually, they stipulated that this should be a private session, without any other LTCB staff. They did not want to cause the Japanese man to lose "face" in front of his subordinates. At the back of their minds, neither Volpi nor Arnold could quite believe that Onogi could have deliberately deceived them about the accounts. When they had started negotiations with LTCB, they had both had the impression that the LTCB managers were an honorable group of men. None of the SBC bankers had ever met Suzuki; indeed, they were barely aware of his existence. However, Volpi and Arnold had greatly liked the men they had met, such as Uehara and Onogi, since they seemed to understand the way that international finance worked. "Onogi was a very charming man and he had a very charming wife," Volpi later recalled. "He came to my house and we had dinners. Onogi likes to cook—he is a very good cook. So he put his apron on and watched my wife doing the cooking, taking notes."

Onogi met the two men in his own room, up on the nineteenth floor of the LTCB tower. He looked tense and tired. In a calm, polite tone, Volpi and Arnold sketched out their deep unease about the outstanding loans to the LTCB subsidiaries. Onogi pointed out that in Japan's system of accounting, parent banks never needed to make provisions for subsidiaries because it was presumed that the parent could not abandon a subsidiary, which meant that they could never fail, and thus had no risk. "In Japan, we don't have to make provisions for subsidiaries," Onogi said. "They are part of our family, our *children!*"

The emotional side of the Italian Volpi welled up. He believed that prudent banking practices would suggest that a bank should make more—not less—provisions for subsidiaries than normal borrowers, because if the subsidiaries face any losses, the burden would fall heavily on a parent company. Just as a father would find it hard to take a knife to kill a child, a parent company could not be relied upon to be brutal toward a subsidiary. "In Switzerland we are forced by law to provision more severely for our affiliates than clients," Volpi said. "The logic being that if you lend to a client you can switch the credit off, but with your son you cannot, so you are stuck!"

"It is a different situation in Japan," Onogi calmly told Volpi and Arnold. Intellectually, Onogi could see why Volpi and Arnold were upset. But Onogi did not believe that he had done anything wrong at all. In his eyes, the use of the subsidiaries was simply a necessary tactic to cope with a temporary problem. He had not lied or broken any law as it was defined in Tokyo, and the Ministry had implicitly approved what LTCB was doing. Somehow, Onogi had presumed that Volpi and Arnold would understand that; after all, he reasoned, they had come to do business in Japan.

Volpi and Arnold discussed what to do next: Should they pull out of the alliance? Or press ahead, knowing that LTCB was potentially bankrupt? It was not an easy choice. Inside SBC there were some bankers who disliked the deal, and would welcome any excuse to pull out. The controller's office of the bank in Switzerland was unhappy about a credit risk that it could not understand. SBC's main fund management operation—a company called Brinson—disliked the deal for cultural reasons. Under the terms of the LTCB deal, this Brinson asset management group in Japan was expected to a play a central role in an alliance. Yet, Gary Brinson, the Chicago-based manager who ran the group and sat on the SBC board, was wary. Asset managers never liked being forced into business deals by investment bankers and Brinson had *hitherto* preferred to focus his energies on America. "The LTCB scheme was really drawn up by Arnold for the investment bank," Brinson later recalled. "And asset management was tacked on by default. We were pretty unhappy about the whole deal. My experience in Japan [from dealing with other Japanese companies] had already showed me that it was incredibly difficult to educate the Japanese with our approach to investing. The cultural gap was just too big."

Katsunobu Onogi as a keen young "salaryman" shortly after he joined Long Term Credit Bank in 1959.

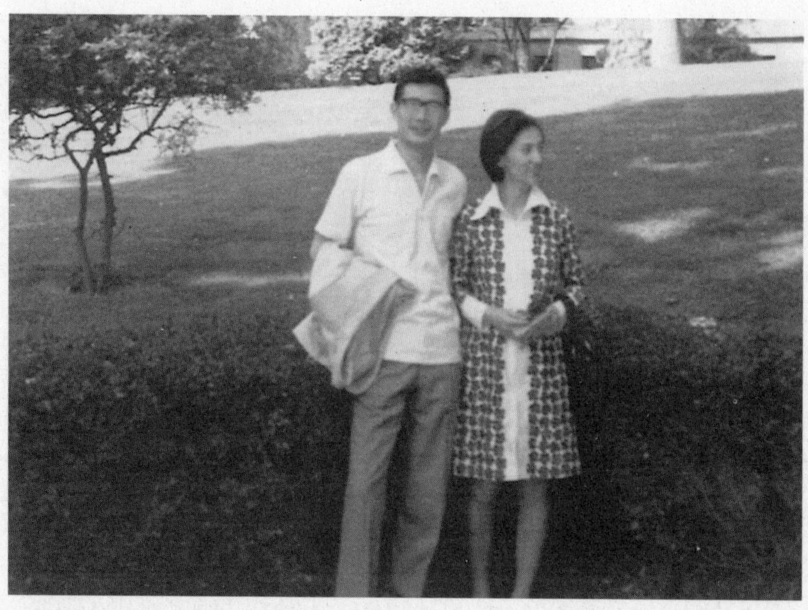

Onogi and his new wife, Yasuko, in London in the early 1970s. He later concluded this was one of the happiest spells of his life.

The young LTCB bankers who established LTCB's London branch in the mid-1970s; Onogi is second from left.

Takashi Uehara, soon after he arrived to run the New York office of LTCB, at the 1989 board dinner of Greenwich Capital markets, the U.S. bond trader that LTCB acquired. Uehara is on the left, Ted Knetzger, the American founder of Greenwich, is third from left.

Bob Burns of the Regent hotel group, standing with a model of the 57th Street hotel that was designed by I.M. Pei.

Photo by Fred R. Conrad/*The New York Times*.

Onogi in 1995 shortly after his appointment to the post of LTCB president.

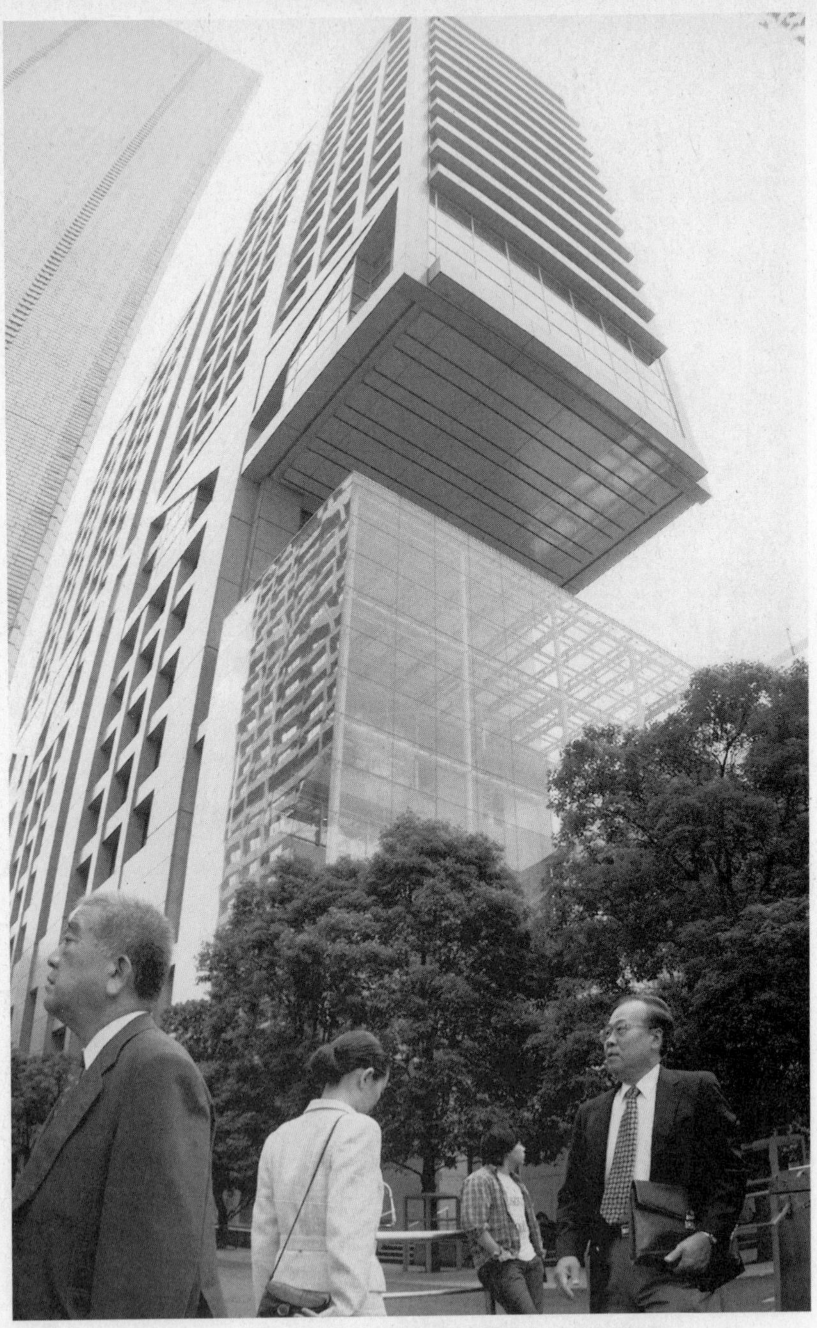

The LTCB headquarters, with its striking 100-foot-high glass entrance; the cost of construction and land was estimated to be more than Y50 billion ($500 million).

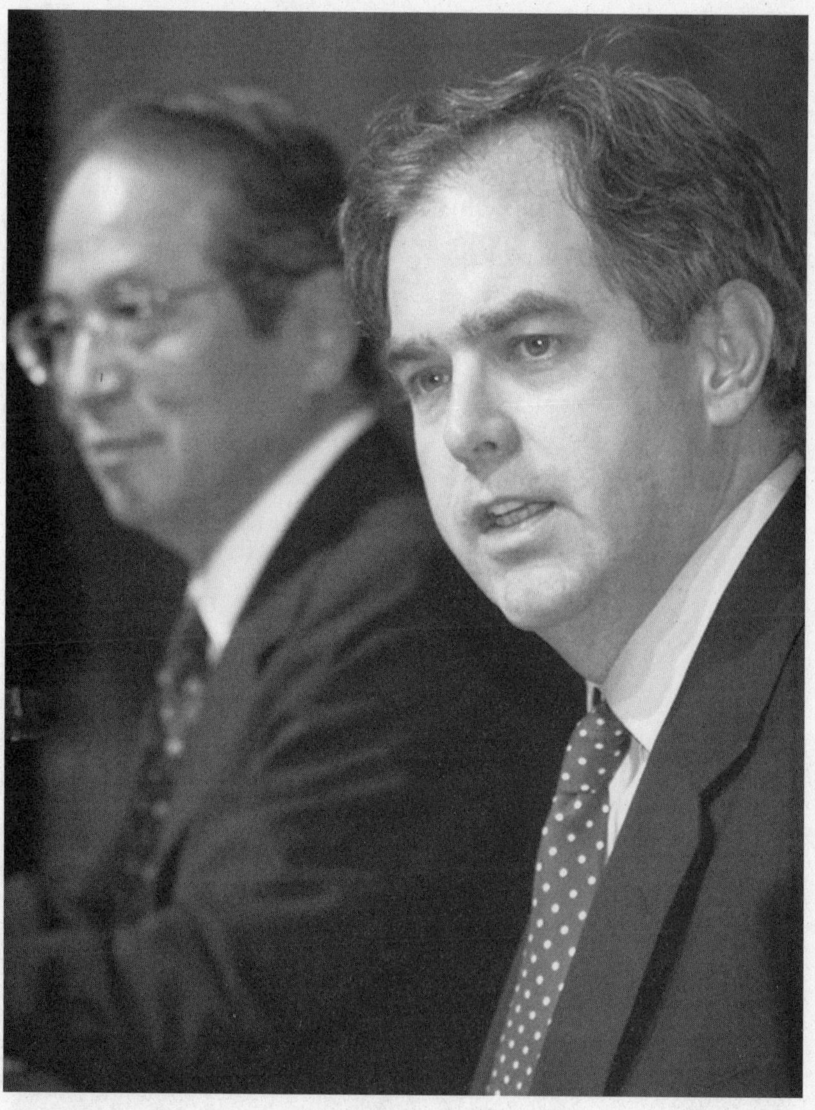

Collins in Tokyo in 1999 announcing the consortium's acquisition of LTCB to the press. Yashiro is seated behind him.

Collins (standing center) in the Sudan in the late 1980s, when he took a break from his job on Wall Street to do charity work in Africa.

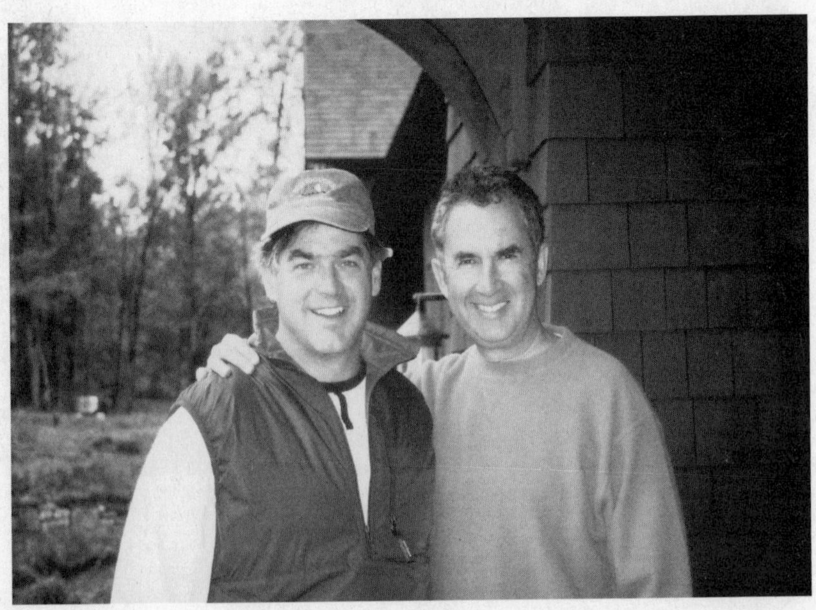

Collins with Gerry Schwartz, founder of the private equity firm, Onex. Collins ran the New York office of Onex in the early 1990s, where he learned the tricks of the private equity business.

Shinsei directors and advisers announce the deal; Volcker was deliberately placed in a prominent position in the center of the podium, along with some of the Japanese "grandees," to impress the Japanese journalists; left to right: J. Christopher Flowers, Timothy C. Collins, Hirotaro Higuchi, Takashi Imai, Masamoto Yashiro, Paul Volcker, Minoru Makihara, Akira Aoki, Hidebumi Mori, and Teruaki Yamamoto.

Vernon Jordan, a close friend of Bill Clinton, who became a Shinsei adviser.

Photo by Robert Giroux.

Paul Volcker, the former governor of the U.S. Federal Reserve, whose lobbying helped clinch the Shinsei deal, talks to reporters in Tokyo in the autumn of 1999.

Photo by Toshiyuki Aizawa.

Flowers (far right) and Yashiro (second from right) shake hands with government officials from the DIC over the deal; Anzai is second from left.

David Rockefeller, the former chairman of Chase, who became a director and enthusiastic supporter of Shinsei bank.

Lawrence Summers, the U.S. Treasury Secretary, who kept pressing for Japanese bank reform.

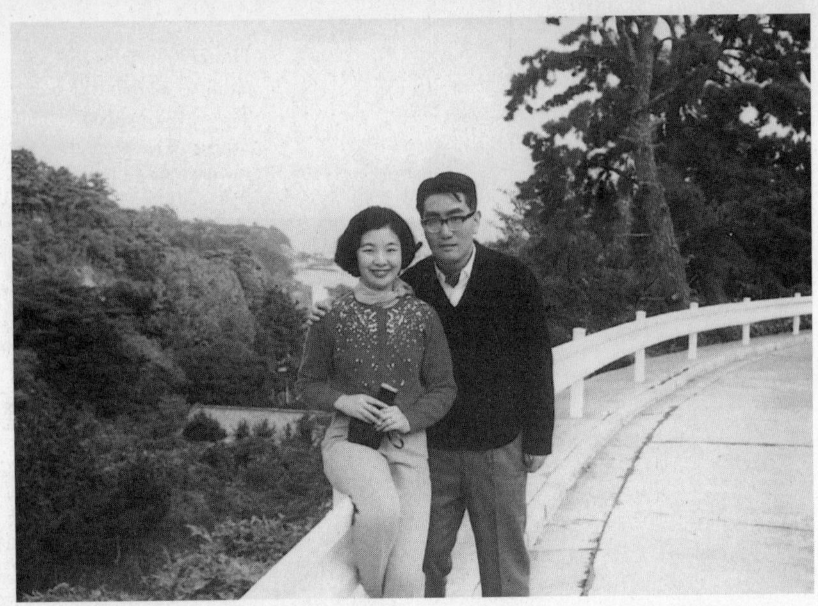

Tadayo Homma, on his honeymoon in the 1960s; as a diligent bureaucrat he chose a honeymoon location close to work so he could return to the office if necessary.

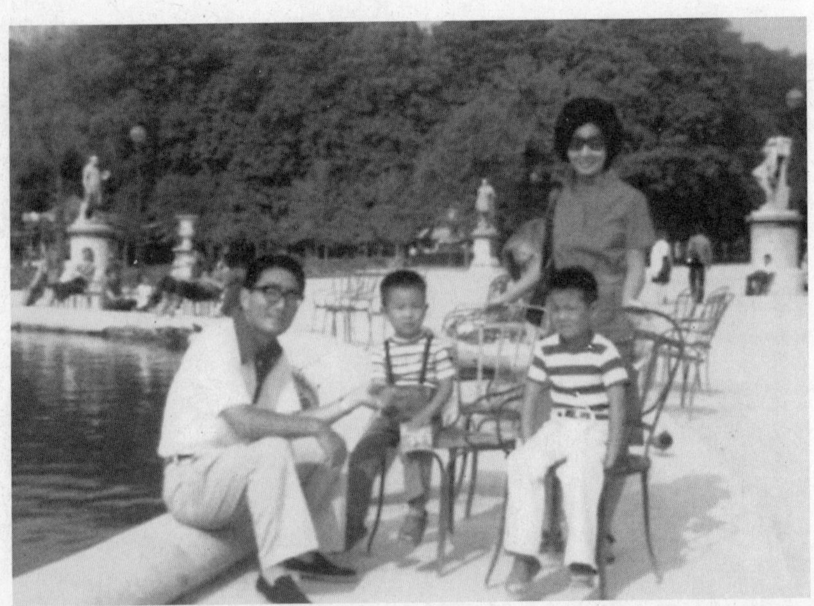

Homma and his family on vacation while he was working at the Bank of Japan's New York branch in the 1970s.

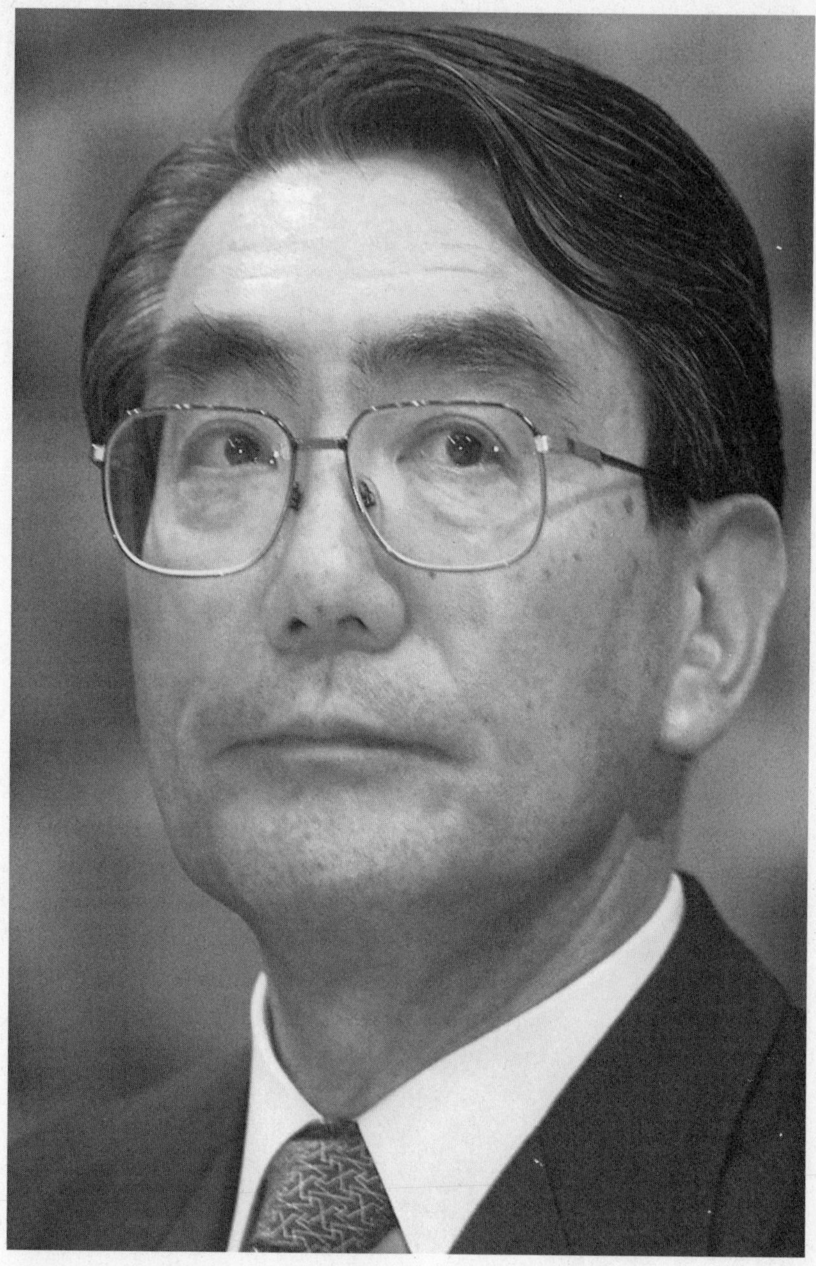

Homma at a press conference to announce the creation of Aozora bank, shortly before he was found dead in an Osaka hotel room.

Yashiro (far left) in the mid-1930s with his family; only he and his brother survived the war.

Yashiro as a young boy (far right) walking through Tokyo, with his brother and a teacher in the 1930s.

Yashiro in 1992 with John Reed, Citibank chairman, at a ceremony marking the 90th anniversary of Citibank's operations in Japan. Yashiro was head of Citibank's retail operations in Japan at that time.

Yashiro explaining his vision of Shinsei to reporters in 2002.

Opening ceremony for the new retail operations at Shinsei bank in 2001 in the remodeled lobby of the bank. Left to right: Satoru Katayama (head of retail), K. Sajeeve Thomas (chief of staff, retail), Yashiro, and Djananjaya "Jay" Dvivedi (head of banking infrastructure).

David Fite, an American banker brought in from Westpac to act as CFO at Shinsei.

Brian Prince, an American banker hired from Lehman Brothers, who became co-head of institutional banking at Shinsei.

Dvidedi, an IT expert and one of three former Citibank senior Indian executives who joined Shinsei, standing in front of the new bank's computers.

The top management team, sitting in Shinsei's airy lobby. Although the press department at Shinsei often tried to persuade the Americans to sit down in official photos, they could not always conceal the height difference. Left to right: Yashiro, Fite, Mori (senior managing director), and Yamamoto (co-head of institutional banking).

Nonetheless, Arnold and Volpi were convinced that the fundamental logic behind the deal was as powerful as ever, even if LTCB was near bankruptcy. Like most Western observers at the time, they were convinced that Japan's economy was poised for a rebound and determined to get a strong presence in the market. LTCB's customer base could still be combined with SBC's investment banking skills to create a financial powerhouse. Indeed, a weaker Japanese partner might benefit SBC. If the Japanese bank was close to collapse, SBC might be able to buy the entire bank at a fire sale price. And if LTCB did not collapse, a sense of crisis might make it more willing to adopt radical, "un-Japanese" measures to revive its business.

"This deal is going to give us extraordinary access to the Japanese markets, which we could not get if we were independent," Arnold insisted. So, after intense discussions, SBC decided to press ahead but with the deal subtly altered. "What we have to do is seek ways of protecting ourselves in case anything goes wrong—the key is to ring fence everything," Arnold told his board in Zurich. SBC insisted that the three joint ventures should be treated as separate entities that were not exposed to the risk inside the parent bank and secretly cut back the cross-shareholding deal from 3 percent to 1 percent. They also agreed to subscribe to only half of the new $2 billion of capital that LTCB hoped to raise, instead of all of it. Under these conditions, the Swiss pressed ahead in mid-September, signing a binding deal to merge the investment banking and asset management operations, and to create a new private bank.

"After we found out about this subsidiary issue, it became a clear political decision about what to do," Volpi later explained. "We did not want to be investors [in LTCB]! But we concluded that it may be possible for the bank to revive itself if we had three years to restructure and change the bank. So we went forward at that point, in spite of knowing that LTCB was in big problems. We told ourselves that even if something bad happens, we have no commitment to rescue them."

Onogi grew uneasy. With the Swiss now only offering a token amount of capital, his problems were as bad as ever. Indeed, in some ways his position was even worse. At the start of 1997, nobody outside the Japanese system had any idea about the scale of problems inside LTCB; now the Swiss had uncovered the rot. Worse still, by allying with the *gaijin,* Onogi had effectively stepped outside the Japanese system and the cozy network of mutual support. He was on his own.

His one source of comfort was the strategic logic of the alliance. Putting a Japanese client base together with international banking skills was the only way forward, he argued; and if the bank was given enough time to put these principles into practice, the joint venture would deliver lucrative earnings. All he needed was another couple of years—and another $2 billion or so.

Unfortunately, the capital raising plans quickly fell apart as well. In late October, with the Swiss bank's help, LTCB drew up plans to issue some $2 billion of bonds and equities. The road show was planned for November. But a few days before the launch, disaster struck. Hokkaido Takushoku, one of Japan's largest banks based in the northern island of Hokkaido, announced that it was filing for bankruptcy. It was the first collapse of a large bank seen in Japan for sixty years and the news stunned the banking world. Although rumors about the problems at Hokkaido Takushoku had been bubbling for months, observers had presumed that the Japanese government would protect the bank, like it had rescued NCB back in the spring. Indeed, the government had initially tried to do that, by bullying Hokkaido Bank, another regional lender, into a merger. However, in the autumn this merger fell apart, leaving the crippled bank in a crisis. The Bank of Japan knew that there was absolutely no appetite among the other financial institutions for a collective rescue of the type that had occurred at NCB. "The whole system of trust and consensus had broken down," Sei Nakai, deputy director of the Ministry's banking bureau, later explained. And, the Ministry did not have any mandate to use public funds to bail out the banks itself, because the concept of using taxpayer money for the banks had become wildly unpopular in the wake of the 1995 public scandals about the *jusen* and EIE. So the bureaucrats decided that they had no alternative but to let the huge bank declare bankruptcy. Secretly, some hoped that shock of the announcement might create a consensus among politicians on the need to use public funds to help the banks—and allow the banks to write off their bad loans once and for all.

The shock had a greater impact than the bureaucrats had guessed; it shook the entire system to its core. Just as Onogi liked to explain in his diagrams, the postwar financial system in Japan had been built on a sense of trust that everybody would always support everybody else, under the wing of the Ministry of Finance. And precisely because everybody trusted the Ministry to protect them, the Japanese system had not needed to develop alternative structures to create trust, such as a strong legal framework and culture of transparency that underpinned markets in countries such as America. The collapse of a large bank had now shattered that old system of trust; but investors discovered that they could not rely on the tools that created faith in the American system either. They had been cast into a new world, without a compass. The laws for protecting creditors in the case of a bank failure were unclear and in the days after the collapse the government admitted that Hokkaido Takushoku's bad loans were more than twice as large as the previously published data. Credit officers at foreign banks started to panic.

Sanyo Securities, a second tier broker, was the next victim. By mid-November, Sanyo found it impossible to raise funds, and declared bankruptcy, defaulting on its contracts in the interbank money markets. A few days later, Yamaichi Securities, the fourth largest broker, declared bankruptcy as well. The broker was already weaker than its rivals and rumors had been bubbling for some time that Yamaichi was manipulating its accounts. Until then, the markets had discounted these tales, presuming that the Ministry would always protect the mighty broker. However, in the new climate such assumptions were wearing thin. As Shohei Nozawa, the Yamaichi president, delivered the news of Yamaichi's failure, he sobbed into the microphone in front of the world's press.

Belatedly, the bureaucrats at the Bank of Japan and Ministry of Finance realized that a full-scale financial crisis was developing, and they rushed to restore some of the trust of the old system. The Bank of Japan issued a solemn statement promising to protect all creditors of failed financial institutions and a shaken Hashimoto delivered the policy shift that the bureaucrats had been hoping to see. He promised that the ruling Liberal Democratic Party would "start to study" ways of using public funds to support the banks, to create a proper safety net. But although the moves helped to push the stock market higher and stop further failures, the repercussions of the "November shock" did not disappear easily. Trust, once shattered, is very hard to restore. And as foreign bankers tried to make sense of why Yamaichi and Hokkaido Takushoku had collapsed, they were beginning to realize that the bad loan problem sitting in the banks was larger than anyone had believed. The type of rude awakening that Volpi and Arnold had suffered at LTCB was being shared by investors across the world as they looked at the Japanese banking system as a whole.

"It is a terrible time to try to sell bank shares," the SBC bankers concluded, as they looked at the markets. By late November, the LTCB share price had fallen below Y200, the lowest level for a decade. Grimly, the Swiss bankers declared that LTCB's plans to raise $2 billion of new capital would have to be postponed. Onogi's lifeline had been pulled away.

On Christmas Day the LTCB board met for its regular meeting up on the twentieth floor of the bank. Onogi looked haggard. On paper, his plans for the beloved alliance with SBC were proceeding and the three joint ventures scheduled to open in the spring of 1998. However, in early December SBC had unexpectedly announced that it was merging its operations with Union Bank of Switzerland, a larger Swiss bank, to create a new bank, also called UBS. This had made the Swiss more wary about the alliance than ever. Meanwhile, LTCB was running out of capital so fast that it might not even be able to pay its normal half-yearly Y7 billion ($70 million) dividend to shareholders. Failure to do that would almost certainly trigger an investor panic and leave LTCB following Yamaichi's fate. Having watched the Yamaichi president sob into his microphone in front of the world's press as he announced his company's collapse, Onogi had no illusion about the humiliation that could lie in store.

One of the men sitting on LTCB's board had an idea to save the bank. Ryuji Konishi ran the market trading section of LTCB and had worked in America for several years. Because he was so close to the capital markets, Konishi knew that LTCB's credibility was slipping. In the autumn of 1997, some foreign bankers such as Bankers Trust had started to demand that LTCB post collateral when it wanted to make any trades, to guard against the risk of a default. Given that, Konishi reckoned that LTCB had nothing left to lose. It was time, he declared in the days before the meeting, for the bank to acknowledge its bad loan problems, drop out of the alliance with the Swiss—and start again. The foreigners, he argued, had betrayed LTCB by refusing to supply any capital, so there was no point in dealing with them anymore. "What we have now is an unequal alliance like the treaty that the Americans imposed on the Tokugawa shogunate back in the nineteenth century!" he declared. "We have to drop this alliance and we should just come clean about our problems; we should all commit *seppuku* [ritual suicide] if necessary!"

Onogi disagreed. At the back of his mind, he continued to believe that if only the bank could buy itself a bit more time by getting the SBC alliance up and running, it could still pull through. And in early December, Yoshiharu Suzuki—the man to whom Onogi had delegated the job of handling the bad loan book—had presented a scheme that appeared to help the bank. Back in 1996, Suzuki's team had started drawing up a new internal system for reclassifying parts of the loan book, in accordance with a new set of guidelines that had been prepared by the Ministry of Finance. In this new scheme, the bank did not need to make one-off large provisions for bad loans to its subsidiaries but could take a more gradual stance, one that projected a stealthy pace of write-offs over many years. The key point was that if the bank used the new system, it would not need to make such large provisions for its bad loans—which meant that it had more free cash in its banks and thus did not look insolvent. Taking a more gradualist stance toward the bad loans, in other words, made LTCB's balance sheet look much better.

Was this the tactic proper? As the LTCB bankers sat around the boardroom table, the matter looked a little gray. The Ministry of Finance had announced in the summer of 1997 that it planned to introduce more stringent standards for the way that bad loans in subsidiaries were measured. Yet the Ministry's guidance to the banks on the matter was still very unclear—and precedent suggested that in practice the bureaucrats were perfectly happy for LTCB to use a more "flexible" scheme for defining write-offs. Indeed, LTCB's own auditors were sufficiently confident that the new scheme was legal that they had agreed to sign off on the accounts.

Moreover, Onogi reckoned that there were the broader interests of the financial system to consider. If LTCB tried to write off all its bad loans—and announced a huge loss that tipped the bank into insolvency—that could shatter investor confidence and potentially trigger another market panic that would hurt *all* the Japanese banks, as well as the economy. But if the bank used the new classification system and continued to pay the Y7 billion dividend as normal, then peace would prevail—or so he hoped. It seemed a tiny amount of money to worry about, given the bigger issues at stake. "[What we did] was within the legally permitted scope," Onogi later insisted to the court.

With a minimum of ceremony, the LTCB board approved the new method of "classifying" the bad loans. Years later, some of the bankers would consider that the moment the Rubicon was crossed.

A few weeks later, Konishi announced that he was resigning from the bank in a small gesture of protest. Onogi was shocked. It was extremely unusual for a director to resign from a Japanese company in a fit of pique. However much men such as Uehara and Mizukami had grumbled about the problems in the past, for example, they had never dared to leave the LTCB "family"; the emotional bonds were too close. Yet Konishi was determined. "As ever, you may find my behavior out the ordinary!" he declared in an emotional resignation speech to the board. "But after I leave I will no longer have any cause to speak to any of you, in public or in private, so this is the last time that you will have to listen to me being ornery. They often quote Shakespeare in speeches in the West. In Japan's it's more common to quote Chinese sayings. So I would like to quote the Chinese proverb: *A man can tell the truth when he is about to die.*" Konishi went on to argue that there were three things fundamentally wrong with LTCB: The bank had lost its business franchise, due to the deregulation sweeping Japan; it had lost a sense of business ethics; and it was dangerously insular. Instead of adopting lessons from outside, it had maintained a "pure, monochromatic" culture, which stifled innovation. "It might be comfortable to stay in this elitist, inward-looking LTCB world . . . but in the end you should know that by doing so you are only hastening your own extinction!"

The other two dozen bankers on the LTCB board listened to Konishi's comments, but most of them shrugged them off. In private, some of the senior LTCB bankers knew that their bank was all but insolvent. But they did not think that their financial situation was different from other banks. Konishi had always had a reputation for being a maverick and most of the senior LTCB executives considered the idea of resigning from the bank as odious as a soldier deserting during a battle. Like the soldiers of Japan's Imperial Army just before its defeat in World War II, the LTCB bankers had a hunch that disaster was looming—yet they continued to hope that against all the odds a miracle would emerge to rescue them. So as they plodded on, they pointedly refrained from talking too much about the bad loans, distracting themselves by narrowing their vision, and focusing on minute details of their individual bureaucratic tasks. "What is the point of talking about depressing matters—we will just become miserable!" the LTCB bankers would sometimes console each other. "What will happen, will happen. It is fate."

The screw tightened. As 1998 got under way the government took a few, wobbly steps toward a large-scale banking "solution." It created a Y30 trillion ($300 billion) safety net to support the banks, and used Y1.8 trillion ($18 billion) of this money to purchase token amounts of preferred shares in the large banks, including a Y180 billion ($1.8 billion) capital injection for LTCB. The Ministry of Finance also released more realistic estimates of Japan's bad loans. These suggested that the broadest definition of "risky" loans in the system could be slightly more than Y70 trillion ($700 billion), 14 percent of all loans. Then, in the early summer the joint ventures with the Swiss finally started. Onogi, Uehara, Volpi, and Arnold all hailed the new alliance in a series of upbeat interviews. "The key thing about this deal is that it is going to give us extraordinary access to the Japanese market," Arnold explained. "And that is something we could not get if we were independent." By the summer of 1998 it had become the conventional wisdom in the international banking world that the fastest way to penetrate the Japanese market—and take advantage of Big Bang—was with a Japanese partner. There were more than a dozen joint ventures getting under way between foreign banks and Japanese partners, with varying degrees of commitment. On the very same day that the Japanese-Swiss investment bank venture opened its doors, June 1, Salomon Smith Barney announced that it was forming its own joint venture with Nikko Securities, which was even more sweeping than the UBS-LTCB tie-up. "I guess imitation is one form of flattery," Arnold dryly joked. "The logic of our deal is compelling."

Yet, within days of the investment bank venture starting, it began to come unstuck. Out of the blue, the *Gekan Gendai,* a tabloid monthly magazine, published a cover story declaring that LTCB was on the verge of bankruptcy. A few days earlier, LTCB had unveiled its results for fiscal 1997, which had painted the picture of a fairly healthy bank, thanks to the usual massaging and the fact that the government had agreed to inject around Y180 billion of public funds into the bank, as part of a broader package of aid to the banking system. LTCB said that its nonconsolidated operations had just recorded its second highest level of business profit, some Y196 billion ($1.96 billion), while net parent profits were Y41 billion ($410 million). The level of gray and bad loans had fallen by Y229 billion ($2.29 billion) in the year to some Y806 billion ($8.09 billion), while its BIS ratio rose to 9.22 percent, one of the highest such ratios among all Japanese banks. LTCB, in other words, looked pretty healthy. Unfortunately, the *Gendai* piece was filled with such startling details about LTCB's bad loans that Japanese readers assumed the figures must have come from a highly placed leak. LTCB's share price plunged 10 percent to below Y200.

Then came a second blow. Traders at LTCB Warburg started offloading LTCB's stock into the Tokyo markets and rumors exploded that the Swiss were pulling out of the alliance. Frantically, the Swiss bank tried to throw water on the fire by declaring that the sales had been made on behalf of a *client*. To Japanese ears, the defense sounded very weak. Culturally, Japanese bankers had never drawn much distinction between trading for a client and for a bank's own account and the Swiss refused to name the client. Consequently, most Japanese concluded that the Swiss were either trying to exit the deal, or deliberately making LTCB bankrupt, so that they could purchase it cheaply.

The share price of LTCB slid lower. Day by day, the European fund managers who had been so charmed by Onogi a year earlier started to dump their LTCB shares. By the middle of June, domestic institutions, such as regional banks and life insurance companies, were discreetly placing sell orders as well. Once, domestic banks and brokers would have considered the idea of selling the shares of an ailing partner to be a terrible breach of Japanese corporate ethics. However, the old loyalties were starting to unravel. LTCB was doubly vulnerable because it had never had a specific *keiretsu* and since it had allied itself with a *gaijin,* it was presumed to have *already* breached Japanese ethics. Thus, regardless of whether LTCB's financial fundamentals were worse than other banks'—and most observers presumed that they were not drastically different—the bank looked weak in a political and social sense. And in Japan, the issue of social support was as important as corporate accounts.

On Thursday June 25, LTCB's share price tumbled to Y50, or par value. The same day, Onogi and the other senior LTCB bankers left the sanctuary of nearby hotels, where they had been holding emergency meetings, and reappeared in the headquarters building for the bank's annual shareholders' meeting. It was held in a large, airy room on the ground floor, packed with depressed employees, angry corporate partners, and *sokaiya*—a type of *yakuza* gangsters. The *sokaiya* were one of the oddest features of Japan's postwar corporate world. They made their living by blackmailing corporate executives and threatening to ask "embarrassing" questions at shareholders' meetings about the company accounts—or aspects of the executives' lives—unless paid a fee. In the past, LTCB—like every other company in Japan—had usually kept the *sokaiya* quiet with discreet payments, because they did not want to suffer any public embarrassment. However, the *sokaiya* had attended every recent shareholders' meeting at the bank and with LTCB in a dire state, the *sokaiya* saw little reason to keep a low profile. Instead, they knew that the LTCB shareholders' meeting could act as a strange marketing ploy for their racket; they had a better chance of blackmailing other banks in the future if they gave a practical demonstration of just how "embarrassing" they could be.

"So, is LTCB bankrupt?" a *sokaiya* heckled from the crowd, as the shareholders' meeting got under way on the first floor of the LTCB tower. The other shareholders remained nervously silent. Everybody knew the bank was in deep trouble, but nobody except the *sokaiya* wanted to point this out.

Onogi batted the question away with dignity. In private, he was exhausted and depressed. However, he was determined to let no hint of emotion leak out on his face. He calmly ran through the financial highlights of the previous year's accounts, pointing out the improvements in the BIS ratio and the core profits. Then he promised to pay the normal Y7 billion dividend to shareholders. It had only been possible to pay the dividend through a second round of "massaging" of the accounts; however, Onogi had convinced himself that what the bank had done was not illegal. He *had* to pay the dividend; he had to protect the system, for the sake of Japan's economy, for the other banks, for LTCB's loyal staff. That was his *duty;* it was the only honorable thing to do.

"This will be your last shareholder meeting, won't it?" screeched the *sokaiya*. Onogi desperately tried to ignore them. But the heckling continued: "The bank is bankrupt! You will never come here again!"

"LTCB is finished!"

— *Chapter 9* —

SCAPEGOATS AND SEEDS

Company executives and bureaucrats are dropping like flies these days, as they commit suicide when faced with bribery charges.

—*Mainichi* newspaper

In the event, the final death throes of LTCB were painfully protracted, like so much else in Japan's banking world. Early in the summer of 1998, UBS—as SBC was now called—made one last, desperate attempt to rescue the alliance. It secretly drew up proposals, optimistically known as the "Phoenix Plan," to purchase parts of LTCB, in conjunction with a *third* partner—Bank of Yokohama, a regional bank. The Swiss bankers were vague about a price tag for LTCB, but stressed that any deal should be negotiated on the assumption that LTCB should first write off at least another Y750 billion ($7.5 billion) of bad loans to become vaguely viable, using another injection of public funds. However, the Japanese government expressed little interest in the idea. Rightly or wrongly, many Japanese blamed the Swiss bankers for the problems at LTCB—and the last thing that the Ministry of Finance wanted to embark on was a frank discussion about the scale of problems of LTCB in front of foreigners.

Instead, the bureaucrats cobbled together another, more traditional Japanese-style rescue plan: In late June, LTCB announced that it was embarking on an alliance with Sumitomo Trust, a medium-sized trust bank. It seemed a distinctly odd idea. LTCB and Sumitomo Trust were not traditional partners, and Sumitomo Trust itself was plagued with bad loans, meaning that it was in no position to "rescue" LTCB by itself. "Merging those two banks is like putting two stones together—they may just sink faster," one UBS banker sourly remarked. Frustrated and betrayed, UBS then decided to withdraw completely from the alliance, by buying LTCB out of the asset management and investment banking joint ventures.

Events then turned from bad to worse for LTCB. To the disappointment of the Ministry of Finance, Sumitomo Trust proved less malleable than the bureaucrats had hoped. The events of November 1997 had badly shaken all the banks' faith in the system, and Sumitomo insisted that it would only proceed with the merger if the government *first* removed the bad loans from LTCB and injected public funds to make the bank viable. The Bank of Japan estimated, on the basis of a new government audit, that about Y2 trillion ($20 billion) was needed to plug the gap. However, parliament refused to provide this money. In mid-July, the opposition parties won an unexpectedly large number of seats in an election, and this left the political process paralyzed. Like most outside economists, the Democratic Party of Japan, the main opposition party, was becoming fed up with the way that the government kept propping up the status quo. Thus, though the LDP wanted to rescue LTCB, the opposition parties were determined to block any deal on LTCB unless the government produced a more comprehensive program of reform.

Through the hot, sticky summer days of July and August, the political paralysis dragged on. With every day of uncertainty, the value of the bank's assets slowly drained away. Worse, the bank was becoming a financial time bomb. LTCB had a vast derivatives portfolio, worth about Y50 trillion (or $500 billion) in gross terms, partly because of the deals it had been doing with banks such as Credit Suisse in recent years to hide the bad loans. The implications of this horrified the Bank of Japan. These derivative trades linked LTCB to most of the major banks in the world and no bank had *ever* collapsed before with so many derivative contracts outstanding in the global markets. It was dangerously unclear whether the counter-parties to the derivative contracts would be protected if LTCB defaulted, since no precedent had been created in the Japanese legal system. "The large derivatives portfolio posed systemic concerns," Hiroshi Nakaso, a senior Bank of Japan official, later explained. "It was feared that if LTCB collapsed in a disorderly way this would constitute a default, which could trigger cross defaults and amplify disruption in other markets." But nobody in Japan seemed able to rescue LTCB; and nobody appeared able to kill it off either. Indeed, Japan's parliament seemed unwilling to take any decisions about anything at all. The bank had turned into a corporate zombie, neither alive nor dead. It was a terrible, chilling parable for Japan's financial system as a whole.

The deathblow occurred in late October—or a full four months after the markets had begun to believe that LTCB was insolvent. It was scarcely a day too late. "LTCB miraculously survived the summer but it could barely have managed another day of funding on its own when it was finally nationalized," Nakaso later admitted. After months of wrangling, parliament passed a new set of banking laws that created a Y60 trillion ($600 billion) safety net for the financial system. As part of this, they also agreed to put LTCB under state control for a period, and while seeking a new buyer. The government claimed that it was a bold new sign of reform. In practice, it seemed like the least bad solution to the deadlock. Japanese bureaucrats reasoned that a sale of LTCB could persuade the DPJ—and the rest of the outside world—that the government was taking radical action to tackle the banking problems; however, it could *also* reassure the LDP that LTCB was not going to be immediately closed in a way that would harm the borrowers. At a stroke, the concept appeared to offer both continuity and change. LTCB would not be killed, but it would not be rescued either. It was a typical Japanese compromise.

So, on October 23, 1998, LTCB called a press conference and announced that it had "voluntarily" applied to be nationalized under these new laws. For good measure, the bureaucrats then announced that they had "suddenly" discovered that LTCB had a capital deficit of Y300 billion ($3 billion) [even though they had hitherto insisted that the bank was solvent]. It was the largest bank failure ever seen in history, by a long stretch.

Then Onogi and the other senior managers quietly gathered on the nineteenth floor of the magnificent LTCB tower. After four months of uncertainty, they felt exhausted, miserable, and defeated. However, Onogi insisted that they should perform one last little ritual. With a small, polite bow, the senior bank managers formally greeted a new arrival to the bank: Takashi Anzai, a senior Bank of Japan bureaucrat, who had been appointed to run the bank while it was nationalized, effectively replacing Onogi.

"Yoroshiku!" Onogi said, politely, using one of those quintessentially Japanese phrases that are extremely hard to translate into English. Technically it means "Please"; in this context it meant, "We are handing this bank to you and we realize that this has left you with a difficult task, but we hope you can make the best of it. We do apologize sincerely for the inconvenience caused by this collapse."

"Yoroshiku, yoroshiku!" It was all that Onogi could think—or bear—to say; Japan was not a culture that liked public emotion. Then he gave another polite bow, poker-faced, and quietly went home.

Seven months later, Takashi Uehara killed himself. On a May evening, he checked himself into a hotel a mile away from his family house in a pleasant suburb of Tokyo. Then he carefully created a noose with the belt of his traditional Japanese gown and hung himself from the ceiling. On the table he left some suicide notes. "I am so sorry. Please forgive me for leaving you," they said. He was fifty-nine.

Few LTCB bankers were terribly surprised. Since the financial crisis had erupted in 1997, a stream of Japanese bankers and bureaucrats had killed themselves after becoming caught up in the financial problems and corruption scandals. Uehara had more reason than most to feel the pressure. The day he committed suicide, the police had indicated they were about to arrest him for his role in massaging the financial accounts in 1997 and 1998. Uehara had always been a proud man, who expected to become president of LTCB after Onogi; being publicly labeled as a common criminal was a humiliating shock.

His age and temperament may have exacerbated his pain. He was just young—and international—enough to have spotted the problems in the traditional Japanese banking model at an early stage of his career. Uehara had worked in America for many years and had been one of the people who had called for radical measures against the bad loans in 1995. But he was also just old enough to have been haunted by the postwar spirit of duty. "Under most measures," Uehara would observe long after he had lost his optimism, "we are already bankrupt." Despite his bleak view of the situation, he never considered leaving the bank. *"Even in the pitch black of night, there is one light shining, so we will go forward!"* he used to tell his friends, quoting an old Chinese proverb. So Uehara plodded on. And during 1998 Uehara's sense of duty apparently became even more intense. Notwithstanding his earlier reform campaign, he became involved in the task of "tidying up" the corporate accounts.

In the months that followed the bank's collapse, his duty turned into a consuming desire to make sense of what had happened. Like Onogi, he had always been an intellectual and precise man, with a strong belief in his own powers of analysis. Tormented, he telephoned Konishi, the pugnacious maverick who had resigned from LTCB back in March 1998. "You were right, Konishi-kun, in what you said. We should have listened to your warnings!" Uehara declared. Konishi was astonished. The two men had never been close since Uehara had always seemed aloof, intent on obeying etiquette, whereas Konishi was passionate and outspoken. "Yes, Uehara-san! You should have *all* listened to my criticisms!" Konishi said with his usual bluntness.

Uehara also called Sei Nakai, a senior Ministry bureaucrat who had tried to organize the disastrous merger with Sumitomo Trust. "I am sorry," Uehara said to Nakai. The bureaucrat tried to offer comfort. He was a decent, sincere man, and he could sense that Uehara was depressed. "It was a mistake to get the politicians involved," he muttered. "But don't worry about it all! We all did what was best. What happened, happened. It was fate."

In the spring of 1999, Uehara appeared to have recovered his spirits. He briefly returned to the LTCB headquarters to attend a small reception in support of a literary foundation that the bank funded. From time to time, he met old colleagues for lunch. Onogi and the other senior LTCB bankers liked to organize these gatherings. After three decades of working together in close proximity, they found it very odd to be separated. "Many of us knew each other better than we knew our own families," one LTCB banker admitted. "We had spent far more time with our colleagues than our wives."

Then the police struck. They first marched into the LTCB headquarters in late October 1998, hunting for evidence that could send the bankers to jail. The collapse of a bank as large as LTCB was a national humiliation and politicians were determined to find scapegoats to blame; they could not admit to themselves or the outside world that the entire system was to blame. Somehow, someone would have to be put on trial. So the prosecutors started with the most junior staff. Through the winter, young LTCB bankers were pulled aside, one by one, and interrogated about their knowledge of the bad loans. "Who hid the bad loans?" the prosecutors asked. Bewildered, the junior bankers did what they had been trained to do, and obeyed a bureaucrat's orders, revealing what they knew. The prosecutors then moved steadily up the hierarchy, questioning more senior bankers. "Your junior colleagues have already told us everything about what you did," they berated the managers. "So there is no use in lying! If you don't help us, we will have to take action against your juniors!" By the spring, many of the junior bankers had become racked with guilt for "betraying" their bosses—and the senior bankers were haunted by their failure to protect their junior staff.

Finally, the prosecutors hauled the top LTCB bankers into police headquarters, telling each banker that their colleagues had already testified against them. Between the questioning, the bankers were forbidden to talk to each other. As they sat at home, isolated, pressure mounted. Many of the bankers lost weight. Some started to drink heavily. Friendships frayed. Every LTCB board member nervously wondered what all the others had said about him. The greatest pressure was on Onogi, Uehara, and Suzuki. The prosecutors were convinced that although Suzuki had been the person who created many of the accounting schemes, Onogi had set the overall policy direction—and Uehara had eventually overseen what Suzuki had done. However, the investigators knew they could not simply charge the bankers with the crime of simply "underreporting bad loans," since that had never been clearly illegal in Japan; that charge would condemn all the banks. So they searched for something that displayed *criminal* intent—and homed in on the Y7 billion ($70 billion) dividend payments that had been approved in 1997 and 1998. The bankers had only made these payments, the prosecutors declared, because they failed to report Y313 billion ($3.13

billion) of bad loans in the accounts. Technically, this breached a small clause in the commercial code, which declared that directors could not pay dividends unless there was enough cash, so the prosecutors prepared to arrest Onogi, Suzuki, and Uehara.

When Konishi, the bank maverick, heard about the prosecutors' plans, he tried to intervene. He knew that personally he had little to fear from the prosecutors, since—in a bizarre turn of the wheel—his decision to resign from LTCB was now considered a good thing by Japanese society, rather than a shameful betrayal. But that did not spare Konishi from the collective sense of guilt that had settled like a heavy cloud on every former LTCB banker. The police put him under huge pressure to testify against his colleagues, and although Konishi refused, he discovered that comments he had made in the press were being used in the prosecutors' case. In an attempt to make amends, he paid a visit to some senior bureaucrats and politicians involved in the case. "This isn't justice—it is a witch-hunt!" he declared. "What the LTCB management did was very bad business judgment, but it wasn't *criminal!*" But the government needed scapegoats. The officials told Konishi that between three and five LTCB bankers would have to go to jail. Then Uehara upset their plans. On May 5, 1999, the prosecutors and police leaked Uehara's name to the newspapers, detailing some of his "crimes." Frantically, one of his friends sent an email to LTCB colleagues. "Let's all quickly get in touch with Uehara-san to tell him that we value him!" The email messages arrived too late: Uehara had already checked into his hotel and killed himself. A few days later, Kazunori Fukuda, fifty-one, the manager of LTCB's Osaka branch, also hanged himself, and left a little note. "I got tired," it simply said.

Over at UBS headquarters in Zurich, Arnold was deeply shocked to hear about Uehara's suicide. He had come to know the Japanese man better than almost anybody else in LTCB, since Uehara spoke excellent English and was deft at dealing with foreigners. Then when LTCB announced its disastrous merger with Sumitomo Trust in the summer of 1998, Uehara had the unpleasant task of negotiating with the Swiss about the future of the ventures. Under the terms of the deal negotiated back in 1997, UBS had the right to buy LTCB out of the joint ventures if the share price of LTCB ever fell to

Y50. It eventually exercised the right and unwound the alliance in a manner that was financially beneficial for UBS. On the LTCB side, it had been Uehara who coped with the messy details of this process. His main priority in the negotiations had been to act like a good corporate "father" and ensure that as many young LTCB staff retained their jobs at the ventures as possible.

"Uehara seemed a very decent person, international and with a lot of integrity," Arnold recalled. The death seemed particularly distressing because Uehara had always projected such a *rational*, Western image to the Swiss bankers. He did not seem a man who would be beholden to old-fashioned Japanese traditions, or concepts of "shame." But had all this been a mask? Indeed, when Arnold looked back on the disastrous alliance with LTCB, he was forced to concede that Uehara's death was just one of many mysterious—and baffling—things.

"I may never understand what happened there—why the political climate changed and LTCB ended up being abandoned and things went wrong," Arnold concluded. "I am still absolutely convinced that Onogi was and is an honorable person. He and Uehara were gentlemen. But toward the end I began to understand that they might have been bound by a complex set of circumstances and obligations, rooted in history."

Like many generations of foreigners before him, Arnold had come to the sad conclusion that LTCB and Japan were not all that they seemed.

Some of the other *gaijin* entangled in LTCB also felt baffled—and betrayed. During 1997 many European and American fund managers had bought LTCB shares, since they deeply admired Onogi's strategic vision. They were subsequently forced to record large losses. The hardest hit was Martin Whitman, the head of the Third Avenue Value Fund in New York, whose main clients were American corporate pension funds. Whitman was a colorful figure, who had made a small fortune in the 1980s by cannily buying shares in troubled Savings and Loan institutions in America. In 1997, Whitman decided that Japan's financial mess seemed similar to the S&L crisis and decided to invest in LTCB because it seemed one way to repeat his earlier success. "I admired the LTCB management because they were reducing their loan portfolio and like the best of the U.S. banks they had made dramatic moves to build up their fee income with SBC. And while we could not do due diligence on the loan portfolio, I felt reasonably comfortable because I was piggybacking Swiss Bank, which had reviewed the portfolio," Whitman later explained. He bought forty-six million shares—or a stake of almost 2 percent. Ironically, that meant the American fund manager owned more LTCB shares than SBC.

During late 1997 and early 1998 Whitman bombarded the LTCB management with letters recommending restructuring plans, drawn from his S&L experience—and an unshakable all-American assumption that an equity stake should give him shareholder rights. LTCB brushed him off. Then, when LTCB announced yet another restructuring plan in August that promised to forgive another almost $4 billion debt to its subsidiaries—without any real demands for restructuring—Whitman sued. "A $3.7 billion debt forgiveness without any consideration! Geez—that would bankrupt Citicorp!" Whitman fumed. Then, he flew to Tokyo to confront the LTCB management directly. "You cannot just go about forgiving debt like that—even if they are your subsidiaries!" Whitman told the senior managers at LTCB.

"But you don't understand, Mr. Whitman. These subsidiaries are our children. We cannot just abandon them," they replied.

"But if your subsidiaries are your children, *what does that make your shareholders?*" Whitman fumed. LTCB did not reply.

Eventually, Whitman wrote off his entire $50 million investment: When LTCB collapsed its shares were effectively worthless. It was easily the largest loss his fund had ever suffered and he was disgusted with the Japanese system. "These LTCB guys are crooks—the whole system is crooked!" he later concluded. "They don't care about shareholders at all. They lie to the investors, they lie to the public. They don't care! They are all a bunch of crooks!"

Another indirect casualty of LTCB's demise was Credit Suisse. A couple of months after LTCB collapsed, Nippon Credit Bank also failed, and when the FSA inspectors started to probe the accounts of LTCB and NCB, they noticed a striking pattern. Both banks had been aggressively using swaps, bonds, *tokkin,* and derivatives products to flatter their accounts in previous years. And the counter-party to a surprisingly large proportion of these deals was Credit Suisse.

In late January 1999, the Financial Supervisory Agency, the new regulator, unexpectedly raided the white skyscraper that served as the Tokyo office for Credit Suisse First Boston and Credit Suisse Financial Products, respectively the group's investment bank and derivatives units. It was the first surprise inspection the Japanese regulators had ever unleashed against a foreign group—and the local staff in Tokyo panicked. With the knowledge of their London bosses, the staff shredded documents, dispatched files to London, and hid other potentially "incriminating" papers in a broom cupboard, which they concealed by altering the floor plans they gave to inspectors. CS staff dryly referred to the offending cupboard as the "Satian room" cupboard, referring to the secret "Satian" compound where Aum Shinrikyo, the secretive Japanese cult, once manufactured chemical weapons.

When the FSA inspectors eventually discovered the "Satian room at Credit Suisse," they were furious—and jubilant. What had started as an exploratory raid had netted a major scalp for the inspectors. The FSA could not pin any criminal charges on CS over the accounting-driven transactions per se, since it had never been illegal to offer these accounting tricks. Still, the inspectors slapped the maximum possible regulatory penalty on the bank for concealing the documents, reprimanded it over the *tobashi,* and forced CS to completely close its Japanese derivatives business; it was easily the most painful punishment ever imposed on a foreign bank in Japan.

The legal punishment fell exclusively on the local Japanese staff—even though these Japanese pointed out in court that they had only been following orders that had ultimately emanated from London. "[What happened] was part of a culture which went to the top," explained Hitomi Gambe, a young female compliance officer. However, the FSA never managed to pin anything concrete on the senior London management and the American and European staff involved in the case in Tokyo left Japan before charges could be filed. A year later, Allen Wheat the head of CSFB, was unceremoniously ousted after accounting scandals exploded in other parts of the world at CSFB. Shortly before that, Chris Goekjian, his protégé, abruptly resigned, citing "personal reasons." Although Goekjian refused to comment on the reasons for his departure, some CS bankers suspected that he had become a scapegoat for the accounting scandals in Japan and elsewhere. Nevertheless, as the junior Japanese staff sourly pointed out, neither man suffered too greatly from their departures since they were both already extremely wealthy. "If there were any winners from the [accounting] game, they were the people like Goekjian," admitted one of his former, senior colleagues from CS. "[It] made some foreign bankers extremely rich."

Onogi's own fallout from the scandals was a more painful affair. In June of 1999, Onogi was arrested and placed in prison for a month. When he emerged, the government launched its criminal case against him and his old friend Yoshiharu Suzuki for their role in covering up LTCB's bad loans, demanding a three-year prison sentence. Suda, another vice president, was also charged, taking the list of LTCB "criminals"—after the death of Uehara—to three. In addition to the criminal suit, the prosecutors also started civil suits that aimed to extract about Y12 billion ($120 million) in fines from a dozen of the senior LTCB bankers. It seemed an impossibly large amount for the bankers to ever pay. Although wealthy by Japanese standards, their salaries were modest compared to their Wall Street counterparts. To add to the financial pressure, the government forced LTCB directors to "voluntarily" return part of their pensions.

After Onogi emerged from prison, he spent his endless hours of free time sitting in his small house in Tokyo, tucked on the plot of land in Aoyama that his father had bought many decades ago. Onogi—unlike many salarymen—was fortunate enough to have a warm and supportive family and good marriage. "Onogi's family has been a great help to him," commented one of his friends. "His wife has been very strong—and he has two little grandchildren that he adores. He spends a lot of time with the grandchildren—they are a real comfort."

Between that, he watched the BBC television news in English and feverishly read books. Like Uehara, Onogi was gripped by a desire to rationalize, explain, and *understand* what had befallen LTCB. He read books by the German sociologist Max Weber and told his friends that Weber's analysis could shed light on the harmful role of the Japanese bureaucracy. He read the Bible, not because he was a particularly religious man, but because he wanted to understand world history. To make the task more challenging he studied ancient Greek so that he could read the New Testament in the original. His favorite verse, he decided, was in St. John: "*Except a corn of wheat fall into the ground and die it abideth alone, but if it die it bringeth forth much fruit.*" Onogi liked to quote that verse to his friends; perhaps, he suggested, the "death" of *his* bank would eventually help to revitalize Japan's economy and pave the way for a healthier banking system in the future.

Yet, as the months passed, Onogi also started to feel angry. In the chaotic days immediately after LTCB's collapse, Onogi was so exhausted that he had given a broad-ranging "confession" to the police, desperately hoping that would help to protect his junior staff. He guessed that was what a samurai was supposed to do. "If I had maintained my innocence it would probably have meant that I alone could escape responsibility . . . but I thought I should assume all of the responsibility [for the problems] and this is the way one should live," Onogi later explained to the court.

Later, he changed his plea to "not guilty." Onogi argued that he was willing to take responsibility for LTCB's bad business decisions; but he did not believe he had done anything *criminal*. After all, he reasoned, plenty of other banks had taken similar measures to move bad loans into their subsidiaries, with the full knowledge of the Ministry of Finance.

The trial of Onogi, Suzuki, and Suda finally opened in November, in a drab room on the fourth floor of the Tokyo district court. It was the same location where Takahashi of EIE had been on trial and where the Credit Suisse bankers would shortly reappear. Suzuki responded to the trial as he had dealt with most things in his life—with pragmatism, stoicism, and a minimum of public words. Onogi threw himself into the case with the same intellectual energy he used to translate ancient Greek. He spent hours reading the legal charges and picking holes in the logic of the prosecution arguments. At court hearings, he turned up clutching documents studded with Post-it notes, to mark the relevant passages. When he was allowed to give a speech to the court, he diligently prepared his case. This was not, he earnestly told his friends, just a matter of self-preservation—there was also a broader issue of history at stake. "I did what I did [with the bad loans] because I thought it was best for the country and because if I did otherwise I thought I could create an economic crisis," Onogi explained to the court. "I wanted to avoid economic havoc. . . . I thought the economy was going to improve. I behaved the way that I thought I was supposed to behave. I don't see how I could have done anything else."

The prosecution didn't see it that way. Nor did most journalists or ordinary Japanese. By 1999 the Japanese public was fed up with the banking problems, utterly confused about why they emerged—and eager to find someone to blame. This reaction had less to do with logic than emotion: In earlier decades, the country had revered its bankers, just as they had admired the postwar economic miracle; now, however, ordinary Japanese felt bitterly betrayed, as if a child had discovered that a revered parent had let them down. The bankers had turned into an object of hate, or ridicule, a lightning rod for an entire generation's sense of disillusionment. "The phrase 'the way one should live' used by Onogi had a grave meaning. But he changed his attitude so easily, I marvel how a person like him could head up a company," Saburo Shiroyama, a popular writer declared. "Men such as Onogi became bank presidents when their institutions had a negative legacy. . . . They took the top posts because they thought they could solve the problems. If they were not willing to assume these responsibilities, they should not have agreed to become president." Or as a revered economic professor muttered: "Sometimes I feel so angry with the bankers I would like to explode! How could these stupid men have done this to our country! How could they be so *weak?*"

Some junior LTCB bankers felt furiously angry with the senior bankers as well. A few of them blamed the bank's collapse on Onogi's bold decision to forge the alliance with SBC; others bitterly complained that Onogi had not been radical *enough*, since he had never clamped down on the bad loans, preferring to delegate it to men like Suzuki. "The top bankers were just cowards! They disgust me!" one mid-level manager bitterly complained. Either way, the sense of shame—and bitter disillusionment—inside LTCB headquarters ran high. The day after LTCB had failed, every single man and woman had turned up to work on time. Many even came in early. Over in America, employees might treat the collapse of a company to be a chance to take a holiday, steal the stationery, or look for a new job; in Japan, however, the staff of a bank could not disassociate themselves from the company in this way. If the bank had failed, they had *all* failed, irrespective of whether the problems were blamed on the senior managers; and the only way to atone for the sense of guilt was to work even harder than before. So the employees sat diligently at their desks in the ensuing weeks, doing what they had always done: answering phones, shuffling bits of paper, keeping the bank running.

As time passed, some of the younger LTCB bankers started to leave. Foreign banks and brokers were keen to boost their staff numbers in Tokyo and the LTCB men were considered attractive hires since many had foreign MBAs. Headhunters buzzed around, offering salaries that seemed bewilderingly large by LTCB standards. Within six months, LTCB alumni could be found at almost every foreign investment bank and consulting group in Tokyo. The older and more domestically orientated staff, however, had no such refuge: Although a few left to work at LTCB's corporate clients, four-fifths of the bank staff stayed on. Indeed, most of the LTCB bankers insisted that they did not want to leave. They had labored together for so many years, as an emotionally entwined "family," that it was difficult to imagine a future apart; they wanted to stick *together* to face whatever came next.

And what would come next? As Onogi sat at home preparing for his trial, he often mulled that question with friends. He liked to hope that somehow LTCB would now pave the way for a new wave of banking reform; Onogi was keen to find some *meaning* in what had happened, a point to the fate that had engulfed his bank. But would anyone really be willing to buy a bank like LTCB, he wondered; was it possible to revive a dead bank? "Except a corn of wheat fall into the ground and die it abideth alone, but if it die it bringeth forth much fruit," Onogi would mumble to himself, from time to time when he felt depressed.

The idea of such sacrifice seemed a comforting one; it fitted with his samurai ideals. And somehow, in the depths of defeat, it also offered Onogi a ray of hope.

PART
TWO

— *Chapter 10* —

AN AMERICAN DREAM

I like to think that free enterprise is what has made this country great. Shinsei and Ripplewood are part of that process.

—David Rockefeller

A few months after Long Term Credit Bank was nationalized, the staff heard a strange rumor: A group of Americans connected to a company called "Ripplewood" had been asking questions about their collapsed bank, apparently with a view to buying it.

"*Ripplewood?*" asked Takeshi Anzai, the Bank of Japan bureaucrat appointed to run LTCB during nationalization. "What is this Ripplewood thing? Is it a town? A person?" The name seemed bizarre, an unwieldy mouthful to pronounce. When Japanese spoke the word, it tended to come out as *Liipuluwuddo*.

Baffled, some of the LTCB staff searched for clues. The only references on the internet to Ripplewood related to a group of American health clubs and holiday resorts. Eventually they discovered some press clippings that suggested that a private equity firm called Ripplewood had recently been buying American auto-part dealers and a muffin maker. In the weeks after the bank's collapse, the LTCB bankers had speculated for hours about their impending fate. Back in October the government had declared that it wanted to nationalize the bank for a short period and sell it to new owners. The LTCB staff hoped this would imply a deal with another Japanese company, perhaps similar to the failed Sumitomo Trust merger.

But the government could be considering something more radical, the once unimaginable step of selling the bank to a foreign bank or a vulture fund. Most of the bank staff had little idea of what a private equity fund was, but they had a vague hunch that a fund often fired workers. The prospect of being invaded by an American vulture sounded terrifying.

"Don't worry!" Anzai told his colleagues. "This Ripplewood thing does not sound so serious." Yet the LTCB remained deeply curious; why, they wondered, was LTCB suddenly attracting so much attention on the other side of the vast Pacific?

It was a question that had been triggering gossip inside the bank for many months. Indeed, speculation about what the Americans might—or might not—be plotting in respect to LTCB dated back to the spring of 1998, when Koichi Kato, the powerful secretary general of the LDP, paid a visit to New York. During that trip, Kato had mentioned to senior American officials, such as William McDonaugh, head of the New York Federal Reserve System, that he was seriously concerned about banks such as LTCB and warned that the Japanese government might soon need to find a "solution" to the problem. Kato subsequently denied that he intended any malice in these remarks. Yet, the meetings put the issue of LTCB on the radar screen of the American establishment, and when news of the conversation subsequently trickled out to the LTCB bankers they were furious. Japan was a country that loved conspiracy theories; and as the weeks passed some bankers and bureaucrats started to wonder whether the Americans and Japanese were secretly plotting some deal over LTCB.

The speculation grew even more intense a few months later. In early June 1998 Lawrence Summers, the U.S. deputy treasury secretary, came to Tokyo for an emergency G7 meeting. Summers did not have any particular interest in LTCB. But what he *was* concerned about was the state of Japan's economy—and its banks. In the spring of 1998 the yen had tumbled against the dollar. This was a cause for great alarm because it had put pressure on the other Asian economies, which were already reeling from a series of currency crises that had swept through Thailand, Malaysia, Indonesia, and Korea during the previous year. The Japanese and other Asians were afraid China would devalue its own currency and pull the bottom out of an already weak region and were begging the Americans for help. Meanwhile, the Japanese economy was stalled. During 1996 there had been signs of a recovery, but by the summer of 1998, this growth had spluttered out, because the government had tightened fiscal policy and the "November shock" in the banks all but wiped out consumer and corporate confidence.

Summers believed that it was extremely important for the region that Japan should return to growth. And to him this required Tokyo to loosen fiscal policy and soothe the financial jitters. Above all, Japan needed a comprehensive banking package, something that removed the bad loan problem for good.

Some economists believed that best way to do this was for Japan to adopt a version of the free-market solutions that America had used when a group of Texas-based Savings and Loan institutions had become engulfed by bad loans in the 1980s. Back then, the U.S. government had dealt with the problem—albeit after several years of procrastination—by letting weak S&Ls fail and vigorously prosecuting bank managers who had broken laws. These S&Ls were then either sold to new owners, or broken up and the assets sold to new bidders in a free auction. The idea behind this whole system was that financial institutions should only be allowed to survive if they were healthy enough to win the confidence of investors; if not, they had to die.

However, Summers was wary of recommending such bitter medicine. He did not want to see a full-scale financial crisis erupt in Tokyo and possibly hurt global markets. Nor did he necessarily believe that the radical free-market solutions would work in Japan. "The S&L crisis was one mess in the middle of a fundamentally healthy American banking system—a small amount of stuff in a big lake, so it could be tackled without hurting the entire system," Summers later explained. "However, the Japanese financial system had problems all the way through—the entire lake was the problem! So I got concerned that if you tried to treat it like the S&Ls you would have a total crisis of confidence, that could make the problem worse."

Yet Summers believed that the Japanese had to do *something*, and the S&L approach was not the only solution. Scandinavian countries had also experienced large, systemic banking crises in the 1990s—and solved this partly with government intervention. In those cases, the state used taxpayers' money to nationalize some banks and then created state institutions to sell the bad loans off. Perhaps that could be a model for Japan. "In many ways, Japan's banking problems seemed much more similar to Scandinavia," Summers said. However, in his mind, the precise details of any cleanup were almost secondary: What the Americans wanted to see from Japan above all else was *action*—almost any action. After a decade of procrastination, Washington believed that it was high time for the Japanese to finally face the facts.

So, the American government cut an implicit bargain with the Japanese: In the days before the G7 meeting, the Americans intervened in the currency markets to stop the yen tumbling, on the understanding that the Japanese would take action to fix the banking system and loosen fiscal policy. The intervention was a success; Summers's mission at the G7 meeting was to ensure that the Japanese now stuck to their side of the deal. "It was a type of quid pro quo," Summers later said. "We orchestrated a lot of theater. First we had the entire G7 come and express their concern. That was kind of weird; it felt like an occupying army coming in to yell at the locals. Then we had the Manila group [of Asian countries] come and tell the Japanese to get their act together as well. I think that was even more weird for the Japanese." Last of all, the Summers team produced a snappy slogan to get the message across to the Japanese politicians.

"What Japan has now is a 'Window of Opportunity'!" Summers declared in the press conference. "What is going to be very important going forward is the steps that Japan takes to take advantage of this Window of Opportunity. It's a 'window.' A real *Window of Opportunity!*"

Like a truculent child, however, the Japanese government obstinately refused to produce what the Americans wanted. Many of the Japanese bureaucrats heartily disliked Summers—and his slogans. "A meeting with Summers was like being lectured," muttered one senior bureaucrat. The only Japanese official who seemed to truly enjoy meeting Summers was Eisuke Sakakibara, the vice finance minister, who had known him for many years. Sakakibara sometimes airily referred to the U.S. minister as

"Larry," to show his Japanese friends how internationally sophisticated he was. Treasury officials, for their part, called the Japanese man "Sak."

Yet even Sakakibara was in no position to deliver what Summers wanted—namely, a banking package—given the political gridlock that had paralyzed the Japanese parliament. Consequently, by the next round of G7 meetings in the autumn, the level of American frustration had risen to fever pitch. The yen was weakening again, the Japanese economy tipping deeper into recession, and the stock market falling. Meanwhile, a full four months after Summers had pleaded for action on the banks, nothing had happened; LTCB was *still* twisting in the wind, neither alive nor dead, creating a festering derivatives risk. In the eyes of central bankers around the world, it almost defied comprehension that the Japanese government should be leaving LTCB to stew when global financial markets were already on tenterhooks: In addition to the Asian financial crisis, Russia had defaulted on its debt in the summer of 1998 and over in New York, the Federal Reserve was fighting a separate bout of market rumors that Long Term Capital Management, a U.S. hedge fund, was on the verge of collapse.

"It is very important that the Japanese government should do *something* to help support market confidence," the American officials urged aides to Kiichi Miyazawa, the finance minister. "Japan needs to show the markets that it is promoting reform." Wearily, Miyazawa tried to explain the strange political deadlock to the Americans. Equally wearily, the Americans tried to propose some potential solutions. In private, many senior American officials were sympathetic to the Democratic Party of Japan, and other opposition groups, for radical free-market reforms. However, they had few hopes that the DPJ's proposals for a radical "hard landing" solution would ever see the light of day. And the Clinton administration did not want to push the Japanese economy into a tailspin at a time when the rest of the global economy was so weak. Nor did Clinton's government want to abandon its "friends" in the LDP by backing the DPJ too forcefully. So, in an effort to break the deadlock, they turned to the issue of LTCB—and instead of demanding its closure, as free-market economists wanted, batted around other ideas. Carefully, the Americans pointed out that if LTCB was nationalized and sold, that would serve as a wonderful sign to the outside world that Japan was embracing reform and becoming more international. "The point we were trying to make was that it would be helpful for them to show seriousness by actually closing an institution or nationalizing it—some kind of act of closure was important," Summers later explained. "What we wanted to see was something concrete."

Summers vehemently denied that this advice represented a direct *demand* that LTCB be nationalized, let alone sold to an American group. Summers had worked as an economics professor before becoming deputy treasury secretary and he was used to batting ideas around in a forceful manner. And the idea of nationalizing LTCB had been first raised by the Japanese *themselves*. Yet, the prism of history through which the Japanese viewed their relationship with America was a peculiar one. Ever since World War II, the American government had felt free to lecture loudly to the Japanese on what economic policies it should pursue, with the self-confidence that comes naturally to a nation built on the concept of "manifest destiny." The Japanese, for their part, usually listened dutifully, keen to avoid public confrontation. When Tokyo disliked the American demands, they simply ignored them; however, when the hectoring served the interests of some factions in Japan, they actually encouraged it. In Japanese culture, change was often considered more acceptable when it was presented as a function of unavoidable, external pressure; thus at times, the American rhetoric could be a useful "excuse" for potentially controversial change, since it was always easy to blame the Americans if anything went wrong.

This had fostered a strange love-hate relationship. The Japanese both loathed *gaiatsu* ("foreign pressure")—and welcomed it. They admired American consumer culture and disdained it. Most importantly, alongside a secret sense of cultural superiority over the Americans, the Japanese often felt desperately insecure on the world stage. They remembered only too painfully their defeat to America in World War II. History had also taught them that Americans could be ruthlessly canny in business: As every Japanese child learned in their history books at school, almost as soon as the first Americans arrived in Japanese waters in 1853, American traders had spotted that Japan had a different exchange rate in gold and silver from the rest of the world—and rushed to exploit this arbitrage, to Japan's cost. What the Wall Street bankers had done in the 1980s and 1990s seemed uncannily similar. It did not take much to convince a Japanese audience that behind every piece of American government rhetoric lay a clever commercial plot.

This pattern soon played out with LTCB as well. Inside the Japanese establishment, some reformers liked the idea of selling LTCB to an outsider, since they hoped that the "shock" of this would promote reform. However, by the time Miyazawa returned to Tokyo after the G7 meeting, senior bureaucrats were dropping hints that they were planning to take the path-breaking step of nationalizing LTCB to appease the *Americans;* if anybody disliked the idea, it was Washington—not Miyazawa—who should be blamed. As these rumors gathered pace, another, darker conspiracy theory started to circulate around the gossip mills: Washington was now scheming to establish a new financial beachhead in Japan, the rumors went; Americans were going to buy the bank.

If Japanese bankers had known anything about the background to the mysterious company Ripplewood that had started expressing an interest in LTCB, they might have been doubly suspicious. Ripplewood was the brainchild of Timothy C. Collins, an entrepreneur whose career not only epitomized the risk-taking, pioneering culture of American capitalism, but also the complex ties that linked money and politics together in Washington and Wall Street.

Forty-three years earlier Collins had been born into the small town of Frankfort, Kentucky. Some of his ancestors had been very wealthy, running vast tobacco plantations, but Collins's father worked as an engineer at a local auto factory and at the age of seventeen, after being expelled from school for teenage pranks, Collins ground crankshafts next to other hard-bitten, blue-collar workers and joined the United Autoworkers Union. "My father's idea was that I should find out what the real world was all about," Collins recalled, "and go and get a real job and find how hard it was for regular people to make a living. In the initial period I was treated pretty harshly and hazed and harassed. But that was a big part of my education, probably one of the most educational experiences in my life."

Collins eventually got himself back onto a white-collar track, and studied religion and philosophy at DePauw, a small midwestern university, and later won a place at Yale Business School, where he studied finance.

After a spell in Chicago working as a management consultant, he went to Wall Street as an investment banker at Lazard Frères.

Ambitious to make a mark on the world, Collins had, in a few short years, become a wealthy New York success story. Along the way he lost any trace of a southern accent. He also collected a dazzling collection of high-profile friends. These ranged from Vernon Jordan, the black political power broker, Richard Rainwater, a Texas financier close to President Bush senior, a host of Wall Street financiers, and Bill Clinton, then the governor of Arkansas and later the U.S. president as well. "I have always had a bunch of guys who were older than me who were big supporters," Collins explained. "I know a lot of people because I have been in a diverse range of things and have a lot of interests in politics and business."

In the late 1980s, Collins gave up the investment banking game to work out what he wanted to do with the rest of his life. He was a Baptist and sometimes wondered whether chasing money on Wall Street really fitted in with his Christian faith. For six weeks he worked in a Sudanese refugee camp and toyed with the idea of doing charity work full-time or even entering the church. "I don't go to church every week but I think my family's religion and my belief are an important part of my view of the world," he later explained.

His friend and fellow Christian, the financier Richard Rainwater, persuaded him otherwise. "God didn't make you a poet or an opera singer or a six-foot-eleven center," Rainwater told him. "But you are pretty good at doing this [business.]" So Collins decided instead to donate a large proportion of his earnings to charity and reemerged on Wall Street—this time to run the New York office of Onex, a Canadian private equity fund. "Rainwater said to me that trying to act as a catalyst for change, by moving capital around the economy, *was* a valuable role in the world. He also said that since business was what I was good at, I would do more good following *those* skills than trying to squeeze into something else."

After learning the tricks of the restructuring trade, Collins broke with Onex and in 1995 he created his own investment company called Ripplewood, named after his family's ancestral tobacco farm back in Kentucky. "We chose the name because no one else had used it. I think my father was pleased. In fact it was probably the one thing of my career that he was truly pleased with."

Within the specialist universe of private equity, Collins liked to present Ripplewood as one of the more "friendly" groups. He hated the word "vulture." His goal, he insisted, was to buy companies in distress that had a core value and then find ways of growing their operations into a new business that he could sell for a profit. "Here at Ripplewood, we want to revive companies and create jobs," he liked to explain. "This is about a process of *creation*, not destruction." The trait that Collins did share with the original "vulture funds" was that he was highly opportunistic. In Collins's eyes, American private equity thus worked a type of alchemy: The process could make entrepreneurs like him very rich; but it could also promote corporate restructuring, which in turn helped to create a more productive, efficient economy. "I really started out with something to prove. I wanted to show that there was a better way to do the private equity business and I was very passionate about trying to create a strategy with an alignment of value, that could allocate capital in a way that could create positive change," Collins later explained. "For me, our returns are the yardstick for how well we have done at creating value . . . but I also want to make the world a better place. This is not just about money for me; what I care about is the record."

Ripplewood started small. Collins raised his first round of finance, worth around $65 million, from friends, before he eventually launched a more formal $450 million fund, backed by dozens of institutional investors, including Travelers insurance, the State of Florida, the State of California, and the Royal Dutch Shell Pensick Fund. He used this money to gobble up numerous diverse companies: a muffin maker in Ohio, a fridge manufacturer in Illinois; a frozen pie company in Arkansas; a collection of auto dealers; and a company that produced the "softening" chemicals used to make bendable toothbrushes or tampons.

Then, Collins raised his game. By the middle of the 1990s, so many new American private equity groups were emerging that it was becoming more competitive to do business. Although Ripplewood was still growing rapidly, it was a minnow compared to the largest private equity names on Wall Street and it needed to find a specific niche if it wanted to compete effectively. So Collins started looking for other, less crowded territories—and became curious about Japan. There was nothing in his background that drew him to Tokyo. Yet he had a hunch that Japan offered the best returns yet. On paper, Japan's problems in the 1990s of unproductive companies, excess debt, and flabby industries looked temptingly similar to America in the 1970s. Collins knew that the patterns of developments in the two economies were unlikely to be exactly the same, but he believed the pattern was sufficiently familiar to take the lessons he had learned in Ohio and Arkansas to Japan. "My approach is a type of Occam's razor of the investing world," he sometimes liked to explain. "There are many parallels, in terms of the process of refocusing and reallocating assets, between Japan and what went on in the United States in the past twenty-five years."

Better still, Collins had a contact who he believed could help him in Tokyo—Minoru Makihara, chairman of the mighty Mitsubishi Corporation, one of the most elite and powerful companies in Japan. During the course of the usual marketing process to raise money for Ripplewood, Collins had approached Mitsubishi Corporation, Japan's mighty trading company. By a lucky chance, Makihara, who was then president at Mitsubishi, had already decided that the Japanese company should learn a bit more about the American private equity business by taking a stake in a private equity group. Although the concept was still almost completely unknown in Japan, Makihara had a hunch that it might be imported from America into Japan one day—and if private equity *did* ever flourish, he wanted to ensure that his company had the necessary skills. So, Makihara was only too happy to take a stake in Ripplewood and a seat on the board. Meanwhile, Collins was delighted to team up with Mitsubishi. Quite apart from the finance, Collins hoped that the connection would one day help him to break into the mysterious market of Japan.

A couple of years after Ripplewood had started Collins began to chase after his Japanese interest with a vengeance. So he approached Makihara and asked if the Japanese company wanted to create a second restructuring fund to explore opportunities in Japan.

Makihara was extremely wary. Inside the world of Japan's corporate elite, Makihara occupied an odd hybrid role. Although Makihara was a blue-blooded Japanese and held one of the most prestigious corporate jobs in Japan, he had been partly educated in America on a U.S. scholarship, studying first at St. Paul's Academy and then at Harvard University. This had left him with a flawless command of English and a network of friends on Wall Street, many of whom Tim Collins knew. With a background like this, Makihara liked to think that he was able to play a type of bridging role, bringing the diverse worlds of Tokyo and Wall Street together. He was also keenly aware that America remained an utterly different universe from Japan, and although Japanese companies could experiment with innovative ideas overseas, it was much harder to do that at home. When Makihara had first embarked on his alliance with Ripplewood, he had done so presuming that it would be limited to New York, safely away from the eyes of Japan's establishment.

"Japan will be very difficult!" Makihara told Collins. "Although we talk about Big Bang it is still a very difficult market to get into. So I would suggest that if you want to go to Asia you should go to Thailand!" Makihara doubted whether Japan was ready to cope with radical restructuring practices.

Collins, however, was not the type of man who could be easily deflected. One of his favorite proverbs in life was the quote from Winston Churchill: *"Never, never, never give up!"* As far as he could see, Japan was virgin territory for vulture funds. Thailand seemed boring by comparison. Over and over again, Collins told Makihara that it made perfect sense to create a Japanese fund. After all, if Mitsubishi's corporate contacts could ever be combined with Ripplewood's financial skills, it could be a winning combination. Eventually, Makihara relented. In the summer of 1998 Mitsubishi and Ripplewood decided to jointly create a tiny Japan restructuring fund, called Ripplewood Holdings Japan, or RHJ. "Tim is a very determined person!" Makihara later laughed. "He can mobilize and attract many people. He is also quite an idealist."

With Makihara on board, Collins turned his mind to working out what he could—or should—buy in Japan. His first instinct told him that he should chase after some industrial companies. After all, manufacturing had been Japan's postwar strength and that was where Ripplewood's previous experience lay. So, in late 1997, as a first foray into the manufacturing sector in Japan, Collins asked McKinsey, the American consultants, to draw up a report on the Japanese economy. The aim was to identify which business sectors would provide the easiest acquisition targets and it yielded a striking conclusion. The real problem in Japan, McKinsey argued, lay not just with the excess borrowing in the corporate sector but in the other side of the coin—overlending by the banks. Almost everything in the economy, including the behavior of small industrial groups, was linked to the activities of these financial groups. The banks were like nails holding the entire rotten corporate structure together. As long as these financial "nails" remained in place, pinning the system together, it would be difficult to implement radical change in the corporate world.

"Why don't we cut to the core, and buy a bank?" Collins idly wondered. On paper it seemed a ridiculously daring concept. One of the first principles of the private equity business was that it was dangerous to move too fast out of familiar territory. Ripplewood had absolutely no experience in Japan. Nor did it have any track record of dealing with banks. Its areas of expertise were auto parts, refrigerators, frozen pies, and bendable toothbrushes. Yet, in American private equity, men made their successes—and money—by thinking the unthinkable. And Collins knew that change was afoot in Japan's banking world: He had lots of contacts with the Clinton government, and he had heard about the American and Japanese discussions over LTCB.

Collins's curiosity might have stopped there, were it not for the fact that he crossed paths with two other men. One of these was Masamoto Yashiro, the elderly former chairman of Citigroup Japan, who had spent the early part of his career working in Exxon. Collins bumped into him one day in September 1998, while he was sitting on a plane headed from New York to Tokyo. Yashiro, sixty-nine, had just attended a board meeting of Arthur D. Little in Boston, since he was a director of that consulting group. Collins had just started his Japan private equity fund and he had already heard about Yashiro from his Wall Street friends. Collins asked Yashiro to dinner and then popped the question: Would he become chairman of Ripplewood's Japan fund? The Japanese man was initially none too keen. He had retired from Citibank a year earlier and was living in London at the time, since that was where his grandchildren were based. He was distinctly uncertain about whether the unknown Mr. Collins had any chance of breaking into Japan. "After we had dinner I wrote [Tim] a letter," Yashiro later explained. "It was quite a polite letter, I think. I said that really I am not interested, but 'thank you for thinking of me and I wish you the best in your venture.' "

Collins was undeterred. He asked to meet Yashiro again. Collins had done his homework on the elderly Japanese man and knew that Yashiro had reformist, free-market instincts. He also knew that Yashiro was renowned for being a patriot with a strong sense of duty. So, Collins cannily presented his plans as a mission: If Ripplewood took its private equity ideas to Japan and promoted corporate restructuring, this could help to revive the country for a second time this century.

Yashiro was hooked. At the age of sixty-nine he agreed to become chairman of the new joint venture fund between Mitsubishi and Ripplewood, envisaging that this would be a part-time role. "Tim Collins did not give up. He was persistent," Yashiro later chuckled. "He is a very determined man."

The second crucial man who crossed Collins's path was J. Christopher Flowers. Flowers, forty-two, was another Wall Street veteran who had spent many years working as a senior deal maker at Goldman Sachs. His character was a sharp contrast to Collins's.

Collins was a gregarious figure, who liked to pontificate about the bigger issues in life, and always denied that his goal was just to get rich. But Flowers was thin and intense. He wore thick tortoiseshell glasses, dull shirts, and carried a battered briefcase and in meetings he always stuck to his agenda. In private, he could often be charming, but in public he had a deadpan delivery and never dressed his comments up with flattery or philosophy. In his eyes, there was only one point of business, namely, making as much money as possible.

Flowers spent his childhood in Boston and later studied at Harvard University before joining Goldman Sachs in 1979. It was a natural home for Flowers's understated but ruthlessly focused style; he zoomed up the corporate ladder, becoming an expert on mergers and acquisitions and the youngest ever banker to win the precious prize of a Goldman Sachs partnership. Flowers enjoyed near-legendary status among Wall Street insiders for his skills at orchestrating deals. By the early 1990s, he was running the powerful Financial Institutions Group—dubbed FIG—which specialized in arranging banking mergers and acquisitions, where he clinched some of the most striking mergers in American corporate history, such as the merger of Bank of America and Nations Bank. It was an intense, high-octane life of billion-dollar finance and twenty-four-hour working days. Indeed, it was so intense that Flowers like to joke that he relished taking long-haul flights, since it was one of the few places in his life where nobody could call him on a mobile phone—and he could relax.

In the summer of 1998, an unprecedented internal power struggle erupted at Goldman and Jon Corzine was later ousted. Flowers had been a protégé of Corzine's and the upheaval hurt his own prospects for promotion. Corzine later made his peace with life by becoming elected as a senator but Flowers had little interest in politics and never considered following Corzine into public service (though he agreed to manage his friend's money while he was in politics). Nor could he see sufficiently enticing jobs at other banks. Instead, he decided to branch out on his own, using his skill at acquiring and restructuring banks. So he created a private equity fund to do this, called—with his usual directness—J. C. Flowers and Co.

By the autumn of 1998, Flowers was scouring the world for banks that he might buy and became interested in LTCB. He had never spent much time in Tokyo and knew very little about the history of the bank. But as far as he was concerned that did not matter. He believed that the world's banks were driven by a set of rules as universal as the Newtonian laws of physics. The point of a bank was to make money—by seeking the highest returns possible on the pool of available capital, wherever, whenever, and however it could. *Rational* was one of his favorite words: In the last resort, Flowers believed that there was a single rational set of economic laws that drove the universe, including LTCB and other Japanese banks.

In the small, gossipy world that is Wall Street, Flowers heard about Collins's interest in Japan. The two men met each other and realized that it might make sense for them to collaborate. In no sense were they close friends. But Flowers had what Collins lacked, namely, a brilliant track record at arranging banking deals. "Chris has arguably got the greatest expertise in the world at doing financial service transactions," Collins later remarked. And Collins had the political skills and delicate charm that were missing from Flowers's life. "Tim's ability to understand how politics work is something he has really brought into this [partnership]," Flowers later remarked. "In style we are different—I could not deny that. But we have the same ideas about where business should go and we make a good team."

In the late autumn of 1998, or soon after the Japanese government nationalized LTCB, Collins offered Flowers space to work in the headquarters of the Ripplewood group. It was a plush office, located on the thirty-second floor of one of the Rockefeller skyscrapers, with excellent views of midtown Manhattan. Collins was careful to explain to anyone who asked that there was no question of Flowers actually *working* for Ripplewood; Flowers controlled an entirely separate, private equity company. "I am just helping Chris out!" Collins declared. But with the two men sitting a few yards away from each other—and Yashiro in the frame as well—their discussions about LTCB heated up. Warily, Collins and Flowers each concluded that somehow they needed to get some serious political clout on their side; if they were going to enter Japan they needed some prestigious American names. One day in late autumn, Flowers walked across the Rockefeller plaza to a neighboring skyscraper about fifty yards away to visit a friend. In those offices he bumped into Paul Volcker, seventy-one, the legendary former head of the mighty Federal Reserve System who served from 1979 to 1986, earning a place in history for his success in taming American inflation. Flowers knew Volcker slightly and he popped by his office.

"So what do you think about the idea of Americans buying a Japanese bank?" Flowers asked. He sketched out in the vaguest terms the reasons why he was interested in LTCB.

Volcker was intrigued. He had already heard through his network of powerful Washington and Wall Street friends what was happening at LTCB, and he had an unusually deep and sensitive knowledge about Japan. His contacts with the country stretched back to the 1960s and 1970s, when he had worked in the U.S. Treasury. Back then, he had frequently flown to Tokyo to hammer out deals with the Ministry of Finance and during those trips, Volcker had become acquainted with many young

Japanese policy makers, such as Kiichi Miyazawa, the man acting as finance minister in 1998.

Still, Volcker freely admitted that he found Japan mysterious at times. Back in the 1980s—or when he was U.S. central bank governor—Volcker had been dazzled by the strength of Japan's economy. Indeed, in 1992 he even coauthored a book called *Changing Fortunes,* which discussed postwar America's decline and Japan's renaissance. But by 1998 Volcker had become deeply uneasy about the state of Tokyo's financial world. During his spell at the Federal Reserve System, Volcker had seen many other countries around the world face banking crises. None of them had ever been as large as Japan's, or dragged on for so long. In quiet moments, Volcker had often racked his brains to work out how the whole saga might end.

Flowers explained the background to LTCB. Was it possible, Flowers asked, that Japan would consider a foreign bid for the bank? Volcker warily pointed out that nothing quite like that had ever been done before in Japan. However, he added that there were signs that Japan was changing—not least because some of his old friends in the Japanese government were talking a great deal about reform. Encouraged, Flowers returned several more times to Volcker's office, swapping gossip and ideas. He could tell that the former American central banker was fascinated. Eventually Flowers popped the question. "If we are going to sit here talking about LTCB, why don't you become an adviser to us?"

Volcker agreed. He was not interested in getting involved in LTCB for the reasons that obsessed Flowers—making lots of money. Although Volcker was not terribly rich—or at least not by the extreme standards of Wall Street—he considered that he had more than enough wealth to be comfortable. What Volcker *did* like, however, was the idea of a new challenge. He had a distinctly idealistic streak and strong notions of public service. Since leaving the Federal Reserve System, Volcker had dipped into some consulting and philanthropic work, including a campaign to help Jewish Holocaust victims to reclaim assets from Swiss banks, and a subsequent attempt to overhaul the operations and reputation of the accountancy firm Arthur Andersen, when it became linked to the Enron scandal. "I am a romantic by nature," he sometimes confessed. The sale of a Japanese bank to American investors could potentially have some fascinating policy implications. It would represent a whole new type of bridge between Wall Street and Tokyo. It might even act as a catalyst to end the sense of paralysis in Japan's financial world and remove the danger that the entire banking system might implode. *That* could be a thoroughly good thing, he reasoned, not only for Japan but also for the broader cause of global financial stability. "Why did I get involved? It certainly seemed that the Japanese banking system needed to change and this was a chance to push it in the right direction, perhaps," Volcker later explained. "I mean you could either sit there and dream about Japan changing, or if this bank was successful it might help push Japan in the right direction. I thought it had very interesting public policy implications. It was an intriguing challenge, an entry into the cultural issues in Japan and it had direct political implications, too. I suppose some people might call it a mission, but I personally don't use that word."

Volcker had no illusions that this lofty vision was what was driving a man such as Flowers. Still he did not see anything wrong with using individual financial incentives to drive a bigger policy agenda: If investors could find a way to get rich by reviving LTCB as a viable bank, in other words, that could benefit Japan as a whole. Although he was not a greedy man himself, Volcker assumed—like most Washington policy makers—that it was sometimes possible to harness individual greed to achieve a greater public good; to align private business interests with policy goals; and use free-market competition to promote a better society. It was a concept that underpinned the way that American capitalism worked. Indeed, most Americans considered it so natural to blend the profit motive with public policy they never questioned it at all; nor did they notice that the Japanese worldview tended to be subtly—but crucially—different.

— *Chapter 11* —

"COWBOY"

Tim Collins is living proof of the truth of that old saying—if you want something bad enough, you can make it happen.

—Vernon Jordan

In late February 1999, Paul Volcker flew to Tokyo to test the political mood in Japan. He started by holding a few informal chats with his old friends, such as Kiichi Miyazawa, the powerful finance minister. Volcker had known Miyazawa for many years, and the elderly Japanese statesman was always more than willing to talk to the former American central banker. "Volcker always wanted to be an American ninja—he kept coming to Japan so much," Miyazawa would sometimes say with an affectionate chuckle. "But he couldn't because he was just too tall!"

The message that Volcker got from these meetings seemed to be unexpectedly reassuring. Over and over again, the Japanese policy makers said this time, in the aftermath of the LTCB collapse, they *were* finally willing to press ahead with financial reform. Encouraged, Volcker then asked for a meeting with Takashi Anzai, the man running LTCB. It was one thing for the Japanese to talk about reform in a vague sense, but Volcker needed to find out if the Japanese were willing to take the extraordinary step of selling a major bank to group of Americans.

On February 23 Volcker duly made his way to the headquarters of

LTCB. It was his first visit to the tower and—like most first-time visitors—he was startled. Even in the days when LTCB was booming, its lavish headquarters had seemed a little excessive; now that the bank had collapsed the white marble and lofty glass atrium looked to Volcker like a giant monument to financial folly.

Anzai, for his part, was also taken aback when he clapped eyes on his visitor. The lanky American had a legendary reputation in Japan for the huge power that he had once wielded over global financial markets. Moreover, physically Volcker was striking; at six feet five inches, he towered like a giant over the Japanese around him. "Volcker is *huge,* like a mountain!" Anzai reflected when he saw him. "I don't think I even come up to his belly button!"

Volcker was shown to a meeting room on the nineteenth floor of the LTCB tower and for a while the two men chatted pleasantly. Anzai tried to crack a joke about their heights, but it fell flat. Although Anzai spoke reasonably good English, he found it hard to explain some of his thoughts or understand everything that Volcker was saying, partly because the American had a habit of mumbling into his shoulder. Then Volcker cut to the chase. "Are you serious about trying to sell LTCB? And resolve the issues [of financial reform]?"

It was a tricky question. When the Japanese government had announced that it wanted to nationalize and sell LTCB back in the autumn of 1998, the concept had seemed like a quick-fix compromise to solve a difficult political impasse. The beauty of the nationalization idea was that it broke the bigger deadlock between the political conservatives and reformers about banking policy—and, as an added bonus, it seemed to silence American complaints that Japan was doing nothing about bank reform. But now that the government was faced with the task of turning reform rhetoric into reality, the idea looked more daunting. *Personally,* Anzai thought that it would be a wonderful idea to sell LTCB to new owners, even foreigners. Like many reformers he reasoned that if a group of Americans took over that might prod the rest of the system into action—and help to import foreign technology and ideas into Japan. By the standards of senior bureaucrats, Anzai was unusually reformist in his thinking. He attributed that to the fact that during his career at the Bank of Japan he had worked in

Hong Kong for a period, where he had seen free markets in action and liked what he saw. Another influence on Anzai was that he hailed from rural, earthy stock in the far-flung Japanese district of Fukushima, rather than the elite, polite world of Tokyo. Even though Anzai had spent decades at the Bank, he still spoke with a coarse Fukushima accent, and had a direct, common-sense approach to dealing with problems, with little patience for the constipated niceties of "polite" Japanese etiquette.

Yet Anzai also knew that the straightforward approach was unusual in Japan. Many parts of the conservative Japanese political world were horrified by the idea of foreign bankers arriving in Japan. So were many Japanese bankers themselves. And since the idea of nationalizing LTCB had emerged as a "quick-fix" tactical response to a political problem, rather than a planned financial strategy, most Japanese policy makers still had little idea of what true bank reform might mean—at LTCB or anywhere else.

So, like most Japanese, he told his foreign guest what he wanted to hear—and what Anzai himself dearly hoped *might* be true. "This time we have made the laws [to reform the banks] and we are fully committed," he said. "As a central banker I know that the bad loans have been shelved for many years and we ended up with the failure of LTCB. But there has been such a big sacrifice, we have created a mechanism to solve this. So, yes, we are serious about reform!"

"I can see that you are serious," Volcker replied. "But when you sell this, will you treat the foreign [bidders] the same as the Japanese?"

"Yes! We will treat the foreigners and the Japanese in the same way," Anzai replied with utter sincerity. "The same, exactly the same!" Volcker was delighted. He tentatively reported back to Flowers and Collins in New York that Japan seemed ready to countenance the path-breaking idea of an American bank buying LTCB.

In the following days, Anzai set to work trying to put his bold promise to Volcker into action. When Anzai had first arrived at the bank in November 1998, and been told to "sort out" the mess at LTCB, he had had little idea about how to go about finding a new owner for LTCB. In the past, it had been the Ministry of Finance that usually organized bank mergers, through opaque discussions in smoke-filled rooms. That, after all, had been how the idea of a Sumitomo Trust–LTCB deal had emerged.

As Anzai settled into his new office on the nineteenth floor of the bank, he was determined that this time it would be different. If LTCB was going to promote reform, then the Japanese government must display high standards, he solemnly declared. And that meant that the Japanese government needed to conduct an open and fair auction to sell LTCB. "I thought that if this huge problem of LTCB could be resolved, it would mark a milestone for the Japanese financial system and set standards that others could follow," Anzai told LTCB bankers. "I wanted to make everything transparent, showing the best possible standards!"

Technically, the task of selling LTCB was supposed to be in the hands of the Financial Reconstruction Commission, a bureaucratic body that had been set up in late 1998 to oversee the government's new Y60 trillion ($600 billion) support package for the banks. Since the funds to nationalize LTCB had come out of this package, the nationalized bank fell under the control of the FRC, which was working in close coordination with the Financial Supervisory Agency, the main regulatory body. However, Anzai was firmly convinced that the best way to create a transparent sales process was to take the whole process out of the bureaucrats' hands and get an outsider to manage the sale. Many reformers in the government agreed. So, in late 1998, Anzai told all the investment banks that the FRC wanted to pick an adviser. Startled, almost every foreign investment bank in town—along with many Japanese—submitted a bid to win the mandate and by mid-December, the government had whittled this down to a short list of seven candidates: Goldman Sachs, Morgan Stanley, Nikko Salomon Smith Barney, J. P. Morgan, Lehman Brothers, and Paribas. There was only one Japanese name involved—Daiwa Securities, which was working in conjuction with Wilbur Ross, an American buyout expert. The lack of Japanese candidates partly reflected the fact that most Japanese banks lacked the international mergers and acquisitions skills to conduct this type of sales process, precisely because it had never been needed before in Japan. However, Anzai was also dubious about whether a Japanese bank or broker would be able to sell LTCB in a "fair" way. Japanese finance was such a tribal world, with all its *keiretsu* allegiances, that the only players in the system who seemed to be truly "neutral" in relation to the *keiretsu* were—ironically—the *gaijin*.

In early January the government asked the seven candidates to make a pitch in a formal meeting on the twentieth floor of LTCB. In theory, the final selection was supposed to be settled by a complex, anonymous voting procedure. In practice, Goldman Sachs seemed to have won the contest almost before it started. Its bankers had been swarming over LTCB ever since the bank had collapsed, like flies hovering around a decaying carcass. That was partly because Goldman Sachs was trying to work out whether it wanted to buy the Japanese bank itself. Goldman Sachs bankers had also guessed early on that the government would need an adviser, and so back in November they had offered to provide free "advice" to the LTCB corporate planning department. LTCB bankers initially tried to fend off Goldman Sachs. However, the bankers working in the corporate planning department were utterly exhausted and overworked; Anzai had asked them to prepare all the logistical plans for a possible sale. So the bankers decided to use some of the U.S. bank's "free help" as a shortcut for their own research—and in exchange Goldman Sachs also got crucial information in advance about LTCB.

A few weeks later, the government committee voted on which bank to chose. Goldman Sachs scored 591 points in a complex scoring system, way ahead of the rest of the pack. Anzai duly announced that Goldman Sachs would now manage the sales process. "We hope to find a buyer in the next three months," he said. "We hope that there are many bids."

When Collins heard that Goldman Sachs had been appointed to manage the sale, he was thrilled. No foreign bank had ever been appointed into such a sensitive role in Japan. Emboldened, on March 3, Collins and Yashiro came to LTCB headquarters in central Tokyo to make their first official pitch to Anzai. "So what is this Ripplewood thing?" Anzai gruffly asked. "Are you vultures?"

Smoothly, Collins preached the gospel of private equity, as practiced by Ripplewood. What his company did, he explained, was to *restructure* companies rather than destroy them. Ripplewood was not a "vulture"; it created new businesses. It brought *good* into the world.

Anzai seemed unconvinced. For a while, the conversation went around in inconclusive—and ominous—circles. Then Yashiro leaped in.

Cheerfully, he explained that he had decided to get involved with Ripplewood because he thought that it could help to reform Japan and promote some badly needed corporate restructuring. "You and I are from the same stock, really," Yashiro told Anzai. "You're from Fukushima district and that's where my ancestors are from, too! So we are both men who know how to talk directly."

"You know, it really ought to be *you* who is sitting here in this president's chair, with your Citibank experience! Not me at all!" Anzai joked to Yashiro. "*You* should be running this bank!"

It was meant as a jest. Yet it was not entirely flippant. Anzai did not particularly like the idea of a private equity fund running LTCB: If it had to be a foreigner, he would greatly prefer to see a foreign bank win the bid, not a fund. But something about Collins and Yashiro impressed him. When Yashiro talked about reform he seemed to be very serious, and Anzai liked many of his ideas. By the time the meeting ended, Anzai had decided that the Ripplewood bid should be given a proper hearing—at least until a better candidate came along.

A few days later Goldman Sachs assembled a formal prospectus on the bank, and secretly drew up a list of companies that might be interested in buying the bank. On the left-hand side of the page were about two dozen Japanese names that included the banks, life insurance companies, and even some nonfinancial groups such as Sony and Toyota. On the right-hand side were most of the major global banks: HSBC, Banco Santander, Bank of Nova Scotia, Deutsche Bank, Dresdner, UBS, ING Barings, ANZ Bank, ABN Amro, Chase Manhattan, J. P. Morgan, Bank One, Credit Lyonnais, Credit Agricole, Credit Suisse, Citigroup, Fortis, AXA, and Aegon. Tucked on the far right side of this internal memo, were ten, less well-known American private equity firms: Newbridge, Blackstone, Bain, Warburg Pincus, Thomas H. Lee, GE Capital, AIG, KKR, Household Finance, and Berkshire Hathaway. These were the funds that Goldman Sachs considered the most credible and obvious bidders for a bank. The unknown Ripplewood was *not* on this list.

As spring wore on, Goldman Sachs quietly contacted all the foreign names. Meanwhile, Anzai visited the heads of almost every Japanese financial company to see if any of them wanted to acquire LTCB. For historical reasons, the banks considered the closest to LTCB were Dai-Ichi Kangyo Bank and Industrial Bank of Japan, but Anzai did not want to revive the old convoy system by encouraging a bid from either of those banks. "If those banks had gone together, there would have been a concentration of risk [in loans and debentures]," he later explained. Instead, Anzai preferred the idea of selling LTCB to an unrelated city bank, such as Sumitomo or Sanwa, or linking LTCB to a large regional bank. His favorite option was a deal with Bank of Tokyo Mitsubishi, arguably the strongest commercial bank in Japan.

When Anzai went to float the idea of a BTM bid in an informal manner in front of Satori Kishi, the powerful BTM president, he received a cutting response. "Kishi immediately said [to me] a firm 'No! I don't want to keep you in suspense by leaving you dangling—please look for someone else!'" Anzai later recalled. Privately, some BTM officials admitted that the bank was terrified of becoming snarled in political controversy. Sumitomo, Sanwa, and the rest of the banks were more tactful in their response, but rejected Anzai's overtures as well. In desperation, he asked dozens more domestic firms. The answer came back over and over again: "No." For decades, Japanese banks had been helping each other out of duty—or fear of the Ministry of Finance. Now the bankers had lost their belief that the MoF would protect them if deals went wrong and they were as suspicious as Sumitomo Trust had been back in the summer of 1998 about the "real" size of LTCB's bad loans. "All the domestic banks and brokers rejected us," Anzai later wailed. *"Everybody."*

By late spring, Goldman Sachs had found just three bids for the bank, none of which seemed ideal. Paribas, the French bank, had expressed interest. This did not appear to be a terribly serious bid, since it was the local office that had made the pitch. J. P. Morgan, the U.S. bank, had also made inquiries, acting in cooperation with Orix, the Japanese leasing firm. This bid seemed more serious than Paribas, and the LTCB bankers liked the idea of working with the U.S. bank, since J. P. Morgan had the type of prestigious image that LTCB had traditionally admired. However, the LTCB bankers were disappointed to see that the American bank did not seem interested in LTCB as a strategic acquisition, or to expand its global network. Instead, the bid was being made by J. P. Morgan's investment arm, which wanted to bid for LTCB's distressed assets, like a vulture fund.

The third bidder was Ripplewood. That was easily the keenest candidate on the list. Throughout the spring, Collins and Flowers had peppered LTCB with well-informed questions and demanded frequent meetings. But Anzai also knew that Ripplewood was utterly undesirable in the eyes of many Japanese. Not only was it American, but it was considered to be a *hagetaka fando* (vulture fund)—whatever Collins might say. Nobody considered that Ripplewood had much chance.

"Are there *really* no Japanese buyers?" Anzai asked, again and again. He did not want to tell the LDP politicians that he had found only three rather undesirable bids for his bank. That would spark criticism that Anzai had failed in his job. Bureaucrats in the FRC and FSA were doubly concerned. "We didn't want only foreigners to bid for the bank, when we had used public funds to revive it. That would have been too embarrassing," one FSA official later explained. Eventually, the bureaucrats turned to some traditional tactics. A bureaucrat telephoned Mitsui Trust Bank, and begged it to make a "voluntary" bid for LTCB. Although the bankers at Mitsui Trust disliked the idea, they were in no position to refuse since their bank was in a very weak financial position, and thus needed Ministry support. Indeed, the bank was *so* weak that the executives had recently decided to merge with Chuo Trust in an effort to make itself large enough to win protection from the Ministry of Finance. "I knew that when Chuo and Mitsui merged, that would be an alliance of weaklings. So I also knew that putting those banks with LTCB was not a good idea," Anzai later explained. "But there were some other people who were keen to have a Japanese bid. So we had that bid as well."

Furtively, Goldman Sachs then deemed that there were *four* bids and assigned each of them a code name in its confidential internal documents. Paribas was dubbed "Fashion," in honor of French sophistication. The reluctant Chuo-Mitsui bid was called "Scan." J. P. Morgan was given the code name "O. J. Simpson," after the American football player who had been accused—and acquitted—of murdering his wife and her friend. Ripplewood was assigned the code name "Cowboy," apparently in honor of the fact that it was American, a rank outsider—and seemed to have arrived in town completely out of the blue, like a solitary interloper in a spaghetti Western.

At the end of March, Japan was rocked by extraordinary news: Renault, the French auto company, had signed a deal to purchase a 36.8 percent stake in Nissan, the troubled Japanese car manufacturer, for $5.4 billion. It was the largest single direct investment that any foreign company had ever made in Japan and seemed to mark a watershed. Although Nissan had been ailing in recent years, it had traditionally been a highly respected company at the core of corporate Japan. The sale thus represented one of the most striking foreign incursions into the Japanese corporate citadel.

The news gave Collins another boost. If Japan was willing to hand partial control of one of its manufacturing jewels to Renault, then perhaps it would be ready to break other conventions—by selling a bank as well. Indeed, all over Japan hints of reform were in the air. Irrespective of the disastrous outcome of the SBC-LTCB alliance, foreign financial firms were still scrambling to link up with Japanese partners. The stock market was rallying, not least because the government had finally bit the bullet in March and agreed to inject almost Y10 trillion ($100 billion) of public funds into the banks' capital bases. Foreign funds managers were scrambling to buy Japanese shares, thrilled by the thought that the country might finally be reforming. By early summer, the stock market was rising toward 20,000. Suddenly Japan was becoming the darling of foreign investors—and Collins was more determined than ever to get a piece of the action.

In mid-May Keizo Obuchi, Japan's mild-mannered prime minister, flew to America for an official state visit to Bill Clinton, the U.S. president. In honor of the event, Clinton hosted a sparkling, formal dinner at the White House, placing Obuchi at the head table, next to Hillary Rodham Clinton. As the Japanese entourage took their places amid a sea of white linen and silver, they noticed another guest sitting nonchalantly at the head table as well—Collins himself.

Collins has always claimed that the seating plan was a sheer fluke. "I don't know how I ended up sitting at Obuchi's table. It was good fortune—story of my life," he later said. However, he had been a supporter of—and minor donor to—the Democratic Party all his life and made no secret of the fact that he knew the Clinton family and its entourage; photographs of Bill Clinton cuddling Collins's youngest child hung in Ripplewood's offices. And Collins was delighted to have the chance to chat nonchalantly over dinner to Hillary Clinton and Obuchi about the issues of the day. He had the impression that Obuchi was keen to talk to him as well: He noted that the Prime Minister had arrived remarkably well informed about the finer details of the bidding process for LTCB.

The Japanese onlookers, for their part, noted the seating plan with awe. Back in Tokyo, journalists always assumed that the power of a businessman could be measured by his proximity to political power. None of the Japanese present could tell exactly how much influence Collins really did—or did not—exert in Washington; the American political process often seemed mysterious to the Japanese. But in Tokyo image and ritual mattered as much as substance; thus if a man such as Collins was able to have dinner at the White House with Obuchi, the Japanese journalists concluded he must be very powerful. Overnight, Ripplewood was starting to acquire gravitas.

Behind the scenes, Collins cranked up the lobbying machine in other ways. He telephoned Deryck Maughan, vice chairman of Citigroup, and asked him to act as an adviser to the group. Maughan's name carried considerable influence in Tokyo, since he had run Salomon Smith Barney's Japanese operations in the late 1980s with enormous success and later forged the path-breaking joint venture between Nikko and Citigroup in 1998. Maughan agreed to help Ripplewood and visited the FSA and other bureaucrats to lobby for the group.

Separately, Yashiro approached some of his old friends in Japan's corporate and political world for help. Then Volcker flew to Tokyo for a second time, to drum up more support for Ripplewood from his contacts in the Japanese government. He visited Miyazawa again, who introduced Volcker to Hakuo Yanagisawa, the head of the FSA, and the man technically overseeing the sale. Volcker then talked to senior politicians in the powerful so-called "Fukuda" faction of the LDP. Another acquaintance was Masaru Hayami, the governor of the Bank of Japan. Hayami seemed well disposed to the idea of selling LTCB to an outsider, since he was deeply frustrated with the slow pace of banking reform, and keen to find "triggers" to break the political paralysis in Japan. Hayami had been furtively watching Ripplewood since the autumn of 1998 through his contacts in New York, and concluded that a feisty foreign fund, backed by a respected figure such as Volcker, could be *exactly* what Japan needed to promote reform of its banks. "In my judgment the American style of business [could] give a good stimulus to the Japanese financial system by bringing more competition," Hayami later explained.

As he did the rounds, Volcker found it easy to get a sympathetic ear. Although the Japanese knew that Volcker had stopped working for the American government back in 1987—and Volcker himself always tried to explain that he was acting as a private citizen—this distinction was not always easy for Japanese officials to grasp. When bureaucrats retired from senior posts in Tokyo, they often remained involved in government affairs as "advisers" and "fixers." Many Japanese thus suspected that Volcker was still operating with the approval of the American government. Moreover, Volcker did not seem to be the sort of man who would be chasing after grubby money or part of a team of marauding "vultures"; he exuded a sense of mission and sincerity. Without the presence of the former U.S. central bank governor, the Ripplewood team looked like unknown adventurers; with Volcker so visibly on board, the group had suddenly acquired prestige. "I have no doubt that it was reassuring for Japanese officials to see me involved during those negotiations," Volcker later admitted. Or as a senior Japanese politician later remarked: "We all have a lot of respect for Volcker. In some ways, you might say that it was Volcker who really influenced the course of the Ripplewood bid."

By midsummer it had become clear that there were only two real candidates left in the game—Ripplewood and J. P. Morgan. So, Goldman Sachs set to work negotiating with the bidders the tricky details of how a sale might be structured. The main person handling this on the Ripplewood side was Flowers. During the spring he had kept a relatively low profile in the negotiations, partly because he had little patience for schmoozing with politicians. Flowers had an added motive for staying out of the limelight: Goldman Sachs, his old employer, was working on the other side of the deal. Flowers did not see any rational reason why that fact should prevent him from making a bid, since he had left the bank back in late 1998 or just before Goldman Sachs won the mandate. Indeed, he insisted the link was a mixed blessing. "My former connection to Goldman Sachs was neither a positive nor a negative. In some ways it helped. But in other ways it really counted against and I think that balanced out," he said. Flowers's background enabled him to speak the same corporate language as the advisers who were selling the bank. He was even able to communicate with the advisers through the Goldman Sachs internal telephone systems, since the bank had inadvertently forgotten to switch off Flowers's voice mail. This advantage was offset by the fact that some senior Goldman Sachs officials in New York deeply disliked Flowers. More importantly, Flowers feared that if Ripplewood was presented as a bid from an ex–Goldman Sachs banker, the Japanese might presume that the bid was an "inside" job. So he had decided early on that it would be easier to leave Collins and Yashiro acting as the official "face" of the bid, and let "Ripplewood" be the name of the group, even though Flowers had his own fund.

Behind the scenes—Flowers was providing the key impetus for the bid. Day after day he sat cooped up in a small conference room at Goldman Sachs in Tokyo, trying to work out what the government wanted to do with LTCB. Sometimes Yashiro or Collins sat in the meetings but Flowers had the main control over the number crunching game. He had spent years of his life acting as a dealmaker and he did not intend to let his first independent deal go wrong in any way. He had too much to prove. Moreover, Flowers could see that even the most subtle details of how a bid for LTCB was structured could be critical in deciding whether the next owners of the bank made lucrative profits—or failed completely. What mattered most in the deal was not simply the upfront price paid for the bank (the issue which is usually most important in a corporate acquisition), but how the *future* risk in the loan book was handled.

The reason for this was that the value of LTCB looked fiendishly difficult to measure. When LTCB had collapsed back in the autumn of 1998, it had almost Y23 trillion ($230 billion) of assets on its books, two-thirds of which were corporate loans. During nationalization, this balance sheet had shrunk dramatically because financial assets were sold, and the government decided to remove almost Y5 trillion ($50 billion) of bad assets to the Resolution and Collection Corporation, a government body designated to handle loans. The government decided which loans to give the RCC on the basis of an audit in early 1999. This left LTCB with Y11 trillion ($110 billion) of loans by the summer of 1999, which were allegedly clean—at least, according to the FSA, which had official responsibility for measuring the bank's assets. But Flowers did not believe for a moment that the government had removed all of the risky assets. Nor did Anzai. Soon after arriving at LTCB, Anzai had realized that the official inspection data was far too optimistic and secretly lobbied for a new assessment. "I knew that there were a lot of problem loans left and personally I thought we should clean those up before we sold it," he later recalled. "But the FRC [Financial Reconstruction Commission] disagreed." Senior LDP politicians and bureaucrats did not want to create more embarrassment for weak borrowers or pressure on the other banks by labeling additional companies as "bad." The Japanese public had already been shocked to learn that there were almost Y5 trillion worth of bad loans inside LTCB. They would be doubly shocked if they learned the real figure could be twice that.

This meant that the bank was riddled with risk—and somehow Flowers had to find a way to offset it. One solution was more due diligence. However, Flowers considered that route impractical, given that corporate accounting was so poor in Japan. "When you have a loan portfolio as big as LTCB's, with $100 billion of loans, it is very difficult if not physically impossible to assemble enough information to accurately assess the problems," he later explained. Another option was to make a pessimistic assessment of the loan book—and pay an extremely low price to compensate for this risk. However, Flowers feared that the bank's price would need to be so extraordinarily low to offset the potential risk as to be politically unacceptable. "It is all very well saying mark everything to market. But it couldn't have been done at LTCB, and even if it could have been done, then it would have created such a huge cost to the people of Japan of tens of billions of dollars."

Consequently, Flowers concluded that the only feasible option was some form of "loss-sharing." This was a familiar concept in the financial world and had already been used to sell collapsed financial institutions in America, and other Asian countries such as Korea. It revolved around the idea that a seller could agree on a price for a bank with a potential bidder but *also* extend a type of insurance policy that promised that if any assets turned bad the potential loss would be split later between both seller and buyer. By using this "insurance" clause a government could sell a bank, even if the quality of assets was unclear. Another attraction was that the new owner of a bank had an incentive to sort out any problems on the loan books themselves, since if they could realize these assets they could reduce their future loss. "Almost every troubled bank deal worth more than $5 billion or $10 billion that has ever been done has been done with something like [a loss sharing]," Flowers later argued. "That is absolutely the most effective way."

In Japan a simple loss-sharing scheme raised problems. The bureaucrats did not like the idea because a form of loss-sharing had been used back in the middle of the 1990s to solve the *jusen* problem, with disastrous results. More practically, there did not appear to be any existing laws on the statute books permitting this. To Western eyes, this did not seem an insurmountable obstacle. "Why doesn't parliament just pass new laws? Isn't that supposed to be how democracy works?" one of the J. P. Morgan bankers asked. J. P. Morgan, like Ripplewood, had also made it clear that they would not bid for the bank unless the government offered schemes to protect against the bad loan risk, ideally in the form of a loss-sharing scheme. Anzai also believed that a loss-sharing system made sense. The bureaucrats were very reluctant to get the politicians involved again; they did not want another public debate about the state of the LTCB loan book, since it still contained too many embarrassing secrets about troubled companies with close connections to the LDP.

"But if we cannot offer the purchasers some protection we are not going to be able to sell the bank!" Anzai wailed, frustrated by the foot-dragging. Eventually FRC came up with another idea. In mid-August, government lawyers produced a flimsy, one-page document that outlined a so-called "cancellation right," or *kashi-tampo* in Japanese. This was a bastardized version of a loss-sharing scheme, albeit potentially far more costly for the government. Instead of promising to split any future losses between the government and Ripplewood, the government promised to provide a moderate level of reserves against loss on bad loans, using public funds. It also promised that during the first three years the purchaser could "return" any loans if they lost more than 20 percent of their value, provided they also returned the relevant reserves. If these reserves did not compensate the loss on the loan, the bank would then be compensated as well. In the jargon of Western investment bankers, this was akin to a financial "put"—or the right to walk away from a deal at a future date in certain conditions, "putting" the loan back to the government. A less technical observer might have called it a right to a refund.

In legal terms, this was an odd proposal. The concept of *kashi-tampo* had first appeared in Japan back in the nineteenth century, when the government created a law to cover street markets and other forms of trading. It offered protection for everyday cases: For example, if a housewife bought a bag of rice thinking that it was edible and later discovered that part of it was rotten, they could return it to the street market and demand a refund, under the *kashi-tampo*. In theory, nobody had ever thought of extending this concept to banking before, let alone treating bad loans in the same category as a bag of rice. "We laughed when we first saw that bit of paper," one LTCB banker later admitted. In the eyes of the bureaucrats, the *kashi-tampo* had one compelling attraction: If they based the LTCB sale on existing Japanese laws—however odd—they would not need to ask parliament to create a new legal framework from scratch. Better still, if the government used the *kashi-tampo*, it would not need to post a large sum of reserves when it sold LTCB. The level of *visible* up-front, public subsidies would thus look small.

The risk of this scheme, of course, was that at a later date the cost of the scheme could rise dramatically. LTCB was still riddled with bad loans, so if the new owners started to return these to the government, the government would need to bear the loss by itself. However, the bureaucrats decided to ignore that problem, hoping that somehow the loans would not turn bad. "I think the put emerged because the government honestly fooled themselves into thinking that things were better than they were," Volcker later observed. "There is this tendency [in Japan] to just keep putting things off."

By the start of September, Ripplewood seemed tantalizingly close to victory. J. P. Morgan had pulled out of the negotiations, partly because it could not stomach the idea of the "put." It was willing to make a bid with a simple loss-sharing scheme, but it feared that if—or when—the Japanese public ever realized the implications of the "put," there would be a backlash against the new owners of LTCB. "We just thought the whole put idea was crazy," a senior J. P. Morgan executive later explained. "We were in a totally different position from a vulture fund and just could not afford that level of reputation risk." Ripplewood, however, *had* agreed to the "put." Flowers could see that the "put" could be very lucrative, if the government honored the deal. And as long as the investors had a legal contract—and the government did not try to rip up the contracts—he reasoned that Ripplewood would be in a watertight position. "There are a lot of ways to do mechanically what the 'put' achieved, but I think it was the right way to proceed," Flowers later insisted.

Rumors swept Tokyo that the Americans had won the bid. Then, some of the Japanese bureaucrats and politicians started to panic. Back in the autumn of 1998, plenty of politicians had been willing to talk about reform in a theoretical way; but now that they were staring a vulture fund in the face, they were getting cold feet. Moreover, by the autumn of 1999, the political climate was subtly shifting. When LTCB had collapsed in October 1998, the mood was swinging in favor of bank reform—partly because there was a sense of economic crisis. Then, during the course of 1999 the economy had started to recover again and the shares of banks had soared. So, in a familiar pattern that had been played out in Japan over and over again during the 1990s, as the sense of crisis ebbed, the reform demands receded as well. By the summer of 1999, with the Nikkei near 20,000, the need to overhaul the banking sector—or appease the Americans—did not seem so urgent.

Behind the scenes, some bureaucrats and politicians dragged Chuo-Mitsui back into the fray. During the summer, the Japanese bank's bid for LTCB had seemed to lose steam, largely because the Japanese bank was blatantly unenthusiastic. It had not bothered to submit any bid at all until July 9—or two months after Ripplewood made its first bid. And when it did make an offer, it filled this with such impossible conditions that the LTCB bankers had the impression Chuo-Mitsui was deliberately torpedoing its chances. As September dawned, politicians and bureaucrats exhorted Chuo-

Mitsui to try a bit harder. "We felt it was unhealthy to not have a Japanese bid," one senior bureaucrat later explained. The hapless Chuo-Mitsui dutifully complied—yet again—and the local media started to run stories suggesting that a *Japanese* bank was now going to win.

Alarmed, Collins and Flowers rallied the troops. They could not bear to have come so close, only to see LTCB slip out of their hands at the last minute. Volcker telephoned Larry Summers, the U.S. treasury secretary, and asked for his support. Yashiro lobbied for help from some of his old friends in Japan's corporate world, such as Hirotaro Higuchi, an adviser to Prime Minister Obuchi, and Takashi Imai, the powerful leader of the *Keidanren,* the main Japanese business association. Meanwhile, Collins tried to activate his friends in Washington, at the senior echelons of the Clinton government.

Then Anzai himself entered the fray, using a tactic that reformers in Japan often employed—appealing for a bit of American pressure. During the long summer months, the president of LTCB had come to know Ripplewood quite well, through endless meetings with Collins, Volcker, Flowers, and Yashiro. These months of discussions had not left Anzai convinced that Ripplewood was necessarily the perfect bidder for LTCB: In an ideal world, he would still have preferred to see a large *bank* acquire LTCB, rather than a fund. But this was not an ideal world and Anzai liked the Ripplewood team, and he needed to sell LTCB somehow, or his own career would suffer. He did not trust the Chuo-Mitsui bid at all. So, in desperation, Anzai discreetly approached officials at the American embassy in Tokyo. Could Summers, he asked, telephone Miyazawa and try to ensure that the bidding process for LTCB was "fair"? Could Thomas Foley, the American ambassador, lobby as well? "There was a rising chorus of people in August saying: "No foreign interests should come to Japan!" Anzai later explained. "I didn't want to be defeated by that process. I wanted to promote reform. So I went to the American embassy, and people like Foley, to say that I wanted to keep this a fair process and not be destroyed!" Anzai was convinced that without that help, Ripplewood would be expelled from the process.

The American embassy was uncertain what to do. The Americans knew that *gaiatsu* was a double-edged sword, since it often rebounded on America as much as it promoted change. And in theory, it went against every principle of the American civil service for the Treasury to *deliberately* intervene in a business auction. America liked to uphold the concept that government and business were separate, and that it was wrong for government to lobby on behalf of favored private sector companies. However, the embassy staff had always known that the sale of LTCB could have broader policy implications. Just as Summers had pointed out to the Japanese a year earlier, if LTCB was sold to outside investors, this could help promote reform in Japan. Indeed, some embassy staff suspected that this type of practical *micro*-level step was likely to be far more effective in promoting change than the stern macroeconomic lectures that Summers periodically hurled at the Japanese. "There was a feeling that talking about the macro stuff wasn't really working, so if we wanted Japan to change we should look at practical micro things instead," said one American official.

Eventually, the American government responded to Anzai's request with a compromise. Summers himself refused to place any calls to Miyazawa. "The Ripplewood guys were always trying to get us to help them but I had a modest distaste in general for the advancement of private interests. I tried to stay out of the commercial and the particular when I was in office so I stayed out of the process at LTCB," Summers later explained. "I said once or twice to the Japanese that you have to have a fair process for selling the bank—you couldn't rule out foreigners because they were foreigners. But that was a general point of principle."

Ambassador Foley had fewer qualms. He strongly supported the free-market, reform ideals in which the Ripplewood team had dressed their bid. Morever, he was well disposed to Collins. Both men were keen supporters of the Clinton administration: Foley had been a congressman in America for twenty-nine years—and had become one of the most senior politicians in the Democratic Party—before serving as ambassador to Japan. By chance, both men also shared a commitment to their Christian faith. Ambassador Foley sometimes attended a discreet Bible study group that met on Thursday mornings in Tokyo. This was attended by an eclectic, but high-powered, group of Japanese working in the business and political worlds. There were relatively few Christians in Tokyo, since the waves of missionaries had never had much success in Japan. Yet precisely because they *were* such a tiny minority, Christians were often adept at maintaining links with each other and there were a surprising number of adherents among Japan's elite. Masaru Hayami, the Bank of Japan governor, for example, often attended these Thursday morning prayer meetings, as did Michio Ochi and Yuji Tsushima, senior LDP politicians, and some senior bankers such as Toru Hashimoto, head of Fuji Bank. "During the meeting everyone prays in front of God and they talk candidly . . . about current issues," Hayami later explained. On Foley's recommendation, Collins soon started to attend the meeting as well. To show "consideration," when the Americans turned up, the Japanese made sure to pray in English.

In September, with the pressure mounting, Foley telephoned Miyazawa and other Japanese officials. Choosing his words carefully, he asked for a fair and open sales process for LTCB and pointed out that the eyes of the outside world were watching closely. If it looked as if the Japanese government was behaving in a xenophobic fashion, Foley warned, this could badly damage Japan's reputation on the world stage. As he delivered his sermon, Foley tried to avoid looking as if he were lobbying for Ripplewood. He chose his words with care to suggest that he was acting on behalf of *all* foreign bidders to uphold the noble cause of reform in Japan. Observing a "fair" procedure was thus presented as something that Japan should do for its own good. "I am sure that Foley does not think he did anything inappropriate," one of his friends later explained. But in a country where symbolism mattered as much as words, his unusual actions had a powerful impact. Rightly or wrongly, by the middle of September many Japanese bureaucrats had leaped to the conclusion that the Washington government was directly backing Ripplewood to buy LTCB; after their experience of the last fifty years it felt like a very familiar pattern.

On September 22 Goldman Sachs submitted its final, confidential sales memo to the selection committee of the FRC, to help it weigh up the two bids. The document was plastered with cheery pictures of scales, as if Goldman Sachs was addressing a class of primary-school children. Below these scales was a list of the different merits of "Scan" and "Cowboy," aka Chuo-Mitsui and Ripplewood. The document was supposed to be a neutral assessment. However, it was clear that Goldman Sachs favored the Americans. " 'Cowboy' is very serious in its intent to buy LTCB and made every effort possible in the negotiations. . . . It has studied LTCB a lot, been very constructive and the first [bidder] to make concessions," the memo declared. Ripplewood had come up with its first concrete business plan in May and was offering to buy the bank for Y1 billion ($10 million) and inject Y120 billion ($1.2 billion) to expand the bank's capital base, while taking over all the LTCB loans. In exchange, it wanted the government to give it Y500 billion ($5 billion) worth of reserves, offer the "put" option, and inject another Y240 billion ($2.4 billion) of public funds into the LTCB capital base. It would pay for this bid by raising finance from companies such as GE Capital, "which mean there could be lots of synergies" for the business at LTCB in the future. "Cowboy has a good management team, including people such as Yashiro and Imai," the memo added. Imai—who was the head of the powerful *Keidanren* business group and a long-standing friend of Yashiro—had already quietly suggested that he would sit on the board of LTCB if Ripplewood won the bid.

The "Scan" bid had none of these merits. Chuo-Mitsui was demanding at least Y1,500 billion ($15 billion) worth of reserves before it would agree to buy the bank, Goldman Sachs explained, *three times* the level demanded by Ripplewood. It had refused to accept the "put" option and it had been extremely vague about its business strategy or management team. Indeed, the Japanese bank had only produced two sets of bidding documents at all. Ripplewood by contrast had revised its bid eight times, in an effort to meet the government's demands.

The FRC committee members, a collection of bureaucrats, academics, and other dignitaries, discussed the documents. Momentarily it seemed as if there might be another option: To the deep relief of the FRC committee, Tokio Marine and Fire, a Japanese insurance company, hinted that *it* might make a bid. But that idea quickly faded, leaving the FRC with a nasty choice: Either it was going to antagonize the Americans and potentially hurt the cause of reform, or it would irritate the conservatives.

So, on September 28, with the battle still hanging in the balance, the commissioners plumped for what appeared to be the least awful option. "We have examined how to best protect the interests of the Japanese taxpayer and had a long debate," Hakuo Yanagisawa, financial services minister, eventually announced, after a tense vote. "We have decided to start exclusive negotiations with Ripplewood."

— *Chapter 12* —

NEGOTIATIONS

One of the fundamental differences between a culture of sashimi eaters and one that enjoys steak [is that] beef-eaters [are] more assertive of their interest in business negotiations.

—Masamoto Yashiro, writing in 1997, using a popular culinary metaphor to allude to Japanese and Americans

On the evening of September 28, 1999, Collins, Flowers, Yashiro, and Volcker called a press conference at the Okura Hotel. Most of the Japanese media had never seen the strange foreigners who had won the bid for LTCB, and they were intensely curious to know what they looked like.

Yashiro and Collins tried to present a calming face. The Ripplewood team had decided early on that it would be best if Yashiro took the lead in handling the public relations in Japan, while Collins dealt with the foreign media. Flowers, as always, wanted to stay well out of the limelight. "We have agreed with the FRC to continue existing loans for three years and to refrain from promptly collecting the loans," Yashiro said earnestly. "We have also agreed to renew loans if existing corporate borrowers require further funding. I have no clue about how the Japanese economy will perform in the next three years, therefore we plan to decide on the loans flexibly and by carefully paying attention to ideas within business circles."

The Japanese journalists asked if Ripplewood had a plan for the bank.

"I want to abandon the businesses distinctive to long-term credit banks and transform it into an ordinary bank as soon as possible," Yashiro declared. In practice, this meant moving into retail banking and investment banking. To do this, the bank would need to unpick the restrictive legal statutes that had hobbled LTCB; however, the Japanese government had promised to let the bank do this, in principle. "I will seek alliances with brokerages and leasing companies . . . which could lead to the joint development of financial products. At the moment, LTCB's net business profit is only about Y50 billion [$500 million] a year and the assets Y10 trillion [$100 billion], implying a return on assets of 0.5 percent. I plan to double that in the next few years," he added. "I plan to launch online services for our clients and to tie up LTCB's automatic teller machines with other financial institutions."

Japanese journalists were moderately reassured. They were very wary of vulture funds and had little idea why the issue of return on assets mattered, since that concept had never been important in Japan. But they liked the idea of "reform" if that meant the introduction of flashy gizmos such as twenty-four-hour ATMs. Cutting-edge technology always won admiration in Japan. Nevertheless, one—tiny—incident from a subsequent press conference jarred. As the Ripplewood team was sitting on the platform, Flowers's cell phone rang. He answered it as one of the Japanese dignitaries was speaking: "Can't talk now—call you back later!"

Flowers never even noticed the incident. When he was conducting tense negotiations on Wall Street, he always answered cell phones, since it was critically important to stay in touch. Some Japanese journalists were appalled. And Flowers had not apologized.

The journalists speculated about his "motives," with their usual passion for conspiracy theories. Some suspected that Flowers had *deliberately* arranged for his cell to ring to show how powerful the Americans were—and add to the sense of humiliation that many Japanese were already feeling over their new American invasion.

Unaware of the offense, Flowers continued hammering out the details of the deal. What the Americans had signed on September 28 was not a binding agreement, but rather a memorandum of understanding (MOU), similar to the first agreement that Swiss Bank Corporation had signed with

LTCB in the summer of 1997. Before this MOU could be turned into a binding deal, both sides needed to satisfy a long list of legal requirements, which included checking the status of the bank's assets, and finalizing the words of a contract.

Due diligence, however, was a tricky matter—just as the Swiss had discovered two years earlier. The FRC had insisted from the very start of the sales process that bidders would not be allowed to check the LTCB assets. Instead, the bidders were supposed to rely on the FSA inspection for data about the loans—and use the "put" option as a type of insurance policy against the risk that this data could be wrong. Flowers had accepted that, but he did not want to finalize the contract without taking a better look at the assets. The Ripplewood team demanded the right to look at the LTCB loan book, and reluctantly the government agreed.

In early October, three different teams from Deloitte and Touche, Deutsche Bank, and Citigroup arrived at the LTCB tower. Ripplewood had hired a team from Citigroup to scan the systems inside the bank, and the quality of the derivatives book. Deloitte and Touche was asked to check whether the assets conformed to the official FSA classifications of bad loans. Deutsche Bank was hired to examine the assets in terms of their "real" underlying value, rather than worry about the FSA categories. This last task was particularly sensitive, since it was only by looking at the health of the borrowers and collateral that lay behind the loans (such as real estate) that Ripplewood could get a sense of whether the FSA data was at all accurate—or not. To make the task easier, Anzai agreed that the advisers could take over a single floor of the bank as a specialized "data room," and start sifting through LTCB files.

As the bankers arrived at the LTCB tower, they were unsure of what they might find. Judging the quality of assets in *any* Japanese bank was a nightmare, and the FSA had repeatedly declared that it did not want the buyer to perform due diligence. However, the LTCB staff seemed more than willing to help the foreigners understand the numbers. By the autumn of 1999 they had suddenly realized that it was in their own interests to give the Americans as much information about the risks as possible, since they did not want the bank to be so weak that it would collapse again; for the first time in recent Japanese banking history, a group of bankers had an *incentive* to come clean. "There was a type of conflict of interest, I suppose," one of the LTCB bankers later admitted. "We knew that if we were going to be sold the new bank should be as healthy as possible." The LTCB employees helpfully explained where the bank had hidden skeletons in the past and suggested the level of "real" reserves that Ripplewood should demand from the government to cover this risk. Belatedly, Anzai realized what was happening—and tried to stop the flow of information. "I was very cross when I found out. I told the staff that *they* were the people being sold, so they really shouldn't be leaking all this information themselves!" But it was too late. By the time Anzai tried to intervene, the LTCB staff had already handed over as many pieces of paper as they could.

In practice, the value of this raw data was often questionable. LTCB had never collected the type of information about its clients that Western investment banks needed, such as data on companies' liquidity levels. Nor did the bank have up-to-date figures on the value of collateral. What was clear was that based simply on the *official* FSA categories of bad loans—which most foreign bankers considered very flawed—LTCB had misclassified a significant chunk of the bank's assets. Loans to the troubled retailer Sogo, for example, had been classified as being nearly healthy, even though these did not even meet the FSA's own—ultraloose—guidelines for "healthy." And if the FSA guidelines were ignored and the real value of the assets was measured, then the picture looked even worse. The Deutsche team suspected that at least seven of the very largest companies on the LTCB client list, which were labeled as entirely healthy, were at future risk of collapse. Large, well-known names, such as Nippon Shinpan, the leasing company, and Kumagai Gumi, the construction group, looked distinctly wobbly. If these went down, they could easily wipe out the bank.

Just before Christmas, Deloitte and Touche and Deutsche Bank presented the results to Flowers, and armed with the data, the Ripplewood team demanded more concessions from the Japanese government. The bureaucrats uneasily debated what to do. They did not want to cancel the deal, given the paucity of other bidders. Failure would look too embarrassing. But the bureaucrats did not want to look as if they were capitulating to the *gaijin*. The deal had sparked a rash of xenophobic newspaper articles, with titles such as: "How the Vultures Could Tear Japan Apart!" And there were ominous hints that the political climate was moving toward a more protectionist stance. In the late autumn, under intense pressure from politicians, the government delayed a step considered crucial to inject market pressures into the banking system—the abolition of the blanket protection for bank depositors. Just before that, Yanagisawa, who had hitherto been seen as a champion of financial reform, had been forced to resign from his post as minister in charge of the FSA and FRC. His replacement, Michio Ochi, was a well-known conservative who did not share Yanagisawa's free-market views at all. "Young Yanagisawa has worked in America and likes the markets. But I think that is a bit naive," Ochi would later explain. "I have more experience and I know that the Japanese way is different."

On a *personal* level, Ochi always stressed that these views did not affect his feelings toward Ripplewood. On the contrary, he was well disposed to the Americans because he—like so much of the elite—had been dealing with Paul Volcker for decades. "I knew Volcker and respected him," Ochi later explained. "Also, I knew that Miyazawa was backing Volcker, and so I knew that I had to support Ripplewood." But Ochi was an astute politician and he knew that it would be hard for the FSA to lose face in front of a vulture fund.

So, the bureaucrats reached for a typically opaque compromise. There was, the FSA declared, no question of reclassifying all the loans at LTCB. Nor would it hand more loans to the RCC. What it would do was furtively agree to raise the level of reserves in the bank from Y500 billion ($5 billion) to almost Y900 billion ($9 billion), to offset the risk of losses on problem loans, which were tentatively agreed to be about Y1,500 billion ($15 billion), or almost a fifth of the entire balance sheet. Then, as negotiations wound on, the FRC tacitly watered down LTCB's commitment to protect its borrowers. Back in September, Yashiro and Flowers had promised that the bank would maintain loans to all its borrowers for the next three years. They had also agreed that LTCB would not sell the loans to other people. However, as the two sides haggled, this promise was slightly modified. Although the main text of the contract preserved the original promises, a tiny note was inserted that stated that LTCB's new owner could ignore its original pledge to protect all the borrowers, if such loans threatened to create losses for the bank.

FSA officials did not pay much attention to these notes. When business was done in Japan, companies usually considered that a legal contract was simply one of many strands that could create a relationship. There was also a presumption that contracts could and should be renegotiated if circumstances changed, since it was more important to preserve a relationship than a single transaction. In many cases, verbal promises were considered to have almost as much weight as a legal document and the bureaucrats believed that Yashiro and Collins had given verbal promises to protect the borrowers. In any case, their main priority was to find a quick solution to any disagreements, even if it meant papering over the cracks—and staving off any disputes to a future day.

The Americans saw things very differently. Wall Street was founded on the presumption that if there was a showdown between a legal transaction and a relationship, it was the transaction and *not* the relationship that should be honored. A contract was not just cosmetic packaging for a deal; it *was* the deal. In the eyes of men such as Flowers and Collins a tiny legal note was thus far more binding than the verbal promises, to which the Japanese were attaching importance. And if the Japanese were willing to concede ground on the details of the contract, the Americans were determined to win all the advantages they could.

While the negotiations dragged on over the details of the contract, Yashiro, Collins, and Flowers were also engaged in the second task of raising funds to finance the deal. They needed slightly more than a billion dollars (Y120 billion), to cover the cost of buying the bank. Although both men planned to put some of their funds' money into the deal, they needed to raise additional support from outside investors. And they were keen to make this group of investors as diverse as possible, to ensure that there would be plenty of powerful voices ready to complain if something in the LTCB deal ever went wrong.

Initially, the Ripplewood team hoped that some of this money would come from Japanese sources, to ensure there was domestic support for the bank. Collins approached Mitsubishi Corporation and asked if it would supply funds. He reckoned that the giant trading company would be a natural backer. Mitsubishi refused. Personally, Minoru Makihara, the Mitsubishi head, hoped that a reborn LTCB could promote reform, but the

LTCB deal had the potential to become very controversial and Mitsubishi executives did not want their company to become tarred by the political risks of a deal. Worse still, some Mitsubishi executives also feared that any involvement with LTCB would contravene the principle of the Mitsubishi *keiretsu*, because Mitsubishi was linked to Bank of Tokyo Mitsubishi. "There was this idea that backing LTCB would be opposed by BTM," one of Makihara's colleagues explained. Mitsubishi executives insisted that the LTCB project should be completely insulated from the Ripplewood fund in New York, so that no Mitsubishi money could be linked to LTCB at all.

Collins and Yashiro then approached some of the other original Japanese investors who had funded Ripplewood's joint venture with Mitsubishi, such as Nikko Securities and Tokio Marine and Fire, the nonlife insurance group. "No Japanese company was interested in investing," Yashiro later laughed. "They said they would not want to get involved for 'reputation' reasons. Isn't that completely crazy? *Reputation!* As if they all had such wonderful reputations to start with!"

Eventually Yashiro and Collins gave up and turned to European and American investors. These, by contrast, seemed positively eager to sign up. Most of the large global banks and insurance companies had investment departments that financed private equity deals—and for years these groups had nervously peered at Japan, wondering if they should put some money there. Until 1998, many had shied away, since Japan seemed so hostile to the concept of private equity. LTCB offered a tantalizing opportunity to dip a toe into the market. The entire project was rooted in a philosophy that Americans instinctively warmed to—the mission of bringing market principles into Japan. Collins's name was already moderately well known on the institutional investment circuit, since Ripplewood had been producing healing returns since it had started. Meanwhile, Flowers had a dazzling reputation on Wall Street for his ability to forge deals and he was trusted by some powerful men, such as Hank Greenberg, the legendary president of AIG. Most important of all, the LTCB deal potentially offered nice returns: Many of the investors calculated, on the back of Ripplewood's data, that LTCB would deliver an internal rate of return (IRR) of 60 percent, implying that the value of investors' funds could more than *triple* over three years. "Collins went around saying that this could be the deal of the century!" one of the investors later explained. "The numbers looked potentially amazing."

These optimistic projections reflected some clever financial footwork by Flowers. Under the terms of the deal thrashed out with the FRC, the investors planned to pay a token Y1 billion ($10 billion) to buy the bank with about Y10 trillion—or $100 billion—of assets on its books, including about Y8 trillion loans. Technically, since the company was bankrupt, LTCB had absolutely no capital to support these assets. Instead, it had a huge *negative* capital position, arising from losses on its equity portfolio and bad loans. However, the government had effectively agreed to wipe out these historical losses by buying the bad assets and then plugging the gap with public funds at an estimated cost of Y3.6 trillion ($30 billion). This included the provision of Y240 billion ($2.4 billion) of fresh capital for the bank by purchasing newly issued preferred shares (without any voting rights).

In addition to that, the government agreed to give another boost to the bank's capital base by "buying" the LTCB's existing portfolio of equity—the cross-shareholdings it had held for relationship reasons—for another Y250 billion ($2.5 billion). On paper, this "sale" was not technically final, since the shares were held in trust and LTCB remained the registered owner of the shares on the stock exchange, with a right to repurchase them. Nonetheless, the government agreed to let the bank count this Y250 billion as "capital" and the fudge suited everyone concerned. LTCB's corporate clients did not want the bank to suddenly sell the cross-shareholdings, since that would cause share prices to collapse—and Ripplewood did not want LTCB to hold equities, since that would create market risk. Meanwhile, from the government's point of view, the scheme allowed it to offer more capital for the bank in a way that the public was unlikely to notice. The Ripplewood team, for their part, promised to buy Y120 billion ($1.2 billion) of newly issued common shares to expand the bank's capital base.

Taken together, that meant LTCB had a capital base of almost Y600 billion, giving the bank a healthy capital ratio of 13 percent. Thus, the investors were paying about $1 billion to buy a bank with almost $100 billion in assets, more than $5 billion in capital—*and* an insurance policy if these loans turned sour. If the investors simply liquidated the bank on the first day, they could—theoretically—make a huge profit, even after repaying the government for its preferred shares. In practice, of course, life was not so simple. The *real* value of the "$100 billion" in assets was crucially unclear and the degree of insurance in the "put" was untested. The investors could not simply seize the value of the capital for themselves. Nor could they drain the bank of cash by paying themselves dividends from the common shares, since the terms of the sales agreement stipulated that the new owners of LTCB had to pay any dividends *first* to the holder of the preferred shares—namely, the government. Thus, the investors could only profit if they eventually found a way to sell all or part of the bank. Collins and Flowers airily insisted this would be possible: There was tremendous value to be unlocked simply by using the "put" and engaging in some financial restructuring of the balance sheet, they argued; and if they inserted a new management, it would be easy to turn the bank's underlying business around as well, particularly if Japan's economy recovered.

Not everybody agreed with this upbeat assessment about Japan's prospects. Chris Flowers knew Robert Rubin, the man who had served as the U.S. treasury secretary between 1995 and 1999, relatively well. Before Rubin joined the U.S. government he worked at Goldman Sachs, and during these years on Wall Street he had become deeply skeptical about the ability of the Japanese government to produce the type of strategy that could solve its problems. His spell in Washington, and his experience of dealing with Japanese bureaucrats and politicians, left him even more scathing. In 1999 he was gloomily predicting in private that the Japanese government was unlikely to turn its economy around soon, let alone fix the problems in its banks. "We talked to Rubin about our plans," Flowers later recalled. "He was a real pessimist on the Japanese economy. He was almost the only guy who stood out from all the people we talked to as being incredibly negative."

Flowers and Collins brushed off Rubin's Cassandra-like warnings. The consensus of most observers on Wall Street was that Japan *was* recovering and had embarked on an irreversible path of reform—and that was the line that the Ripplewood team badly wanted to believe. "Japan has been declining for a decade. It cannot keep going down forever," Collins said cheerfully. "Eventually the economy has got to pick up. And when it does this bank will be perfectly placed to benefit!"

Nobody noticed that Collins's words closely echoed what Luqman Arnold at Swiss Bank had said two years earlier, when he embarked on his own unfortunate adventure with LTCB; indeed, no one in the Ripplewood consortium had ever looked too closely at the history of LTCB. The culture of Wall Street tended to focus on the *present*, not the past, since it assumed that the world could be constantly remade anew, that it was possible to rebound from a defeat and start again. That was not how most Japanese viewed the world: To them, the present was inevitably anchored in the past, with ties that could be ignored in polite company, but *never* entirely severed. In Japan, a slate could rarely be wiped clean. Yet to the Ripplewood team, the whole point of an LTCB deal was that a failure could create a fresh start; and it was a concept that was central to the philiosophy of creative destruction.

Mellon Bank, the Pittsburgh-based bank, was one of the first American banks to become hooked by the sales pitch. The senior managers knew Flowers very well, since Goldman Sachs had worked on several mergers and acquisitions that involved Mellon Bank. "Flowers is a genius at deals," one of the senior Mellon executives explained. "He is the kind of guy you love to have sitting on your side of the table in a deal, and hate to be sitting across the room!" Mellon was already interested in Japan because it wanted to expand Mellon's asset management operations there. It hoped that a deal with LTCB would provide a way of testing the market, as well as offering lucrative returns. Even before the MOU was signed, the bank offered $100 million for the project—the maximum it *ever* invested in a single project.

Mellon then brought ABN Amro, a Dutch bank, into the deal for a similar amount and Deutsche Bank, the German group, joined the consortium as well. This was part of an implicit quid pro quo that had emerged when Ripplewood had hired Deutsche to do due diligence on the LTCB portfolio back in the autumn. Two other large European investors came on board as well. Banco Santander Central Hispano (BSCH), a large Spanish bank, offered $100 million, partly because it hoped that a deal with LTCB would expand its knowledge of Japanese distressed real estate. Jacob Rothschild also made another large investment via a British-based investment fund he controlled, St. James Place Capital. Collins—true to form—had got to know Jacob Rothschild a few years earlier. "We got involved in this deal primarily for investment reasons," Rothschild later explained. "We thought that given the way it was structured the downside risk was quite limited and the upside was quite considerable. Strategically we wanted to deepen our knowledge of Japan as well. We felt, like everybody else, that it was timely for reforms to take place in the Japanese financial sector. It is an important investment for us."

David Rockefeller, the former chairman of Chase Manhattan Bank, also became involved, primarily for ideological reasons. The Rockefeller family had had close ties with the Japanese elite—including the Japanese imperial family—over many decades and David Rockefeller had been passionately arguing for years that Tokyo needed to embrace market reforms in order to revive their economy. He fervently hoped that an American-run bank could provide a model for these changes. "Free enterprise is part of what has made America great! This [Shinsei project] is part of that process," Rockefeller liked to say. Indeed, Rockefeller was so excited by the whole plan that he tried to persuade Chase Bank, which he had once run, to invest. When Chase refused, Rockefeller invested some of his own money into the project instead. "Not *that* much—just a few millions of dollars," he later explained. "But it was my own money. I felt strongly that I should support this."

The project also attracted other rich American investors, such as the Malkin family, a dynasty that owned the lease of the Empire State Building. The Malkins knew virtually nothing about Japan and had little strategic interest in the deal. They got involved simply because Flowers's projections for the returns on LTCB were better than U.S. property at the time. Bank of Nova Scotia, the Canadian bank, also came on board. Then Paine Webber, the U.S. financial conglomerate, offered $100 million more funds, partly because it knew Chris Flowers. "From Paine Webber's point of view, the [project] was a solid investment. Paine Webber was already thinking about Japan from an investment and business standpoint," Donald B. Marron, CEO of Paine Webber explained. "The challenge of bringing American financial and management methods to a Japanese bank was exciting and we hoped the deal would provide a set of relationships and opportunities to Paine Webber." Marron, like many Americans, also hoped that the sale of LTCB could be the first step of a broader wave of financial reform, of the type that had been triggered by the Resolution and Trust Corporation in America after the 1980s Savings and Loan debacle. "I thought our purchase of Shinsei would demonstrate that reform was occurring—if investors could buy the bank on the terms they wanted to buy it, this would indicate structural reform was taking place in Japan's economy and financial system."

Collins and Flowers also attracted three corporate giants who were already heavily involved in Tokyo in their own right: AIG, Citigroup, and GE Capital. In political terms, these three investors were arguably the most crucial of all. AIG had been investing in Japan for decades and dominated niches of the country's insurance industry. It was also powerful in congress. GE Capital employed nearly 12,000 people in a sprawling Japanese empire that included consumer finance operations, leasing, and its own private equity arm. Meanwhile, Citigroup employed a similar number in a retail bank, consumer finance group, and ran the only successful investment banking joint venture between a Western and Japanese firm, Nikko Salomon Smith Barney. This existing exposure made the three American giants distinctly nervous of becoming entangled in any new political risk. They were thus determined to keep a very low profile. However, all three American giants recognized that a success at LTCB could potentially help them; if the Ripplewood team could show that it was possible to revive a collapsed Japanese bank, that might make it easier for *all* investors to operate in Japan. Similarly, the presence of these three giants in the team added to LTCB's political weight. With groups such as AIG, Citigroup, GE Capital, Mellon, and Paine Webber on board, this was no longer simply a Ripplewood deal; suddenly half of Wall Street was on board. If something went wrong at a later date at LTCB, in other words, there were now plenty of Americans who would have a vested interest in creating a diplomatic and political storm.

By late December 1999, Collins and Flowers were in the happy position of having generated so much excitement about the deal that they had actually raised too *much* money. Yet they did not want to exclude any single name from the lineup. So they asked the large investors such as Mellon, Deutsche, ABN Amro, and Paine Webber to cut their subscription by about 20 percent (or from $100 million to around $80 million) and with the minimum of ceremony, the lawyers and investors gathered in New York and created a new company called the "New LTCB Partners" to act as a vehicle for this finance. This was headquartered in the Netherlands to reduce the potential tax bill if the group ever realized any profits. The consortium was formally signed into existence shortly after Christmas Day 1999. "It was a pretty amazing lineup of names," one of the investors later laughed. "The largest single investor, after the government, was Flowers himself."

Then, Collins, Yashiro, and Flowers set to work putting in place the last strand of their political insurance strategy: creating a powerful board for the bank. Traditionally, the boards of Japanese banks had been made up of dozens of men, almost exclusively internal managers. Ripplewood was determined to bring in as many prestigious external names as possible, drawn from both sides of the Pacific. On the Japanese side, Yashiro's old friends Takashi Imai, the chairman of Nippon Steel and influential head of the *Keidanren,* and Hirotaro Higuchi, the honorary chairman of Asahi Breweries, both agreed to sit on the board. A third—and more surprising—Japanese participant was Makihara of Mitsubishi. Not many people inside Mitsubishi initially knew that Makihara had agreed to hold this post and some were horrified when they found out, given that Mitsubishi had so pointedly refused to invest in the deal. Collins had asked Makihara to sit on the board and the maverick Japanese man had eventually agreed, partly to demonstrate support for reform—but also because he wanted to keep a close eye on the venture. "I made it clear in the initial board meeting that I was acting in a personal capacity and I think that is clearly understood by everyone," Makihara later explained. "I felt that compared with the other directors I could play a particular role in seeing that the situation in Japan would be clearly understood by the shareholders. My role on the board is to see that Mr. Yashiro is doing a good job."

On the non-Japanese side, there were also some heavyweight names. Martin G. McGuinn, chairman of Mellon Bank, Emilio Botin, the chairman of BSCH, and Marron of Paine Webber, all represented key investors. Rockefeller was another, highly enthusiastic board member. "I want to support this project all I can—what they are doing is good for Japan!" he explained. Another member was Michael J. Boskin, a professor at Stanford University and a former chairman of George Bush senior's Council of

Economic Advisers. Collins reckoned that a few Republican Party connections could be useful if the Democrats lost control of the White House in late 2000.

Flowers and Collins also urged Rubin to join the board but he firmly declined. Rothschild also turned down an invitation, citing his lack of knowledge about Japan and dislike of long plane flights. Volcker was also reluctant to join the board. "I didn't want to become a director because that would imply levels of detail and responsibility that I wasn't in a position to take," he later explained. However, he did agree to become an "adviser" to the board, which implied that he would still promote the bank's interests and remain heavily involved in the venture.

Then Collins produced a second "adviser"—the imposing figure of Vernon E. Jordan Jr., a prominent black former civil rights activist who had carved out a second career as an investment banker, but was renowned for being a powerbroker in Washington. In some ways, Jordan seemed a most unexpected addition. In America, Jordan was mostly known as a player on the *domestic* American political and corporate scene. Indeed, by late 1999, Jordan was to become famous—or infamous—for having helped his friend Bill Clinton during a scandal about Clinton's relationship with Monica Lewinsky, a White House intern. But he had known Collins for years, since the two men were both trustees of DePauw University in the American Midwest and Jordan worked as a counsel to Ripplewood. The presence of Jordan would add to the aura of White House ties.

Jordan, for his part, was rather tickled by the idea. Back in the late 1980s, when Jordan was working as a civil rights activist in Washington, he—like everybody else—had greatly admired the strength of the Japanese economy and felt rather nervous about the speed at which the Japanese were buying American assets. In 1989 Jordan had even traveled to Tokyo and delivered a speech to the *Keidanren* that stressed the importance of foreign investors blending into the culture—and appealed to the Japanese to adopt some local, American values, such as gender equality. "To effectively counter anti-Japanese sentiment it is not enough for you to condemn Japan-bashing or to educate the public to the benefits of free trade and investment or even to negotiate more open markets," Jordan had solemnly told a group of Japanese business leaders. "Foreign-based multinationals must ensure that their American subsidiaries are seen by their workers, customers, and communities as operating in all important respects as American companies, equally committed to American corporate expectations."

Back then, Jordan had never imagined that one day the tables would turn and American companies would end up making acquisitions in Japan—meaning that it was now Americans who needed to fit into local *Japanese* culture. Nor would he have guessed that as a black American he would end up being an adviser to a Japanese bank. "I mean, we used to think that Japan was so strong! Something has been going on that we don't quite understand." But Jordan hoped that somehow the LTCB project might do some good. "What Ripplewood and the others are doing with LTCB is a truly wonderful thing for the world," Jordan later explained, with the practiced patter of a politician. "I like to think that what this bank shows is that we are all part of a great big global village! Isn't that the way that the world should work in these troubled times? American and Japanese together breaking down those borders that divide us! Isn't that a nice idea?"

On March 1, after months of negotiations and last-minute changes in the contract, Ripplewood finally took control of the bank. The following day, some of the foreign investors turned up at the bank for the first official meeting of the directors and shareholders. Collins arrived early and as he milled around the corridors he bumped into his friend Jordan and another American banker, David Fite, who had been appointed a managing director of the new bank.

"Why don't we go and have lunch in the staff canteen?" Collins suggested. He liked to pride himself on having the common touch. Whenever he bought a company in America, he usually tried to go around and shake the workers' hands, to show "I haven't got horns," as he liked to say. It was the type of populist gesture that went down well in the heartland of America. He hoped that would work in Japan as well; after all, Collins had told himself that he was coming to *help* Japan; he was trying to fix their problems—while also getting rich.

The three men descended to the eighth floor of the bank, and walked into the staff canteen. The Japanese staff clutching their chopsticks could barely believe their eyes. Foreigners had rarely been seen inside their canteen before. This was not because of any official *rule* banning foreigners, but simply because visitors to the bank were always shepherded away from the "private" eating space to special "guest" rooms. At LTCB a rigid hierarchy governed the lunchtime universe, like everything else—and everybody was supposed to keep to their allotted place.

Now, however, a huge black man had arrived in the canteen, shattering the usual sense of order. At six feet five inches tall, Jordan towered over the Japanese around him. Fite and Collins seemed almost as large. "I guess the new invaders have arrived," one of the LTCB managers later wryly reflected. For months the staff had been nervously wondering what the American investors wanted to do with their bank. Few of the Japanese employees sitting in the canteen were old enough to have personal memories of Japan's shocking defeat in World War II themselves. The image of victorious American soldiers stomping into Tokyo after the war, a foot taller than the local population, was etched on Japan's cultural memory. To some of the Japanese at LTCB, the arrival of the new Americans felt uncannily similar.

As Jordan stared back, he felt distinctly disconcerted as well. Back in America, when employees ate their lunch they usually did so in an anarchic, relaxed manner. The LTCB lunchroom, on the other hand, had a hushed sense of discipline: The workers sat in neat, quiet rows, in a clear pattern. Some tables were filled just with women, wearing matching, "office lady" uniforms; others were exclusively men, wearing dark blue suits. Although Jordan did not know it, this distinction had less to do with gender per se, than status: The women all held the lowliest jobs, so they tended to sit together, at the bottom end of the hierarchy. "I mean, I have seen segregation before," Jordan later recalled. "I grew up with segregation. I'm from the American South. So there ain't nothing you can tell me about segregation! Oh no, no! But when I looked at that canteen, it was like a whole new type of divide . . . like nothing I have seen before!"

"So where shall we sit for lunch?" the three men wondered. Jordan could tell that a hierarchy was at work in the room. However, he had spent his whole life fighting against segregation. He believed in democracy, not hierarchy. "I am a free man! I am a man of the people!" he liked to declare.

He cheerfully sat down at the first seat that grabbed his egalitarian fancy—right in the middle of the youngest and most junior office ladies. It was the lowest point possible in the LTCB lunchtime hierarchy.

With a big grin, Jordan tried to strike up a conversation with the tiny women around him.

The women froze. Eventually Jordan gave up trying to make conversation and the Americans ate their lunch, chatting among themselves. Furtively, the Japanese peeped at them. Equally furtively, Collins, Fite, and Jordan glanced back at the sea of frozen faces and tried to guess what on earth the Japanese were thinking.

PART THREE

— *Chapter 13* —

YASHIRO'S DREAM

Success for Shinsei is guaranteed as long as we do just exactly the opposite of what traditional Japanese banks have been doing. I have a great textbook that tells me what not to do.

—Masamoto Yashiro

On June 6, 2000, the reborn bank officially opened for business with a minimum of ceremony. At 9 A.M., Masamoto Yashiro, the new CEO of the bank, unveiled a small plaque at the front of the old headquarters tower, with the word "Shinsei" written in Chinese characters. The bank management had decided to discard the old name, Long Term Credit Bank of Japan, to make a clear break from the past and had chosen the Japanese words *shinsei* because it meant rebirth, renaissance, or—most literally—new life. They had also chosen to use traditional characters for its name, to reinforce the idea that it was still a *Japanese* bank. Next to the characters stood the bank's new logo, however, a cerulean globe with an "S" running across the orb, which was intended to convey a sense of international connections. It looked oddly similar to the Citibank logo.

Yashiro also congratulated all the staff on the launch of the bank by sending an email from the computer in his new office. He had chosen to work out of the very same room on the nineteenth floor that had once been Onogi's office. The only immediate visible sign of change from the old days was that Yashiro had removed a collection of vases and a vast television set, and installed a slim new computer. Most Japanese bank presidents rarely gave any sign to visitors that they did work, but Yashiro spent hours at his computer, leaving it only reluctantly. He had become a frenetic emailer working for American companies and started each day at 5 A.M. by firing off long messages around the world, in both Japanese and English. "This is a most exciting moment!" Yashiro told local journalists. "We are creating a new type of bank." He meant it.

In some ways, Yashiro's entire life had been preparing him for his new role. Indeed, there were few other people in Tokyo who seemed quite as well qualified. Outwardly, Yashiro displayed the trappings of an elite Japanese business leader: Like Onogi, he had been to the best universities, was a childhood friend of some of the most powerful men in the country and had a strong sense of duty. Yet, *unlike* Onogi—and the vast majority of Japanese—Yashiro also had a defiantly individualistic streak. It was a rare combination of traits, and Yashiro had had a rather unusual life.

Born on February 14, 1929, in Tokyo, he was the youngest of three children in a family that hailed from the rural district of Fukushima. While Yashiro was a small child, his father worked as a pharmacist in Tokyo and he was sufficiently wealthy to send Yashiro to a relatively prestigious school, the First Tokyo Prefectural Middle School, tucked next to the Japanese parliament.

Yashiro's classmates included men such as Takashi Imai (the future head of Nippon Steel and *Keidanren*); Tatsuro Toyoda (future head of Toyota); Yuji Tsushima (a senior LDP politician); and Atsushi Mano (a senior figure at Sumitomo Electric). However, the First Tokyo Prefectural Middle School was also considered to be unusually liberal and before the explosion of virulent Japanese fascism in the late 1930s, it tried to inculcate the pupils with an international outlook. "[The school] followed the British educational philosophy of trying to bring people up as gentlemen," Yashiro later explained. "My older brother went to the same school and before the outbreak of the Second World War every pupil was given a foreign name in the English language class. My brother was called 'Hugh.'"

The war shattered this idyll. When it started, Yashiro, barely a teenager, was too young to be drafted. Still, in his second year at Middle School, he was sent to work, first at a naval supply depot and then at a factory in the Kamata region, where he was ordered to inspect steel gyroscopes used in locating submarines. In 1945 Allied bombers destroyed the factory. "I remember clearly, as though it was about ten in the morning, that the shadowy silhouette of numerous American bombers circling overhead and the black smoke billowing from burning homes had transformed the sky into twilight," Yashiro later wrote in an autobiographical essay. "Against that darkness, the incendiary bombs that came raining down on the city appeared like swords of light. Frighteningly, the holding bolt from an incendiary bomb landed with an incredible thud no more than a meter away from where we had taken shelter behind a wall. It is a miracle that no one in our group was injured."

His father and sister died during the war, but Yashiro himself survived. Then, just a few days after the war ended, his beloved mother died in Kyoto. Yashiro never forgot the desperate sense of loss. "The war had just ended and the whole country was in a state of chaos," Yashiro later wrote. "I caught the night train to Kyoto and cried the whole night through. Until four or five years ago I used to have a recurring dream about my mother in which I screamed: 'Mother, don't die!' Sometimes my own wife resembles my mother to me. I suppose I must be a classic example of someone you would describe nowadays as suffering from a mother complex."

Shocked and exhausted after the war, Yashiro initially had little desire to return to school. His parents had left him modest savings, but much of that was wiped out by hyperinflation. But the memory of his mother haunted Yashiro and he knew that she valued education. "I could hear her saying, 'Mah-chan, don't give up!'" So he returned to Kyoto, her birthplace, and eventually graduated from high school.

Yashiro then won a place to study law at Kyoto University and paid for his course by working as a telephone switchboard operator for the American army, connecting Japanese supply lines with troops in South Korea. Then in 1952 an event occurred that changed his life: Yashiro won a place to participate in a U.S.-Japan student peace conference in San Francisco, followed by a United Nations scholarship to travel to Europe. He became passionately interested in overseas cultures. So he started graduate research in international relations at Tokyo University, where he wrote an earnest thesis about Asian trade. Along the way he married a suitable Japanese woman called Yoko. She bore him two daughters, whom Yashiro utterly adored and insisted on spoiling as much as he possibly could, giving them every bit of luxury and security that he had been denied during his own teenage years. Indeed, his indulgence was so extreme that it ended up causing serious strains in his marriage. "Once my wife declared that she couldn't bear to be with a man who spoils his children so much and came close to divorcing me," Yashiro admitted. "I have been told any number of times by non-Japanese that it's best to be strict with children. I am nonetheless convinced that there is nothing at all wrong with pampering your children as much as you like."

In 1958 Yashiro entered the workforce, finding a job at the Tokyo office of Standard-Vacuum (Stanvac), an American oil company. It was a very unusual choice at the time. "[In those days] since most students pursued careers in the civil service or with Japanese firms, anyone who opted to work for a foreign company was assumed to be odd or incompetent," Yashiro admitted. But Yashiro's determination to act as an individual meant that he flourished in the American environment. He was sent to New York for a spell. Then, when the company split itself into two parts in 1960, Yashiro returned to Japan and joined the part known as "Esso," later renamed "Exxon." In 1964, at the age of thirty-five, Yashiro was put on the board of directors of Esso Sekiyu, the Japanese branch of the American group affiliated with some local oil suppliers. It was considered a shockingly high promotion for such a young man in Japan.

During the next twenty-five years, Yashiro gradually rose from post to post inside Exxon's Asian operations, including a seven-year stint in Houston. As he flitted back and forth across the Pacific, he became adept at juggling the radical differences he saw between American and Japanese business culture, such as the contrasting attitudes toward legal contracts. Another difference was that Americans placed a heavy emphasis on making profits—no matter what. Along the way, Yashiro also became adept at fighting with Japan's bureaucracy. As an American group, Exxon was hobbled by numerous restrictions in Japan, and from the 1960s onward Yashiro was locked in endless skirmishes with the Petroleum Division at the mighty

Ministry of International Trade and Industry, trying to win equal treatment for non-Japanese groups. The wearing battles left Yashiro convinced that one of the worst features of the Japanese economy was its bureaucracy; in his eyes, there was absolutely no reason for government to control the corporate world.

By the time he retired from Exxon in 1989 at the age of sixty, Yashiro was a prominent member of Tokyo's business community, although still too much of a loose cannon to have broken into the very inner citadel of the corporate elite. He was not ready to stop working. Harvard Business School offered him a post as a lecturer—but he turned it down. Then Yashiro bumped into John Reed, who was then the head of the American bank Citibank—and Reed hired him to run retail banking in Japan. "Reed said to me, 'We want to open consumer banking in Japan,' " Yashiro later recalled. "So I said, 'What, you mean selling consumer banking services like selling gasoline?' "

It was the start of an unlikely friendship. Yashiro was more than ten years older than Reed. But since Yashiro was completely new to banking, he looked up to the American as a teacher, or *sensei*. Reed, for his part, was delighted to cultivate Yashiro as a quasi "protégé," since it provided him with a loyal guide and "fixer" in the mysterious world of Japanese banks. The bond between Reed and Yashiro was reinforced by the fact that Citibank was going through tumultuous times. In 1991, Citibank recorded a record loss due to a huge overhang of bad loans and seemed to be on the verge of collapse. Reed managed to turn the bank's fortunes around by implementing a savage restructuring package, with the close collaboration of his global managers, such as Yashiro. The experience left Yashiro impressed by Reed's leadership skills and convinced that the key to being an effective manager was to take firm, bold decisions.

"Yash and I have become older and wiser together over the years," Reed later explained. He always called his friend Yash. Indeed, during their long friendship, the Reed family as a whole had come to know Yashiro's wife and children well, and whenever he traveled to Tokyo to see Yashiro, Reed took his wife Cindy along as well. "We went through the crisis at Citigroup together and the thing I have always loved about Yash is that he sees the big picture. A lot of people are too immature for that. But with Yash I could always share things that I was worried about. So for years and years we have been dealing together with problems that don't always have obvious answers. He is a fascinating character, perhaps one of the few people who can bridge the Japanese and American worlds.

"But Yash never forgets that he is also very *Japanese,* just as deep down I am an *American,*" Reed carefully added. "Ultimately, Yash loyalties are clearly to Japan."

In 1997, at the age of sixty-eight, Yashiro retired for the second time. He had more than earned a rest. During his eight-year period at Citibank, he had built a thriving retail business in Japan that was easily the most successful consumer banking enterprise of its type. He had achieved this by ruthless cost-control, clever marketing, and introducing innovations, such as twenty-four-hour ATM machines. By the standards of Japanese—and even many Americans—Yashiro's management style was unusually forceful. "He could act like a little dictator at times," one of his former American colleagues observed. Or as Reed explained, more tactfully: "Yash has a directive management style. When we were in Citigroup we would agree what to do and he would get the plan done, in a distinctly Japanese way. It was quite invisible to us Westerners what was going on. He surrounds himself with his own people. It is a very personal way of working."

Reed himself claimed this reflected a particularly "Japanese" approach to management. It was perhaps more accurate, however, to describe this as *one* strand of Japanese culture. On a day-to-day basis, most Japanese subscribe to the ideal of consensus decision making. But on the rare occasions when leaders try to break out of this mold, they often go to the other extreme—and become distinctly authoritarian, precisely because they are unchallenged. In Yashiro's case, this authoritarian streak was usually tempered by his charm and multicultural approach. He prided himself on always trying to learn from the opinions of others, irrespective of age, race, or gender. Yet, he made no secret of his frustration with Japan's consensus-driven business culture. And when these frustrations boiled over, a self-righteous streak sometimes emerged that startled some of his colleagues.

Reed did not worry about such foibles; he was simply grateful to have found a Japanese manager who could produce results. And these were stunning: When Yashiro took over the American bank's tiny consumer business in Japan, it was losing $30 million a year; by the time he left, he had transformed it into a business that was earning $100 million in profits. By the benchmark of banking that mattered in Wall Street, in other words, Yashiro was a great success.

After a flurry of farewell parties Yashiro moved to London. One of his beloved daughters had married an English banker and Yashiro wanted to live close to his grandchildren. He based himself in a pleasant apartment in the district of Kensington, near Hyde Park, and spent his days visiting art museums and giving the odd lecture at the London School of Economics. "It was a pleasant life. I was quite happy, walking in the park and that sort of thing!" And yet Yashiro remained restless. So Reed was not at all surprised when Yashiro announced that he wanted to start a *third* career, working with Ripplewood. And when Yashiro—true to form—asked Reed's advice about the move, the American encouraged him to go back to work. "I recognized that for Yash to do something for Japan was fulfilling . . . probably more fulfilling than messing around with history classes in England," Reed explained. "Yash has a real sense of duty. He is like a hero, perhaps a Greek hero sometimes. And I think he felt that he was one of the few people in Japan who was able to bridge the Japanese and American worlds."

However, the events that actually propelled Yashiro into the seat of Shinsei president did not quite turn out as he had expected. When he had first agreed to help Collins, Yashiro had expected to run an *industrial* restructuring fund, in a part-time job, rather than become involved with a bank. "I thought I could live in London and travel back and forth," he later said of his plans to work at Ripplewood. "Then when my daughter moved to Hong Kong I thought I would be based there and get involved with Collins's private equity thing on the side."

Indeed, when Collins and Flowers started looking at LTCB, Yashiro was distinctly lukewarm about the idea. During the years that he had worked at Citibank, Yashiro had had endless opportunity to observe LTCB at close quarters and he believed that the long-term credit banks were trapped in a dying franchise, given that interest rates in Japan were so low and the country stuffed with troubled borrowers and banks. "[At first] I did not see much future for LTCB," he admitted. But he poured through the prospectus for LTCB, and gradually changed his mind. Although the traditional LTCB business of lending had no future, the bank had two potentially interesting assets. One was a large pool of employees. The second was a highly valuable web of relationships with corporate borrowers, regional banks, and other financial institutions across Japan, of the type that no foreign bank could ever hope to create. And this, in Yashiro's eyes, created an exciting opportunity. He was convinced that as time passed, Japanese companies and consumers would start to demand more sophisticated financial services. He also believed that Japanese banks were ill-equipped to offer these new services—and though the foreign banks could provide these skills, they lacked the contacts to sell them. So if he could find a way to marry LTCB's Japanese relationships with international-standard products, he would have a winning formula. It was exactly the same logic that had attracted the Swiss bankers to LTCB two years earlier.

In practice, Yashiro and the Shinsei investors believed that this implied a three-pronged strategy. Yashiro knew that he could not afford to jettison the traditional lending business since it was these loans that created the all-important relationships. Somehow this lending needed to be maintained, even if it was not a profitable business. But Yashiro wanted to use these links to sell a new range of higher-margin products, such as asset management and investment banking services. And by offering these new services, he hoped that the bank might offset the low profitability of the traditional corporate lending business. "Perhaps it is easiest to imagine the bank like a plane," he liked to say. "The fuselage is the business we have done since the old times [making corporate loans], with the right wing being the retail banking and the left wing investment banking. We would not be able to fly unless we attached them to the wings. All the parts fit together."

Of course, this model would only be viable if LTCB could find a way to make the corporate lending business vaguely solvent. If the loan book ended up incurring massive losses, then no amount of higher earnings from investment banking or retail banking would ever be able to make the bank "fly."

In the autumn of 1999—or just as Ripplewood was winning the bid—

Yashiro finally agreed to become CEO of the new bank. Nobody else seemed as well qualified to run the new bank and he was becoming increasingly excited about the whole idea of creating a new model of banking in Japan. During his years at Exxon and Citibank, he had become convinced that the only way to overcome the stagnation in Japan's economy was to create a more entrepreneurial, competitive, risk-taking spirit in the corporate world. Somehow Japanese businessmen had to stop being so timid and reliant on government. Yashiro also believed that it was time for the banks to stop believing that they were somehow "special." Why, he fumed, should banking be so protected from global pressures when so many other parts of Japanese industry—including the oil sector—had already been forced to adapt to global competition and international economic swings. "Back in 1995 the heads of most Japanese banks rather confidently said that they had put the bad loan problem behind them," Yashiro fumed. "And what has happened?"

That did not mean, Yashiro stressed, that he blamed the individual bankers for the financial mess; he blamed the system. "Sorting out good and bad companies is very difficult for Japanese businesses to do, partly because they have traditionally looked on their subsidiaries as children, but also because businesses are not used to segment analysis and looking at how capital is deployed and returns on capital. I learned how to analyze the use of capital forty-five years ago after I joined Exxon's Japanese affiliate. But most Japanese businessmen did not." Indeed, Yashiro was well acquainted with many of the bank presidents and he knew Onogi and the other former LTCB bankers quite well. Back in the early 1990s, Yashiro sometimes took Reed to meet the LTCB bankers or hosted dinners for them all. In the autumn of 1997, Onogi had even held a little retirement lunch party for Yashiro up on the twentieth floor of LTCB to say "thank you" for years of close cooperation between LTCB and Citibank. At that lunch Onogi had asked Yashiro how Citibank had extracted itself from its bad loan problems in the early 1990s and two men had discussed how much they both loved England. "Onogi is a *nice* man, a very nice man," Yashiro always said, with defiant emphasis. The two men were close in age.

Yet now that Yashiro was sitting in Onogi's old chair, he believed that Japan needed more than a "nice" approach to banking. "Nice" policies might have worked back in the immediate postwar years, when the Japanese were working together in harmony, pursuing a common goal, or in the 1980s when the economy was booming, money was plentiful, and life was easy. But now Yashiro believed that Japan's bankers had to get tough; they had to make hard decisions; they had to fight. Above all else, Yashiro believed that it was time to treat banking as a *business*, not a public service.

Could a Japanese bank president actually do that? At the Japanese car company Nissan, the Brazilian born manager Carlos Ghosn was also trying to revive a shattered company. What Yashiro was pledging was potentially even more ambitious than what Ghosn had promised. At Nissan, Ghosn was primarily seeking to make Nissan better run; Yashiro wanted to not only make his bank more efficient, but also to change the entire concept of what a bank was about. He knew that it was a tough mission. Yet Yashiro also knew that he had considerable advantages. When mavericks at LTCB had called for change, they had always been squashed because they were isolated. Yashiro, by contrast, had his investors behind him, who were demanding radical reform with an urgency that reflected their financial incentives. And Yashiro believed the *gaijin* affiliation of LTCB could make change more acceptable. Japan had a long history of letting foreigners get away with practices too shocking for a Japanese group to perform, and Yashiro knew that some reformers in the Japanese government had decided to sell the bank to Ripplewood precisely because they thought that only a group of empowered foreigners stood much chance of breaking the mold.

Yet, the one thing that Yashiro did *not* think he was trying to do was to build an American bank. On the contrary, the very suggestion made him cross. To the outside world, Shinsei was often described as an "American" venture, since it had been launched by investors such as Collins. However, in Yashiro's eyes, it was not really "American" at all. Or, more precisely, though men such as Collins had been a catalyst for the entire venture, Yashiro believed that the next stage of the Shinsei project was about competing *Japanese* visions of change. What Yashiro wanted to do—with the Americans' backing—was build a new vision of banking that was different from the old convoy system, but also *Japanese*. "I never felt this was an American bank or that I wanted to make this an American bank," Yashiro later explained. "When I arrived I knew that we could not follow an American model but we could not follow the old Japanese model either. So we had to create something *new*—a new way of being a Japanese bank. That was my hope."

A few weeks after Yashiro sent his email to the bank staff celebrating the launch of Shinsei, he also paid a visit to a shrine next to the old headquarters of LTCB, over in the Tokyo district of Otemachi. It was dedicated to Masakado, the samurai who had lost his head nine centuries earlier. Like most Japanese, Yashiro had a highly pragmatic approach to the spiritual world, cheerfully observing some *shinto* and Buddhist rituals. So when he heard the legend of Masakado, he decided that there was no point in needlessly risking the wrath of a headless samurai ghost. He left some money on Masakado's shrine and prayed for the spirit's blessing to help him in his momentous challenge of reforming Shinsei, and creating a bank that was Japanese—but in a new way. He reckoned he would need all the help he could get.

— *Chapter 14* —

CULTURE CLASH

These days I feel like one leg is in the old-LTCB, but the other leg—or the other half of my body—is in Shinsei management! Sometimes it is like being pulled in two.

—Hidebumi Mori, Senior Managing Director, Shinsei Bank

As Yashiro settled into his new office on the nineteenth floor, the bank staff nervously wondered what would happen next. About 2,000 former LTCB employees—or two-thirds of the staff—had stayed on at the bank, demoralized and defeated, but glued to their places by intense bonds of mutual loyalty. During 1999 wild rumors had regularly swept the bank that Ripplewood was about to unleash some dreadful things, including sacking workers. The speculation became even more intense when a local television station screened a fictional drama about a Japanese company taken over by foreigners, which showed women in senior management roles—bossing men around. "We all watched that program and talked about it," confessed Takei Tamiwa, a former LTCB "office lady." "I wondered if that would happen to us as well—a company with a woman in such a leadership job! It was a very shocking TV program."

Most of the staff had little real idea what to expect, however, since nothing like Ripplewood had ever been seen before in Japan's banking world. So, as they waited they feared for the worst, but tried to hope for the best; they were ready to give Yashiro a chance.

It did not take long for the shocks to start. A few days after he arrived, Yashiro announced to the staff that he planned to attack two of the most hallowed pillars of the Japanese corporate world: the planning and human resources departments. To build a modern bank, Yashiro believed he needed to change not only the strategy but also the corporate culture. The old LTCB—like almost every other large Japanese company—had been a homogeneous and hierarchical place, where rank and salary was largely decided by age. Bankers had traditionally been assigned to their roles by a centralized human relations department, which rotated the staff every two to three years, creating a culture of generalists. Moreover, the direction of business strategy had been set by a centralized planning department, which created policies based on what the bank wanted to offer—rather than what customers demanded.

Yashiro, backed by the Shinsei investors, wanted to create a flat, decentralized organization, where business development was driven by the needs of customers. So he effectively abolished the corporate planning department and emasculated the human relations department; in the new bank, staff would be appointed to positions on the basis of merit, rather than age, and each department would be encouraged to develop its own team. Then Yashiro attacked two more taboos. Two hundred new specialist outsiders were hired, including Americans, Indians, Chinese, and Koreans, marking the biggest single incursion of "outsiders" that Japanese banks had ever seen. The old rigid boundaries between female clerical clerks—or so-called "office ladies"—and the male bankers were also eliminated. For the first time in any Japanese bank, Yashiro declared, all women would be allowed to apply for managerial jobs, if they wanted. "Just like the television drama!" Tamiwa noted, with awe. She, at least, was impressed. She was doubly amazed when she herself was appointed to a management job a year later; that was something she had never, ever dreamed of seeing in her lifetime.

In the early summer, Yashiro summoned the bank's chief financial controller to his office. He knew he needed an effective flow of information. So a good place to start his reforms was with the data systems.

"Did we make money last month?" he asked the controller, one of the former LTCB bankers who had stayed on at the new Shinsei bank.

"We don't know," the controller replied.

"Why don't you know?"

The controller explained that when the bank was called LTCB it had never attempted to collect profit and loss data on a monthly basis, since it only ever looked at the figures every six months. That was the usual practice in Japan. Since the corporate planning department drew up business plans on a five-*yearly* basis, nobody saw the need for monthly data.

"Can you give me your best guesstimate?" Yashiro asked. A few days later the controller complied, with a number for profits in April.

"What's the confidence level in this number?" Yashiro asked.

"Maybe twenty percent, or thirty percent, up or down," the hapless official replied.

Yashiro was appalled. "We have got to know where we are making money!" he bellowed in frustration. "What products with which customers, how much and what risk we are incurring!"

Then Yashiro tossed the problem over to two senior Indian executives he had just hired to work at Shinsei. Both men already had long experience of managing information systems at banks. Equally importantly, both men had known Yashiro well since his Citigroup days. In the 1990s, the American bank had employed a large number of Indian systems experts in the bank's global operations (a group sometimes called the "Indian mafia"), and Yashiro got on unusually well with these Indians. When word later leaked out that he was recruiting for Shinsei, three of them secretly approached Yashiro. One was Dvivedi—known as "Jay" to his friends—who had run the IT operations for Citigroup in Tokyo, New York, and Singapore. Another was Sajeeve Thomas, former treasurer of Citigroup in Tokyo and latterly head of risk management at the global corporate division. The third was Janak Raj, a skilled operations man who had been working for Citigroup for twenty-five years.

When the Citigroup executives found out that the Indians were planning to desert, they were furious, particularly since the Indians were threatening to take their entire teams as well. Deryck Maughan, the international chairman of Citigroup, called Tim Collins to complain and faxed a list of the men who Yashiro had "poached." "This has got to stop!" Maughan declared. He felt doubly irritated, since back in 1999 Maughan had lobbied on Ripplewood's behalf, to help it buy the bank. Yashiro tartly replied that he was *not* poaching the Indians.

Either way, the talented systems men provided an important boost for Yashiro. He had always preferred to work with respectful acolytes, and his team of Indians offered a level of loyalty that was unusual in the international banking world. "When I worked with Yashiro-san [at Citibank] I realized that he is truly one of the most extraordinary men I have ever met," said Dvivedi, explaining why he had moved across to Shinsei. "He is a very powerful blend of Japanese thinking and American experience—he thinks long term."

Thomas and Dvivedi set to work, trying to put Yashiro's orders into practice. Dvivedi's first task was to get the information technology systems up to speed. In the past, LTCB—like other Japanese banks—had run its IT operations on "mainframe" systems, managed by a closely linked subsidiary of the bank. The computers themselves were always bought from Fujitsu, a traditional borrower from LTCB. The system was fifteen years old and the bank maintained two expensive old computer networks, one of which was used for exchanging data and the other for accounting. The two systems could not talk to each other and could not offer real-time analysis. Worse, customer accounts were processed branch by branch, meaning that there was no central database. "This was the type of system that American banks had twenty years ago," Yashiro declared.

The usual technique to change such a system was to replace an old mainframe with a new one. But as Dvivedi looked at the problem, he developed a grander plan to discard the mainframe *completely*. Indian software developers had recently linked lots of small pieces of software into one large matrix via the Windows operating system. Flexcube, an Indian company partly owned by Citigroup, was at the forefront of this development and Dvivedi believed their system would be cheaper and faster to introduce since much of the work could be subcontracted to Indian software specialists. "In every sense," Dvivedi later explained, "this made more sense."

Dvivedi took over a large "planning space" on the fifth floor of the bank's headquarters and called a meeting to announce his plans to the former LTCB bankers. They were appalled. No large company in Tokyo had ever tried to abandon a mainframe system before, or been bold enough to change an entire computer system in just a few months: the normal time frame for change was *years*. More shocking still, no large bank had hired outsiders to install the systems. The final straw came when Dvivedi coolly told the former LTCB staff that he planned to bring new teams of Indians into the bank. "In the beginning we had lots of problems because the foreigner and Japanese didn't understand each other at all," said Michiyuki Okano, an IT manager at Shinsei.

There was a subtler cultural problem, too. Back in the old days of LTCB, the senior managers had generally not attempted to implement a policy by simply issuing orders. Instead, the usual pattern was to execute policies by *nemawashi*, or the traditional Japanese process whereby a middle manager would create a consensus in an organization *before* implementing any action, by lots of private debate and discussion. This process gave considerable power to middle managers. "In the past what happened was that the senior managers heard our opinion, and then it was presumed to be OK for us to do it," Okano said. "Of course the managers showed the goal for us, but after the former management had shown up this goal, the middle and junior people would create a report based on their discussion, which might be different from what the management thought."

It was now clear that Yashiro had no intention of running Shinsei like a democracy. Nor did Dvivedi. After he received his orders from Yashiro, Dvivedi then issued orders to his staff. Sometimes, to save time, he did this via the Indian subcontractors.

The Japanese dispatched delegations to Yashiro's office to complain. Dvivedi tried to make amends. He convened face-to-face chats with the staff members, in small groups—complete with cookies and chips—to explain his IT dream. Dvivedi hoped that the snacks would help them relax.

The move backfired. Although they were used to going out drinking with colleagues in the evening outside the bank, the former LTCB bankers had never encountered the idea of talking about business while also eating in an *office*. "We are not accustomed to eat such snacks at a business meeting," Hidehiko Arakawa, general manager in the operations department, explained. "Therefore we tend to say 'no' when they are offered. I know foreigners do such things. But it makes us uncomfortable." Then Yashiro started attending some of the meetings himself. That shocked the staff even more than the cookies; senior bank managers had never appeared without warning back in the LTCB days. "Yashiro-san appears everywhere, even when we least expect it!" explained Arakawa. "Sometimes the junior staff will be meeting and Yashiro will suddenly appear, find out what they are talking about, and express his views and agenda on the spot. We have witnessed that several times and it is absolutely amazing—he says things without prior planning!"

The biggest shock of all was the arrival of the Indians. Men such as Arakawa had never traveled outside Japan in their entire life, let alone *worked* with foreigners. But by the autumn of 2000, several hundred Indians were roaming the bank buildings. These Indians spoke little or no Japanese and though the Japanese tried to communicate with them in English, they found it difficult to understand the English the Indians spoke. In an attempt to be friendly, some of the LTCB staff pointed out that their canteen served "curry rice," the Japanese fast-food dish named after "curry" (though it bore little resemblance to the Indian dish). But the Indians refused to eat it. "They thought our curry rice was horrible!" Arakawa explained. "We learnt that they were vegetarian, so they had to be careful about what they ate."

On the fifth floor of the bank headquarters, next to Dvivedi's IT revolution, a second cultural experiment was also under way. This aimed to create a new retail bank and it was a mission particularly dear to Yashiro's heart, given his past triumph at Citibank. During the postwar years, consumers had been encouraged to leave the vast majority of their savings in bank deposits, which paid virtually no interest. And though consumers had briefly become more adventurous in the 1980s, when the stock market crashed, households rushed back to bank deposits, that on average paid a mere 0.03 percent interest a year. "If you put Y1 million into a bank and left it there for a year, at the end you would only have Y340 interest—not even enough for two bus tickets!" Yashiro liked to say. "Consumers are so badly served in Japan, that there is a mass of opportunity!"

The other major Japanese banks, such as Bank of Tokyo Mitsubishi, already had enormous retail banking operations. But LTCB did not have a retail base. Although nearly 200,000 households owned its debentures, they had bought these in an anonymous manner and the bank had no data about clients. Moreover, the former LTCB bankers had never been trained to deal with customers, since most of the male bankers disdained retail banking. "The entrance of the lavish headquarters was more like a mausoleum than a retail bank. [On] my first day at the bank I walked in at three P.M. one day in March through the empty lobby, that vast glass atrium," Thomas later explained. "I thought: Boy, how can you have a bank with an empty lobby?"

And still Yashiro was undeterred. He reasoned that in the age of the internet, physical branches were less important. The other banks were not offering a good service to consumers, no matter what their size. Moreover, he believed that the old LTCB bankers could be *retrained*. So Thomas and Satoru Katayama, a former LTCB manager, assembled a 100-strong team, drawn from the ranks of the old LTCB staff, to act as the basis for a new retail bank workforce. "We wanted people who could think," Thomas explained. "We kept insisting that we wanted women. Initially none of the branch managers wanted to send any women at all, but Yashiro insisted on it. In this country women control a lot of financial decisions."

The bankers were divided into groups, and asked to write down how they thought a retail bank should operate, nominate companies they admired for customer services, and discuss how Shinsei could copy them. One admired model was Starbucks, the American coffee shop chain that had taken Japan by storm in the previous few years. Other popular choices were 7-Eleven, Uniqlo, a Japanese clothing store, and Sony, the electronics group. On the basis of this debate, the bankers then proposed four new themes for the retail bank: Empowerment; A Unique Identity; Accessibility; and Fun.

All of these themes seemed alien to Japanese banks. Traditionally, when customers visited a Japanese bank they were greeted by rows of desks, behind which bankers sat counting money or shuffling forms. Thomas decided to abolish this. He remodeled the branches to look like showrooms, with the branch manager standing at the front of the office to welcome new clients, and hired an American design company, which normally specialized in producing plans for shopping malls, to create new interiors for the bank's branches, and logos.

Then he set to work tackling the hardest task of all—changing the way that the old LTCB bankers operated. "One of our biggest challenges was that people believed that the old rules had to stay in the new business," Thomas said. "Traditionally if you came to the bank and deposited Y2 million, for example, the bank staff would count it, and hand it to someone else at the back who could also count it, and then probably hand it to someone else again. That is OK if you have all day. But we didn't. So we had to change the rules. But how do you tell a general manager who had been here for fifteen years to let someone who has just arrived at the bank receive Y2 million? That was a challenge."

In the investment banking division, there was an even bigger cultural battle under way. Yashiro's corporate strategy for Shinsei was predicated on the assumption that the bank would retain most of the old LTCB lending relationships—which covered some 5,000 companies and 900 financial institutions—and use that to sell more sophisticated, higher margin services. It looked like a brilliant idea on paper, if the bank had three things: a team known as "relationship managers" who could maintain the old corporate relations; a group of bankers familiar with the new financial services, or "product" specialists; and—most important of all—a system that would force both teams to work together, happily.

The bank was already full of people who could act as relationship managers, but there was a shortage of product specialists. The former LTCB bankers who had stayed on to work at Shinsei were overwhelmingly those who had previously worked on the *domestic* wing of the bank and most of those LTCB bankers who understood capital markets had left, since they were attractive "catches" for foreign banks. To fill this gap, the

Shinsei investors hoped to hire product specialists from outside the bank. They knew that they could not hope to attract outside employees to the bank if they offered the traditional Japanese pay system, since salary levels had traditionally been far lower than a Wall Street bank would pay. So early in the process, they decided to create two distinctly different salary systems. One system was used for old LTCB bankers, and offered a job for life but a relatively low salary. The second system, which was used for outsiders, offered short contracts with less job security—but the potential for large remuneration via a bonus, like a Wall Street bank. The first set of employees was known as "Ps" ("permanent staff"); the second "Ms" ("market hires"—though some Japanese sourly labeled these "mercenaries" instead).

Flowers had led the search for suitable investment bankers, offering lucrative pay packages as an incentive. One early catch was Brian Prince, the former head of Lehman Brothers distressed debt team in Tokyo. Prince brought the rest of his team from Lehman Brothers with him. Prince took the leap because of the pay packet and the logic of Ripplewood's arrangement. At an American bank such as Lehman Brothers, it had been difficult to build a large-scale distressed-debt business, because foreigners had access to only a small pool of distressed assets in Japan. Shinsei's web of contacts could potentially yield a significant harvest. Prince then telephoned a friend, Robert Sheehy, a genial American who ran a securitization team at Bear, Stearns. "Why don't you come over?" Prince asked. Sheehy agreed and pulled over his team as well. "The frustration of working at a foreign bank in Japan is that it doesn't have an extensive client list," Sheehy later explained. "Here we have the clients and more balance sheet than a foreign bank would have and we have the technical competence."

With these two teams on board, plus a motley selection of other bankers, Shinsei had the kernel of an investment bank. So the bankers started to sniff around for deals in distressed debt or financial engineering. LTCB's old clients were stuffed with distressed assets that they needed to off-load and many were also keen to find ways to raise funds or sell assets, which made them natural candidates to buy capital market products, particularly as an alternative to regular loans.

Prince and the other senior managers set to work trying to create these synergies. But it proved fiendishly difficult to get the product specialists and relationship managers to work together. The new design of the bank placed the product specialists on the fourteenth and sixteenth floors of the Shinsei headquarters. But the relationship managers sat on a different floor and the two groups almost never voluntarily visited each other. This partly reflected an ideological gap. To the product specialists, such as Prince and Sheehy, it appeared to be overwhelmingly obvious that Japan needed to move away from indirect finance to direct finance. But the former LTCB bankers had spent their entire careers making corporate loans. They did not understand the new products and did not think their clients really needed them.

There was also a cultural chasm. The relationship managers were mostly Japanese men, who spoke limited English. Prince and some of the other investment bankers spoke limited Japanese. They were used to a brash, aggressive style of working, where bankers debated with each other in an open, frank manner about how to do deals. "All these Americans seemed terribly short-term in their thinking. They just talked about profits and were terribly rude," one Japanese relationship manager later admitted. The distinctions between the pay scales caused added resentment. "It felt like a caste system was developing," one middle-aged Japanese manager grumbled. "At the top were the foreign investors, then the foreign managers at Shinsei, then the Japanese who had been hired from outside, and then us." They were doubly piqued when the bank introduced "swipe cards" to improve security at the bank; though common on Wall Street, it made a mockery of the hallowed idea that companies such as LTCB were "families." "The new investors show they don't trust us. I want to throw away my swipe card," one grumbled. "I hate, hate, *hate* it!"

The Americans found dealing with the Japanese staff equally frustrating and baffling. To them, the former LTCB bankers seemed frustratingly passive and risk-averse. Worse, the former LTCB staff rarely volunteered opinions. For men such as Prince, this was deeply irritating. He was an emotional, passionate man, who had spent much of his career on Wall Street and joined Shinsei because he believed it could offer interesting business opportunities. But day after day, his proposals would be met with just a polite bow; nobody would "bat ideas around" with him. After a few months of working at the bank, Prince noticed that he had become obsessively talkative when he saw his wife in the evenings. It was the only way he could cope with the baffling daytime silences at Shinsei.

In the late spring of 2001, Yashiro was finally ready to open his new retail bank. It seemed a stunning triumph of project management. When Dvivedi had first announced his plans, nobody had believed he could change an IT system in just eight months. But by the spring of 2001, the new system was in place, at a cost of only Y6 billion ($60 million), about a tenth of what Japanese banks usually spent. These dramatic savings came by using the Indian "Flexcube" system and buying cheap computers from the American computer group Dell, instead of using Fujitsu, a "traditional" partner of LTCB. And the switch had gone *so* smoothly that it had even converted some of the former LTCB workers to the idea of reform. "In a typical Japanese corporation," Okano, the IT manager, later recalled, "the idea that you could change something in a month would be impossible. So when we were told things were changing, we could not believe that it could be done that fast! But instead of receiving excuses of why we cannot do it, we got notice up front of when it would happen; division by division we got a list of the dates. When we saw the new PCs arrive on our desks, it was the first real sign for the staff that the new management would be different."

Yashiro's consumer bank also looked impressive. The branches were full of innovative features such as internet banking that allowed consumers to access a whole range of financial services by using a single software program. Although standard in American consumer banks, none of the other Japanese banks were able to provide this service. Better still, the new branches provided tangible evidence of change. In the old days, the 100-foot-high entrance to the LTCB had been as deserted as a mausoleum, decked out in gray walls, glass ceilings, and white marble. The staff was forbidden to enter the building through it, in case they messed up the sense of "order." But by the early summer of 2001 it had turned into a riot of color. The staff had been ordered to use the entrance to create a "buzz" of people, and Thomas's team had placed an enormous Bloomberg terminal in the atrium and a dazzling orange, red, and blue 50-foot picture of a man, reaching triumphantly to the sun. Next to it stood a banner that summed up the message that Yashiro wanted to proclaim: *Welcome to a whole new world of banking!* A few months later, a Starbucks coffee stall was installed as well as a Yahoo! internet café.

Yet, as Yashiro looked at his new lobby, with its joyous burst of color and life, he did not feel particularly triumphant. On the contrary, although these glossy signs of "success" were striking, they still seemed dangerously cosmetic. Away from the retail bank, a much darker tale had also been unfolding in Shinsei during the first year that could potentially undo everything Yashiro seemed to have achieved.

The same issue that had proved to be the undoing of Onogi and so much of Japan's financial world was still bubbling—what to do about the bad loans.

— *Chapter 15* —

THE SOGO SHOCK

Now, with Shinsei, Japanese people have seen the predatory face of capitalism—a type of capitalism that lives by the law of the jungle.

—Banri Kaieda, DPJ politician, talking to local journalists

"Sogo has just come to us asking for debt forgiveness!" A banker came running to Yashiro in the early summer of 2000. It was just a few weeks after he had arrived at the bank, brimming with optimism about his plans to create a new banking model. Nervously, the banker explained that the retailer Sogo had just asked Shinsei to cancel Y98 billion ($980 million) in loans, or about half of the total Y205 billion outstanding with the company. "What shall we do?"

Yashiro pondered his options. He knew that if LTCB had received such a request, it would have immediately agreed. Sogo was one of the most prestigious retailers in Japan. It had a 170-year history and a clutch of high profile stores including at Number One Rodeo Drive in Beverly Hills. Since Sogo was also a long-standing client of LTCB, Shinsei was considered a quasi "parent" of the company, along with IBJ. The request for debt forgiveness was part of a larger IBJ-orchestrated restructuring plan that had seventy-three banks forgiving Y630 billion ($6.3 billion) of Sogo's outstanding Y1.9 trillion ($19 billion) in debts. A refusal by Shinsei could trigger Sogo's collapse—which in turn could create losses at the *other* banks. In traditional Japanese thinking, to refuse would be utterly "selfish."

Yet the IBJ "restructuring" plan also epitomized everything Yashiro disliked most about the traditional banking world. Japanese bankers had known for years that Sogo was effectively bankrupt. During the 1980s bubble, the retailer—like many in Japan—had expanded its operations with giddy haste, borrowing almost Y2 trillion ($20 billion) to purchase overpriced real estate in Japan and overseas. Since the early 1990s, the value of its real estate had declined by Y100 billion ($1 billion) a year, and sales were poor. IBJ and LTCB had become so uneasy that back in 1993 they dispatched their own officials to help run Sogo. Still, both banks continued to pour loans into the group, to prop it up, sometimes offering funds simply on the name of the Sogo president, Hiroo Mizushima. "I am living collateral for these loans!" Mizushima used to declare.

What most appalled Yashiro was that this forbearance had continued even *after* LTCB fell under state control. By 1999, it was clear the retailer could never repay its debts. But when the FSA had conducted its audit of the LTCB loans in early 1999, it labeled the Sogo loans as almost normal. Ripplewood subsequently challenged the classification but the FSA refused to reassess the loans. Instead, the bureaucrats quietly agreed to give the bank an extra Y100 billion of provisions to keep the Sogo loans on its books. This made a mockery of the FSA's own rules, since "near normal" loans were not supposed to need such a high level of provisions.

The request for debt forgiveness put Yashiro in a bind. He did not want to signal to the rest of the world that he was going to be a soft touch. In theory, if Shinsei agreed to the debt forgiveness scheme, this would simply "use up" the Y100 billion of reserves than the FSA had already furtively given the bank for the Sogo loan—meaning that the bank would not suffer an immediate loss. But this would still leave Y100 billion of Sogo loans on Shinsei's books that would need new reserves. A prudent calculation suggested the reserves should be about Y28 billion, about the same level as the bank's net profits for that year. "If we make reserves for Sogo," Yashiro concluded, "we wipe out our profit for this year."

Worse still, the rules of the sale contract between Ripplewood and the FSA stipulated that Shinsei could not return loans to the government if the loans had been extended to companies that Shinsei had also given debt forgiveness. If Shinsei agreed to the IBJ request, it lost insurance on the remaining Sogo loans.

Yashiro decided to stand up to the status quo. On June 28, Shinsei informed the Financial Reconstruction Commission that it would refuse to extend debt forgiveness to Sogo. "We cannot continue to make loans to companies with a high risk involved," Yashiro explained. "If I carry on doing business in the old way, this bank would go bankrupt again." Then he exercised the "put" option for the first time, returning the Y205 billion Sogo loans to the government, together with the Y100 billion in reserves. He hoped it was a clean way out. The staff at Shinsei presumed that once the loan was back in the government's hands, the government *itself* would extend the debt forgiveness—effectively taking Shinsei off the hook.

Two days later, the FRC secretly convened a meeting at the Bank of Japan. The FRC had known ever since it agreed to the sales contract with Ripplewood that Yashiro would have the right to return bad loans. Many FRC members had also known that Shinsei's books were riddled with troubled borrowers. Still they had optimistically hoped that the economy would recover, or presumed that if the loans *did* turn sour, then Yashiro would refrain from doing anything tough, since that would be "un-Japanese."

Now, however, Yashiro had tossed the problem back into the government's lap, in a particularly uncomfortable manner. It did not take long for the committee to decide to save Sogo. The FSA bureaucrats were vehemently opposed to letting Sogo collapse, since the losses on the loans would create problems for IBJ and other banks. The retailer also employed nearly 10,000 people, with a further 40,000 employed in the 10,000 small companies that supplied Sogo. The bureaucrats insisted that Sogo's core business would pick up when the economy recovered. "Eventually Sogo should be able to repay the remaining debts," the FSA bureaucrats declared, with their usual optimism that economic salvation was around the corner.

Thus far, events seemed to be going as Yashiro and the Shinsei investors had expected. But then news about Yashiro's bold move dribbled into the Japanese press. In normal circumstances, it might have attracted little criticism. But just a week earlier, in late June, the ruling Liberal Democratic Party had suffered a severe loss in the Lower House parliamentary elections. The LDP had still managed to hang on to power but the opposition Democratic Party of Japan was feeling unusually confident—and looking for opportunities to embarrass the government.

Sogo was perfect ammunition. Mizushima, the honorary chairman of Sogo, was a rotund, shady character, who had murky links to the LDP, partly through IBJ. He had also once been a close "friend" of Yoshio Kodama, the right-wing postwar politician who was tightly linked to the *yakuza*. Indeed, Kodama had once given Mizushima a twenty-carat diamond to express his gratitude for mysterious "favors."

"Why is the government rescuing a man such as Mizushima with public money?" the head of the DPJ, Yukio Hatoyama, asked rhetorically. "Is this a good use of public funds? This rescue scheme for Sogo is a shameful example of the worst type of nepotistic back-scratching!" The newspapers echoed this line. "This FRC decision is far from an acceptable plan," the *Asahi* newspaper solemnly declared in an editorial: "The government must reconsider the loan write-off plan, along with Sogo's overall rescue plan that the IBJ has prepared. The trustworthiness of the rescue plan is not known. . . . It should not be forgotten that as much as Y3.6 trillion of public money has already been spent to cover the liabilities of LTCB. The government's haste in putting the matter behind it [with the Sogo decision] looks as if it is trying to sweep something shady under the rug."

More embarrassing details about Mizushima and Sogo tumbled out. It emerged that the banker LTCB had sent to monitor Sogo's finances had recently committed suicide. It also came out that Mizushima had received a Y4.4 billion ($44 million) salary from Sogo during the previous decade. Though unremarkable by Wall Street standards, it was considered shocking inside Japan. If Sogo was bankrupt, the journalists reasoned, Mizushima should plug the gap by selling his own assets. Hadn't he promised to be the "living collateral" for the loans?

Eventually, at 4 P.M. on July 11, Shizuka Kamei, head of the LDP's powerful research council, made a telephone call to the Sogo executives. Kamei was a canny politician. In excruciatingly polite Japanese, he delivered the execution order. "Why doesn't Sogo proceed with reconstruction. Why don't you use your own strength to rebuild yourself?" The next day, Sogo's board declared that it would "voluntarily" apply for bankruptcy.

The LDP's U-turn sparked even greater political uproar. Policy makers could see that the Sogo debacle was just a foretaste of what could happen if Shinsei took the same approach to the other companies on its balance sheet. For a decade the banking system had been sustained on mutually supporting deception—and optimism that an economic recovery would eventually wipe the problems away. Shinsei could reveal that the emperor had no clothes.

The politicians angrily summoned the people they considered responsible for the mess to testify in parliament: the bureaucrats at the FSA and FRC and Yashiro himself. They also summoned the mighty American bank that had written the sales contract between Ripplewood and the FRC in the first place—Goldman Sachs.

At Goldman Sachs's offices in the Tokyo district of Akasaka, the invitation came as an unpleasant surprise. Back in 1999, winning the management of the LTCB sale seemed a great coup and Goldman had agreed to perform the work for a below-market fee, less than $10 million, just to have the marquee business. In this heady excitement, the bank never anticipated being dragged into parliament. "In retrospect, that whole LTCB deal was probably one of the worst things we ever did in Japan," a senior Goldman Sachs banker later admitted. "We didn't even cover our costs."

Even before the Sogo row erupted, there had been signs that the climate for Goldman was turning a little sour. During 1999 the bank had won a stream of lucrative advisory deals in Japan, built up a large proprietary business to acquire Japanese distressed assets, and developed a large mutual fund business, too. "Professionally this has been an extraordinary time for me, and an amazing time for Goldman Sachs!" Mark Schwartz, Asia chairman, declared at the start of the summer of 2000. "Right now Japan represents one of the most important opportunities for us globally. We have doubled our staff in the last few years . . . are likely to double our staff again in the coming years." But that blatant display of success had also made Goldman Sachs vulnerable. Japan was not a country that liked overt displays of *individual* achievement. Nor did it warm to investment banks, let alone American ones. "When I look at Goldman Sachs, I think they are very arrogant," a senior Ministry of Finance official complained in the spring of 2000. "Arrogant like Nomura was at the peak of the Japanese bubble! We in Japan don't like that."

Worse, Goldman Sachs kept fueling this resentment with its own clumsy behavior. Early in 2000 Masanori Mochida, the aggressive head of investment banking at Goldman Sachs, deeply antagonized a key female bureaucrat at the Ministry of Finance during the preparation period for a sale of shares in NTT, the government-owned telecommunications group, with his allegedly "arrogant" behavior. The Ministry responded by threatening to cut Goldman Sachs out of the deal. Then local bankers and politicians griped that the American bank was exploiting conflicts of interest, by getting involved in deals both as adviser to its clients—and as an investor. Around the same time that Goldman Sachs was arranging the sale of LTCB in 1999, it also arranged the sale of Japan Lease (a LTCB subsidiary), bought several billion dollars of liabilities held against Japan Lease (another LTCB subsidiary), and a large chunk of Nippon Landic assets (yet another affiliated group). Then, when the government announced that it wanted to sell the failed Nippon Credit Bank, Goldman Sachs popped up as the adviser to Softbank, the main company that was bidding for NCB. Cheekily, Mochida used exactly the same team of advisers for NCB as he had used at LTCB. Since the government was selling NCB with the same model that it had used to sell LTCB, this prompted accusations that Softbank had inside information on the government's stance while making its bid. Eventually, the FRC itself became so uneasy about conflicts of interest that it nervously forced Goldman Sachs to change its advisory team.

Goldman Sachs blamed the criticism on jealous carping by rivals. "There is a proverb in Japan about the nail that sticks out furthest getting hammered down," commented Henry Paulson, chairman of Goldman Sachs, by way of explanation. "The only thing that is worse than being in that [prominent] position is not being in that position."

Whatever the truth, by the summer of 2000 the Goldman Sachs bankers had absolutely no desire to head into any *more* controversy over the LTCB deal. No foreign bank had ever before been pulled into parliament to testify. Worse still, the Goldman Sachs bankers knew that they would be in a difficult position if anybody asked too many questions about the "put." Contrary to the assumptions of most Japanese politicians, it had not actually been Goldman Sachs that had produced the concept of the "put": instead, the idea had emerged because the *government* had requested it, to avoid revealing the rotten state of the LTCB loan book. And the golden rule of Goldman Sachs's culture, drummed into the head of every new recruit, was *the client came first, no matter what*—even if the client behaved stupidly.

Uneasily, Goldman sought the advice of its lawyers, who informed the bank that it could not be forced to testify in the *diet* (parliament) unless there were clear indications of wrongdoing. Goldman Sachs decided to face the politicians down and indicated that they would not attend the *diet* debate. The politicians interpreted this as more evidence of Wall Street "arrogance"—and decided to press ahead anyway.

On July 17, 2000, the finance committee of the Lower House convened for a debate about the Sogo affair. As the television cameras whirred, the politicians grilled Shoji Mori, the head of the FSA, and Noboru Matsuda, head of the Deposit Insurance Corporation. Why, they asked, had the whole debacle with Sogo—and Shinsei's controversial "put"—emerged?

"My guess is that when the government created the 'put' option nobody ever really imagined a situation like the one with Sogo. Is that correct?" asked Takumi Nomoto, a young LDP politician. Although the opposition party, the DPJ, was dominating the attack on the government, young LDP politicians privately shared the opposition party's unease about what had happened. "By getting involved in Sogo loans, the government has become responsible for deciding which companies are going to survive and which not. But is that a good thing? This is a huge policy issue. So can you explain to us, Mori-san, whether that was what you expected to happen when you agreed to the 'put'?"

Mori waffled. He could not admit that the bureaucrats had created the time bomb of the "put" as a short-term tactic to avoid admitting the scale of bad loans. "It seemed to me that there was no option other than what we did in this case [of Sogo]," he lamely offered.

"It seems to *me* that you [the FSA] were totally overwhelmed in the negotiations with the Americans when you sold the bank!" declared

Yoshito Sengoku, a DPJ politician. "The problem is just getting bigger and bigger. The Americans made you conclude this absurd deal because you defined the assets as being appropriate when you shouldn't have. But why did you make this agreement with Ripplewood with this 'put'? What was Goldman Sachs doing? I have heard that you have paid a Y1 billion advisory fee to Goldman Sachs for their work on the sale. What was *that* about? You are using taxpayers' money! Frankly, I think you should cancel the contract and simply not pay that Y1 billion to Goldman Sachs!"

Matsuda of the DIC pointed out that he could not simply rip up the contracts with Goldman Sachs or Shinsei. "We have already agreed the put option. We cannot cancel the contract now."

"Well, I think we *should* just cancel the contract," Sengoku insisted. "It doesn't matter if we end up being sued in court by Shinsei. . . . The whole put option is stupid."

"Goldman Sachs does not seem to have seen the implications of this contract, so they have a huge responsibility for all this," charged Fumihiko Igarashi, another DPJ politician. "What were these advisers doing? They have violated their duty."

"Goldman Sachs was in charge of finding the bidders and laying down the foundation of the negotiations," Mori admitted. "But the 'put' was not invented by Goldman Sachs."

"But surely the job of an adviser is to warn of the dangers in a deal. [Goldman Sachs] was advising the government and representing the government's interests, so it should have tried to warn the government that including a `put' option could increase the burden on the taxpayers. If Goldman Sachs could not even manage to perform a simple task like that, then Goldman Sachs should pay us back the money!" Sengoku wailed. "The government just does not seem to care how much money it is using to prop up the financial system."

"In fact, on the Goldman Sachs thing, there are lots of questions and concerns!" Igarashi added. "Did Goldman Sachs fix the bidding process [so that Ripplewood would win]? Why is Goldman Sachs representing Softbank in its bid for NCB? That's like a lawyer working for both sides of a case! Why are we spending all this taxpayer money for this deal with Ripplewood anyway?

"Wouldn't it have been better and cheaper to just liquidate LTCB in the first place?"

The next day, the debate moved to the finance committee of the Upper House of parliament. This time, the politicians summoned Yashiro for questioning as well. Unlike the Goldman Sachs executives, Yashiro knew that he could not refuse the "invitation," since the government technically owned about a third of the bank. In any case, it was not Yashiro's style to run away. As far as Yashiro was concerned, he had done nothing wrong; refusing the debt forgiveness was the only rational thing to do; and it had been the government—not Shinsei—that had actually pulled the plug on Sogo.

The politicians started the debate—once again—by lashing out at Goldman Sachs. To them, the bank had become a symbol of everything the Japanese disliked about Wall Street. "The government hired Goldman Sachs to get advice because they are supposed to be specialists. But they didn't provide proper advice," argued Keiichiro Asao, a DPJ politician. "They don't seem to be very good at their job when they couldn't even spot the problem with the 'put'!"

Japanese journalists and politicians were beginning to ask whether the whole Shinsei deal was a Wall Street conspiracy. Wasn't it a strange coincidence, they asked, that Chris Flowers had worked at Goldman Sachs—just before Goldman Sachs sold him the bank? Did he get inside knowledge to make his bid?

Yashiro vehemently denied that anything untoward had taken place. "As far as the bid for Shinsei was concerned, Flowers had no connection to Goldman Sachs." Mori, the head of the FSA, backed Yashiro up. "According to our findings, LTCB made the financial adviser contract with Goldman Sachs to sell the bank on February 1, 1999. But from what I have heard, Flowers had already resigned in November 1998," he said. Mori was deeply embarrassed at being dragged into the public spotlight in that way; however, he could see little option except to defend the deal.

The DPJ remained suspicious. The consumer finance company Life, another large Shinsei borrower, had also recently collapsed. GE Capital, a key investor in Shinsei, had recently been trying to buy Life and many

Japanese onlookers suspected that Shinsei had deliberately forced Life into collapse, so that GE Capital could swoop in and grab the assets cheaply.

Yashiro vehemently denied that, too. "We only make contracts with investors at arm's length. Just because GE Capital is buying Life doesn't mean that GE Capital gets treated in an advantageous way—or that Shinsei would influence Life!" Defiantly, he tried to point out that Life had been completely rotten, well before Shinsei or GE Capital had got involved. When Shinsei had looked through Life's books, after the collapse, the bank had discovered Y50 billion ($500 million) of net losses sitting on Life's books—*even though the accountants had previously said that the company was solvent.* "Those liabilities were not shown on Life's balance sheets before, but then they suddenly appeared!" Yashiro protested. "I suppose that was partly because consolidated accounting was adopted in March 2000 in Japan, so although Life's problems were not seen on a parent basis, it had problems on a consolidated basis . . . but I know some huge companies that have 700 to 800 subsidiaries and most of them do not produce profits at all!"

What, the DPJ asked, did *that* mean? Would dozens of other large companies be poised to collapse just like Life and Sogo? Was Shinsei going to start pulling the plug on all of its troubled groups?

"We are hoping that all these companies, including other medium- and small-sized companies, will revive . . . and that the Japanese economy will recover," Mori said. It was the bureaucrats' perpetual refrain.

As the pressure mounted, Shinsei attempted to seize back the public relations initiative. In early August, it issued its first annual report. "I believe that Shinsei Bank can make a unique and important contribution as the Japanese economy moves toward recovery," Yashiro explained in a letter, next to a perky portrait of himself standing in front of a globe. However, the move backfired. As politicians and bureaucrats leafed through the report, they noticed a footnote titled *Related Party Transactions*. This revealed that the bank had just paid Y1.1 billion ($11 million) each to Ripplewood and JCF, respectively Collins's and Flowers's funds, as a fee for "advisory services." The bank had also paid Y2.69 billion ($27 million) to New LTCB, the Dutch company that was the vehicle for the investment consortium. Even by the standards of Wall

Street, the move seemed sharp. Politicians and journalists were outraged. It seemed further proof that American investors were pillaging Japan.

In a frantic attempt to offset the damage, Yashiro promised to amend the contracts, so that the payments to Collins's and Flowers's funds would no longer be made directly from Shinsei, but from the investors instead, via New LTCB fund. However, the politicians demanded yet another debate in parliament. "In the last couple of days I have been reading Shinsei's annual report and saw these transactions. . . . I think it is strange that Shinsei bank should pay Y2.69 billion to New LTCB partners," Banri Kaieda, a DPJ politician, said as the Lower House finance committee convened. "Why did Shinsei make this payment?"

Yashiro explained that the payments were intended to cover the legal fees, translation, and due diligence costs for the LTCB acquisition. It was quite normal to make these payments, he added; that was how international finance worked. "We got consulting services from about seventeen different entities during the deal and we had about seventy accountants working for us in various ways over ten months."

"But New LTCB was the investment consortium. So why did *you*—Shinsei bank—have to pay for these services, rather than the investors?" Kaieda asked. "This is outrageous!"

"In a corporate acquisition the people who buy the company are what we call 'shareholders.' Japanese people tend to have difficulty in understanding the notion that shareholders are the owners of the company. But based on this notion it was appropriate for the company to pay for the services," Yashiro explained. He pointed out that LTCB itself was going to use the consultants' finding as well as the investors.

"Perhaps these types of payments are common in America. But that is why it is up to *you*, Yashiro-san, to tell those Americans that the case of Shinsei is greatly different from America!" Kaieda retorted. "You know the distinctions of how business is done in Japan and how it is done in the United States—so you should know how the politicians here, who represent the Japanese citizens, feel about this. You should have taken the lead in Shinsei's board of directors and told the Americans that these payments were impossible.

"That is not how business is done here! You should tell the Americans that!"

In mid-August, after one last, brief debate about Shinsei, parliament broke for its annual summer holiday. The DPJ politicians had eventually realized that they did not have any legal grounds to take action against Shinsei or Goldman Sachs. So they dropped the issue and returned to their constituencies. Japanese politicians tended to have extremely short memories, and most of them were still confused about who—or what—was to blame for the banking problems, at Shinsei or anywhere else.

Yet as the Shinsei investors mulled the implications of the "Sogo shock"—as pundits labeled it—they could see that the implications were alarming. When the Americans had bought the bank, they had assumed that the government was tacitly backing the deal. They had also assumed that if loans to companies such as Sogo turned bad, the bank would be able to hand these back to the government. Yet now the Shinsei investors had discovered—like the Swiss bankers two years earlier—that politics could be a very deceptive game in Japan.

On the one hand, parliament was unwilling to let the government bail out troubled companies such as Sogo. On the other hand, they seemed to hate the consequences of *not* rescuing troubled borrowers. The debate in parliament had failed to confront the real problem facing the Japanese government and the banks. Sogo was simply one of dozens of troubled borrowers with which the banks were confronted. In April, Nihon Building, a small construction company with loans from Shinsei, had failed. Then Dai-Ichi Hotels, a vast hotel group that had been ailing for years, ran into problems, Life, the consumer finance company, declared bankruptcy, and Seiyo, a real estate group, collapsed as well. Shinsei's combined loans to Dai-Ichi and Life alone totaled Y170 billion ($1.7 billion). Meanwhile, Hazama and Kumagai Gumi, two huge construction companies with large loans from Shinsei, were in a dire situation and asking for debt forgiveness as well. "If another case like Sogo turns up [and we exercise the 'put'] the government will have a serious problem about what to do," Yashiro mused in the following weeks. "If the government turns it over to the RCC [the body that handles bad debt], that will trigger the bankruptcy of the borrowers and the government doesn't want to be blamed for that. But if they forgive it, they may get blamed as well. The political atmosphere that has developed this summer has made it impossible for the government to offer debt forgiveness. Of course, the sensible thing would be to work out a restructuring plan. But the government finds that hard to do as well."

There was another option—namely, that the other Japanese banks could shoulder more of the burden, by buying the bad loans. Indeed, that appeared to be happening at Hazama and Kumagai Gumi; DKB and Sumitomo had respectively offered to buy Shinsei out of its loans, to avoid a repeat of the Sogo debacle. But that merely emphasized the horrible dilemma of Shinsei's position. If the bank did not clean up its balance sheet, it might collapse; but if it tried to clean up the bad loans by itself, this would cause big problems for the rest of the banking industry and the government. As Onogi had always liked to explain, Japan's postwar financial system had been built on a mutually supporting system of trust, in which the behavior of one bank had immediate implications for every other player in the system. If one bank started playing by different rules, it could destabilize the entire house of cards.

"This job is harder than I expected," Yashiro concluded.

— *Chapter 16* —

HOMMA'S DEATH

In some ways, my husband's death was a tragedy that reflects a bigger tragedy of our society.

—Michiko Homma

A few weeks after the parliamentary debates, Yashiro received a telephone call while he was in the company car: *"Homma-san is dead!"* Tadayo Homma was the president of Nippon Credit Bank, the other large bank that had collapsed in 1998 and—like LTCB—then been sold to new investors. He had just been discovered in a hotel room in Osaka with a noose around his neck. The police blamed suicide; some of his colleagues suspected that Homma, sixty, had been murdered. There were lurid rumors that Homma had been threatening to deal with NCB's deadbeat borrowers and speculation that this had somehow angered the *yakuza*.

Yashiro was deeply shocked. He was not a close friend of Homma, who had spent most of his career as a bureaucrat in the Bank of Japan before becoming president of the bank. But in the clubby world of Tokyo, the two men's paths had often crossed. Back in the early 1990s, when Yashiro was working at Citibank, Yashiro often visited Homma, who was the central bank's branch manager in Osaka. More recently, fate had thrown them into oddly similar roles. After NCB collapsed it was also placed under state control and then sold to a new consortium in the summer of 2000, using a structure almost identical to the LTCB deal. The key members of this consortium were Softbank, the internet group, Tokio Marine and Fire, the Japanese nonlife group, and Orix, the leasing company. UBS, Lehman Brothers, and Cerberus investment group also held minority stakes. Cerberus was represented on the board of the new bank by the former U.S. vice president Dan Quayle: The American investors hoped that he could add diplomatic gravitas to the venture, just as men such as Volcker had done at Shinsei.

The bank had started life on September 1, 2000, under a new name, "Aozora"—or "blue sky" bank—with Homma as president. However, Homma was a very different character from Yashiro. He had never worked in the private sector before, and had tumbled into his new role almost by accident. Indeed, when he was first approached for the job, after some of his colleagues recommended his name to the investors, he was reluctant to take it. His last job at the Bank of Japan was executive director overseeing the banking system, which meant that he knew a lot about NCB. Nonetheless, he was an ambitious man and he felt that he had a "duty" to help NCB. Back in 1997, when NCB had been on the verge of collapse for the first time, Homma had overseen a disastrous attempt to rescue NCB by using Y80 billion ($800 million) of Bank money. The Bank lost the money and Homma always felt guilty about that loss. He was a decent and conscientious man, and consequently found it difficult to turn down a request to help NCB. The investors, for their part, hoped that Homma's government connections would make it easy for their bank to deal with the government over issues such as the "put" option.

Almost as soon as Homma arrived at Aozora, however, he realized that he had been thrown into an impossible position. Intellectually, Homma could see—just as Yashiro had spotted at Shinsei—that his bank's balance sheet needed radical surgery to survive. The bank had historically specialized in real estate lending and had a shady political reputation. NCB had initially been set up as a bank serving the Korean colonies of the Japanese empire in the early part of the twentieth century and this had left it with extensive links to the Korean community in Japan, including the North Korean community. It subsequently became closely linked to the Tanaka faction in the LDP, and some senior politicians in that faction had used the bank to channel illicit funds in the past, allegedly with *yakuza* links.

Homma did not have the stomach for a fight to clean up this mess. Like most Japanese bankers and bureaucrats, he was a gentle intellectual who believed in supporting the consensus of the group. "When my husband became president of Aozora," Michiko Homma, his charming wife, later explained, "I think he really wanted to bring good things to the bank and promote reform and a new vision. But he wanted to do that in a way that respected the Japanese traditions. He respected *giri* and *ninjo* [obligations and human relations]." She had married her husband in a wedding arranged by a senior Bank of Japan official in the 1960s. For three decades she had loyally tended home, while her husband worked slavishly hard, climbing the ranks of Japan's bureaucracy. "In fact, my husband was a very Japanese person in many ways. He had a very Japanese heart and precisely because he had a Japanese heart he found it very difficult and painful when he saw bankruptcies and things like that."

In the weeks before he died, Homma confessed to some of his friends that it seemed impossible to square that circle. "He became very tired and quite downbeat," Michiko recalled. "He said to me: 'I had no idea how hard this would be! That this bank was so troubled!' " The culture of the Japanese bureaucracy was intensely group-oriented, and although Homma had faced difficult jobs at the Bank of Japan, he had always been part of a team. In his new job, he was more isolated than he had ever been in his life. The old NCB staff regarded Homma with suspicion and the investors were squabbling among themselves about what the bank's strategy should be. "At the Bank of Japan we always supported each other, we were close like a family, so however difficult things were we knew we could overcome," one of Homma's colleagues explained. "At Aozora, Homma was alone."

A few days before he died, Homma visited Yashiro at LTCB. "I could tell he was tired and somewhat worried," Yashiro later recalled. Uneasy, Yashiro asked Homma to dinner to discuss the situation. It made sense for the two bank presidents to cooperate closely, since they shared many troubled borrowers. If nothing else, Yashiro reckoned that he could offer Homma some moral support. But before the dinner arrangements were set, Yashiro received the telephone call telling him that Homma was dead. Any offer of help was too late.

The death of her husband devastated Michiko. She raged against the system, perplexed that life could have turned so sour after all the years of dutiful service. Eventually, her family placed her in a hospital to "calm her down." Meanwhile, Tokyo's banking world buzzed with rumors about what might—or might not—have happened. Many of Homma's colleagues suspected that *yakuza* or Korean mobsters had murdered the gentle bureaucrat or threatened him into committing suicide, because he had stumbled across dirty political secrets on the bank's loan book or threatened to call in loans. Tabloid newspapers claimed that hotel guests in rooms next to Homma that night had heard screams. A spokesman for the hotel admitted that it was difficult for a man to hang himself from a curtain rail, as police alleged. The police refused to publish their investigation. The body was quickly cremated.

When Michiko eventually emerged from the hospital, however, she had reverted to her normally gentle—dutiful—self. "After he died I was very sad and could not see things clearly. But now I have recovered and I have come through the dark times and learned that it is possible to do that," she said. "I am very grateful for everything from his old friends at the Bank of Japan and other places. And I am very sorry that this caused a disruption and embarrassment for Aozora Bank." She agreed with the police that her husband had committed suicide. She said she thought the cause of her husband's death was simply the tremendous difficulty that Japanese faced in reforming the banks in a "decent" way. Perhaps the *Americans*—or any other group of empowered outsiders—could overturn decades of banking tradition; but the challenge had simply swallowed up her conscientious husband.

"For somebody like Yashiro-san, who has a really very American way of thinking, perhaps things are different," she said. "But my husband was not like Yashiro-san—he was very Japanese and my husband was not able to act in the American way like Shinsei. Maybe acting in a new way is the only way now—maybe that is the way of the twenty-first century since we have to overcome these twenty-first-century problems. But my husband's ways were the ways of the twentieth century, you might say, not the twenty-first century. He himself could see the contradictions of all this. But I think he knew that no one else would take on this risky and difficult job [at Aozora]. In some ways this was a tragedy that reflects a bigger tragedy in our society. He has almost been like a sacrifice—part of the samurai tradition."

When Homma's body was found there had been a suicide note addressed to his family. "I am so sorry," the letter had said, next to some little cartoons. During his long years of slavish service to the Bank of Japan, Homma had always been devoted to his children, but like most Japanese men he found it hard to express emotions in words. So, Homma had developed a habit of scribbling cartoons as a way of indicating his love for his family. Michiko guessed the sixty-year-old banker had added the scribbles to his suicide note as a tender way of expressing the inexpressible—and saying a tender "good-bye."

When he heard about Homma's death, Flowers and Collins started to worry about Yashiro. In theory, Shinsei was supposed to be protected from any *yakuza* risks since, when Ripplewood had purchased LTCB, it had inserted a clause in the contract that stipulated that if any loans were found to have "antisocial connections," these would be returned to the government. This type of "*yakuza* put," as it was known, had first been developed by banks such as Goldman Sachs and was commonly used by foreign financial groups dealing with distressed debt in Japan. In the event, however, when Yashiro's team looked at the LTCB book, they could barely see any *yakuza* problems. Some bankers suspected that was because LTCB had had a much cleaner reputation than NCB. Others guessed that the government had transferred any *yakuza*-loans to the Resolution and Collection Corporation, the government institution created to deal with bad loans. Although most Japanese grudgingly tolerated the presence of the *yakuza* in their society, they wanted them to stay in their correct "place" in the social hierarchy—and not embarrass the country in front of foreigners. The RCC was thus considered a convenient dumping ground.

Flowers and Collins did not want to take any chances, and uneasily asked Yashiro if he would like to have a bodyguard. "I was concerned with all these rumors about Homma being murdered," Collins later explained. "I mean, we didn't seem to have any complications on our books and I don't have any knowledge of it myself. But if one tenth of the stories you hear are true . . . "

Yashiro stubbornly turned down the offer. He did not know exactly what might—or might not—have happened to Homma. But the experience of being bitterly criticized in parliament during the summer had not cowed him; on the contrary, the more he came under pressure, the more defiant he became. Perhaps the threats might scare some people, he vowed, but Yashiro had survived the war and the death of his parents, before the age of sixteen. At the age of seventy-one, he did *not* want to be seen running away from anything or anyone. Indeed, some of his friends suspected that a hint of messianic fervor was creeping into his stance. "If I start something, I finish it!" Yashiro declared. "I am proud to be a *fighter!*"

— *Chapter 17* —

THE FIGHT WITH THE FSA

Yashiro is the central player in a very strange play. At some level he must sometimes wonder if he has got himself into a Greek tragedy that will have no good outcome for anyone involved, even though it started with good motives.

—John Reed, speaking in the early summer of 2002

The tension inside Shinsei mounted. In the aftermath of the "Sogo shock" it had become clear that the idea of "creative destruction" remained anathema to the Japanese establishment. Yet there were still dozens of loans to deadbeat companies sitting on the bank's balance sheet and the American investors were utterly convinced that somehow, the bank needed to act. After all, they reasoned, the reason why LTCB had failed in the first place—and the entire Japanese economy was so weak—was that the country was refusing to take action against deadbeat borrowers. Moreover, the bank did not have much time to waste: at the end of February 2003, its "put" option would expire, which meant that it would lose the insurance policy for its bad loans. If Shinsei did not deal with its problems before that deadline expired, it would need to bear all the remaining losses on the bad loans itself—which would sink the bank.

Getting a handle on the state of the loan book was a complex, technical affair. Responsibility for this task fell indirectly to David Fite, the bank's head of finance, and the most senior non-Japanese at the bank. A tall, sporty-looking American in his late thirties, with striking blue eyes, Fite had forged the early part of his career at the World Bank and Bankers Trust and then moved to Sydney in the mid-1990s, where he helped to restructure Westpac, a troubled Australian bank. He had engineered this turnaround with such success that he eventually rose to become number two there. Then in 1999 Flowers had approached Fite and persuaded him to leave Westpac for Shinsei, by offering a pay packet considerably more attractive than the A$2.8 million Fite was earning. The idea was that Fite would use his Westpac experience to sort out the operations of Shinsei. Flowers—like most of the Shinsei investors—did not give much credence to the idea that Japan needed to be special. Money was money anywhere in the world, and if Fite had helped to clean up a bank in Australia, there was no reason why the same approach could not be repeated in Japan.

Even before Fite arrived in Tokyo, he knew that the Shinsei loan book was likely to be a mess. It was common knowledge in Sydney's financial circles that LTCB had financed some spectacularly stupid projects in Australia back in the 1980s, such as Sanctuary Cove, a lavish coastal resort built by EIE, which later collapsed and became an eyesore on the coast. "When I moved up here a lot of my friends said: 'Hey, can you sort out that mess at Sanctuary Cove?' Fite later recalled. But what Fite finally saw in the loan book was even worse than he imagined. The information LTCB traditionally collected about corporate clients was not really the type of data that a Western bank wanted to see. "The LTCB style was to analyze companies like equity analysis," Fite said. "The bankers would write reports saying the company has a great product or a good market share. But we needed hard data for credit decision, data on cash flow. At the end of the day what we had to know was 'will we get our money back?' "

The managers set about trying to change this culture. In November, the bank created a new division to handle the most troubled loans and changed the team of relationship managers that were handling these companies, since Fite figured—in sharp contrast to the old LTCB—that the bankers with historical relations with a company were *not* the best people to clean up bad loans. A new credit control committee met every Thursday morning to review the loan book. Any loan over Y100 million ($1 million) had to be passed by this committee. The idea was to remove the responsibility for making a loan—or cutting somebody off—from relationship managers and put it on a more scientific basis. In the past, lending decisions had essentially been binary: If a company was a favored client it got money; if not, it did not. However, Fite wanted to create a *spectrum* of mathematical data that expressed the profitability of Shinsei's lending relationships. He changed the lending forms, demanding precise details about collateral, and introduced a detailed credit system that measured default risk on a scale similar to Moody's bond ratings, and then mapped this risk against the interest rates. "We tried to get across the message that if someone comes to you and asks for more money because they cannot repay the old loan, that is probably *not* a good reason to extend more money," he later explained. After a few months of working at Shinsei, Fite had taken to describing the old culture as "Monty-Pythonesque."

As the results of this number-crunching poured in, Fite became increasingly alarmed. When the Shinsei investors had bought the bank back in March 2000, they believed about Y1,900 billion ($19 billion) of the Y7,700 billion ($77 billion) loans were risky. These were protected by about Y900 billion ($9 billion) of reserves. However, the new analysis suggested that the "real" level of risky loans was Y2,600 billion ($26 billion). The increase had occurred partly because the government had completely misclassified companies like Sogo. However, the economy was also deteriorating faster than expected. This meant that companies that were merely "troubled" a year earlier were now on the verge of collapse. The upshot of that was that bad loans were now at least Y700 billion higher than reckoned when the bank had calculated what level of reserves would be needed at the bank. *Seven billion dollars*. Even for Japan, it was a shockingly large number. It was also more than the entire capital base of the bank—and seven times what the Ripplewood team had invested.

What could the bank do? The management was divided. Some of the foreign investors and management were convinced that Shinsei had to recover its money from risky borrowers as quickly as possible. With seven billion dollars of extra risk, the bank did not have a moment to waste. And there was a broader philosophical issue. The older generation of LTCB bankers had spent years avoiding painful decisions, and ended up creating even greater problems as a result. Shinsei did not wish to fall into the same trap. Yet rapid action also carried a risk. If Shinsei savagely demanded repayment from troubled companies, that could hurt its reputation and discourage *all* clients from dealing with the bank. Some Shinsei managers feared that would deal a deathblow to the bank's business.

The discussions rumbled on—and to his colleagues, Fite seemed torn about what to do. Meanwhile, Yashiro appeared oddly complacent about the issue. "Yashiro just didn't seem to share our sense of urgency," one American observer explained. "He had made this grand gesture over Sogo, which was great. But then it seemed to slip off his radar screen a bit. He was distracted by the retail bank and he had never dealt directly with distressed debt before."

Yashiro subsequently denied that he *had* taken his eye off the ball. "From the beginning, when I arrived at the bank, I told everyone that I had no experience dealing with and little knowledge of the bad loan issues in Japan. And precisely because of that I paid a lot of attention to those issues in the early days!" Yet as time passed and the frustration grew, the American bankers at Shinsei increasingly started to look to Flowers—*not* Yashiro—for leadership. It had been Flowers who had hired most of them in the first place, and even after Shinsei started life, he remained very involved in the internal operations of the bank, often dominating discussions in the credit committee. However, Flowers, by nature, was not a manager: He had built his career cutting *deals*, rather than running banks. And Yashiro had absolutely no desire to relinquish control, to Flowers, Fite, or anybody else. Ever since his Citibank days, his management style had had a distinctly authoritarian streak, and he had arrived at Shinsei expecting that the Americans would treat him with devotion and respect.

Eventually, some of the Americans snapped. Fite appealed to Flowers for help and they convened a meeting of the Japanese relationship managers. At the meeting they announced that the bank was going to immediately review its loans to its main 4,000 clients, applying new standards of risk introduced in late 2000. If any loans did not meet Shinsei's new profit standards, relationship managers were told to offer the clients three stark choices: repay the loan; pay a higher interest rate on the loan; or offer better collateral. If any troubled company refused to do that, Shinsei would then withdraw funding or hand the loan back to the government. Effectively, the bank was putting a gun to the head of weak corporate clients.

To the Americans such as Fite and Flowers, it seemed the only rational thing to do; indeed, the type of thing that *all* Japanese banks should be doing. The Japanese relationship managers were horrified. Their careers were tightly entwined with many of the core clients and they considered them to be like members of the family. In some cases, the executives at these corporate clients *were* members of the LTCB "family." "In the old days, it was common for LTCB bankers to be seconded to the companies the bank lent money to and they often stayed there as well," explained a senior executive at First Credit, one of LTCB's old affiliates. "It helped business because we all knew each other well and had worked together."

The former LTCB bankers did not dare to openly express their opposition—or at least, not in a clear-cut way that the Americans might understand. "That man Flowers is very scary when he shouts," one banker said flatly. And Yashiro himself subsequently insisted that he had been unaware of what was going on. "Suddenly a highly theoretical approach [to the bad loans] was advocated by expatriate staff. I only became aware of this *after* problems surfaced," he later said, by way of explanation. "This theoretical approach was advocated by people looking at the portfolio, but not directly involved in dealing with customers, and the people who were actually dealing with customers found it very hard to respond to senior managers regarding the new approach. They should have brought all the issues for open discussions with me at the time. [But] our relationship managers and branch managers are afraid to say 'no' to senior people, particularly senior expatriate staff."

In the spring of 2001 the 250 relationship managers unhappily fanned out to tell their clients that the Americans had decided that Shinsei was going to dramatically change its lending policy.

It was almost certainly the most dramatic collision that had ever occurred between the set of values that had ruled Japan's corporate world for the past five decades, and the type of "rational" policies that foreign economists were now pressing Japan to adopt.

It did not take long for the borrowers to fight back. They started complaining to their local politicians that their bank was behaving "unfairly" and these politicians then expressed their anger to the bureaucrats. At the start of 2001, the Financial Reconstruction Commission had been abolished and its functions moved to the Financial Supervisory Agency, creating a new organization called the Financial Services Agency (also known as the FSA). It was this new FSA which now had responsibility for dealing with Shinsei—and it did not take long before the complaints about the bank reached Shoji Mori, the main bureaucrat in charge of the FSA, and Hakuo Yanagisawa, the politician in charge of banking policy.

The news put Yanagisawa and Mori on the spot. Even without Shinsei, they already had plenty of reasons to be defensive. Back in 1999, Mori and Yanagisawa had briefly become heroes in the eyes of foreign investors when they had taken the bold decision to sell LTCB to Ripplewood. But by the summer of 2001, most foreigners had lost their faith in the FSA's ability to implement banking reform. The banking sector had undergone a wave of consolidation during 1999 and 2000, as most of the largest banks merged with each other to form four so-called "mega banks": Mizuho (formed out of IBJ, Fuji, and DKB); UFJ (Sanwa and Tokai), Sumitomo-Mitsui (Sumitomo and Mitsui), and Mitsubishi Tokyo Financial Group (the various Mitsubishi financial companies). This consolidation process had not prodded the banks into better behavior, however, nor had it spurred them to clean up their rotten balance sheets; by the spring of 2001 the banks remained as dangerously short of capital and overloaded with bad loans as they had been in 1999.

Whenever he was given a chance to comment on this growing criticism, Yanagisawa angrily insisted that he *was* still a reformer—and the FSA determined to clean up the banks. "I do not believe that the traditional convoy system should be used today in Japan. We should use market mechanisms to resolve issues . . . only the fit should survive," he liked to say. But Yanagisawa was in a trap that illustrated the shortcomings of Japan's political process. When the FSA had burst onto the scene back in 1998, it had been a brand-new organization—and Yanagisawa had thus felt free to attack all the practices of the past. By 2001, the FSA had become the status quo. Japan was not a country where it was assumed that policy makers should keep learning from mistakes or that policy *naturally* needed to be remade all the time. Unlike America, a state of stability was considered the norm—and ideal. Thus if policy needed to be changed, it was usually blamed on an external factor or attributed to somebody's failure.

So, by the spring of 2001, the FSA felt that it had no choice but to insist that its past policies were perfectly adequate. It argued that the total level of truly bad loans at the banks was a mere Y12 trillion ($120 billion) and that the banks had all the capital they needed. Most independent analysts, however, put the problem loans nearer to Y100 trillion ($1 trillion). And when the International Monetary Fund pointed this discrepancy out, the FSA was furious.

Shinsei's new credit policy threatened to raise the pressure on the FSA even higher. If it pushed companies into bankruptcy, that would create new losses for the other banks and reveal that the other banks had badly underestimated the level of risk held in their loan books. Daiei, the giant retailer and one of Shinsei's biggest headaches, was a classic example. The company had a debt burden of more than Y2 trillion ($20 billion), but a market capitalization of barely Y30 billion ($300 million) and annual profits of just Y70 billion ($700 million). Fite and Flowers saw that Daiei was deeply troubled and didn't want to keep lending it money. However, Daiei's other large lenders, Mizuho, UFJ, and Sumitomo-Mitsui had labeled it as a "category two" loan—or only slightly risky, and they were reluctant to call in their loans or downgrade their debt since that would create a heavy new burden. If Shinsei pulled the plug on Daiei—and hundreds of other similar borrowers—it would send an earthquake through the whole system.

On August 10, Shoji Mori summoned Yashiro for a formal meeting. The bureaucrat explained that the government had received dozens of complaints from politicians about Shinsei's behavior and it was unhappy about the bank's tough new lending stance.

"Shinsei should behave in line with other banks," Mori said.

Yashiro was unpersuaded. "We cannot simply afford to keep problem loans on our balance sheet," he replied, pointing out the obvious.

Mori was unconvinced. He pointed to four large borrowers that he was particularly concerned about, which were "category two" companies. Inside the Japanese banking industry, it was generally accepted that banks had a right to take a tough action on loans to bankrupt or virtually bankrupt borrowers (companies labeled as "category four" and "three"). What Japan had never really accepted was that banks had a right to get tough with companies like Daiei, which were deeply troubled but had not yet collapsed, even if they survived only because the banks kept propping them up. Technically, these companies were known as "category two"; Westerners often called them "zombies." And the crucial rub was that these "zombies"—and *not* the "category three" or "four" companies—accounted for the bulk of "nonperforming" loans in Japan.

"I would like to reiterate that if possible Shinsei would support these borrowers . . . so that they can improve," Mori insisted, highlighting some of the "category two" companies he was worried about. "Shinsei should be concerned about its reputation risk, as anything can happen down the road." He asked that Yashiro pass the warning on to the investors in New York.

Yashiro did so. But the strains inside the Shinsei team were getting worse. When Yashiro had found out what Fite had done in the spring, he considered it a direct challenge to his authority. It also offended his sense of style. Yashiro believed that he was as passionate as anybody else about the need to clean up Shinsei's balance sheet. But he wanted to adhere to this broader principle in a *Japanese* manner and Japan was a culture that hated abrupt action. Thus, if Shinsei was going to cut off its borrowers, he fumed, it needed to broach the idea gently with prior planning, rather than produce sudden ultimatums. "I don't compromise on principle. But I do use *finesse*—and that is different from compromising," Yashiro later explained.

Yashiro's misgivings cut little ice with some of the foreign staff. The Americans were convinced that Shinsei had to take radical action. They did not want to wait for another decade for change; they wanted to clean up the bank and float it. Indeed, to some *gaijin* it seemed as if the fundamental problem with Shinsei was that the bank was reforming far too *slowly*, not too fast—not just in the loan book but in every other area of the business. They were doubly furious that some of the bank's own relationship managers had appeared to oppose them. "People here are in job preservation mode and life preservation mode," one American executive complained to a researcher from Harvard Business School. "Some of the old guard thinks: 'This too will pass.' A number of these people have been churning in passive resistance, thinking that they are going to wear me out . . . but from my American perspective there is going to have to be consequences to those sorts of actions."

Or as Fite grimly noted: "Our path is one of deliberate speed . . . but right now I think we are verging on not moving quickly enough to transform this bank. We must be the only turnaround company in the world that has not fired a single person."

The FSA slowly cranked up the pressure. First, the bureaucrats started to drag their feet on the *kashi-tampo*, the "put" option or "cancellation" clause. In the year to March 2001, the bank had used this cancellation clause to return about Y200 billion ($2 billion) of loans to the government, most of which had been linked to Sogo and its affiliates. The bureaucrats had paid out the compensation, as the original contract stipulated, hoping that Shinsei would not dare to keep returning *more* loans in 2001. Between April and June 2001 Shinsei handed back another Y100 billion ($1 billion) of loans and indicated that it had Y300 billion ($3 billion) more in the pipeline. These included loans to Life, the consumer finance company, which had provoked furious debate in parliament the previous year because many politicians suspected that Shinsei *itself* had pushed Life into collapse. In Japanese eyes, that made it particularly distasteful that Shinsei should dare to ask for compensation for its losses on Life. When Shinsei tried to return the loans, bureaucrats at the Deposit Insurance Corporation complained that the Y100 billion in loans to Life did not meet the criterion of the cancellation clause, since they had not really fallen in value by 20 percent.

Then, the FSA regulators started an inspection of Shinsei's operations. In theory, such inspections were routine affairs. In practice, it seemed that the FSA was hunting for technical transgressions with which to bully the bank. It quickly found some. Back in the spring of 2000, the government had demanded that Shinsei produce an official business plan and in this it had promised to maintain its loans to small companies. As the FSA inspectors scoured Shinsei's files they discovered that Shinsei's actual loans to small companies were 13.5 percent lower than the original plan had projected. They also declared that because the bank was failing to roll over many of its short-term loans to deadbeat borrowers, this had broken the original term of the sales contract, in which the bank had promised to "provide credit sufficiently and smoothly." In practice, this initial promise had always been very ambiguous. Most of the short-term loans on the

Shinsei books were only of six or three months' duration—implying that the bank had no legal obligation to extend loans after that period had ended. Moreover, the contract that Ripplewood had hammered out in 1999 specifically stated—in the footnotes—that Shinsei was allowed to suspend credit when it had serious concerns about the health of a borrower. However, Japanese officials had never paid much attention to the footnotes and in Japan's corporate world there had always been an assumption that "short-term" loans were not really short-term anyway, but would be automatically rolled over, in perpetuity. Thus, in the eyes of the FSA bureaucrats, Shinsei's threat to withhold new short-term loans *was* tantamount to "cutting" credit. The FSA ordered the bank to raise its level of small-company loans, rewrite the credit policy, and issue a formal press statement that humbly promised to change Shinsei's lending policies.

For a few days, Yashiro wondered what to do. The Americans were outraged by the FSA request. But though Yashiro shared some of this anger, he knew that the FSA did have grounds to reprimand Shinsei about the loans to small companies, since the bank had pledged to maintain these loans in a written document. He also believed that the switch in lending policy in the spring had been clumsy. Somehow, the bank needed to redefine its new credit policy in a way that caused less offense, to the FSA and everybody else—and causing the bureaucrats to lose face was not the best way to proceed. So, after a tense internal debate, on September 7 the bank caved in to the FSA and issued a press release, just as the bureaucrats had demanded. "We deeply regret that various constituencies have reported on and criticized our lending posture toward corporate customers. . . . We accept the criticisms that our posture in the recent past may have been rather straightforward, and caused some anxiety to customers," the statement declared, using language that some Americans found distinctly bizarre. "We will strengthen our support to customers where we can actively accommodate demand for loans. For customers where we have concerns about credit standing, we will have sufficient discussions on their restructuring and repayment plans, paying attention to smooth financing and taking the likelihood of their short-term and medium-term improvement into consideration."

The FSA was still unhappy. As September wore on, the bureaucrats demanded that Shinsei rewrite its internal credit guidelines. It was "government policy," the bureaucrats explained, for banks to support "category two" companies, however risky they might seem. Shinsei staff retorted that if it complied, this might be interpreted as a breach of fiduciary duty—and prompt lawsuits from the angry American investors. To back up their point, they pointed to the case of Mycal, a large retailer. When the government had classified the loans at Shinsei in 1999, it had judged that the bank's loans to Mycal were "normal," and thus the bank did not need to make provisions. Most of the other banks had also taken a lenient stance. In early September, Mycal declared bankruptcy with debts of Y1.7 trillion ($17 billion), *sixty times* its operating profits, creating huge losses for the banks.

The FSA shrugged the argument off; they were determined that Shinsei *should* keep supporting the category two companies. Yashiro yet again felt trapped, under attack from both the FSA and some of the American investors. "I want to make sure that whatever we finally agree [upon with the FSA] can be defended as good business practice and also against possible suits that can be brought against Shinsei management by investors," he told a group of senior Shinsei staff in an internal email. "There may be still some wording changes [to our credit policy] that we can live with while more or less satisfying the FSA."

Events then turned from bad to worse. In late September, the *Wall Street Journal* published an article about the saga that described Yashiro's dealings with Mori, citing internal Shinsei emails. Yashiro vehemently denied that he had leaked the story, but the bureaucrats concluded that the Americans were deliberately trying to whip up diplomatic support for their case and were furious. Mori, the chief bureaucrat at the FSA, was particularly angry. He was closely identified with Shinsei in the public eye, since he had overseen the initial decision to sell the bank to Ripplewood. Moreover, he had *defended* the decision to sell the bank to Ripplewood in parliament back in 2000. Now Mori felt that Ripplewood had betrayed him by "embarrassing" him in the foreign media. He angrily told some of his colleagues that he never wanted to talk to Yashiro again.

— Chapter 18 —

STALEMATE

We must tell the public that there are no financial problems and that the situation in the banks is quite normal.

—Memo circulated around the LDP, April 2002

In mid-January 2002, John Reed, the former chairman of Citibank, flew to Tokyo to offer moral support to his friend. Yashiro was delighted to see the American. Back in the spring of 2001—or when the row over the bad loans was first erupting—Yashiro had asked his old boss if he would get involved in the Shinsei project as an "adviser." Yashiro deeply trusted Reed and considered him the ideal person to help him navigate the conflicting demands between the FSA and the Wall Street investors. It was Reed, after all, who had pulled Citibank back from the brink of its own bad loan catastrophe in the early 1990s.

Reed agreed to help. He was intrigued by the path-breaking project, and could spot that his friend was in a difficult position, caught in the cross fire between the American investors and Japanese bureaucrats. "Talk about a culture clash," Reed later laughed. "You had the Japanese government on one side and his investor group on the other—and quite frankly that investor group was *not* the easiest in the world to deal with." But although Reed agreed to help Yashiro, he stipulated that the help would be on *his* terms. Reed did not want to receive any payment for the role of adviser to

Shinsei, nor did he want to attend the bank's board meetings. As far as he was concerned his role was to aid Yashiro personally, *not* the Wall Street investor group as a whole. "My prime role for Yash is that I am an experienced voice with whom he can speak. He doesn't do everything that I say. But my loyalty is totally to him. When he leaves Shinsei, I leave."

Reed first visited Yashiro in the summer of 2001, and for a few days in mid-July the two men swapped ideas about Yashiro's dilemma. Reed was distinctly alarmed for his friend. "Yash put a good face on the problems, because he always does. He is a straight guy and is determined to get his job done. I knew he was not going to stay and pretend everything was OK—or commit suicide.

"But I think on one level Yash must have been thinking, 'Jesus, did these guys know what they were getting into when they bought the bank?' Is it going to be possible to have a happy ending to this tale?"

What made the pressure particularly pernicious was that the criticism was so personal and emotional. Reed suspected that was partly because Yashiro was Japanese and not *gaijin*. At Nissan, Carlos Ghosn, the Brazilian-born executive from Renault, was also implementing a wave of painful changes to make the troubled automotive group's operations more profitable, primarily by demanding new efficiencies in the supply chain and selling noncore businesses and cross shareholdings. However, in sharp contrast to what was unfolding at Shinsei, these reform moves had been widely praised and Ghosn was considered a hero in Japan. Some observers attributed this difference to Ghosn's superior public relations skills, or the fact that Nissan's reforms only hurt a small segment of society. However, Ghosn also had the advantage of being a *gaijin:* when he had started in his new job he had been acutely aware that he faced cultural minefields and so he had bent over backward to make cosmetic gestures toward the local culture. The Japanese had had such low expectations that Ghosn's behavior could only surprise them on the upside. Yashiro, by contrast, was Japanese, and thus judged by a different, much higher set of *Japanese* standards, which he constantly flouted. And as time passed—and Yashiro came under more pressure—his comments sounded harshly messianic to Japanese ears. "I don't think you could have had a *gaijin* at the bank, given that you need to handle bank customers," Reed observed. "But there again, maybe it is easier for Ghosn. He is a Brazilian and they have a way of dancing around relationships, like how they play soccer. As *gaijin*, the Japanese have less expectation of us—we are known to be cannibals so they are not surprised when we start eating people."

The visit in January 2002 was Reed's second trip. Once again, he started by brainstorming about the state of the bank with Yashiro and then visited some Japanese bankers, politicians, and bureaucrats, trying to heal the breach with the FSA. He followed that up with a formal letter, urging the Japanese bureaucrats to stick to the original sales contract and honor the "put" option. "The letter basically said that you shouldn't sign agreements and then not live up to them—that is not a good idea," Reed later explained.

By January, and to his relief, Reed judged that Yashiro's spirits were rising. After twenty months in the firing line, Yashiro was becoming almost resigned to attack. He also had a few modest success stories to show Reed. The retail bank was slowly expanding. The investment banking business was settling down. Shinsei had enjoyed a morale-boosting success in the capital markets. In late 2001 it repackaged part of its loan portfolio as bonds, the first such deal ever struck in Japan. A local newspaper dubbed this "raising finance the American way"—and, in typical fashion, the FSA promptly told Shinsei that it hated the whole idea. To bureaucrats, it seemed distinctly "un-Japanese" to water down the relationship between a bank and its borrowers, by turning them into bonds. When the first issue took place in December, investors rushed to buy the bonds and the *International Finance Review* named the deal "Best Japanese Securitization of 2001." For once, Shinsei—and capital markets logic—seemed to have triumphed. Yashiro was thrilled.

Yet, as Reed looked at Shinsei's businesses in detail, he could see that the bank was still riddled with problems. Though the retail bank was growing steadily, it was not growing as fast as Yashiro had expected, since the Japanese economy was still very weak. There was relatively little demand for Shinsei's investment banking services. Most ominously of all, there were still more than ten billion dollars of bad loans on the books, the government was still refusing to pay compensation for Shinsei's losses on its loans to Life, and it had started quibbling about whether the "put" could be applied to other loans as well. In November, Yashiro had been hauled back into parliament again, for another bruising debate about Shinsei.

"I think that Yash thought that when the Japanese government sold the bank to the investors, it was signing up a certain vision of change. He thought that the Japanese government had recognized that there was need for a cleansing mechanism in Japan, and it wanted LTCB to be a catalyst for this cleansing mechanism," Reed observed. "But the Japanese haven't been willing to let that happen—they have just not embraced the logic of constructive deconstruction. And the model of reform that we used in Citibank in the early 1990s doesn't really work if the customer doesn't play along. When Yash goes to a client and asks them how they will repay the loan, they go to a politician and complain. It is like trying to play tennis with a guy who won't hit back the ball.

"I think there could be a great crisis," Reed added. "My guess is that the whole [Shinsei] deal may end up being renegotiated. But Yash's time is running out."

A few weeks after Reed's visit, Collins also flew to Tokyo hoping to patch things up with the FSA. During the first year of the bank's operations, the American entrepreneur had tried to stay out of the internal operations of Shinsei, partly because he knew that he did not know much about banks. But when tensions developed between Yashiro and some of the Americans, Collins tried to smooth the row by meeting the loan officers at the bank and had thrown himself into the task that he had always been good at—lobbying. Even at the best of times, Collins believed that it was important to spend time with politicians, bureaucrats, and journalists. As the controversy around Shinsei smoldered, he frantically tried to stamp out the fire. He scurried around Washington, meeting officials in the Treasury Department and political world, urging the American government to back Shinsei in its dispute with the FSA. The officials in Washington were sympathetic, but wary of becoming publicly involved. At the start of 2001 a new Republican administration had taken control of the White House, and these had fewer links to Wall Street—and Ripplewood—than the previous Clinton administration. The U.S. Treasury argued that it could only intervene if Ripplewood could provide concrete proof that the Japanese government had broken a legal contract. The Shinsei investors pointed to the case of "Life."

In Japan, Collins also made a point of meeting with as many senior LDP politicians and bureaucrats, desperate to lessen the anger. He drew the line at going out in the evenings with Japanese to raunchy bars, even though he knew that was a common way to forge business relations. Collins's Baptist beliefs left him appalled by the sex-soaked culture of Japanese entertainment. However, he frantically explored as many other lobbying routes as possible. When the opposition Democratic Party of Japan started making particularly spiteful comments about Shinsei, Collins dropped a note to Keiichiro Asao, one of the leading DPJ critics, and asked to discuss the criticism face-to-face. Asao was pleasantly surprised by the overture: When the DPJ had criticized Goldman Sachs, the American bank had refused to meet the party members at all. Collins visited Asao in his scruffy little office in parliament, and while the meeting did not lessen Asao's disapproval for the Shinsei project, he became a little more sympathetic to Ripplewood's dilemma. "I suppose that it is not really Ripplewood's fault the way they are behaving—it is only to be expected that investors want to make money," Asao admitted. "But I still think the government was wrong to have sold the bank like this."

Collins's most important goal was to keep the conflict between the FSA and Shinsei from spiraling out of control. So, together with Flowers, he requested a formal meeting with Yanagisawa, the head of the FSA. To boost their chances of a rapprochement, Flowers and Collins took David Rockefeller along to the FSA meeting as well. After years of working on Wall Street, linked to one of America's most prestigious and wealthy families, Rockefeller had numerous powerful acquaintances in Tokyo, such as Kiichi Miyazawa, the finance minister. Prince Hitachi, a member of the Japanese Imperial family, was another long-standing chum, since the two men shared a passion for collecting dead beetles. "I have got the largest beetle collection in the world, and I think Prince Hitachi has got the second largest collection," Rockefeller said. "So we always take care to have a good chat whenever I come to Tokyo."

Collins, Flowers, and Rockefeller arrived in Tokyo in late February and they all checked into the prestigious Okura Hotel. Prince Hitachi promptly sent an Imperial dinner invitation to Rockefeller's room, together with a vast bouquet of flowers and a plate of lavishly expensive giant strawberries, each the size of a small plum. "Ooh, how lovely!" Rockefeller cooed, when he saw it.

On February 27, Rockefeller, Flowers, and Collins set off to meet the bureaucrats. They found Yanagisawa looking stiff. He started by reading a long list of familiar complaints: Shinsei was abruptly cutting off loans; it was not observing Japanese banking practice; it did not have a viable business franchise. During the past two years the Shinsei loan book had shrunk dramatically, because the bank had been trying to remove its bad loans—and refusing to extend new credit to troubled borrowers—and to the FSA, that decline looked very odd. "Our intent [when we sold the bank] was that Shinsei should maintain its relationships with creditors as much as possible," Yanagisawa later said. "Of course if the creditors are already bankrupt there are exceptions to this and then a bank can go ahead and process these companies. However, our basic idea is that the lending business should be maintained as much as possible. If the borrower is about to become bankrupt or has collapsed, then these losses should not be born by Shinsei Bank. But now we hear that some of these companies are collapsing not because of social and economic reasons, but because Shinsei *itself* pulled the trigger to cause their collapse! If a collapse was inevitable, then the government [would] take back the loans. But if the collapse was caused by Shinsei it is another story."

The Americans tried to present the counter case. For the umpteenth time, they pointed out they had a legal contract that guaranteed compensation for loans that had lost their value; how could the government dispute that?

Eventually Yanagisawa put down his list of complaints, and appeared to relax. Privately, he was thrilled to be meeting Rockefeller. "It is important to be *calm*," he insisted. The two sides batted around the issues, trying to find out whether there was any ground for a compromise. What about extending the deadline for the "put" option beyond 2003? What about encouraging the banks to share more of the burden of Shinsei's loans?

Then the American investors floated another, potentially more controversial idea. Back in the autumn of 1999, the Ripplewood group had told their investors that they wished to do an IPO "within the next three years"—or 2002. Indeed, behind the scenes Collins and Flowers had already told some of the senior Shinsei staff that they were aiming to float part of the bank on the Tokyo Stock Exchange in July 2002 and appointed Morgan Stanley and Citigroup as the underwriters. They hoped to float about 20 percent of the bank, which they reckoned could be worth about $1.5 billion to $2 billion, implying that the entire value of the bank was about $10 billion, or ten times what the investors had originally paid for it.

But would it be possible to actually list the bank while FSA was so cross? Nervously, Collins and Flowers asked whether the government would let an IPO go ahead in the summer of 2002. What if the investors started by floating the stake that the government held in the bank—so that it would be the government, not the Americans, who made a profit first?

Yanagisawa was very unhappy about the idea. He did not want to see any sale of the bank until well after 2003, or after the controversial "put" had expired. He knew that there would be protests from politicians if the Shinsei investors were seen to make a large profit while they were still reaping the benefit of the cancellation clause. When the FSA had agreed to the Ripplewood deal back in 1999, the Japanese had realized that the foreigners would make *some* money from the deal. However, they had never expected this to reach billions of dollars. Japan was not a culture that assumed that greed could be good—or harnessed to serve the public interest. Many bureaucrats instinctively felt that if the Shinsei investors were going to make a big profit, they should share this with the bank's corporate clients, by offering them cheap credit.

"The key issue that everyone needs to consider is whether Shinsei is attractive enough to list itself," Yanagisawa explained. "Public funds should not be part of what makes the company profitable." In bureaucratic parlance the message was clear: The FSA was determined to block any plans that Ripplewood had to list the bank in the summer.

"Fuck," said one of the American investors, when they heard the news. On paper, the investors believed they were sitting on a potentially fabulous deal; but the gains remained only potential, until they could actually sell part of the bank. They wanted to do that sooner, rather than later. Moreover, they considered FSA's objections to be utterly ridiculous. Americans took it as a God-given right that free investors were the best people to judge the value of a company. So why, they fumed, did the bureaucrats think that they were in a position to judge the merits of Shinsei's business model? Couldn't the bureaucrats see that if a sale of Shinsei went ahead it might help to boost international confidence in Japan? What made the dispute doubly baffling—and infuriating—for the Americans was that the Japanese government itself was likely to make a tidy profit from a sale. The government held a 33 percent stake in Shinsei, because it had subscribed to Y240 billion ($2.4 billion) in preference shares back in 2000. The investors had a strong motive to sell this government holding early, since they were not able to pay proper dividends to the ordinary shareholders while these preference shares remained in place. In the original sales contract, the government had agreed to cap the profits it could take on these shareholdings when the bank was sold, meaning that the government did not have as much upside potential as the investors. Yet the government was still likely to double its money when a sale took place. "Those morons don't seem to have a clue," one investor complained. "I mean, here we are—we are offering the government the chance to make some money! After years of them throwing money down the drain bailing out the other banks, we are offering money on a plate. Don't they want to take that? Are they *totally* fucking nuts?"

The FSA refused to budge. For the bureaucrats, the prospect of the government making profits was not a particularly big incentive at all; they were more concerned about the criticism they might face if foreigners made large profits. Moreover, the bureaucrats knew the IPO gave them leverage. The key source of power for bureaucrats in Japan had never derived through the bureaucracy's ability to issue direct orders; instead, it arose from a type of negative power—namely, the fact that bureaucrats were able to block almost anything that a businessman might ever want to do. As long as the IPO issue grumbled on, the bureaucrats knew they had a powerful weapon that they could use to control the unpredictable foreigners.

Uneasily, the investors wondered if they had any weapons with which they could hit back. On paper, the FSA did not have the legal powers to block an IPO indefinitely: If Shinsei was banned from doing a sale in Tokyo, it could list in New York or London instead. In practice, it looked extremely difficult to conduct a sale in the face of FSA disapproval. As long as the FSA kept dragging its feet over the use of the "put," there were still billions of dollars of bad loans hanging in the balance and it would be difficult to float a bank with this uncertainty. But the investors had some other weapons. They could threaten to blow the whistle on the rot in the other banks. They could also use diplomatic pressure to "embarrass" the FSA. After all, they pointed out, if the FSA had broken the original sales contract, the Shinsei investors had the right to sue. "The future of this bank will be closely watched by global investors," Yashiro told journalists. "If Japan is perceived to be a difficult country to do business in, this will really harm the country. However if Japan is seen as a place that accepts the rule of law and rational business behavior, more investment will come."

Yashiro himself was wary of turning the whole issue into a public row. So was Volcker. "I would hate to see the American government become involved in a purely commercial argument," he admitted. Uneasily, Volcker tried to float some compromise ideas. Perhaps, he suggested, the investors should simply decide to delay the IPO plans for a few more years and focus their attention on building a viable bank first. Or perhaps the government could agree to extend the "cancellation" clause, so that it didn't run out in February 2003, but a year or two later instead. Volcker figured that this type of extension would reduce the pressure on Shinsei to clean up its balance sheet by 2003, and thus might lead to less confrontation over the troubled borrowers.

Most of the investors did not like the idea of delaying the IPO; they wanted to get their money out as fast as possible. And, to Volcker's surprise, Yanagisawa himself was strongly opposed to any extension as well. The bureaucrats knew that they could not change the contract without another parliamentary debate, and the last thing they wanted was more public scrutiny of the whole Shinsei deal. "It is true that we are discussing many possibilities with the Shinsei investors at the moment, including an extension of the put option," Yanagisawa explained. "However, I think it would be extremely difficult—well, almost impossible, in fact—to have an extension."

That left the two sides in an increasingly dangerous stalemate. "In theory it ought to be easy to find a solution to the conflict between the FSA and Shinsei because neither side has much to gain from a bust-up. But theory doesn't always match reality," Volcker admitted. "Personally, I would have thought that the whole [situation in the banking system] would have come to a climax by now and that would help Shinsei in a way. But the Japanese still seem to think that they can keep muddling on. It doesn't surprise me that they want to keep muddling on—but what surprises me is their confidence that they *can* get away with it! Somehow the system survives. It keeps staggering on and on."

The mood in the FSA became increasingly truculent. A few weeks before the end of the fiscal year on March 31, the FSA unexpectedly tightened the rules that governed short-selling in the Japanese equity markets. In normal circumstances, the rule change would have aroused little interest. The guidelines for short-selling were an arcane matter and the new rules that were being introduced into Japan were similar to existing American practices. However, the timing of the changes suggested that the Japanese government was going back to its bad old habits of meddling in markets. The FSA announced the move with almost no advance warning, which meant that Western banks had no chance to change their systems—and were thus forced to suspend their dealings in short sales in the critical last few days of March, triggering an artificial equity market rally. Before that rally, the Nikkei had been sliding sharply toward 9,000. This was half the level it had been at two years earlier and the decline was threatening to trigger a new financial crisis. However, as a result of the clampdown on short-selling, the market shot up to almost 12,000. That meant most banks were able to revalue their equity portfolios on March 31 at a reasonably high level and thus did not need to post capital losses. Yet again, Japan had avoided a shakeout of its banking sector.

The FSA denied that this was a backlash against reform. However, the claims rang hollow. And some of the politicians frankly admitted that they were trying to boost share prices. "In early February everyone was saying that there would be a financial crisis so I personally pledged that I will prevent any crisis in March," admitted Michio Ochi, a senior LDP politician who had briefly been the minister in charge of bank policy in late 1999. "I said to my colleagues that what we must do is raise stock prices to help the financial institutions, and so we did that, which was good!"

Then in late March a strategy paper was circulated around the LDP, which appeared to have been prepared by senior officials at the Ministry of Finance and the FSA. This explicitly declared that the best strategy for the government was to talk up the markets. "Finance is based on trust. So the government needs to tell everybody that the financial problems have been solved," the paper said. "We must make it clear that this government is not going to let any bank go bankrupt. . . . We must also argue against injecting public funds. In support of the argument against injecting public funds, we should ask people if they really want to see a second Shinsei?"

The memo also had a distinctly xenophobic streak. "Foreign investors are only interested in making short-term profits for themselves with their 'short-selling' rather than creating mid-term profits by promoting Japanese stocks," the paper continued. "So we need to introduce full-scale measures to stop this and the political message must be very strict, warning that we are considering banning short-selling. Most foreign investors are considering pulling out of Tokyo and there is a danger that they will run away without paying for what they have eaten. So in some cases we need to think of imposing punishments on the individual bankers at foreign firms, not the firms themselves."

There were other hints of an anti-*gaijin* backlash. In the spring of 2002, the internet company Softbank indicated that it wanted to sell the stake it had acquired in the nationalized bank Aozora back in 2000. The collapse of the global internet bubble had left Masayashi Son, the charismatic chairman of Softbank, desperately in need of more cash. There was a willing buyer: Cerberus, another American private equity fund similar to Ripplewood, which already owned a small stake in Aozora. Then, just as Softbank was about to strike a deal with Cerberus, the FSA intervened. The bureaucrats declared that they did not want a second American fund controlling a major bank.

Ochi himself blamed the LDP's unease on the timing of a sale. "Son says that he wants to sell the shares, but that that seems very selfish to us. We don't want the consortium at Aozora to break apart after just a few years—that would be like a part-time marriage, like the marriages Americans have! We want to place more strict controls on investors, particularly if they are investing in banks. We do not want investors to run away."

In the eyes of Ochi, there was also another reason why a sale to Cerberus seemed undesirable. Two years earlier, it had been Ochi himself who had overseen the last stage of negotiations between Ripplewood and the Japanese government. He had never been entirely thrilled by this sale plan, which had largely been drawn up by his predecessor Yanagisawa, since Ochi was by nature a conservative politician. But Ochi had pressed ahead with the sale partly because he knew and liked the Ripplewood team—and back in 1999 there was a mood of reform in Japan. But now, after two years of watching Shinsei, Ochi had come to the conclusion that the sale had been a very bad idea.

"Back in the old days, LTCB had lots of loans and influence, and so when I sold it I hoped that the bank would become a model for Japanese institutions," Ochi admitted. "But what did they do? Well, they introduced lots of Indians who are good with computers, but I don't hear any voices saying that the bank has become a good role model for Japanese institutions! The original aim of the bank was to provide long-term funds for investment, but now at Shinsei the only thing the Americans are interested in is short-term profits and getting the returns they promised their investors. That affects their entire strategy and thinking.

"So can they be a good role model for Japan? I have lost my faith in that idea."

— *Chapter 19* —

SUCCESS?

What Shinsei is doing is what all Japanese banks should do. Shinsei points the way forward for Japan.

—Robert Grondine, former chairman of the American Chamber of Commerce in Japan

The Americans got it all wrong—we Japanese don't like the capital markets; we like our banks!

—Hisayoshi Teramura, Chairman of Nichiryoku, a Shinsei client

In late May 2002, Yashiro made a ritual visit to the Bank of Japan to deliver Shinsei's annual results. The ceremony was a peculiar local quirk. In America, when a bank releases its results to the media it stages a press conference at any time that suits its fancy—and journalists presume they have a right to attend. In Japan, the official reporting process is a tightly controlled, group affair. The banks have traditionally reported their results simultaneously, and the presidents of these banks address the local media via the press cartel—or *kisha* club—attached to the Bank of Japan. Each bank is permitted thirty minutes to speak and only members of the *kisha* club who obey its rules are allowed to attend, lodging their questions through a single, central representative of the club. Foreign journalists are often excluded.

From time to time, the American bankers at Shinsei would discuss whether they should buck this system. Should they present their results on a different day to show a flash of independence? Should Yashiro refuse to visit the *kisha* club? He concluded that there was little point in stirring up any additional media ire, given the public relations challenges that already existed. So twice a year he made the pilgrimage into a stuffy little room in the Bank of Japan to present Shinsei's results on the same day as the other banks.

When it came to Shinsei's allotted spot on May 24, 2002, however, Yashiro was almost pleased to visit the *kisha* club. The other bank presidents who had visited the room earlier in the day had all delivered dreadful news. For five successive years, the major banks had posted huge losses as they wrote off bad loans. Each year they had declared that it would be the last year of these losses. On May 24, the largest banks announced another Y4 trillion ($40 billion) of losses—and they admitted that they were *still* drowning in a sea of bad loans. Mizuho was in a particularly dire position: Just a month earlier, the bank had officially started its merged operations and the computing systems had spectacularly collapsed, prompting a flood of complaints, an FSA reprimand, and additional costs. Shamefacedly, the Mizuho president bowed in abject apology to the *kisha* club.

Yashiro, however, chirpily unveiled some *good* news. In the year to March 2002, Shinsei had recorded net profits of Y61 billion ($610 million), almost double the level of core profits the previous year. It was a dramatically better result than Shinsei had predicted back in 2000. And while most of the other Japanese banks were struggling to reach a BIS ratio of 8 percent—and had only achieved it by using accounting tricks, such as the use of deferred tax payments—Shinsei's ratio stood at 17.04 percent. "Our strategy was the key to our overall profitability, allowing us to exceed our original plan!" Yashiro declared, with a huge, perky grin. "We are convinced that our business model is the right model for the future."

Flummoxed, the Japanese journalists tried to make sense of the results. They knew perfectly well that politicians such as Ochi were muttering that it had been a mistake to sell the bank to the Americans. Yet now the bank had unveiled results that put the rest of the sector to shame. What was going on? Were the American investors simply scavenging off the

Japanese taxpayers? Or was something going right with the bank's business model at last?

The truth lay somewhere in between. Part of the reason for Shinsei's profits lay in its protection from bad loans. In the year to March 2002, most of the other banks had recorded a modest level of operating profits, but these had been wiped out by the need to post new provisions for bad loans. Shinsei, by contrast, had barely needed to make any new provisions at all. Despite the fight over the "put"—and the fact that the government had rejected several hundred billion yen worth of loans—the bank *had* managed to return about Y780 billion ($7.8 billion) of loans to the government by the summer of 2002, receiving about Y400 billion ($4 billion) worth of compensation. Without doing that, its profits would have been devastated.

The "put" did not tell the whole tale. Encouraging change was also under way at the bank. In the old days of LTCB, the bank had earned almost all of its profits from corporate lending. In the year to March 2002, 30 percent of profits came from *non*lending activities, up from 15 percent the previous year. Moreover, the corporate loan book had shrunk dramatically. Back in 2000, outstanding loans totalled almost Y8 trillion ($80 billion); by the spring of 2002, they had fallen by 40 percent to just below Y5 trillion ($50 billion). This partly reflected a decline in bad loans. The bank had also been refusing to extend new loans, unless they made commercial sense. Instead, Shinsei had been frantically searching for more lucrative ways to use its capital. It had channeled some of this to investment banking or proprietary trading of bonds and distressed loans. However, since it could not find enough attractive outlets, it had also left a large part of its capital sitting unused on the balance sheet, invested in short-term bonds, which explained the high BIS ratio. It was a damning indictment of Japan's stunted financial world: Even when a bank had money, it was hard to spend it wisely. But the Shinsei investors reckoned that leaving money idle was better than pouring into hopeless borrowers.

An equally striking shift was under way in the funding area. In the old days, Shinsei had raised almost all of its funding by issuing debentures, or traditional five-year bonds. By the summer of 2002, a quarter of the bank's funding—or almost the same level as the debenture finance—came from the cash collected in the retail operations. Another chunk of funding arose from the so-called "CLO" (collateralized loan obligation) program that the bank had started in late 2001 to repackage its loans as bonds. Thus far, Shinsei had only issued about Y200 billion ($2 billion) of these bonds. However, the bank had prepared the legal framework to securitize up to Y1,400 billion ($14 billion) of its loans in the future—or a fifth of the entire loan book. "The greatest value of a CLO program is that it means that we can fund anytime and anywhere," Robert Sheehy, head of the securities division, explained. "It is designed with the idea that we can issue in any term and in any currency." Debentures were becoming redundant.

Added together, this had eviscerated the old long-term credit bank model—exactly as the investors had wanted. LTCB had been created to provide long-term bank loans to industry; Shinsei had become a child of the capital markets. LTCB had operated with a binary credit culture, in which companies either got virtually free finance or nothing; Shinsei was trying to create a credit world built around a *curve*, where it would lend to risky clients—but only at a high price. Similarly, instead of raising finance—or not—in the debenture market, Shinsei was shopping around for its funds, driven by the idea that money always had a comparative price.

Was this a good thing? To foreign observers, the answer was self-evidently "yes," not just for Shinsei but all banks. In a world of near-zero interest rates it was difficult to make profits on loans. It made business sense to put this capital where the bank *could* make returns. It also made sense to be seeking to create a credit curve—or a middle ground between the virtually free finance offered by large banks and the exorbitant rates charged by the loan sharks. "Shinsei is well on the road to doing to Japanese banking what Nissan did to Japan's car industry: raise overall efficiency and demonstrate to the world that Japan can still compete," said Jesper Koll, chief economist at Merrill Lynch in Tokyo. "If Shinsei Bank can use taxpayers' funds as a building block for a higher profitability, why are the other banks that received public funds still lagging behind?"

Yet the Japanese bureaucrats had been raised to believe that the fundamental business of a bank was lending—and they were convinced that any new reforms should be tacked *on top* of that basic business, rather than replacing it completely. Although the Wall Street investors considered the money inside a bank to be almost as fluid as water and assumed that the point of this capital was to earn *more* money, by utilizing it in the most productive way, wherever the bank could, the Japanese had not traditionally thought of money as being a detachable resource. Instead, loans were like the beams of a house supporting an industrial structure. They could imagine that a bank might want to move some of this money around; they did not want to see dozens of financial "beams" redeployed, since the entire structure might collapse. "The way Shinsei is behaving is like a giant hedge fund," a senior official at the Ministry of Finance sniffed. "I don't understand why those Americans bothered to buy a bank at all, if they were going to act like that."

Shinsei's clients also had mixed emotions. Some large companies welcomed the shift. Nissan, for example, the giant motor company that was under the control of Renault, was a great fan. LTCB had not been a traditional main bank for the car company. However, the Nissan executives deliberately raised finance from the bank, partly as a gesture of support to Shinsei's ideological aims, but also because Nissan considered the bank to be much more flexible and responsive than some of its competitors, with its mix of capital markets and banking products.

Shinsei's weakest Japanese clients—unsurprisingly—disagreed. "Those Americans are greedy and they just want to grab profits," complained a Daiei executive. Even relatively healthy companies were uneasy. Nichiryoku, for one, was a classic example of the challenge Shinsei faced. The company, tucked into a neat four-story building next to a railway line in a far-flung Tokyo suburb, made gravestones and employed about 100 people. Traditionally, the company had funded itself through regular bank loans, raised from LTCB, Mitsui, and other banks. However, in late 2000, a relationship manager at Shinsei discovered that Nichiryoku had a problem. The company needed to borrow about Y3 billion ($30 million) to finance a new graveyard development in Yokohama, but did not want to increase the total level of its borrowing, since this was already Y7 billion, compared to annual sales of Y6.4 billion.

The relationship manager contacted the Shinsei product specialists and together they drew up a plan for Nichiryoku that raised finance off the balance sheet. Effectively, this created a special purpose company located in the Cayman Islands that issued bonds on Nichiryoku's behalf, backed by the potential stream of earnings from the Yokohama graveyard. "At the beginning I was very happy when this young man from Shinsei explained to me how it worked. None of the other Japanese banks could do this," Hisayoshi Teramura, the chairman of Nichiryoku explained. "So I agreed to use the scheme."

By the summer of 2002, Teramura had come to regret his actions. The Yokohama graveyard did not perform quite as well as he had hoped, and the financing costs were more expensive than he had expected, running at about 4.5 percent a year. Teramura thought that in those circumstances, Shinsei should offer to show its "sympathy" by offering concessions. However, the bank refused. "This is tougher than having a loan. I don't have a good feeling about Shinsei anymore because they just want to get profits. Also, the other banks don't like Shinsei so they won't help. Usually in Japan the banks all work as a group, but when Shinsei is involved the other banks ignore it," he explained.

"Yashiro has a face like a Japanese but his brain is really American—and the problem is that the Japanese and American systems are so different," Teramura added. "The Americans like gambling and risk and profits. But we don't think like that. When Japanese banks and companies make a loan there is a sense of balance, so that no one makes extreme losses or profits. But Shinsei doesn't want to share—it wants to keep its profits! Next time I need any money I am definitely going back to a normal Japanese bank for a normal Japanese bank loan! The Americans came here and thought that they could take over our economy with the capital markets. But these Americans got it all wrong. They didn't realize that we Japanese don't really like the capital markets—we don't like what Shinsei is doing. We like our Japanese banks!"

Shinsei managers shrugged off such criticism. It would be unrealistic to expect corporate Japan to be converted to the new methods overnight, they muttered; *they* were going through a process of adjustment themselves. During the first year of Shinsei's life, there had been endless bickering between the (mostly Japanese) relationship managers and (mostly foreign) product specialists. However, as time passed, some of these tensions abated. The bank had implemented a sweeping restructuring, which combined the relationship managers' department with the investment bankers into a single unit, forcing them to work together. More importantly, by the summer of 2002 even some of the old LTCB bankers had slowly become comfortable with the commercial strategy of the bank. This did not mean that all of the former LTCB bankers necessarily *liked* the Americans; most presumed that the Americans would soon go home, just as the American military administration had done, after running Japan for a few years after World War II. Yet, some had absorbed Yashiro's sense of mission. "In the past three years I have had to face lots of conflicts—sometimes I feel like a punching bag!" explained Hidebumi Mori, a former LTCB banker who was the Shinsei senior managing director. "However, what makes me excited is that our mission to be a new bank takes priority over these conflicts. I think that my role is to try to interpret the ideas of the foreign investors into a Japanese context. But Shinsei is *not* just about bringing foreign ideas into Japan. The things we are doing are the things that the managers and employees of banks—most of whom are Japanese—think they should do as well."

Another convert was Teruaki Yamamoto, fifty-one. Before the American investors had arrived, Yamamoto had spent his banking career hopping between traditional jobs at LTCB, working closely with Yoshiharu Suzuki, the old "king" of the domestic loan book; however, by the summer of 2002 he had been appointed as cohead of the institutional banking group with Brian Prince. The two men were an utterly unlikely team: Prince was outspoken and forceful; Yamamoto reserved. Meanwhile, Yamamoto stood a full foot shorter than the American (although the bank tried to disguise this in photographs by getting Prince to sit down).

Almost against the odds, the two men forged an unlikely bond, largely because Yamamoto adopted the new restructuring creed with a quasi-evangelical zeal. Some of Yamamoto's old colleagues from LTCB cynically suggested that was simply a ploy to earn promotion; but Yamamoto denied this. "I am not sure how long it took me to really understand what the Americans were trying to do with the corporate business, but it was probably near to one year," Yamamoto explained. "The greatest change in thinking compared with the past is how we evaluate risk return and credit risk. Due to the overbanking situation in Japan, you can only find risk-adjusted returns in a very limited number of situations.

"It is true that it took some time to get people in corporate business, including myself, to understand this, but this is the core issue. So I think that our clients look on us in two different ways: If the company is flourishing or adapting to the new economy, they rate us highly, but if the company is struggling, it looks on us harshly," Yamamoto added. "BTM, Sumitomo-Mitsui, and others are starting to demand risk-adjusted rates, so I think we are not an anomaly anymore! There are companies that appreciate our stance towards lending and my impression is that the number is increasing."

But would this increase occur fast enough to allow Shinsei's business to flourish? The issue was still far from clear. When Yashiro had presented the data in the Bank of Japan *kisha* club, he had hailed a surge in investment banking revenues. On closer inspection, it seemed that most of the profit growth had come from just one source: proprietary trading in distressed loans. This was the practice whereby Western bankers would purchase distressed assets at a knockdown price from Japanese companies and realize their value either by collecting part of the debt or collateral, or selling it to another party. In itself, it was not particularly surprising that Shinsei had engaged in this business; most of the other large foreign banks, such as Goldman Sachs and Morgan Stanley, also relied on the loan trading business for a large part of their Japanese revenues. What worried some analysts looking at Shinsei, however, was that loan trading seemed a highly volatile, unpredictable game. If the loan trading business suddenly dried up, in other words, there was a risk that the bank could quickly find itself losing a large part of its revenues. It was one thing to make one-off profits by scavenging from corporate distress; it was another task to create a profitable, repeat business with clients.

And there was still only patchy evidence that the rest of the nonloan business was producing a more stable stream of earnings growth. The bank's retail operations were slowly growing, and had attracted 130,000 accounts, with some Y550 billion ($5.5 billion) of funds, but it was unlikely to become profitable before 2004. Meanwhile, the investment bank was still struggling to find a vibrant pool of demand, since those Japanese companies that did want to use investment bank services tended to be the big groups, and thus were used to dealing with established brands.

David Fite, the head of finance at Shinsei, insisted that the bank could still find a niche by targeting the "upper-middle" pool of companies that were often ignored by the large Western banks. "There is no doubt that our franchise is smaller than it would have been before the nationalization. The controversy over the cancellation right has shrunk it as well. But the real question people should be asking is do we have more access than other Western firms? Absolutely! The key thing to realize is that our cost structure is so much different from a Western bank—there is a lot of business in Japan, like a Y3 billion [$30 million] securitization, that the other banks will not do because it is too small. But a Western bank will have some employee being paid half a million dollars a year, and we will have a chance manager being paid $70,000. So we can do lots and lots of small deals that no one else will touch."

However, some of the rating agencies remained uncertain about whether these deals would be enough to create a viable business. "Shinsei has still not fully recovered from the damage [caused by nationalization] . . . it is uncertain whether it will be able to achieve stable operating bases in the future," S&P, the rating agency, warned in a report that summer. "In its strategic business areas . . . it faces intense competition from major banks, regional banks, securities companies, foreign-owned financial institutions, and other companies. At this stage, it does not possess strengths that provide it with advantages over these competitors."

Meanwhile, the bad loan problem still hung over the bank. Two years after the bank started, the total level of problem loans on its books remained at Y1.1 trillion ($11 billion), or 20.8 percent of the total, a horrifyingly large level by international standards. Yashiro insisted that the bank would bring this below 5 percent by the spring of 2003, or when the "put" ran out. "We have largely dealt with the big borrowers and we can expect to write these loans off our books soon," he told the journalists in the Bank of Japan club in late May. But it seemed a fantastically optimistic promise, given the row about the "put"; and if Yashiro did not remove these loans before the "put" ran out, the bank's finances could unravel. "I am not blaming Shinsei for this," commented Koyo Ozeki, a credit analyst at Merrill Lynch. "But there is no doubt that for various reasons, including opposition by some politicians to foreign ownership of financial institutions, the bank is in a challenging situation."

In late July, John Reed visited Yashiro in Tokyo again for another pep talk. In the sticky summer heat, the two men reviewed the bank's strategy. Reed hailed the growth in the retail bank, progress in the corporate lending department, and the rising morale of the staff. He thought Yashiro now had a good chance of turning the bank around and realizing his strategic vision—if only the government stopped harassing Shinsei and the bank was able to clean up its balance sheet.

And if that did not happen? Reed was forced to admit that the situation looked precarious. Three years earlier, Onogi had discovered that if the bad loan problem was not resolved, this could wipe away even the best strategic vision in the world. In a way, this had become a chilling metaphor for Japan as a whole. Now Yashiro was facing the same terrible logic: If he did not clean up the balance sheet by the spring of 2003, his bold new banking vision could crumble into ashes. "Frankly, things seemed rather in the balance that summer," Reed later admitted. "I was hoping that everything would turn out OK for Yashiro and he was trying very hard. But a lot depended on what the government did next. It looked to me as if the situation was at a point where it could tip either way."

— *Chapter 20* —

THE BAD LOAN SURPRISE

Cleaning up bad loans isn't a boxing match. It is a barroom brawl.
—Brian Prince

In early September 2002, Junichiro Koizumi, the Japanese prime minister, made a state visit to America. The timing had been arranged to coincide with the first anniversary of the terrorist attack of the World Trade Center, on September 11, and security issues dominated the agenda. However, as Koizumi chatted to U.S. president George W. Bush, the American government felt sufficiently uneasy about Japan's banks to deviate from military matters. What, the American officials asked, was the Japanese government planning to do about the fact that an entire decade after the bubble had burst, its banks were *still* plagued by bad loans?

Koizumi produced the rhetoric he knew the Americans wanted to hear. "Reform is on track. We are preparing to speed up the cleanup of bad loans!" He promised the banks would remove all their bad loans by the spring of 2005.

The Americans did not believe him for a minute. For years Japanese prime ministers had been trooping over to Washington, promising to fix the financial problems. Yet none of them had delivered on their rhetoric. And Koizumi was a particular disappointment. He had been unexpectedly catapulted into power back in the spring of 2001 in an internal LDP election, and the outside world had initially hailed him as a "reformer," because he liked to produce snappy slogans about the need for "change" and sported long, wavy hair. In a world of bland, expressionless men, Japan had finally produced a politician who looked *memorable*. Bush soon declared Koizumi "my good friend," in the jovial buddy-to-buddy manner that Americans liked to adopt.

But in his first year in office, Koizumi seemed unable—or unwilling—to turn his rhetoric into action. Time and time again, the Bush economic team urged the Japanese government to take action to lessen the unease in the financial system. They had a nasty feeling that the problem was—if anything—getting worse, not better. By 2002, it was no longer possible to blame the entire bad loan problem on the collapse of the real estate bubble; instead, new bad loans were emerging that reflected the grinding deflation that was plaguing the economy and the fact that Japanese companies were losing competitiveness on the world stage. Some American economists concluded from this that Japan's real priority was thus stopping deflation, before even worrying about structural reform. Indeed, a school of thought argued that tackling the bad loans on their own would be a mistake since it would actually worsen the deflation. However, as far as American officials such as Glenn Hubbard, the chairman of the Council of Economic Advisers, was concerned, the real problem was that the deflation and banking woes were feeding off each other: Deflation might be creating bad loans but one reason why prices were falling was because there was so much spare capacity in the economy, and banks kept propping up deadbeat borrowers. One of the essential problems was that Japan had never let markets establish any natural "clearing price"—or a point where investors believed that values could not fall further, and were thus willing to purchase assets. Instead, because the government had repeatedly meddled in markets to artificially raise prices, investors did not trust that prices reflected real value. There was a gnawing sense of unease in the markets—and a fear that prices would fall further in the future. Deflation and bad loans had created a deadly cocktail.

Given that, the Americans tried to persuade the Japanese to adopt a *combination* of policies, that wove together monetary easing, bank support, and corporate reform. "What is needed is coordinated policies," argued

Hubbard. More specifically, some American officials suggested that it would make sense to inject public funds into the banks, or use the type of tactics that helped clean up America's S&Ls; namely, letting the weak banks collapse or selling them off. The White House team was particularly fond of preaching about that episode, since it had been Bush Senior who had presided over this "cleanup," and the S&L crisis had taken place in Texas, the Bush family state. Moreover, the Americans believed that the tale had an important political moral: Bush Senior had succeeded with the S&Ls because he had acted immediately after arriving in office, while there was still plenty of political momentum behind him. If Koizumi was ever going to clean up *his* country's bad loans, the Americans argued, he needed to act while he still seemed popular.

But the Koizumi government appeared paralyzed. That was partly because Koizumi lacked the powers of a U.S. president. But his economic predicament was also worse. When American banks had cleaned up their bad loans in the early 1990s, they were enjoying high earnings. At the time there was a steep yield curve, and a large gap between the (very low) interest rate that banks paid to depositors—and the (relatively high) rate that banks charged borrowers. However, in Japan, interest rates were so low that the yield curve was extremely flat. Thus it was difficult for the banks to earn profits from lending, which meant they had few resources with which they could tackle the bad loans. Worse, the banks faced little market pressure to act quickly: With interest rates so low, in the short-term it cost the banks almost nothing to leave the bad loans on the balance sheet.

What was desperately needed, in other words, was a clear political initiative to break the logjam. Uneasily, the American government—and Shinsei investors—wondered if Koizumi could ever produce that.

A few days after Koizumi returned to Tokyo, one unexpected glimmer of hope did emerge. Out of the blue, Masaru Hayami, Bank of Japan governor, suddenly announced that the Bank planned to start purchasing part of the banks' equity portfolios. The idea behind the move, he explained, was to help the banks reduce their shareholdings, since the Bank did not believe that it was a good idea for banks to hold so much of their capital in the form of equities and feared that if the banks sold shares rapidly this would depress the market.

By the standards of financial history, it was a bizarre step for a central bank to take. Behind the scenes, however, Hayami had come to share the American government's unease about the paralysis in the Japanese banking world—and he was desperate to break the deadlock. For Hayami was a rather unusual man. In the past, Bank governors had usually been staid, senior bureaucrats drawn from the ranks of the Ministry of Finance or the Bank itself. Though Hayami had spent the early part of his career working as a Bank bureaucrat, he later left the Bank in the 1980s to work at Nissho Iwai, a trading company. Normally, this type of pedigree would have excluded him from the post of governor. However, when a corruption scandal exploded at the Bank in the spring of 1998, forcing the last governor to resign, the Bank's senior leadership decided they needed a "clean hands" replacement, so instead of picking an internal bureaucrat, it appointed an "outsider," Hayami.

In the event, Hayami turned out to be more of a loose cannon than anyone expected. Before his appointment, he had never had much interest in the details of monetary policy, and he arrived at the Bank presuming he could delegate that to other staff. What he *was* deeply interested in, however, was bank reform and corporate change. Hayami's experience in the private sector had left him passionately convinced that Japan needed to undergo radical corporate restructuring and he disliked heavy government intervention. Indeed, from the moment he arrived in office, Hayami had quietly urged the banks to clean up their bad loans and deal with their deadbeat borrowers, with a zeal that seemed to be influenced by the fact that he was one of Japan's tiny minority of practicing Christians. Many Japanese have a relativist moral universe, in which concepts of "good" can shift and it is presumed that an individual's conscience should reflect the dynamics of the group. Hayami, however, believed in absolute ideas of good and considered it incumbent on everybody to act according their individual conscience.

"In both banking and religion I have strong beliefs," Hayami explained. "Looking back I think I have been in the quest for rationality and efficiency in all my life and whenever I have had a strong responsibility I have tried to act. I think that is like a calling from God. . . . The word I always keep in mind is the serenity prayer of Reinhold Niebuhr: *God grant me the serenity in accepting the things I cannot change, the courage to change the things I can; and the wisdom to know the difference.*" More specifically, in Hayami's eyes, the excesses of the bubble era had not simply been unfortunate, but *wrong*, and Japan required a period of cleansing repentance, to courageously clean up the banking problems. "The way I think of the pursuit of efficiency and rationality and accountability is sometimes different from Japanese thinking. In that way I think there is some impact of Protestantism [on my economic views]."

By the autumn of 2002, Hayami was feeling isolated and frustrated. Soon after he arrived in office, responsibility for overseeing the banks was handed to the FSA, which meant that Hayami had not actually been in charge of the financial system during the last three years. That had forced Hayami to tone down his public comments about the banks. However, he believed that the banks were undercapitalized and needed to take more radical measures to tackle their bad loans than the FSA had suggested. And since Hayami was not allowed to express his views in a *direct* manner, he chose to implement them in the only manner he could—monetary policy. By the autumn of 2002 most Japanese bankers and bureaucrats believed that the Bank should maintain as loose a monetary policy as possible, to stop deflation. However, Hayami argued that a loose monetary policy created a "moral hazard," since it helped the banks to prop up deadbeat borrowers. He insisted that what the country *really* needed to do was to embark on structural reform—and clean up its banks. "Monetary policy alone will not boost the economy. Japan needs to wake up!" he sternly insisted. But, this stance backfired. The more that Hayami refused to loosen monetary policy, the more that the politicians insisted that deflation—not structural problems—was the source of the bad loans. Hayami, for his part, retorted that it would be useless to loosen monetary policy until there was a clear program of structural change. But politicians argued that it was pointless to take tough policy measures until Hayami relented. It was a classic pass-the-parcel game of blame.

The equity purchase scheme was a last-ditch attempt to break this deadlock. On paper, it went against most of Hayami's instincts about how the economy should be run, since it risked creating even more moral hazard in the system. However, Hayami believed that the system needed a "wake-up" call—and he shrewdly guessed that the scheme would signal to the outside world that the Bank was becoming alarmed about the bad loans. So, on September 20, with no prior warning, he announced the Bank's startling plan to purchase "several trillion yen" of bank equities. The markets were so stunned by the move that it was nicknamed the "Hayami hand grenade."

Just as Hayami hoped, the "hand grenade" raised the stakes in Japan's banking debate. Until that point, Hakuo Yanagisawa, the minister in charge of financial policy, had vehemently insisted that Japan's banks were healthy and did not need more capital to deal with their bad loans. Hayami's move was an implicit challenge to that view. And Hayami was not the only skeptic: Heizo Takenaka, the economics minister in the Koizumi cabinet, was also worried. Takenaka was a mop-haired economics professor who had worked in American universities, where he had come to know men such as Hubbard. Takenaka shared the American government's frustration at the slow pace of bank reform and he firmly believed that it was time for Japan to nationalize or close its weakest banks and inject public funds into the system.

Alarmed at this policy split, investors started to sell their shares in Japanese banks and their largest corporate clients. The Koizumi cabinet wondered what to do. Yanagisawa himself had absolutely no intention of backing down in the face of Hayami's challenge and injecting more public funds into the banks. The Koizumi cabinet knew that they could not simply sit on their hands, when the markets—and the American government—were clearly pressing for more action on the banks. So eventually, Koizumi acted: as September turned into October, he sacked Yanagisawa. Then, in a turnabout that stunned the financial markets even more than the "Hayami hand grenade," Koizumi announced Yanagisawa's successor: Takenaka himself. Overnight, a man who proclaimed radical reform views and seemed to be a good friend of the American government had been put in charge of banking policy.

And Takenaka then swung into action, with a sense of melodrama that made the "Hayami hand grenade" seem almost tame. Within days of his appointment, Takenaka airily declared that the laws of free-market economics meant that "no large Japanese bank was too big to fail," suggesting he was preparing to nationalize one of the so-called "megabanks." Then Takenaka assembled a task force to produce a new bank reform plan. This, he indicated, would force the banks to stop flattering their capital with tax breaks; introduce a much stricter system for assessing bad loans; and take criminal actions against any bank manager who had been massaging the accounts. Any bank that failed to meet the minimum BIS standard of capital adequacy would be forced to accept a new injection of public funds—or be closed. Suddenly Japan seemed to be heading toward a new bout of banking reform.

The Shinsei investors were thrilled. The financial markets, however, did not react as well. In theory, foreign investors had been arguing for years that what Japan needed was a radical dose of reform. In practice, however, investors could see that what Takenaka was proposing could deliver some unpleasant short-term shocks, since nobody could assume anymore that Japan's "zombie" companies and banks were protected. Nervously, investors rushed to sell shares in banks and their troubled corporate clients, sparking a sharp slide in equity prices. By mid-October the equity market had tumbled to below 9,000, the lowest level that it had touched for almost twenty years.

Hubbard tried to shrug off the market reaction. In the short term, he argued, there might be some pain; but the laws of free-market economics meant that in the long term investors would welcome any efforts to remove the "zombie" companies and make the Japanese economy more productive. Most Japanese saw things differently. To them, the fall in share prices suggested that Takenaka's reforms were a very bad idea. And the decline was getting worse by the day. By November, the value of the banking sector had fallen by 30 percent, compared to where it had been before the Hayami "hand grenade." Rumors had exploded that Japan could be heading for a new financial crisis. Then, when Hiroshi Okuda, the head of the Toyota motor company—and the mighty *Keidanren* business group—told British journalists that two big banking groups were on the verge of collapse, the share price of Mizuho and UFJ plunged.

Dusting off a well-worn script, the conservative elements inside the Japanese establishment rallied their forces for a backlash. The banks hated

Takenaka's reform plans, because Takenaka wanted to hold bank managers accountable for misrepresenting their bank accounts: Having seen what happened to Onogi at LTCB, none of the other bankers wanted to risk suffering that type of shame themselves. The conservative parts of the LDP hated Takenaka's ideas, because they did not want to let favored companies—and LDP donors—go bankrupt. Meanwhile, many of the FSA bureaucrats were irritated, since Takenaka's initiatives were a direct challenge to the idea that bureaucrats—not politicians—created policy in Japan.

Takenaka grimly battled on in the face of this tide of criticism—loudly backed by the White House. "The U.S. government continues to believe that Takenaka is an excellent reformer," Hubbard declared. However, the lower the stock markets fell, the more the conservatives fought back. And when Takenaka finally produced his "radical" plan at the end of October, he had been forced to water down his most striking proposals. Back in the autumn Takenaka had hoped to stop the banks from artificially boosting their capital bases by using deferred tax assets and other forms of "phony" capital. However, under fierce opposition by the banks, he dropped that idea. He also shelved the concepts of prosecuting bankers who misrepresented their accounts and injecting public funds into the banks. Then the Ministry of Finance derailed Takenaka's proposals for dealing with the banks' troubled borrowers through a radical shakeout by producing an idea of its own—a government-controlled "Industrial Revitalization Corporation." The idea behind this new state body, bureaucrats explained, was to decide which troubled companies were worth saving, and then impose a restructuring plan on "viable companies" and close down hopeless enterprises. The Ministry claimed this would promote restructuring; pundits, however, nicknamed it the "zombie hospital," since it seemed designed to keep propping up the weak companies.

Takenaka's aides and friends attempted to put an optimistic face on these policy defeats. "There are some positive elements in the [new Takenaka] plan, but there is also a significant amount left undone," admitted Hubbard. "Is there everything we had hoped? Certainly not. Is it a step forward? I think so." More specifically, Takenaka supporters insisted that the mop-haired professor *had* made progress in pushing the bank debate in the right direction. As winter wore on, there were signs that Japan was getting tougher in its assessment of the bad loans. There were also indications that the banks themselves had started to feel a little more urgency about the need to tackle the problems. Indeed, the four "megabanks" were so uneasy that they all rushed to find ways to boost their capital bases before the end of the fiscal year on March 31, so that they could write off more bad loans. Yet, no amount of cosmetic tinkering could quite disguise the underlying truth: Yet again, a would-be reformer had been emasculated, and the Japanese establishment had missed a chance to tackle the banking woes.

Back inside Shinsei, the bank management tried to work out what this emotional roller coaster meant. The "Hayami hand grenade" and "Takenaka tempest," as investors liked to call them, showed that opinions about the banks were becoming more and more polarized. Back in 1998, most Japanese intellectuals had been willing to admit that the old banking system was not working anymore, and it was fashionable to use words such as "Big Bang," "globalization," and "market competition." However, by 2002, Japanese officials believed they had glimpsed one alternative to the old status quo—and decided they did not like it very much. To them, market "reform" was associated with bankruptcies and stock market falls, rather than tangible *positive* benefits. The American corporate scandals that exploded during the summer of 2002 had reinforced the Japanese establishment's suspicion of American capitalism—and left Japanese officials less willing to tolerate lectures from Washington about the need for reform. "Back in 1998 and 1999 we agreed that the Japanese financial authorities should break with a convoy-fleet approach of pressuring strong banks to support weaker peers. Instead, it felt that the fate of strong banks should be left to the market," explained Asahiko Isobe, a former member of the Financial Reconstruction Commission, the government body that had sold LTCB to Ripplewood. "But now I am not sure that we were right. Stock prices do not always reflect the true state of a company's financial standing."

And public xenophobia was rising. By late October, rumors were flying around Tokyo that the White House was promoting bank reform so that America could dominate Japan's economy. "The so-called 'Takenaka' shock appears to have been developed in an essentially freelance manner, without serious political discussion in advance," Alex Kinmont, a strategist at Nikko Salomon Smith Barney, gloomily noted. "Yet the manner in which this policy was developed, and the unfortunate fact that it received public backing from U.S. policy makers, has had the unintended consequence of convincing almost all shades of opinion [in Japan] that the evil intentions of foreign vulture funds can be discerned behind Mr. Takenaka's statements, and the consequent fall in stock prices and the attendant troubles of the banks." Or as Ryo Takasugi, a best-selling author, wrote in a column in the Sunday *Mainichi:* "I think that Mr. Takenaka is a pawn being used by foreign capital. American officials in the White House, the Treasury and the State Department are using vulture funds to try to beat down prices [for distressed assets]. It is no wonder that they support Mr. Takenaka."

The vitriol seeped out to infect Shinsei as well. A few months before Takasugi wrote his column in the Sunday *Mainichi*, he published a book called *Za Gaishi (The Foreign Securities House)*. This purported to be a fictional account about how a failed Japanese bank was acquired by an American consortium. However, it was clear that the bank in question was modeled on LTCB, and the American fund—known as "Appletree" in Takasugi's novel—was supposed to be Ripplewood. The Japanese characters in *Za Gaishi* were consequently portrayed as weak-willed men, who had been seduced and corrupted by the dangerous temptations of the Western world and thus forgotten their Japanese spirit. Meanwhile, the Americans were uniformly portrayed as evil and rapacious. The most unattractive foreign character of all appeared to have been closely modeled on Chris Flowers. "Shinsei is a child of evil!" Takasugi thundered.

Yet—almost perversely—some observers took a measure of comfort from the shrill rhetoric: If nothing else, it suggested that the conservative elements in Japan had reason to feel more defensive. For though Takenaka had failed to achieve his grandiose plans to clean up the banks, what he *had* done was to shift the margins of the debate about banking reform and bad loans. As time passed, the idea that rotten companies should collapse was slowly seeping into public consciousness. This did not yet add up to a revolution, let alone any wholesale embrace of the reform ideas. There were still as many signs of opposition to reform, as reform itself. Yet, in a subtle manner, it seemed that the debate was shifting; Shinsei was losing its ability to shock. Or that, at least, was what the Shinsei bankers liked to tell themselves. For, against all the odds, as the autumn rumbled on, the Shinsei bankers believed that they were starting to see signs of progress, and in a most unlikely place—the bank's own loan book.

Back in the summer of 2002, Yashiro had cheerily promised that by the time the bank's "put" option ran out—on March 1, 2003—the bank would have brought the proportion of bad loans down to less than 5 percent of the balance sheet. At the time, most observers had viewed this pledge with deep skepticism, given that bad loans accounted for 20 percent of the total loan book. Yet, while the media's attention was distracted by Takenaka's public policy storm, something remarkable started to unfold. Behind the scenes, Shinsei quietly worked through a remaining chunk of its bad loans, with a speed that few outside observers had ever expected to see. By the time the bank reported its half-year results in late November, the bad loan total had fallen by half. Then, as spring approached, the level kept falling. Just when analysts were becoming gloomy about the macrosituation, on a microlevel inside Shinsei the ice had cracked.

When the Shinsei staff subsequently tried to explain how this turnabout had occurred, some attributed it to a shift in the FSA. During the summer and autumn, relations between the bureaucrats and Shinsei had started to improve; or, more accurately, they did not deteriorate to a point of a public political crisis. Some observers attributed that to the fact that Takenaka had replaced Yanagisawa; others guessed that the Shinsei investors' threats had eventually persuaded the Japanese government to back down, to avoid losing face. As always in Japan, the tipping point for action tended to occur when it became more embarrassing to do nothing, than something.

There seemed to be another, more basic factor at work: during the summer of 2002, Shoji Mori, the head of the FSA who had felt so bitterly betrayed by the bank, left his office and another bureaucrat, Shokichi Takagi took Mori's place. Takagi's ideological views were not very different from those of Mori and he had also spent his career in the bureaucracy; but Takagi had no *personal* reason to feel emotional antipathy to Shinsei. Nor did Takenaka. "In our thinking we are still often very far apart from the

FSA, but the current relationship between the FSA and Shinsei is very cool," Yashiro explained in late 2002. "*Cool* is the important word—not 'cold'! My point is that I can have a very reasonable discussion with the FSA now in a very *rational* atmosphere and that is good. Now they can say where they stand and we can say where we stand, and as long we continue these logical approaches we can make progress." Indeed, by the spring of 2003—in spite of all the political protest—Shinsei had finally managed to return almost Y1 trillion ($10 billion) of bad loans to the government.

However, the shift in the government attitude told only half the turnabout tale. As time passed, Shinsei was increasingly finding ways to clean up its loan book *without* using the "put" at all. Sometimes Shinsei did this by persuading the other banks to buy Shinsei's loans to troubled companies; sometimes Shinsei persuaded its own clients to repay the loan, or offer better collateral against continuing loans. On other occasions, Shinsei also persuaded the company to pay a higher rate of interest or agree to a restructuring plan. Either way, the net result of all these methods was the same: inch by inch Shinsei *was* slowly managing to clean up its balance sheet.

This partly reflected changing attitudes outside the bank. The Sogo saga back in the summer of 2000 had terrified the rest of Japan's corporate world and during 2002 a few more cases emerged that demonstrated that the bank meant business. In early 2002, Shinsei forced First Credit, a troubled consumer credit group and long-standing LTCB client, into bankruptcy. It was the first time any Japanese bank had ever forced an involuntary bankruptcy on a client. Then, Yashiro became involved in a public dispute with Daiei, a troubled retailer, over its failure to cooperate in a restructuring plan with Shinsei or repay loans. The resulting public dispute was deeply embarrassing for Daiei. The retailer eventually backed down and repaid most of the loan and Shinsei then sold the rest of its loans to Daiei to other banks, ending its exposure. By earning a reputation as the neighborhood bully, in other words, Shinsei was forcing a modicum of cooperation from the rest of the system.

But an equally important reason for the shift was a change in attitude *inside the bank*. Back in the spring of 2001, when Shinsei had made its first disastrous attempt to clean up its balance sheet, it had been Americans such as Fite and Flowers who were driving events—and shaping them according to *gaijin* logic. As 2001 wore on, the bank management slowly modified this approach—and tried to learn from its earlier mistakes. Fite decided in the summer of 2002 that he was leaving the bank. Ostensibly this was for family reasons; however, the tension between Fite and Yashiro had never abated and Fite had become thoroughly fed up with being an internal scapegoat for the damaging events of spring of 2001. Meanwhile, Flowers and some of the remaining *gaijin* searched for ways to undo the damage caused by the clumsy policy shift in 2001. Though Flowers was a militant adherent to the American creed of market logic, he was canny enough to realize that he was on a steep learning curve in Japan—and willing to do whatever it took to ensure that the bank (and his own investment) made money. So, as time passed, Flowers and the other *gaijin* explored a range of ways to make the loan collection process seem more in tune with Japanese culture—at least in a cosmetic sense.

The Japanese bankers inside Shinsei started to exert greater influence over the process of loan collection—and ensure that loans were collected with more deference to Japanese sensibilities. Whereas in the spring of 2001, for example, the bank had threatened to cut clients off with almost no notice, by 2002 the bank had installed a new credit procedure that required multiple meetings with clients before any decision was made. A special "relationship fund" had been created, to offer subsidies to troubled clients for a temporary period, if these clients were willing to be cooperative in developing restructuring plans. Moreover, the bank offered a host of new restructuring "advice," or creative solutions, that might help companies to wriggle out of their situations. In some situations, for example, Shinsei securitized the assets of a client to enable them to repay a loan. Sometimes, they even offered new loans in exchange for a proper restructuring plan or a stake in the company. The net result of these schemes was usually the same: namely, that the bank ended up getting its money back, or a higher degree of security behind its loan. The process was more subtle, opaque, and gradual. In Japanese eyes, it was thus more acceptable; in its own way, Shinsei was becoming slightly more "Japanese."

Yashiro himself liked to take credit for some of this shift in the approach. "After I became aware of the issues [in the collection of bad loans]," he said, "we changed the process and since then we have experienced less problems with the customers and politicians." But equally important was a shift in middle management. As the internal operations of the bank had slowly settled down, the battles between the relationship managers and product specialists ebbed away. And as time passed—and the American Prince and Japanese Yamamoto, the coheads of the institutional banking group, worked together—something inside the loan department started to "click." After all the months of procrastination, foot-dragging, and bitter rows, the Shinsei loan team finally started to pull together in tackling the issue of bad loans. "Once people in the bank bought into the idea of cleaning up the bad loans," Prince said, "the implementation was a piece of cake. In the American system, less time is spent getting consensus, but implementation can take longer. Here it takes a lot of time to build consensus, but implementation is quicker."

In optimistic moments, Prince sometimes liked to think the tale could have implications for the rest of the system: namely, that if the other Japanese banks *did* ever decide to act on their bad loans, a turnabout could occur very fast. More importantly, if the experience of Shinsei was any guide, the "tipping point" for this change could sometimes be a subtle one, that could emerge when the outside world least expected it. "It sends a pretty encouraging message to the rest of the Japanese financial system and the world," Prince noted. "When people pull together in Japan, the results can be fantastic."

Yet the parable also came with a more pessimistic caveat. Shinsei had only succeeded in cleaning up its bad loan book because it had a clear sense of leadership. Moreover, this leadership was willing to endure bitter controversy and short-term pain—and squarely face up to the problems. Thus far, however, these qualities were still in woefully short supply in Japan; that at least, seemed to be the sad message from the Takenaka saga.

— *Chapter 21* —

SAVING THE SUN?

Young people in Japan know that when things don't work they should hit the reset button.

—Kenichi Ohmae, author and consultant, suggesting that Japan's leaders need to emulate the "reset" spirit of young Japanese who love to play computer games

In mid-September 2002 Onogi walked into courtroom number 104 in the central court in Tokyo for the conclusion of his trial. He had aged dramatically since his arrest in 1999: His face was taut, frame-thin, and he kept his gaze fixed on the floor or directly ahead, ignoring onlookers. At one end of the court sat three black-cloaked judges; at the other end a desultory audience of middle-aged men bedecked in suits. Some were journalists; many were friends of Onogi or fellow bankers who nervously wanted to find out whether the government considered LTCB to have acted in a criminal manner—or not—by concealing the bad loans.

In a flat monotone, a judge read out the verdict: "guilty," with a three-year suspended prison term for Onogi and two years for Suda and Suzuki, his two LTCB colleagues. Then, he read a statement explaining the decision. It took almost three hours to articulate. Ponderously, the judges noted that when Onogi and the other LTCB executives had "massaged" the bank's accounts, they had been acting in accordance with the accepted standards of behavior at the time, with the knowledge of the Ministry of Finance. "We have some sympathy with the defendants," the judge noted. However, he then insisted that Onogi had behaved in a criminal fashion. "The executives ended up generating bad debts on a large scale, when they should have been disposing of the bad debts, in their roles as a president and vice presidents of LTCB. Onogi in particular is guilty of particular misconduct, since he was a top executive at the bank."

Onogi was utterly poker-faced as he listened. He had no intention of trying to point out the obvious: namely, that if *he* was a criminal, so was almost everybody in the Japanese government and banking world, given that the entire establishment had tried to run away from the problems for a decade. Onogi was not going to complain in public about his fate. Yet he remained convinced that it was ridiculous to label his actions at LTCB as wrong, given the broader national issues at stake. It would have been completely impossible, he sometimes muttered to friends, for LTCB to have blown the whistle on the bad loans or cut off bad borrowers back in 1998, without hurting the rest of the financial sector. If anybody doubted that, he fumed, they only needed to look at the experience of Shinsei, and all the anger and controversy that Yashiro had created! Would the Japanese government have wanted LTCB to go around behaving like Shinsei back in 1998, trying to create a "hard landing"? Was *that* really a better way of fixing Japan's problems?

Of course, Onogi hastily added whenever he talked to his friends about the matter, he did not want to criticize Yashiro personally. Onogi liked his successor and tended to assume that it was the Americans, not Yashiro, who were to blame for the "coldhearted" stance. However, he felt a palpable sense of disappointment. In 1999, he had comforted himself with the hope that the death of LTCB was going to act as a "seed" to promote Japanese-style reform; but by 2002, he had lost this faith. To him, Shinsei was *not* the answer; perhaps the "American" way might be more efficient in a narrow economic sense; but it risked sacrificing the values that were most precious in Japan: ideas of harmony, respect, and consensus. Indeed, Onogi sometimes doubted whether Shinsei was even the answer in an "economic" or "business" sense: It was one thing for one bank to clean up its loans quickly; but if all the banks went around behaving like Shinsei, that would trigger a terrible, unnecessary recession. If Shinsei alienated all its clients, it would lose business.

In Onogi's eyes, that did *not* mean that he was denying the need for reform; he desperately wanted to see some broader vision in the country. Yet, why did reform mean that Japan needed to implement a dramatic shakeout or become an economic outpost of the American financial empire? Living standards were dramatically better than anything that Onogi's generation had grown up with, in the decades after World War II. The nation remained fabulously rich: On paper, it still had some Y1,400 trillion ($14 trillion) of savings and an enormous current account surplus; it was not Korea or Argentina. So why not aim for a steady pace of *Japanese*-style change that used this wealth to cushion the blow? Sooner or later, the economy would recover. And when that happened, the banks' problems would go away—just as Onogi still believed that they would have evaporated at LTCB, if he had only been given a bit more time.

In the last resort, Onogi remained convinced that evolution, not revolution, was the best way to "save" what was important about Japan, even if it meant sacrificing a bit of economic growth.

And if the last three years were any guide, it seemed that most of his compatriots agreed.

Yashiro, however, did *not* agree; when he looked back at what had happened in Japan in the last three years, he felt buffeted by optimism—and despair. As far as Shinsei itself was concerned, he felt proud about what he had achieved. By March 2003, the level of bad loans had fallen to a mere Y233 billion ($2.33 billion), or about 5 percent of the total. In three years, the bank had removed Y2.7 trillion ($27 billion) in bad loans, using the "put" to clean up Y990 billion ($10 billion) and removing another Y1.7 trillion ($17 billion) itself. There were still a few loans outstanding whose status was in dispute due to technical arguments about the use of the "put." However, by most measures Shinsei had managed to clean up most of its balance sheet. "A year ago the situation was problematic—they were at a clear fork in the road and there was a feeling that the thing could go in one direction or the other," Reed observed. "But in the last six months the situation at the bank has changed. Yash has achieved a real breakthrough on the bad loans."

This turnabout did not yet guarantee commercial success for the bank in the future, let alone ensure that the bank could conduct an IPO anytime soon. The bank had notched up three years of healthy profits, while it was protected by the "put," but this protection had now run out. The questions that had hung over the bank in the summer of 2002—namely, could it sell its investment banking and retail services on a large enough scale to generate high profits—were still relevant. "Yash's problem now is making sure that he has a good solid business base. From a business point of view he has got a reasonably decent base, but it is not entirely stable," Reed admitted. "That is the issue going forward."

Yet, what Yashiro *had* done was create the platform on which the future Shinsei managers could implement a new banking model. And that made the bruising battle worthwhile. "I don't regret having taken the position of president of Shinsei. It has been much harder than I expected and I have had *so* much criticism. But I truly believe that eventually the rest of Japan will appreciate what we have done at Shinsei and realize what all the Japanese banks should be doing!" Yashiro liked to say. Or as Reed echoed: "Yash thinks that he has created something that will be useful to Japanese society. He now has a real sense of satisfaction." At the age of seventy-four, Reed reckoned that his friend more than deserved it.

What Yashiro did not feel, however, was much satisfaction about the rest of Japan. He liked to hope that the past three years showed that Japan was beginning to move in the right direction. "Japanese society is changing its perspective and becoming more accepting of business failures. It is going through a learning process. The fact is that Japan just needs more time than any other industrialized country to adjust and adapt to a changing world, partly because for forty years the old system seemed so successful."

But the critical question remained: Was Japan changing *fast enough?* The challenge for the world's second largest nation was not simply to "change," but to do so at a speed that could make its economy sufficiently productive to offset all the other factors that were dragging the country down. And these pressures were formidable. The self-reinforcing cancer of deflation and bad loans was eating away at growth. The country was losing competitiveness to its neighbors such as China, and many of its best manufacturers were fleeing its shores. The level of national debt was rising toward 150 percent, as Japan kept spending more and more money to prop the old system up. The population was aging at a horrifying speed: By the year 2020, the ratio of dependent people to those in work was projected to rise from 44 percent in the late 1990s to 65 percent, a development which could crush the rate of growth. Japan was like a swimmer moving against a tide: If it just made token signs of action, it could only hope to stay still, at best.

In the eyes of outside economists, this posed frightening questions about Japan's long-term financial stability. In the short-term, Japan was easily able to service its huge national debt because most of the debt was held by domestic savers, who were more than willing to buy low-yielding bonds and less alarmed by the type of economic analysis that worried international investors. As long as this domestic demand for bonds continued, the government was able to keep spending money on propping the old system up, which in turn reduced the sense of crisis, and ensured that savers were happy to keep buying government debt. Japan was trapped in a cycle of complacency and wealth. Yet the combination of an aging population, deflation, and slow growth suggested that it would be almost impossible for Japan to repay this debt in full unless it dramatically raised its rate of growth, which it was unlikely to do without radical structural reform, and probably a wave of immigration as well. Eventually the government was likely to default on the debt it owed to its own population, either directly or indirectly (through hyperinflation). And if that occurred, the illusion of calm could shatter, triggering a violent market upheaval. What worried macroeconomists, in other words, was that Japan's own obsession with preserving "stability" was—ironically—sowing the seeds for terrible financial *in*stability in the future.

Yashiro expressed his unease with simpler metaphors. He was not a macroeconomist by training. But, he *was* a deep patriot and he deeply grieved for what might soon befall his nation. As a child, Yashiro had witnessed Japan's military expansion into Asia, followed by its humiliating defeat and destruction. As an adult, Yashiro had brimmed with pride at his country's amazing subsequent renaissance on the world stage. At the age of seventy-four, he found it deeply distressing to imagine that this was going to crumble into ashes again. "If we don't change here in Japan, we will just keep slowly declining as a nation. We *have* to change our way of thinking if we want a better future," he sometimes muttered. "By avoiding short-term pain we just keep creating a longer-term cost. The way we have been dealing with the problems of the last ten years in this country will lead to a continuous decline of this country, not only economically but also politically.

"And Korea and China are going up as Japan is going down. If this [muddling through] continues, Japan will keep slowly declining and declining until it is in a position *under* China. If this continues we will end up being just an eastern province of China in fifteen years!" To Yashiro—like most Japanese—that seemed the ultimate humiliation.

"I am not saying that because I think it is inevitable, but because it could happen if we don't change.

"And when I think about that I feel very sad."

For his part, when Collins reflected on the state of Japan he would also get a little downhearted. In some respects, the past five years had been a distinctly humbling period for the American entrepreneur. When he had first planned the purchase of LTCB back in 1998, he had assumed that one of two things would unfold: Either Japan would recover and post a healthy rate of growth (which would help the bank), or it would tip into a recession, which would in turn force a broader shakeout of the corporate world (and also benefit Shinsei). What Collins had *not* imagined was that Japan would continue to muddle through, with neither a recovery nor a dramatic corporate shakeout. Nor had he expected the shifting world of political currents on Japan to be so perfidious. "I have been stunned by the [anti-*gaijin*] backlash," he admitted.

Yet, irrespective of these setbacks, Collins had never lost his conviction that Japan's economy had amazing potential and that the best way to save it from decline—indeed the *only* way—was to embark on a bout of creative destruction and radical corporate reform. And, against all the odds, he remained convinced that *eventually* some type of shakeout would occur. For however paralyzed Japan might seem at the macro level, there were lots of encouraging signs of microlevel reform. Companies were going bankrupt at a faster rate than ever before. Foreign investors were slowly entering new sectors of the economy. A new generation of Japanese was growing up with subtly different attitudes from their parents: They were willing to change jobs; they were less obsessed with the idea of duty; and they had less emotional angst toward foreigners. Indeed, in Collins's eyes, the last three years at Shinsei provided tangible, concrete proof that change could occur—and sometimes when least expected. "I think the genie is out of the bottle; there is no other managed centrally planned solution that is going to work [except corporate reform]," he concluded. "Change is inevitable and it is just a question of when and how bad things have to get before the change occurs."

So, with all the dogged optimism, opportunism, self-confidence—and sheer entrepreneurial energy—that had historically made America's brand of capitalism so extraordinarily vibrant, Collins kept clambering back into the first-class section of an airplane to make the fourteen-hour journey to Tokyo and preach the gospel of restructuring. Sooner or later, he liked to tell listeners, Japan simply *must* realize its need for corporate reform; one day the government would understand that the path of Shinsei was right. Somewhere in the corner of his heart, he even hoped that Japan would eventually hail him as a hero.

But in the meantime—and even amid adversity—Collins remained convinced that he could make money.

EPILOGUE

[Shinsei] may be the most profitable private equity deal of all time.

—David Rubenstein, co-founder of Carlyle,
the global buyout group, speaking in March 2004

On February 19, 2004—or almost four years after LTCB started its new life as Shinsei—the investors finally conducted their long-awaited IPO. This time the government did not attempt to block the listing. And the sale went off with a bang. The consortium sold 476 million shares, about a third of the outstanding common stock of the bank (excluding the portion that the government could own in the future, if it converts its preference shares) for about Y250 billion, or a price of Y525 a share. In the run-up to the IPO, the three investment banks chosen to underwrite the deal—Morgan Stanley, Nikko Salomon Smith Barney, and Nomura—had initially suggested selling the shares at a much lower price level, around Y435. But demand for the shares was extremely heavy, both in Japan and overseas. So the underwriters eventually set the IPO price at the very top of their provisional price range. On opening day the share price soared even higher to Y827 and then broke above Y850 in subsequent weeks, pushing the total market capitalization of the bank above Y1,000 billion. After all the twists and turns of the previous years, the IPO looked like a stunning success.

The high demand for Shinsei shares partly reflected the macroeconomic environment. During 2003, the Japanese economy had embarked on a cyclical recovery, due to a stronger global economy and a new effort by the Bank of Japan to loosen monetary policy. This, in turn, had reduced the sense of crisis across the Japanese banking sector. For as the economy improved, the Japanese stock market rose, which raised the value of the Japanese banks' equity portfolios—and thus, their capital bases. Meanwhile, fears of a financial crisis were alleviated when it became increasingly clear that the government was not willing to let any large bank collapse. During early summer 2003, the government stepped in to rescue Resona with an injection of almost Y2,000 billion of public funds after its capital adequacy ratio plunged so low that the accountants refused to sign off on the accounts. Separately, the Bank of Japan also kept flooding the markets with so much liquidity that there was little danger that any bank would ever run out of funds, however weak it might be. "The banks are insolvent but very liquid," says Brett Hemsley, associate director at Fitch, the credit rating agency. "It is only illiquid banks that fail."

These macroeconomic factors left investors more willing to hold bank shares in general. But the reason they were interested in buying Shinsei stock in particular was that by the time the IPO took place, the bank looked clean and well run—and doubly so when compared to the dismal standards of its competitors. By early 2004, the government liked to claim that Japan's banks had put the worst behind them. And in some respects this was true: The upturn in the economy meant that the banks were finally starting to make some headway in reducing their bad loans, and some were even on track to post profits for the year. Nevertheless, the banks had still not truly resolved the basic question hanging over the sector: namely, how could they make money on their lending business when interest rates were so low? And the asset problems seemed unlikely to disappear for several more years, given that the banks still had plenty of bad loans on their books—irrespective of any progress in reducing the total—and relatively little capital by international standards.

At Shinsei, however, the bank was posting its third consecutive year of net profits, of around Y60 billion. And though it was finding it difficult to make any profits from its traditional corporate lending business, it was reaping earnings from its nonlending businesses, such as loan trading. Meanwhile, the bank's capital adequacy ratio was running at around 20 percent, and its bad loan ratio was a mere 4 percent. "Many people thought that the reason we were doing well was because of the cancellation clause—they thought when that expired, we would not do so well," Yashiro said in the spring of 2004. "But we have shown now that is not true!"

In the longer term, the bank still faced big challenges. Corporate Japan remained wary of Shinsei's investment banking services. Meanwhile, the bank had so much spare capital on its books that there was a risk that management might be tempted to make silly investments in the future. During late 2003, for example, it emerged that the bank had suffered some losses on unwise investments that it had made in U.S. corporate bonds during its first few years, while it was seeking places to invest its capital. Meanwhile, the bank remained dogged by management upheaval: In the summer of 2003, for example, the Tokyo financial community was startled to hear that Brian Prince was suddenly leaving the bank. His departure meant that the two most senior American bankers who had been present at the outset of the Shinsei saga had now left. And it was far from clear that all the fights between Shinsei and the government had ended. During the IPO, the investors had tried hard to persuade the government to sell its 33 percent stake. However, it refused, ostensibly because it remained uncertain whether Shinsei had a truly viable business model. Suspicions abounded that the government was not yet willing to stop meddling at the bank.

But by the time the IPO took place, most investors were willing to overlook these uncertainties. "I think the reaction from investors shows that the markets think what Shinsei has done is the right thing," declared Yashiro shortly after the IPO. Or as Marc Desmidt, head of investment at Merrill Lynch, said, to explain why investors were scrambling to buy shares: "This is a bellwether event. Shinsei is a bank that has emerged from rehabilitation under foreign control, and it is clean." In investment banking terms, in other words, Shinsei was an easy story to sell.

But did a successful IPO mean that the Shinsei experiment as a whole could be called a success? On that point, as about almost everything else in the bank's history, opinions remained very mixed. Over on Wall Street, where success is judged in terms of profits, the answer was a resounding yes—at least for the investors. By selling their 35 percent stake for some Y250 billion, the investors had roughly doubled the $1 billion they had spent to purchase the bank. Better yet, the paper value of the remaining stake they still held in the bank was extremely valuable, theoretically worth around $8 billion at the share price seen in late March. Of course, there was absolutely no guarantee that the share price would stay that high. As the history of Japan had shown in the last decade, share prices could fall as well as rise. However, by the spring 2004, most investors were celebrating an internal rate of return of about 70 percent. And while this type of IRR was not in itself a record in the private equity business, when it was combined with the sheer scale of the original investment, it made Shinsei potentially the most profitable deal ever seen anywhere in the history of private equity—if the share price remained high. Or as David Rubenstein, co-founder of Carlyle, the global buyout group, said at a conference on private equity in Germany shortly after the IPO: "This may be the most profitable private equity deal of all time."

The biggest winners in this bonanza were Flowers and Collins. Back in 1999, they had structured the deal in a manner which meant that about 20 percent of the profits would be split evenly between Collins's Ripplewood and Flowers's private equity company. At the listing price, that created a joint unrealized gain of about $1.2 billion (or nearly $2 billion, if this was calculated according to the share price in subsequent weeks). However, of the two men it was Flowers who made the most money. For in addition to his 10 percent stake of the profits, Flowers had raised his exposure to the bank back in 2003, by buying equity from one of the deal's original backers. This left him one of the largest shareholders, which meant that his potential profit from the deal was heading toward $1 billion—at least if the share price stayed high. Even by the standards of Wall Street, this was a stunning coup for any one individual.

The other key investors also recorded large gains, with groups such as Mellon, Citigroup, and Deutsche all estimated to have enjoyed some $50 million of profits after the IPO. Another big winner was Banco Santander Central Hispano, the Spanish bank. Back in 2000, BSCH had taken a 6 percent stake in the bank. But in 2003, the Spanish bank doubled that stake after ABN Amro, another early investor, quietly decided to sell its shares to BSCH. BSCH then went on to sell a third of this 12 percent stake in the IPO, netting itself a capital gain of ∈109 million. Its remaining stake in the bank was theoretically worth about ∈500 million.

But although these heady profits made Shinsei look like a clear-cut success to Wall Street, inside Japan itself the verdict was more mixed. By the spring of 2004, the level of public criticism of Shinsei had died down, compared to the vitriol the bank had attracted during 2000 and 2001. That was partly because the bank had finished most of its difficult work in cleaning up its balance sheet and was no longer threatening to trigger a wave of corporate bankruptcies. Equally important, after four years of bitter battles, many of the ideas that had sounded radical when first mooted by Shinsei were starting to become more widespread. The concept that Japanese banks needed to be solvent was becoming more accepted. So was the idea that banks should price money.

However, this new climate of grudging tolerance did not mean that the Japanese establishment had really learned to love Shinsei. Nor did the government want to see the experiment repeated too widely. Since 2000, three other Japanese banks in addition to LTCB had fallen into the hands of Americans: Cerberus, the U.S. private equity group, had taken control of Aozora, buying out the stake held by Softbank; Lonestar, another private equity group, owned Tokyo Sowa bank, a regional group; and Kofuku, another regional bank, had been acquired by Wilbur Ross, a third private equity player. However, few observers expected to see more sales soon. Indeed, the government's move to rescue Resona in the summer of 2003 appeared to mark a deliberate decision to avoid embarking on another bank sale—or creating a repeat of the Shinsei saga.

This unease about Shinsei was fueled by controversy about the IPO. Japan has never had a culture with a strong concept of risk and reward. Consequently, many ordinary Japanese felt distinctly uneasy about the idea that foreign investors should make such massive profits from a bank deal, particularly when the deal had been organized by the government after a massive injection of public funds. Indeed, by the spring of 2004, some government officials estimated that the total amount of money that had been spent supporting LTCB over the years had risen to more than Y7,000 billion. This staggering sum included the money spent cleaning up the bank's balance sheet, purchasing preferred shares, providing reserves, and subsequently purchasing bad loans.

To make matters worse, in early 2004 it emerged that the consortium would not pay any Japanese tax on their profits since the group they had used to make the investment—New LTCB partners—was based in the Netherlands. (Existing laws meant that Dutch-based investment vehicles generally are not liable to Japanese tax, although in the Shinsei case, the investors may eventually pay tax in their home countries.) "There is a perception that foreigners have got rich at the expense of Japanese taxpayers," admitted one government official. "That is unfortunate for the cause of reform."

The government tried to shrug off this criticism, arguing that the high profits generated by the deal were simply a natural reward for the high levels of risk. "Japanese banks could have bought [Shinsei] if they wished," said Junichiro Koizumi, Japan's prime minister. "The fact is that it was worth taking that risk." Meanwhile, defenders of the deal pointed out that it was wrong to assume that the Y7,000 billion injection had somehow helped the Shinsei investors per se. Most of the funds had been spent well before the Americans even arrived—which meant that if anyone had benefited, it had been Japanese borrowers or debenture holders. Meanwhile, the amount that the government had spent to acquire LTCB assets was likely to be recouped, in part, from the sale of these assets in the future. The LTCB equity portfolio, for example, could potentially be valuable. And the government holds two swaths of preference shares, which it has to convert into common stock by 2007 and 2008, at a share price of Y360 and Y600–800. At market prices in the spring of 2004, this implied a Y500 billion-odd potential gain. "The government may make money [on the assets] if the economy continues to improve," says Yashiro. "People say that Shinsei cost the Japanese taxpayer all this money, but that is simply not true!"

These arguments did not entirely remove the sour taste felt by many Japanese observers about the whole Shinsei saga. Most Japanese commentators did not blame the Ripplewood consortium itself for this. On the contrary, by the spring of 2004, there was a grudging acceptance among many Japanese intellectuals that Shinsei investors had simply been acting in accordance with the terms of the 1999 deal. When bankers, journalists, politicians, or pundits looked at the deal, on the other hand, there was a growing sense of anger at the government. Or as the *Asahi Shimbun* wrote: "Critics who are miffed by a foreign consortium cashing in on the rehabilitation of Shinsei Bank miss the point: The fault lies with the government . . . the root of the problem was clearly careless government management based on a flawed loan assessment . . . and the government has still got to learn the lesson."

And what of the characters who became swept up in the LTCB and Shinsei saga? These days, Collins and Flowers continue to chase new deals. Flowers has acquired a 22 percent stake (currently worth about $50 million) in Enstar, an American reinsurance run-off company, and is expanding its global business. His private equity fund has also acquired an American company that finances mobile home purchases, and it heavily invested in Allianz, the German insurance group. More controversially, since 2001, Flowers has also been trying to buy Bankgesellschaft, a deeply troubled German bank, in a move that would replicate the Shinsei deal. In 2003, the Berlin government rejected this bid. But Flowers remains keenly interested in doing financial deals in Germany.

"Germany and Japan are similar in that capital markets are dominated by banks rather than the securities markets, which results in a more opaque market, with more opportunity for the accumulation of bad debts," he explains. "In both countries you have large financial institutions at the heart of the financial system which have serious problems, [so] I believe what I have learnt from Shinsei will be very valuable should we end up investing in a major German bank or insurance company."

Separately, Collins continues to expand Ripplewood's operations, both in America and Japan. The company now employs some fifty staff, has raised more than $2 billion in funds for American investments, and has generated an average IRR of about 60 percent from the deals that have been completed in America. In Japan, Ripplewood is expanding via the RHJ fund, or the joint venture with Mitsubishi, which has raised $1.2 billion for investments. Thus far RHJ has now bought seven distressed Japanese companies, including Niles Parts (an auto supplier linked to the Nissan empire),

Columbia Music (a record label); Phoenix Seagaia (a sprawling resort complex in the south of Japan), and Denon and Marantz (two electronics groups, which Ripplewood merged). Collins hopes to revive these distressed companies by teaming up with other leading business executives. At Nippon Columbia, for example, the restructuring effort is being lead by Strauss Zelnick, the American music executive.

Some of the Japanese projects have made progress: Columbia recently recorded the first operating profit for several years, and Niles has increased its EBITDA by more than 4.5 times. Other projects, like Seagaia, have had more mixed results. Nevertheless, Collins remains optimistic that his other investments in Japan will repeat the Shinsei success. And in the summer of 2003, he pulled off his biggest purchase to date: a Y230 billion leveraged buyout of Japan Telecom. This was not only the biggest deal of its kind ever seen in Japan, but it also makes Ripplewood easily the largest private equity player there. Collins likes to tell his investors—with his usual chirpy optimism—that the Japan Telecom deal will end up producing even *more* profits than Shinsei.

Yashiro, for his part, is plotting his retirement. He plans to leave Shinsei in the summer of 2005—by which time he will be seventy-six years old—and has already hired his successor: Thierry Porte, the former head of Morgan Stanley's operations in Japan. Although he hails from an American bank, Porte has spent many years working in Japan, is fluent in Japanese, and knows the Tokyo elite well. The hope is that Porte will thus be able to offer another way of "bridging" the different Japanese and Wall Street business approaches, particularly since Porte and Yashiro are expected to work together for around eighteen months before Yashiro leaves.

What Yashiro himself will do next remains unclear, but he will probably not live in Japan. Like many people who have challenged the system in Japan, or simply spent a considerable period of their lives outside the straitjacket of Japanese society, Yashiro and his family now feel more comfortable living outside his homeland. So he is thinking of returning to London, or even heading to New York, where his dogged individualism will not attract criticism anymore. Nevertheless, wherever he lives, he is likely to do so in some style: His years at Shinsei are believed to have left him very wealthy.

Onogi, by contrast, faces vastly reduced circumstances. He is now appealing the guilty sentence in the criminal case against him, and the case is likely to reopen in 2004. Meanwhile, the prosecutors have launched civil suits against most of the former LTCB management, to reclaim billions of yens' worth of damages over their role in the collapse of the bank. If the prosecutors win their case, it is highly unlikely that the former LTCB management will actually be able to pay any fine in full. Still, the legal process is likely to take many years, perhaps beyond the lifetime of most LTCB managers. For many, it is a dismal way to spend their final years.

The men linked to EIE are now trying to stage a surprising renaissance. In the mid-1990s, Harunori Takahashi was given a suspended four-and-a-half-year prison sentence for false accounting. He immediately appealed the sentence, and just a few days after the conclusion of Onogi's trial, in the autumn of 2002, Takahashi trooped into a court, as well, just a few yards away from the room where Onogi had appeared. The atmosphere in Takahashi's hearing was very different: Whereas the onlookers at Onogi's trial had been sober middle-aged men and the LTCB men had been afforded three lawyers, the audience at Takahashi's trial was a brash, talkative group, and no less than *nine* lawyers were helping Takahashi to fight his case.

Their defense rested on a strategy of blaming everything on Onogi and LTCB. "The matter of Takahashi is fundamentally about LTCB and the conspiracy that LTCB conducted," one of these lawyers solemnly told the court. "Compared to Onogi, Takahashi did nothing wrong." The courts did not entirely accept this. Yet, Takahashi's arguments had some effect: In 2003, the Japanese court reduced his sentence, effectively leaving Takahashi a free man.

Takahashi then took an even more startling step: In early 2004, the administrator of EIE International launched a massive lawsuit against Shinsei bank, demanding some $7 billion damages as compensation for the way in which LTCB had sold off the Regent Hotel assets back in 1992. Credit Suisse First Boston and Shearman & Sterling, a U.S. law firm that had been involved in this Regent deal, were also sucked into the litigation, which had been bubbling in various forms for several years.

To casual observers, this case seemed almost laughably bizarre, if not opportunistic. After all, Shinsei itself had never had any direct dealings with EIE. Indeed, until the lawsuit exploded, most of the Americans involved with Shinsei knew little at all about EIE—or Takahashi. Wall Street was a world that preferred to focus on the future, not the past, and when the Shinsei investor consortium had acquired the bank back in 2000, most of its members assumed that the murky history of the bubble years had little relevance to their business plans. However, Takahashi's legal team argued that because Shinsei was the surviving entity to LTCB, it should thus inherit the legal liabilities for LTCB's alleged wrongs. More specifically, EIE claimed that LTCB's decision to dispose of the Regent Hotel group assets, such as the 57th Street hotel in New York City, back in the early 1990s had been tantamount to fraud, since these sales took place even though LTCB never took formal legal control over EIE. To back up their claim, they presented documents that they had seized from LTCB and Shearman & Sterling, the U.S. law firm which had been the EIE lawyer during this period.

These documents described how LTCB staff had drawn up a scheme—code-named Project Penthouse—to secretly strip the Regent group of its assets. By the standards of Japanese banking, what LTCB had allegedly done was not particularly unusual: After all, Japanese banks had usually assumed that they controlled their borrowers, irrespective of whether they had any legal documents to show this. The EIE team was convinced that by the standards of American law courts, LTCB's behavior was tantamount to fraud. "[The documents] say things like they are going to 'empty EIE' out and 'quietly hold a funeral for it,'" explained Ed Calvo, part of a team of American lawyers retained by EIE to fight the case in American courts. And in the summer of 2003, Shearman & Sterling took the highly unusual step of issuing a public apology to EIE over the way that it had sold off the Regent Hotel assets, such as the New York 57th Street hotel. "Shearman & Sterling has been informed that the law firm's efforts did not help EIE International," this apology said. "Shearman & Sterling is deeply sorry."

At Shinsei itself, most of the investors and managers initially paid relatively little attention to the whole affair. They doubted that Takahashi's case would get legs, and assumed that even if it did, the bank would be protected from the cost of any damages, since back in 2000, the DIC had pledged to indemnify the bank against any action taken by LTCB before 2000 and compensate it for any legal damages over Y5 billion. However, after EIE International lodged its lawsuit against Shinsei in early 2004, some DIC officials appeared to have second thoughts about this clause. In particular, they argued that the government did not face any obligation to meet the costs of a future legal bill created by Takahashi, since Shinsei had failed to inform them about the scale of the EIE suit. If the bank did not accept this, the DIC bureaucrats muttered, *they* would take the bank to court as well.

By the spring of 2004, it was still distinctly unclear how this tangled tale would develop. Collins and Flowers were embroiled in discussions with the DIC, trying to force the Japanese government to accept its liability. Meanwhile, Shinsei itself was seeking to force EIE into a process of independent arbitration inside Japan, to keep the case well away from costly American law courts. But however the tale ends, one thing is clear: The saga of Takahashi shows that history had a nasty way of biting back in Japan, even—or especially—when foreign investors least expect it.

As the lawsuit rumbles on, observers say that Takahashi is living comfortably even though he has no visible means of employment. "Takahashi does fine," Ishizaki, his former aide at EIE, explains. "He has friends who help him—that sort of thing!" The identity of the friends remains mysterious. Meanwhile, Ishizaki, for his part, now runs a small company that specializes in the import of health food from the Pacific island of Tonga. It is based in Ginza, almost next door to the old EIE office. Iwao Nomoto—the third key member of the EIE team and the "logistics man" who helped Takahashi—has also carved out a new business career for himself: He runs a new real estate company and dreams of building his own hotel empire one day.

Bob Burns of the Regent group is flourishing. To this day, he remains angry about the way that LTCB sold his beloved Regent hotels to the Four Seasons group back in 1992. Yet he has plenty to console himself with. He recently got remarried to a much younger wife, and in 2001, at the age of seventy-three, became a father for the first time. He splits his time between a palatial apartment on New York's Park Avenue and a delightful corner of northern Italy, where he has bought an old villa that Mussolini, the Italian dictator, once used as a summer retreat. Funded with some of the $200 million in proceeds from the Regent sale, Burns has remodeled this villa into a luxury hotel called the Villa Feltrinelli. It is the first hotel in his career that he has developed without any interference from fickle bankers, and he adores the place, perhaps more than any other hotel he has ever owned. He spent ten times more on the lavish hotel furnishings than he actually spent on acquiring the property.

The hotel on 57th Street in New York is also flourishing, under the name The Four Seasons New York. In the mid-1990s, it was finally sold to a consortium of Hong Kong Chinese investors for about $150 million (or about a quarter of what it cost LTCB to build). The Chinese investors then cannily sold it for almost twice that price to Ty Warner, a fabulously wealthy, highly secretive, Chicago-based businessman, whose main occupation in life is running the company that produces the Beanie Baby toy.

Under Warner's control, the hotel has become a favorite spot for power lunches, classy dinners, or meetings among the elite of New York. And Warner reportedly adores the hotel; so much so, that his company has even designed a new line of Beanie Babies to honor Isadore Sharpe, the owner of the Four Seasons group. These are called Izzie Babies and are sometimes placed in the 57th Street hotel as souvenirs for guests, along with promotional literature praising Sharpe. These leaflets never mention the tangled tale of Bob Burns or EIE, let alone LTCB or Shinsei. Indeed, very few New Yorkers have any idea about the hotel's tangled past. Nor, until recently, did Ripplewood: In a particularly ironic twist, Collins's private equity group has sometimes held its own meetings at the 57th Street hotel in recent years.

The UBS bankers who became entangled with LTCB in 1997 and 1998 have also gone on to new pastures. In the months after the collapse of LTCB, the Tokyo office of UBS buzzed with rumors that the leaders of the failed alliance might be sacked. Western investment banks are cruel, Darwinian places that rarely tolerate failure. However, Volpi was later promoted to head up the combined Japanese operations of both SBC and UBS, and he now runs private banking for UBS in Milan. He retains a keen interest in Japan and recently published a book calling on Japan to reform. "I think that there is a huge capacity for self-delusion among the Japanese," he says. "This country is dangerous because they cannot rationalize things. There is just this huge self-deception about reality."

Meanwhile, Arnold rebounded from the setback in an even more startling manner. He left Japan in the autumn of 1998 to become chief operating officer of the entire UBS group back in Zurich and later became CEO of the bank (although he was later ousted from UBS in a boardroom dispute in late 2001 and now runs Abbey, a British savings group). Some bankers suspect Arnold survived the LTCB debacle due to lucky timing. Just before LTCB failed, financial markets were rocked by the collapse of Long Term Capital Management, a U.S. hedge fund based in New York. UBS was heavily exposed to LTCM. In the midst of that, the UBS board in Zurich had no time to worry about a Japanese bank with a confusingly similar name. "In a sense, Japan is the perfect place to screw up, because people are very willing to blame the country and culture, and not you," admitted one senior UBS banker.

However, there was another factor at work: In spite of all the controversy, the Swiss ended up doing quite well from the deal, in financial terms. Although the bank lost about $50 million on the shares that it had held in LTCB, it more than recouped this loss in huge fees it subsequently earned from investment banking deals that arose from the alliance.

Like most of the *gaijin* who had ever dealt with LTCB, in other words, Arnold and Volpi had emerged having made a profit. Yet, like generations of foreigners before them—and to come—they still have a lingering sense that Japan is a baffling place.

NOTES

x the entire British economy: This Y100 trillion estimate represents a rough rule of thumb, calculated by adding existing nonperforming loans (NPLs) to loans already written off. For more details see "Notes on Bad Loans."

3 "please take care to be ready!": Due to an ongoing legal process Onogi was forbidden to talk to journalists in an official capacity about events that occurred after 1999. However, the author knew Onogi relatively well for several years before this date and has drawn on comments from these interviews. She has been helped by Onogi's friends and others. For more details see the acknowledgments.

4 to spare their family "shock": In fact, some Japanese consider it "selfish" to hang oneself in a hotel as well, since hotels often demand large compensation from families when suicides occur. Irrespective of this, by the end of the 1990s these suicides had become so common that some hotels were deliberately designing rooms without any rails that could support a man's weight in an attempt to stop this.

5 since these cost Y30,000 (about $80): The postwar dollar–yen exchange rate was fixed at Y360 to the dollar until the early 1970s.

8 brothels to serve the incoming American troops: Nippon Kangyo's role does not appear to have reflected any prior connection with the sex industry. It became involved in this initiative simply because it often funded government initiatives. Japan has always had a tolerant attitude toward the sex industry, and the outgoing Japanese government deliberately created these brothels in 1945 to prevent Americans from raping local women. The policy appears to have contributed to a relatively low level of postwar violence although, as the historian John Dower points out, it also reinforced American sexual stereotypes about Japan that have continued to the present day. See Dower: *Embracing Defeat*, p. 126.

8 in the face of heavy state control: For an excellent discussion of the prewar financial system, see Hoshi and Kashyap 2001. As these authors point out, evidence from Japan's prewar period suggests that there is nothing intrinsically "un-Japanese" about capital markets. On the contrary, features now considered intrinsically "Japanese," such as the dominance of banks or job-for-life culture, only emerged under the military rule of the 1930s and 1940s.

9 the main source of finance in the economy: Between the 1950s and 1970s companies raised about 80 percent of their finance from the banks, while Japanese savers placed around 70 percent of their money in banks. See Hoshi and Kashyap, pp. 117, 119.

9 there was a unique function for shares: This pattern was not entirely isolated to Japan: Elements of this so-called "cross-shareholding" system were also found in Germany. However, Japan's system was more extreme than anywhere else in the industrialized world.

17 together with its samurai bankers: Not all senior bankers in Japan come from samurai backgrounds. However, a significant proportion do and many of the old samurai values—namely, disdain for commerce and a focus on public duty—have infused Japan's bureaucratic and banking elite. These values differ from the more commercial culture of Osaka, and it is intriguing to imagine what might have happened if it had been the Osaka merchants, rather than the old samurai, who had risen to dominate the government in the late nineteenth century.

19 in just a decade or so's time: See Richard Katz, *The System That Soured*, pp. 55–61.

22 there were fewer restrictions outside Japan: In late 1983, the Ministry of Finance grudgingly announced a few minor "reforms" in a bid to quell the bankers' complaints. LTCB and the other Japanese banks were permitted take part in underwriting corporate bond issuance in the euro-markets via securities subsidiaries in London and New York. However, they were still banned from doing this inside Japan.

23 to live in Latin America: Millions of Japanese emigrated to Latin America between the late nineteenth century and the middle of the twentieth century. Many were poor peasants, trying to escape the economic hardship in Japan; some, however, had elite backgrounds, as Mizukami's family did.

24 the LTCB plan said: LTCB 5th Long Term Management Plan, 1985.

31 thought that Trump's business projections were not profitable enough: In fact, the LTCB New York office turned down a number of property projects because it considered these risky. Some American observers argue that these standards of credit control were still lower than at other Western banks; however, the practices of the New York office differed so sharply from what was happening in Tokyo that when LTCB collapsed a decade later, the New York Federal Reserve expressed bafflement at the contrast between LTCB's (moderately healthy and well-run) American loan book—and the bank's rotten balance sheet in Japan.

33 who made frequent trips to the United States: This is the tale of EIE's origins according to the former EIE staff such as Nakamatsu and Ishizaki. However, the earliest parts of this story are extremely murky. It was difficult for Japanese to travel overseas immediately after World War II without official backing and extremely unusual for a Japanese woman to run a company. Thus some observers suspect that EIE was initially a front for other activities. In the 1950s and 1960s the CIA was channeling funds to favored Japanese politicians to fight communism, and initially used small "import" companies to do this. EIE might possibly have initially been linked to this. However, this is purely conjecture and whatever its origins, EIE staff insist that by the 1970s the company had a bona fide import business.

33 over the law in the stock market: These events are very murky. Nakamatsu declines to discuss who might—or might not—have been backing the Takahashi family. It should be noted that friends of the Takahashi family strenuously deny that they were linked to the *yakuza*, and the Japanese establishment is also apt to suggest that anybody who challenges the accepted system is "*yakuza*," irrespective of whether they have formal *yakuza* links or not.

34 "I didn't have a chance": In fact, Nakamatsu did not suffer too greatly. After he left EIE he went on to run his own company and subsequently became one of the most successful inventors in Japan, garnering more patents than any other person in global history. His inventions include an early form of the floppy disc, for which IBM still pays him royalties. He has won numerous awards from American inventors' clubs and been admiringly featured in American magazines. He almost never mentions his past connection with EIE in these interviews.

34 "Luck, luck luck!": Takahashi's comments are based on recollections from Bungo Ishizaki, his aide.

36 limited need for cash *inside* Japan: By 1985, for example, net household savings were equivalent to more than 10 percent of GDP. However, net corporate investment was only 4 percent of GDP. This created a huge 6 percent gap of surplus cash. See Katz, pp. 212

36 take the money outside Japan: Of course, this is not the only "solution." Other ways to mop up this excess cash is to fund a government budget deficit (which Japan did), or to introduce massive restructuring so that the economy can produce newly productive ways of absorbing investment (which Japan did not).

36 on a massive scale: Between 1985 and 1990 Japanese companies raised Y85,000 billion ($850 billion) through the stock market alone, in what seemed at the time like virtually free financing. See Woods, *The Bubble Economy,* p. 6.

37 "strengthened against the dollar": In the early 1950s the outgoing American administration created a fixed foreign exchange regime for Japan, which set the yen at Y360 to the dollar. This was partly lifted in 1971 and in the late 1970s the current exchange briefly touched a high of Y183. However, during the early 1980s the G7 countries aimed to keep the yen around Y250 to the dollar.

37 LDP politicians who introduced Nomoto to EIE: More specifically, Nomoto was introduced to EIE via a family friend, Seichi Ota, the LDP politician. Ishizaki met Takahashi because both men were friends of Toshio Yamaguchi, another LDP politician.

37 Nomoto later explained: Except when specified, the material on EIE is drawn from extensive on-the-record interviews with Ishizaki, Nomoto, Burns, and Kahane, and off-the-record interviews with key players. Takahashi declined to be interviewed. However, the author drew on interviews Takahashi had previously given to Japanese journalists.

38 “everybody else”: John Bond says that he does not remember this deal or anything about EIE or Takahashi. However, he does confirm that he dealt extensively with Bob Burns, later EIE’s partner, during this period.

41 quarreled with two of his original partners: Burns’s other partners at Regent initially included George Rafael and Adrian Zeccha, who later founded the Rafael and Aman luxury hotel groups, respectively. The two men owned a 30 percent stake in the Regent hotel group in the early 1980s. When they left in the mid-1980s Burns bought them out, which left him owning most of the company, save for a 5 percent stake held by HSBC.

49 Ashikaga Bank, and Sumitomo Trust: This is according to mortgage documents filed with the City of New York.

49 the building was initially valued at just $375 million: For a stream of statistics describing this shift see Peter Hartcher’s excellent book, *The Ministry;* pp. 69–72. Mitsui deliberately overpaid by $235 million simply because it wanted to get into the *Guinness Book of Records* for striking the most expensive deal in the world. See Hartcher, p. 60.

50 for a single Van Gogh painting: These statistics are taken from Taggart Murphy’s book, *The Weight of the Yen,* which has contributed heavily to the macroeconomic analysis in this chapter.

52 “and so it begins”: Takahashi interview with Peter Hartcher as published in the *Australian Financial Review,* March 3, 1995, and *The Ministry,* p. 93.

55 “take a commission on the deal”: Interview with Peter Hartcher, in *The Ministry,* p. 79.

55 stay that way indefinitely: One indication that Takahashi was confident this situation would last—namely, that Japanese interest rates would stay below American rates—was that he raised the initial loan to build the Four Seasons hotel in New York in yen, even though American projects were usually funded in dollars.

56 wielded enormous power: The Chinese characters used to spell “Yoshiharu” can also be read to create the sound “Katsuji,” which is how the second name arose.

57 more than Y300 billion ($3 billion) loans to EIE: Data on EIE’s total debt is hazy, partly because the company itself did not keep very good track of these figures and the loans were split between dozens of different projects and banks. Further complicating the matter, many banks did not lend money to EIE directly, but via subsidiaries, and after 1990, banks such as LTCB kept pouring money into EIE, to plug the gap. Chris Wood in *The Bubble Economy* (p. 58) writes that EIE's total debt was almost Y700 billion ($7 billion) in 1990. Other observers put it at Y1,000 billion ($10 billion). Meanwhile, Nemoto of EIE calculates that he personally handled loans worth $4 billion for the international operations, which were half the EIE business. Either way, LTCB accounted for well over Y300 billion ($3 billion) of the loans.

60 "have caused problems for their cash flow": "Japanese Banks Gather to Back a Maverick," Robert Thomson, *FT*, January 9, 1991.

62 waiting to be sold: Wood, p. 52.

62 additional Y260 trillion ($206 trillion) of credit: The Y260 trillion statistic is drawn from the Bank of Japan and Merrill Lynch credit research.

62 the Bank for International Settlements: One of the changes was that under the BIS rules the Japanese banks were only allowed to count 45 percent hidden equity gains as capital. These "hidden" gains were the gap between the book value of shares and market value and this gap was often considerable, since many of the shares had been acquired by banks in the 1950s, and thus were worth only a tiny fraction of their 1980s value. Until the new BIS rules were introduced, banks had thus used the hidden gains as a core part of capital.

63 had slashed the banks' lending margins: The pressure from this was not immediately visible in the 1980s, since the banks sold equities in the second half of the 1980s, which ensured that the sector as a whole posted a 13 percent rise in profit growth each year between 1984 and 1990. However, by 1989, nearly half of the Tokyo banks' profits came from these securities gains, which dried up after 1990. Again, see Wood, p. 22, for an excellent discussion of this.

64 "we had to do it again!": This comment is taken from a former LTCB banker who does not want to be identified; the author had no way of verifying this incident independently, but it appears to be consistent with the story presented by other former LTCB bankers.

65 or Showa 28: The graduates who joined the bank in its founding year—known as the *ni-ju-hachi-nen gumi*—were all told that they would become presidents one day, to reward their loyalty. Since it wasn't possible to make them all the president of LTCB, many were thus posted to run subsidiaries.

67 known as *tokkin*: The idea of using *tokkin* trusts to massage corporate results had actually first arisen in the late 1980s—ironically, to *reduce* profits, because some life insurance companies wanted to avoid revealing the vast earnings they were enjoying. It was thus a natural development for the foreign banks to produce a scheme with the reverse aim later. Although they were often called "derivatives" schemes, "derivatives" were not the critical issue; what made these schemes effective were the *accounting* laws, above all else.

68 ignore this in its official bad loan data: For a detailed discussion of the *jusen* issue, see Hoshi and Kashyap, pp. 269–271.

68 that could be potentially risky: The material in this and subsequent chapters on LTCB's treatment of bad loans from 1991 to 1998 is drawn from three sources: interviews with former LTCB staff; materials provided to the court during the trial of Harunori Takahashi; and (most importantly) the internal investigation of LTCB commissioned by Anzai in 1998. Part of the investigation was published on December 16, 1999, by LTCB ("General Report Based on Reports Submitted by the Internal Investigation Committee"), but much of the report was never officially published. This chapter draws on a wide selection of the Anzai report.

71 of which half were bad: In fact, the outstanding level of LTCB exposure appears to have been twice as large, since some of the lending had occurred through LTCB-controlled affiliates. Moreover, LTCB's exposure had risen quite sharply from 1990, as it tried to cope with EIE's problems by giving it more and more money.

72 were pulling the loans: "A Maverick Takes to the Golf Course"; Robert Thomson; *Financial Times*, July 13, 1993.

73 credit unions and their affiliates: These figures and subsequent details about the credit unions and their links with EIE are taken from the extensive press coverage in the *Financial Times, Asahi, Mainichi,* and *Yomiuri* at the time. See, for example: "Outcry Grows Shriller"; Gerard Baker, *FT*, February 15, 1995; "Audits Signalled Credit Unions' Demise"; *Mainichi,* February 27, 1995; "Bad Loans Continued Through Credit Probe"; *Asahi,* February 28, 1995; "Small Wave Washes over Banking System"; Gerard Baker; *FT*, April 7, 1995.

73 Ishizaki later said: Peter Hartcher, *The Ministry,* p. 32. See also, "Inside the Secret World of EIE," by Peter Hartcher, *Australian Financial Review,* March 3, 1995.

75 the *Shukan Gendai* tabloid: "Revealing such luxurious treats; the parties of the finance ministry bureaucrats in Kyoto"; *Shukan Gendai,* May 1995.

77 "It is completely unfair!": Takahashi's thinking and comments are drawn from interviews that he had with Japanese journalists at the time. I am grateful to Hiroshi Yoshitsugu, a Japanese journalist who interviewed Takahashi extensively, for generously sharing some of his thoughts about these interviews.

79 stop the candidacy of Mizukami: More specifically, the factor that affected Mizukami was a long-standing rivalry between Masuzawa and Horie, respectively LTCB's chairman and president in the early 1990s. The two men had joined the bank back in 1953, its founding year, and for four long decades they had jostled to become LTCB president. Eventually, Horie won the post in 1989, but in the interests of "fairness," Masuzawa became chairman as well. Both men knew that they needed to present a united front to survive, and the one issue that united the two men was that they both resented Sugiura's continued influence at the bank, like brothers faced with an overbearing father. They were thus opposed to the idea of Mizukami taking the reins of power because this would extend Sugiura's power. It should be stressed that this type of internal struggle was typical of many Japanese institutions, and reflected the fact that so few employees ever actually left their corporate family (even when they lost internal power struggles).

83 more and more funds into them: During the course of 1994, for example, the LTCB board discreetly agreed to provide another Y400 billion ($4 billion) of aid for Japan Lease and other large affiliates.

83 hidden gains: The "hidden" gains on the equity portfolio arose because Japanese banks had large quantities of equities on their portfolio that were booked at the price they were initially acquired at. This "book" price was very low, since the shares had often been acquired several decades ago. Thus the gap between the market price of these equities and the book price was considered to be a "hidden" resource that banks could potentially use if they fell into difficulties, and banks were allowed to count part of this as their "capital."

83 to write off bad loans: In fact, the internal investigation commissioned by Anzai in 1999 concluded that by the spring of 1995, "the bank did not have enough strength to revitalize the group as a whole," meaning that on paper its capital resources were *already* too low to handle the bad loans. However, this is a theoretical concept and judging when a bank is or is not potentially bankrupt is a notoriously slippery exercise. LTCB report 1999, p. 125.

89 earning virtually no profit: A survey the bank conducted in 1997, for example, indicated that more than Y3,000 billion ($30 billion) of the healthy loans were earning less than 50 basis points returns, or about the same as their costs.

90 competitive on the world stage: Many Japanese observers suspected dark political motives as well. According to one popular conspiracy theory, Hashimoto was trying to reduce the Ministry of Finance's control over the financial system; another rival theory suggested that the Finance Ministry had produced the idea of "Big Bang" to distract attention from its mishandling of the economy and the banking system.

92 *"omiai":* In Japan, when marriages are arranged, a matchmaker traditionally acts as a go-between, performing the introductions, or *omiai.*

93 to his native Italy: The parallels between Italy and Japan in the postwar period are fascinating (albeit very understudied): In both countries, the gangster and political worlds are tightly entwined and many of the battles for power tend to occur outside the channels of party politics. This may reflect the fact that the current political structures were imposed on the country after World War II by the American government, which then used covert financing to ensure that the country's political direction remained in line with Cold War aims.

93 "Most charming!": Interview with the author.

94 "to take a tremendous leap": Interview with the author.

94 were very reluctant to help NCB: In fact, the powerful president of Nippon Life, Japan's largest life insurance company, initially refused to rescue NCB, because he knew that the published data about the bad loans was inaccurate. It only came on board in the end when the Ministry provided written guarantees that NCB would not collapse. As a further carrot, the Bank of Japan discreetly provided another Y80 billion ($800 million) of funds to help the bank and a Y291 billion ($2.91 billion) recapitalization plan was put into effect. However, NCB eventually collapsed eighteen months later, and the BoJ and everyone else lost their money.

98 on the main balance sheet of the bank: General Report based on reports of the internal investigation committee; LTCB 1999, p. 126.

98 of which Y350 billion ($3.5 billion) were seriously bad: This is taken from the annual report 1997. The definitions that LTCB used in this report were slightly different from the classification used by MoF and BoJ inspectors. It divided loans into "nonaccrual" (Y840 billion); "restructured" (Y12 billion); and "loans to supported companies" (Y336 billion).

100 reform catalyst than Japan needed: In fact, Sakakibara's own intellectual views have sometimes seemed fluid in recent years. Early in his career, he appeared to endorse free-market views; in the late 1980s he then wrote a highly influential book suggesting that Japan had developed a distinctive economic system that did not need free markets. However, in 1997, Sakakibara became an enthusiastic supporter of Big Bang, and the arrival of foreign banks in the Tokyo markets.

102 Gary Brinson: Interview with the author. Brinson's asset management company had formed an alliance with Yasuda Marine and Fire in the early 1990s. Brinson had found it extremely difficult to persuade the Japanese side to adopt American fund management techniques, particularly since Brinson investment philosophy was based on a type of value investing that was utterly alien to Japan.

104 Sei Nakai: Interview with the author.

106 On Christmas Day the LTCB board: Details of this meeting are drawn from interviews with LTCB bankers and some of the statements made by LTCB bankers to the prosecutors in June 1999, as reported by the Japanese press. See, for example, "LTCB reportedly hid bad loans," *Yomiuri*, June 9, 1999; "Ex-LTCB Chiefs Grilled over Cover-up," *Mainichi*, June 9.

107 Tokugawa shogunate: When the American navy arrived in Japan in the middle of the nineteenth century, they concluded a trading deal with the old Tokugawa shogun that was extremely advantageous for the Americans. The Japanese later accused the Americans of exploiting their *naïveté* and forced a renegotiation.

108 Comment drawn from Onogi's interview with *Asahi* in early May 1999, published June 11, 1999, in "Dividends Were Essential."

108 Konishi announced that he was resigning: These comments are taken from an interview with Konishi and an unpublished study of LTCB produced by Harvard Business School on August 23, 1999.

109 Y70 trillion: This Y70 trillion ($700 billion) figure arose from a new system designed to help banks assess their own bad loans, which divided loans into four categories of risk. However, the banks continued to use additional classification systems as well. One of the least confusing guides to this quagmire can be found in Hoshi and Kashyap (1999).

109 Salomon Smith Barney: SSB pledged to buy up to 25 percent of Nikko's shares as well as merge the Nikko investment banking arm with Salomon's Tokyo operations. This gave SSB a seat on the Nikko board.

109 *Gekan Gendai:* See *Gekan Gendai*, July 1998.

110 on behalf of a *client*: Some former UBS executives have subsequently indicated that the client was M&G, a British fund. Apparently it asked to sell $5 million of LTCB stock in London and junior staff passed this order to Tokyo without realizing the implications of it. It seems a credible explanation, since M&G was a big UBS client and many British pension funds held shares in LTCB, partly because they admired Onogi. However, UBS has never confirmed this explanation and some LTCB executives do not believe it.

111 *sokaiya:* The *sokaiya* problem is endemic in Japan. In an effort to minimize their impact, companies try to hold their shareholder meetings on the same day. However, they are often tolerated by the police and some are so brazen they even advertise their services on the internet.

114 vast derivatives portfolio: The *net* value of these derivatives trades was far smaller, since most of the positions were interest rate swaps and effectively canceled each other out. When investment bankers and hedge funds look at derivatives, it is usually the net value of a book that they care most about since this shows the potential for losses. However, the financial press—and the regulators—often look at the much larger gross number instead. For reference, the gross position of LTCB's book was about half the size of the portfolio held by LTCM, the hedge fund that collapsed in the autumn of 1998.

115 Hiroshi Nakaso: For more details of this extraordinary episode see the paper that Nakaso subsequently wrote: *BIS Papers* no. 6, October 2001; "The Financial Crisis in Japan During the 1990's." The crucial issue was that Japan lacked a netting agreement, which meant that if LTCB had collapsed, investors might have been forced to unwind each and every derivatives contract separately, creating enormous disruption instead just netting them off against each other, which is the usual practice.

117 Konishi: Interview with the author.

117 Sei Nakai: Interview with the author.

119 UBS had the right to buy LTCB: In practice, UBS did not end up suffering financially. It lost almost $50 million on the LTCB shares it held; however, when the Swiss bank took control of the joint ventures, it gained access to a number of LTCB clients and later sold them investment banking services. UBS bankers calculate that these deals, which included deals such as a large equity block trade completed for Bridgestone, garnered more than $80 million in fees. UBS also took control of LTCB's asset management venture for a knockdown price, which left it with Y2,000 billion ($20 billion) in assets, twice what it previously controlled.

120 Martin Whitman: Interview with the author and Whitman's correspondence with LTCB.

122 Credit Suisse: For full details see "The Hidden Truth Behind the Mask," by Gillian Tett; *Financial Times,* June 18, 1999.

123 Although wealthy by Japanese standards: A senior Japanese banker typically received an annual salary of around Y30 million and Y50 million ($300,000 and $500,000) a year, and when he retired he received a modest pension and lump sum bonus worth several times the annual salary. This left him wealthy compared with many Japanese, but not by Wall Street standards. However, it should be stressed that—unlike in America—money was not necessarily the most valued perk of office: nonfinancial perks such as golf club membership were considered equally valuable. Typically, Japanese bankers kept these after retirement; the LTCB bankers lost them.

124 Onogi later explained: As quoted in "Ex-execs of Failed Banks Recant"; *Yomiuri,* June 5, 2000.

125 "should not have agreed to become president": Ibid.

130 Koichi Kato: Kato has insisted in an interview with the author that he mentioned LTCB in his conversations with the Americans to illustrate a bigger point, namely, that Japan's biggest priority was not tackling fiscal policy (as the Americans had been insisting in late 1997) but dealing with the banks. Kato denies that he meant to focus on LTCB in particular: In fact, he was alarmed about the state of *several* major banks at that stage.

131 Larry Summers: Interview with the author.

133 backing the DPJ too forcefully: Indeed, as Katz points out, Clinton actually ended up supporting Obuchi against the DPJ reformers by seeming to endorse Obuchi's claim that the DPJ had been blocking bank reform. This shocked the DPJ, since they had assumed that America wanted to impose more market reforms and would support their case. See "Japan's Slow Road to Recovery," *Christian Science Monitor,* September 29, 1998.

135 Collins recalled: Interview with the author.

136 "pretty good at doing this [business]": "Gaijin at the Gate," *BusinessWeek,* December 10, 2001.

137 Ripplewood started small: In fact, since its inception Ripplewood has launched a series of funds, including a first American fund ($450 million), a Japanese fund ($1.2 billion), and a third $1.2 billion American-focused fund.

141 Yashiro later chucked: Interview with the author.

143 Flowers later remarked: Interview with the author.

145 Volcker later explained: Interview with the author.

147 "up to his belly button!": Interview with the author.

150 Goldman Sachs scored: The results of this voting process were never published. However, internal government documents show that Morgan Stanley scored 498 points, NSSB 468, J. P. Morgan 436, Lehman Brothers 425, Daiwa 369, and Paribas 319.

152 When Anzai went to see Satori Kishi: This detail is based on the recollection of Anzai, LTCB officials, and government bureaucrats at the time. Kishi says he has no recollection of receiving a formal request to purchase LTCB.

153 "O. J. Simpson": This acronym was apparently chosen as a handy way of referring to Orix–J. P. Morgan (i.e., another O.J.). However, it was subsequently considered distasteful by some of the American bankers involved in the deal.

156 Hayami later explained: Interview with the author.

157 Flowers had his own fund: For ease, in this book I use the words "Ripplewood team" to refer to the consortium that acquired LTCB, since this is how they often referred to themselves in casual conversation (although Flowers had a separate fund).

159 loss-sharing scheme: In fact, the J. P. Morgan Japanese lawyers argued that there were ways to conduct a loss-sharing scheme under the existing legal framework in Japan. However, the FRC rejected these arguments.

163 There were relatively few Christians: When the Portuguese missionaries first arrived in Japan in the sixteenth century, they initially succeeded in converting some Japanese before the shoguns later banned Christianity and killed many of the converts. Some pockets of Christianity secretly survived, particularly in the south. However, most of the modern-day Christians are descended from conversions that took place after American and European missionaries reached Japan in the nineteenth and twentieth centuries.

164 one of his friends later explained: Foley declined repeated requests to comment on this episode.

166 Yashiro said earnestly: "Boss to Turn LTCB into a Commercial Bank"; *Yomiuri;* October 1, 1999.

167 cell phone rang: Although it may sound far-fetched to American ears, some journalists were convinced that Flowers had "conspired" for the phone to ring and Ryo Takasugi, a popular novelist, echoed the suspicions some Japanese felt when he wrote a book loosely based on the Shinsei story, *Za Gaishi.*

170 Ochi would later explain: Interview with the author.

170 Y1,500 billion: This was the figure floating around in the discussions in mid to late 1999; by the early summer of 2000, however, the "official" level of NPLs was considered to be Y1.9 trillion ($19 billion).

170 main text of the contract: The main text of the Share Purchase Agreement between the government and foreign investors (known as New LTCB Partners), signed on February 9, 2000, states in article 7 that: "For the Reprivatized LTCB to maintain good relationships with borrowers of loan-related assets, Partners represents that it will have the Reprivatized LTCB manage its loans based on the following basic policies for at least three years from the Closing. Specifically, unless compelling reasons otherwise require, the Reprivatized LTCB (i) will not sell the loan-related assets, (ii) will not collect loans abruptly, and (iii) will meet the proper finance needs of borrowers by, for example, renewals and provisions of seasonal funds." However, a note to this agreement then goes on to explain that: "Instances of compelling reasons . . . shall mean in the case of (I) arranging loan participations, securitization of loans and other similar activities that are undertaken for providing supplementary sources of financing for the Reprivatized LTCB and are not contrary to the intent of protecting the borrower. In the case of (ii) and (iii), compelling reasons include circumstances where it is reasonably foreseeable that the Reprivatized LTCB would incur losses if it did not collect or it consented to renewals."

172 no Mitsubishi money could be linked: Ripplewood decided to invest $50 million from its general U.S.-based fund into the deal. However, it structured this in a way that ring-fenced the project from any funds Mitsubishi had previously given to Ripplewood. Makihara of Mitsubishi has never commented in public on why Mitsubishi was reluctant to take part in the deal and the information on this is drawn from multiple sources.

172 deliver an internal note of return (IRR) of 60 percent: The Ripplewood team has neither denied nor confirmed this projection, since private equity groups are notoriously secretive about their returns. A projected 60 percent IRR is considered relatively high for a private equity deal, but not extraordinarily so.

173 an estimated total cost of Y3,600 billion: The sums worked roughly like this: when LTCB collapsed it was believed to have negative equity of about Y3,500 billion ($35 billion). The government injected money to plug this gap and the shareholders were all wiped out. The Resolution and Collection Corporation took over bad loans with a face value of Y4,600 billion ($46 billion) from LTCB, whose value had declined to almost nothing. Then the government "paid" Y250 billion ($2.5 billion) to buy the equity portfolio from LTCB and subscribed to Y240 billion ($2.4 billion) in preferred stock, which could be converted in five to seven years to a maximum of 33 percent of the outstanding equity.

173 the government agreed to let the bank count this: This scheme was effectively an extension of an accounting game already widespread in Japan. Japanese banks often pretend to "sell" pools of shares to a specially created trust around the end of the fiscal year, so that they can record capital gains and boost their BIS capital ratio, only to buy them back at a later date.

175 Jacob Rothschild: Interview with the author. The structure of the Rothschild group changed halfway through the completion of the LTCB deal and though the investment was initially made by St James Place Capital (and this was the name listed on the documents), it was eventually handled by Ritcap, Rothschild's international arm.

177 "Japan's economy and financial system": Interview with the author.

179 told a group of Japanese business leaders: "Corporate Social Responsibility the American Way"; *Keidanren* speech by Vernon E. Jordan, January 11, 1989.

181 foreigners had rarely been seen: During the late 1980s and early 1990s some foreigners did work at LTCB headquarters, and occasionally appeared in the canteen. But these had all left by the middle of the 1990s.

185 traditional characters: There are three writing systems in Japan: Chinese characters, and two phonetic alphabets. One of these, namely, the *katakana*, is used specifically to write words with foreign associations. Thus, Shinsei's decision to use Chinese characters was unusual and came—ironically—as most of the other Japanese banks were going in exactly the *opposite* direction, using "foreign" letters to create a more "progressive" image.

187 Yashiro later wrote: *My Career Chronicle,* p. 11.

187 "from a mother complex": Ibid, p. 8.

187 "Mah-chan": "Mah-chan" is the diminutive, affectionate form of Masamoto.

188 "came close to divorcing me": *My Career Chronicle,* p. 6.

189 Reed later explained: Ibid, p. 87.

192 "I did not see much future for LTCB": Interview with the author; quotes cleared.

199 said Dvivedi: Interview with the author.

199 Fujitsu: It was common practice in a *keiretsu* for banks and related companies to buy all their parts from each other. Thus, because Fujitsu was a favored corporate client, it automatically supplied the computers for the database system.

199 Yashiro declared: "A Bank That Is Living Up to Its Name," *BusinessWeek,* May 30, 2001.

201 Hidehiko Arakawa: Interview with the author.

202 "women control a lot of financial decisions": Foreign companies in Japan often try to hire women, since they are often more willing to work for foreigners and better at adapting to new business models than men, precisely because they have been effectively excluded from the old Japanese corporate system in the past.

204 Sheehy later explained: Interview with the author.

210 the FRC secretly convened a meeting: Drawn from committee minutes of FRC meeting on June 30, 2000, and an FSA website report on Sogo.

211 for mysterious "favors": *Yomiuri;* July 17, 2000.

211 "shady under the rug": *Asahi;* July 3, 2000.

211 committed suicide: Yasuji Abe, a former LTCB banker and Sogo vice president, sixty-three, committed suicide in April 2000. A few months later, Yukio Nazakazawa, another vice president, also killed himself.

212 below-market fee: Neither Goldman Sachs nor the FRC ever confirmed this fee; this figure is drawn from data supplied to the author by bureaucrats involved in the deal.

212 Mark Schwartz: Interview with the *FT,* published August 5, 2000, but conducted in early July.

213 Paulson: "Capitalism, Consensus and Conflict: Goldman Sachs"; Gillian Tett and John Willman, *Financial Times,* June 12, 2001.

214 asked Takumi Nomoto: The comments are taken from the Lower House Finance Committee debate on July 17, 2000, parliamentary session number 148. The dialogue has been greatly condensed.

216 politicians started the debate: Upper House Finance Committee transcript from July 18, 2000. Parliamentary session 148.

218 as the Lower House finance committee convened: Lower House Finance Committee; August 3, 2000. Parliamentary session 149.

222 key members of this consortium: Softbank owned 49 percent, Tokio Marine and Fire and Orix each owned 15 percent, and the foreign investors each held stakes between 0.5 percent and 5 percent. A group of Japanese regional banks also held a small stake.

222 shady political reputation: It is difficult to tell to what degree NCB's reputation was grounded in fact or prejudice. The Japanese are very racist toward the Koreans and are apt to presume that anything linked to the North Korean community in Japan is criminal, sometimes unfairly. However, NCB was widely believed to have ties with murky aspects of politics: When Shin Kanemaru, a senior LDP figure with underworld ties, was arrested in a corruption scandal in the late 1980s, for example, it emerged that he had chosen to hold his wealth in the form of gold bars—and NCB debentures.

223 Michiko Homma: It is unusual for the wife of a suicide victim to talk on the record in Japan and Michiko Homma deserves enormous credit for her courage in doing this. She says she decided to do this—after clearing comments with other members of her family—as a way of honoring her husband's sacrifice and in the hope that it can promote better understanding of Japan's banking challenges.

224 to call in loans: In Japan the *yakuza* will sometimes bully a victim into committing suicide; for this reason, it is not always easy to distinguish between murder and suicide.

224 Tabloid newspapers: For descriptions of these allegations, see "Buried in the Books" by Benjamin Fulford, *Forbes,* January 8, 2001. These allegations were commonly echoed in Japan. However, the police deny these tales and the author has no proof at all that criminal elements were ever involved.

225 "*yakuza* put": In recent years most foreign banks have had to confront the *yakuza* issue in some way in Japan, either through their involvement in distressed debt or real estate, or because some of Japan's entrepreneurs, particularly in the internet sector, have had *yakuza* links in recent years. The "*yakuza* put" is simply one the coping mechanisms used.

225 The RCC was thus: The RCC has become the key institution that deals with *yakuza* loans. The banks have often been keen to get rid of the problem by passing it on to the government, and the first head of the RCC was a crusading lawyer who made it his personal mission to combat the *yakuza*. This has sometimes distracted the RCC from other jobs, such as creating a liquid market in distressed loans. However, the RCC takes pride in its admirable bravery in standing up to the *yakuza*. Officials at the RCC state that 18.4 percent of its loans have *yakuza* links, although some observers consider this an underestimate. Estimates of what proportion of total bank loans are *yakuza*-linked vary wildly, between almost nothing to 25 percent. For more details on the RCC role, see "Japan May Field New Weapons in Bad Loan Battle"; Gillian Tett, *Financial Times,* October 23, 2001.

228 pay packet: Details of Fite's salary were reported in "Westpac Doctor Takes Off to LTCB"; SMH.com, March 3, 2000.

228 such as Sanctuary Cove: In practice, the Sanctuary Cove mess was not Shinsei's responsibility: All the EIE loans were moved from the LTCB to the RCC and Sanctuary Cove was sold to new developers at the start of 2002, a decade after its collapse.

228 "get our money back?": Interview with the author.

232 Yanagisawa angrily insisted: Interview with the author. There was another, more subtle, issue that also shaped Yanagisawa's thinking: He feared that if the banks were given more capital, they were more likely to squander this on propping up deadbeat companies, rather than changing their lending practices. Given the experience of history, this seemed a reasonable concern; however, this also meant that Yanagisawa had boxed himself into a position where he could not accept the reformers' demand for capital injections and a new evaluation of bad loans.

233 "Shinsei should behave": Quoted from the Shinsei transcript of this meeting cited in "Authorities Tell Shinsei to Ease Up," *Wall Street Journal*, September 26, 2001.

233 "category two" companies: For details of this four-part system, see "Notes on Bad Loans."

234 researcher from Harvard Business School: See Harvard Business School Study on Shinsei Bank, A–D. 9-302-036, October 2001.

235 loans to Life: Shinsei has never officially revealed how much of a loss it would bear on the Life loans if the DIC does not accept them. S&P suggests that the potential loss to Shinsei from Life without the put is about Y20 billion ($200 million) since it holds some collateral ("S&P DIC rejects Shinsei Loan Repurchase request," July 30, 2001).

236 issued a press release: "Regarding Our Posture on Lending," Shinsei Bank press release. September 7, 2001.

237 leaked the story: The nature of the documents leaked suggests that the source was a relatively senior person within the bank. However, Yashiro, Collins, and Flowers all vehemently deny that they leaked the emails, or know who leaked them.

240 "raising finance the American way": "Shinsei to Get Cash the U.S. Way"; *Asahi*, October 25, 2001.

242 Asao admitted: Author interview.

243 Yanagisawa later said: Yanagisawa's comments are based on a subsequent interview with the author, in which he described in general terms what he had told the American investors, not a specific transcript of this meeting. However, officials present have indicated this dialogue was broadly correct.

247 The guidelines for short-selling: This is the practice of borrowing shares that an investor does not already own, to sell them with an agreement to repurchase them at a later date. If share prices fall, a short-seller makes money. Thus this tactic is used by traders when they presume that the market is declining—and the sheer act of selling can actually help to push the market lower as well, since it creates a bearish climate.

247 the claims rang hollow: The local media reported that bureaucrats had placed calls to Japanese brokers and life insurance companies, trying to curb the short-selling business. See *The Japanese Phoenix*, Richard Katz, p. 199.

248 a strategy paper: The origin of this memo, titled "Is There a Financial Crisis?" is controversial. The FSA has always denied any official role in its production and it is unclear whether the memo represents simply the summary of a meeting between senior bureaucrats, or a specific manifesto. However, Japanese journalists attribute it to senior bureaucrats.

250 *kisha* club: The exclusion of foreigners from the *kisha* clubs triggered a U.S.–Japan trade dispute in the early 1990s. After this dispute, the *kisha* clubs removed any specific rules banning foreigners and some news organizations, such as Bloomberg, are now members of the *kisha* clubs. However, most *kisha* clubs are reluctant to accept foreign nationals as members—and foreign newspapers are often reluctant to join the *kisha* clubs, since they do not want to observe the rules. The BoJ *kisha* club refused to let the author attend the Shinsei press briefings in person.

251 net profits: Net profits in the year to March 2001 were Y90 billion ($900 million), and thus higher in an overall sense than in the year to March 2002. However, the first year's results were distorted by a one-off gain of Y55 billion ($550 million) on sales of equities to the DIC.

251 BIS ratio: By the summer of 2002, almost all the large banks claimed to have a BIS ratio of about 8 percent. However, a large part of this capital was credits on the theoretical value of taxes that the banks would pay in the future if they ever made a real profit again. This was essentially an accounting trick: If the tax credits were excluded, then some of the banks had almost no capital left at all.

252 its profits would have been devastated: S&P notes that by the end of December 2001, Shinsei had handed back Y605 billion ($6.05 billion) in loans to the government and received Y358 billion ($3.58 billion) of compensation. S&P suggests that without the put, Shinsei would have suffered a Y179 billion ($1.79 billion) loss, more than twice its Y68 billion ($680 million) profits in that period. "Revitalizing Japan's Banks," *S&P*, May 2002.

253 said Jesper Koll: "Shinsei Bank Showing the Way Forward"; by Jesper Koll. *Yomiuri Shinbun,* May 9, 2002.

255 Teramura, the chairman of Nichiryoku: Author interview.

257 trading in distressed loans: This is a particularly odd business that reflects the distinctive nature of Japan's financial world. In theory, there is no practical reason at all why Japanese lenders could not collect these loans themselves, and it would be cheaper for them in financial terms to do this. However, the Japanese banks often feel that it would be too "embarrassing" to engage in this business and prefer to use Western bankers as third party intermediaries—even if the Western bankers do nothing more than buy one set of loans from a party and then sell them to another. In that sense, Western banks play a role in Japan's financial system akin to "untouchables" in Hindu society, paid to fulfill an unpleasant task. Or to put it another way, what Western banks are doing in this situation is not so much a financial arbitrage, as a strange type of *cultural* arbitrage.

258 commented Koyo Ozeki: "Shinsei's Way"; Charles Smith, *Institutional Investor,* August 1, 2002.

264 in Hayami's eyes: Interview with the author.

264 he could—monetary policy: In fact, by the autumn of 2002 the BoJ's monetary policy was loose by the standards of most Western countries. The nominal overnight money market rate was almost zero and the Bank was regularly flooding the financial markets with more than Y10,000 billion ($100 billion) of liquidity each day. However, since prices were falling, the *real* level of interest rates in the economy—as opposed to the nominal rate—was still around 2 percent. Thus, some economists believed that the Bank needed to take more unorthodox measures to fight deflation and create a radically loose monetary policy, such as purchase large quantities of government bonds or other assets. Hayami argued that there was no reason to believe that these tactics would actually feed through to the rest of the economy because the banks were in no position to extend new loans, even if they were given more cash (in normal economic circumstances, the way that monetary policy affects the real economy is through the process of credit creation by banks). Many Western economists disagreed.

264 equity purchase scheme: The scheme was not actually dreamed up by Hayami at all, but by a couple of midlevel Bank officials. However, Hayami decided to back it for the reasons outlined above.

266 Hiroshi Okuda: Okuda subsequently blamed the *gaijin* for "misinterpreting" his comments. "It may be better to not associate with foreign [media] people. You never know what they might say," Okuda declared, in an effort to appease the rest of Japan's corporate world. However, most observers believed that Okuda had simply stated the obvious.

267 Hubbard declared: "U.S. Jumps to Defend Takenaka's Reforms"; *Asahi Shinbum,* October 14.

269 "I think that Mr. Takenaka": As quoted in *The Economist,* "Yankee Plotters," November 9, 2002.

272 family reasons: Fite left in November 2002 and was replaced by John Mack, formerly a senior banker at Bank of America. Fite said that the reason for his departure was that his wife was pregnant and wished to have the baby in Australia, not Japan.

NOTES ON BAD LOANS

The term "bad loan" has been used in a broad-ranging fashion in this book. However, the definition of a "bad" loan—or a "nonperforming loan" (NPL) to use the more correct technical term—is complex, and estimates of the size of Japan's problem have varied wildly in recent years. The following points may be helpful for a general reader.

When a bank lends money to a client, there are *two* factors that determine whether that loan is "good" or "bad": first the ability of the company to repay the loan out of cash flow or its reserves; second, whether the company has posted collateral that could be seized in case of default. Defining a "bad" loan is thus not a precise science, since loans to bankrupt companies may still be valuable, if the collateral can be collected. The time perspective also complicates the issue. Until recently, banks in Japan only revealed the loans with which they had *already* experienced collection problems; however, most modern international banks also estimate how many loans will turn sour *in the future,* since prudent banking requires them to post financial reserves to offset the risk of losses (like a "rainy day" fund). Projections of future losses can be highly subjective and vary according to the value of collateral and reserves. Japanese banks tend to take a very optimistic view of the future health of the economy; most independent economists do not.

Deflation also muddies the issue. When prices are rising, the relative size of a debt problem shrinks over time; however, if prices are falling, it steadily becomes harder for borrowers to repay debt and makes it difficult to measure NPLs with "normal" bank classification systems. In countries such as the United States, banks usually judge whether a company will repay a loan according to whether it can maintain interest payments. However, Japanese interest rates are so low that companies can cobble together funds to make interest payments—even when they have no hope of ever repaying the loan in the future.

For this reason, recent estimates of the scale of Japan's bad loans have ranged between Y12 trillion ($120 billion) [the government's estimate of loans which have already turned bad among major banks] and Y235 trillion (Goldman Sachs's estimate of all potentially problematic loans in the economy). This variation reflects both underreporting and differing definitions of the problem. The Japanese establishment has used no less than three different NPL classification systems in recent years, and independent observers have devised their own systems.

The best-known official system today in Japan was introduced in 1998 and divides loans into four groups. Loans "that cannot be collected" are labeled "category four" (these are generally to bankrupt companies); loans where there is "serious concerns about their ultimate collection" are considered "category three" (to virtually bankrupt companies); loans "subject to specific management risk" are "category two" (to troubled but operating companies). Loans to healthy companies are labeled "category one." However, the "category two" loans have recently been subdivided into two groups (one very risky; one slightly risky), and the government has modified this system to take account of the quality of collateral. The Japanese government usually defines loans in category four, three, and the lower tier of category two as "NPLs"; there were Y40 trillion ($400 billion) of these in September 2002.

As a very rough rule of thumb, the government data suggests that the problem has topped Y100 trillion over the last decade, since in addition to the current Y40 trillion NPLs, the banks claim to have *already* dealt with more than Y80 trillion NPLs since 1992, by posting reserves to cover the possible loss and/or selling of the loan, and/or recouping the collateral. The banks have already made provisions for some of the remaining Y40 trillion of bad loans. However, as Kashyap (2002) points out, many Western bank analysts believe that the government is still underestimating the problems and calculate that it will cost banks between Y20 trillion and Y70 trillion ($200 billion to $700 billion) to write off all the remaining bad loans. If correct, this implies that many banks are insolvent since the projected cost of writing off their bad loans is likely to be far bigger than their capital or earnings.

SOURCES AND BIBLIOGRAPHY

The information in this book is primarily drawn from more than 200 interviews that I conducted around the world, mostly during 2002. However, I have also been aided by press reports in English and Japanese, mostly notably the *Nikkei, Yomiuri, Asahi, Mainichi, Sentaku,* and *Shukan Gendai;* and the *Financial Times, Wall Street Journal, IHT, Economist, Institutional Investor,* and *Business Week.* Other sources include memos written by former LTCB staff including Kozo Tabayashi and Ryuji Konishi; case studies of LTCB and Shinsei by Harvard Business School; the website of the Financial Services Agency, which includes extensive information about the parliamentary debates on Shinsei; the FSA's treatment of Sogo and Shinsei's business plans; the findings of the internal investigations into LTCB's activities between 1990 and 1998 commissioned by Takashi Anzai in 1999; and some internal documents from Goldman Sachs and the Japanese government that were made available to me at various stages of my research. I also drew on a broad range of existing literature on Japan. The English language ones include:

Aoki, M., and Hugh Patrick, eds. *Japan's Main Bank System: Its Relevance for Developing and Transforming Economies*. Oxford: Clarendon Press, 1995.

Atkinson, David. *Totally Rethinking Japanese Asset Quality,* pp. i–x. Tokyo: Goldman Sachs, 2001.

Bayoumi, Tamin, and Charles Collyns, eds. *Post-bubble Blues: How Japan Responded to Asset Price Collapse*. Washington, D.C.: IMF, 2000.

Bergsten, Fred, Takatoshi Ito, and Marcus Noland. *No More Bashing: Building a New Japan–United States Economic Relationship*. Washington, D.C.: Institute for International Economics, 2001.

Ian Buruma. *Inventing Japan. 1853–1964*. New York: Modern Library, February 2003.

Calder, Kent E. *Crisis and Compensation: Public Policy and Political Stability in Japan*. New Jersey: Princeton University Press, 1988.

———. *Strategic Capitalism: Private Business and Public Purpose in Japanese Industrial Finance*. New Jersey: Princeton University Press, 1993.

Cargill, Thomas F., Michael M. Hutchison, and Takatoshi Ito. *Financial Policy and Central Banking in Japan*. Cambridge, Massachusetts: MIT Press, 2000.

Dattel, Eugene R. *The Sun That Never Rose: The Inside Story of Japan's Failed Attempt at Global Financial Dominance*. Chicago, Illinois: Probus, 1994.

Dower, John W. *Embracing Defeat: Japan in the Wake of World War II*. New York: W. W. Norton, 1999.

Fingleton, Eamonn. *Blindside: Why Japan Is Still on Track to Overtake the U.S. by the Year 2000*. Boston: Houghton Mifflin, 1995.

Grimes, William W. *Unmaking the Japanese Miracle: Macroeconomic Politics 1985–2000*. Ithaca: Cornell University Press, 2001.

Harner, Stephen M. *Japan's Financial Revolution and How American Firms Are Profiting*. New York: M.E. Sharpe, 2000.

Hartcher, Peter. *The Ministry: How Japan's Most Powerful Institution Endangers World Markets*. Boston, Massachusetts: Harvard University Press, 1998.

Hayes, Declan. *Japan's Big Bang: The Deregulation and Revitalization of the Japanese Economy*. Boston: Tuttle, 2000.

Hoshi, Takeo, and Anil Kashyap. *Corporate Financing and Governance in Japan: The Road to the Future*. Cambridge, Massachusetts: MIT Press, 2001.

———. "The Japanese Banking Crisis: Where Did It Come From and How Will It End?" *NBER Macroeconomics Annual*, 1999.

Kashyap, Anil. *Sorting Out Japan's Financial Crisis*. Federal Reserve Bank of Chicago Economic Perspectives, 4th quarter 2002.

Katz, Richard. *Japan: The System That Soured—The Rise and Fall of the Japanese Economic Miracle*. Armonk, NY: M. E. Sharpe, 1998.

———. *Japanese Phoenix: The Long Road to Economic Revival*. Armonk, NY: M. E. Sharpe, 2003.

Kerr, Alex. *Dogs and Demons: Tales from the Dark Side of Japan*. New York: Hill and Wang, 2001.

LaFeber, Walter. *Clash: U.S.–Japanese Relations Throughout History*. New York: W. W. Norton, 1997.

Lincoln, Edward. *Arthritic Japan: The Slow Pace of Economic Reform*. Washington, D.C.: Brookings Institute, 2001.

Maruyama, Masao. *Thought and Behavior in Modern Japanese Politics*. Oxford: OUP, 1970.

Mason, Mark. *American Multinationals and Japan: The Political Economy of Japanese Capital Controls 1899–1980*. Cambridge, Massachusetts: Harvard University Press, 1992.

McClain, James L. *Japan: A Modern History*. New York: W. W. Norton, 2002.

Mikitani, Ryoichi, and Adam S. Posen, eds. *Japan's Financial Crisis and Its Parallels to the U.S. Experience*. Washington, D.C.: Institute for International Economics, 2000.

Mikuni, Akio, and R. Taggart Murphy. *Japan's Policy Trap; Dollars, Deflation and the Crisis of Japanese Finance*. Washington, D.C.: Brookings, 2002.

Murphy, R. Taggart. *The Weight of the Yen; How Denial Imperils America's Future and Ruins an Alliance*. New York: W. W. Norton, 1996.

Patrick, Hugh. *From Cozy Regulation to Competitive Markets: The Regime Shift of Japan's Financial System*. Columbia University Center on Japanese Economy and Business Working Paper, no. 186. At *http://www.gsb.columbia.edu/japan/pdf/wp186.pdf*, 2001.

Porter, Michael E., Hirotaka Takeuchi, and Mariko Sakakibara. *Can Japan Compete?* London: Macmillan Press, 2000.

Sakakibara, Eisuke. *Beyond Capitalism: The Japanese Model of Market Economics*. Lanham, MD: The University Press of America, 1993.

Schlesinger, Jacob M. *Shadow Shoguns: The Rise and Fall of Japan's Postwar Political Machine*. California: Stanford University Press, 1997.

Smith, Patrick. *Japan: A Reinterpretation*. New York: Vintage, 1998.

Tamaki, Norio. *Japanese Banking: A History 1859–1959.* Cambridge, U.K.: Cambridge University Press, 1995.

Van Wolferen, Karel. *The Enigma of Japanese Power: People and Politics in a Stateless Nation.* Tokyo: Charles E. Tuttle, 1993.

Volcker, Paul, and Toyoo Gyohten. *Changing Fortunes: The World's Money and the Threat to American Leadership.* New York: Random House, 1992.

Wood, Christopher. *The Bubble Economy: The Japanese Economic Collapse.* London: Sidgwick and Jackson, 1992.

Yashiro, Masamoto. *My Career Chronicle* (appeared in the *Nikkei Keizai Shimbun* as *Watashi no Rekisho*). Tokyo: Toppan, 1997.

Yoshino, Michael Y. *Shinsei Bank*; *Case Studies A–D.* Harvard Business School 9-302-036, October 11, 2001.

Japanese Books

Kyodo news journalists (a collective work). *Chogin nissaigin funshoku kessai jiken (Chain Reaction—The LTCB and NCB Window-Dressing Fiasco).* Tokyo: K. K. Kyodo News, 1999.

Nikkei news journalists (a collective work). *Kinyu meiso no junen (Ten Years of Erratic Finance).* Tokyo: Nihon Keizai Shimbun, 2000.

Nishino, Tomohiko. *Kensho Keizai meiso—Naze kiki ga tsuzukunoka (The Erratic Economy—Why Does the Crisis Drag Ou?).* Tokyo: Iwanami Shoten Publisher, 2001.

Takasugi, Ryo. *Shosetsu Za Gaishi (The Foreign Securities Company).* Tokyo: Kobunsha, 2002.

Takeuchi, Masatoshi. *Jitsuroku Chogin butenchokaigi (Commentary: The Meeting of Department/Branch Chiefs of LTCB).* Tokyo: OS Publishing Co., Inc, 1999.

Yanai, Noboru. *Moto yakuin ga mita chogin hatan (The Bankruptcy of LTCB, As Seen by a Former Executive).* Tokyo: Bungei Shunju, 1999.

ACKNOWLEDGMENTS

This book was first triggered by a mysterious death. To be precise, I was first inspired to write it back in the autumn of 2000 when I heard that Tadayo Homma, formerly an executive director of the Bank of Japan, had been found dead in an Osaka hotel room with a noose around his neck, shortly after becoming president of a Japanese bank. The police blamed his death on suicide, but there were unsubstantiated rumors that *yakuza* gangsters may have been involved. He was sixty.

I had been working in Tokyo as a financial reporter for three years by then, and had met Homma several times. He had always struck me as a mild-mannered, shy, rather typical Japanese bureaucrat; in short, a most unlikely person to end up hanging in an Osaka hotel room, for whatever reason. The news of his death left me sad and baffled—and doubly so, since most of the Japanese establishment was determined to avoid discussing the case in public.

It also crystallized a sense of unease I felt about the way that Japan's financial issues were being analyzed. In the last decade, many (often admirable) books have emerged that discuss Japan's problems from a macroeconomic perspective. Indeed, in recent years, the country's problems have become akin to a bizarre laboratory test tube for Western economists. However, in the midst of this analysis—and "prescriptions" to fix Japan's woes—the *people* behind the financial woes have often been forgotten. Though the country is full of tales such as Homma's, they tend to be swept under the carpet, perhaps because the Japanese prefer to present a neat "face" to the outside world. Yet these tragedies are not mere footnotes to Japan's financial tale; in a sense; they are an essential part of the story, precisely because Japan's "economic" woes are about far more than mere economics, but deeply rooted in cultural, political, and social issues.

So a few months after Homma's death I decided to try to write a book that explored the "people" side of Japan's banking tale, drawing both on my experience in financial journalism and an earlier academic background in social anthropology. The easiest way to tell this complex tale was to focus on one bank, and I chose LTCB/Shinsei, since I had been dealing extensively with the bank since early 1997, and thus already knew it well.

It should be clearly noted that this book does *not* pretend to be an authorized history of LTCB and Shinsei; it has not been approved or initiated by personnel linked to the bank. Indeed, when I informed people linked to the bank's history that I hoped to write a book, many initially reacted with unease or horror. That was understandable: The tale of LTCB and Shinsei has been an emotional one for the key players, and the controversy continues. Yet, in spite of this—entirely understandable—caution, I received an extraordinary degree of help during my research and I am deeply grateful to all concerned. Indeed, I ended up conducting more than 200 interviews around the world, mostly off the record but sometimes on the record as well. Wherever possible, I have offered the key people in the book an opportunity to present their perspective on incidents described; only four people specifically refused. As far as possible, I have tried to base dialogue on "on-the-record" interviews. However, in a few places, I have reconstructed short passages of dialogue from "off-the-record" sources. I realize that some academics might disapprove of this approach. However, this book aims to balance two goals: to create a narrative that makes Japan's opaque financial world as accessible as possible to a non-Japanese audience; and to be generally accurate.

Among the Shinsei-related characters, Timothy C. Collins, J. Christopher Flowers, and Masamoto Yashiro graciously tolerated my endless (albeit sometimes unwelcome) questions and offered on-the-record comments on some issues. Other Shinsei investors and directors offered opinions, including Takashi Imai, Minoru Makihara, Donald Marron, John Reed, David Rockefeller, Jacob Rothschild, Vernon Jordan, and Paul Volcker. At Shinsei itself, the staff of the press office—Yoshihide Nakagawa, Kazumi Kojima, and Connie Marshall—arranged multiple formal interviews with senior bank staff. I am most grateful to them and am aware that this consumed a considerable amount of their time, since they sat through these interviews as well.

Among the former LTCB bankers, Katsunobu Onogi was unfortunately unable to talk to the media in any official capacity after his criminal trial started in 1999. Thus there are no direct comments in the book from him on recent matters. However, I have known Onogi since 1997 and enjoyed numerous conversations on and off the record with him before his trial started (indeed, he was one of the very first people who I ever interviewed as a journalist in Japan). My material draws on these numerous conversations over the years, supplemented by extensive discussions with his friends to explain recent events.

Separately, a large number of former LTCB staff talked to me. Some are reluctant to be highlighted, since they are now in new jobs or enmeshed in legal proceedings. However, I must thank Koji Hirao for offering much wise and thoughtful advice on the history of LTCB and Japan's financial system. Kozo Tabayashi for providing an invaluable memo on the history of LTCB, which influenced early sections of this book; Ryuji Konishi, who also shared some of his insightful memos; and Rikushi Kawakami, an indefatigable and irrepressibly cheerful source of help. Outside LTCB, Shigeo Abe, Robert E. Fallon, and Hiroshi Nakaso provided guidance at critical moments, and Takashi Anzai was extremely helpful in describing his role in the sale of LTCB. Luqman Arnold, Gary Brinson, Vittorio Volpi, and other past and present UBS staff, helped to explain the events of 1997 and 1998; Bob Burns, Bill Kahane, Iwao Nomoto, and Bungo Ishizaki provided their perspective on the "bubble" era.

Outside LTCB, Michiko Homma deserves enormous respect for having the courage to talk about her husband's death; she specifically chose to comment on the record (after checking the quotes with her family) in an effort to improve international understanding of Japan's banking challenges and her husband's sacrifice.

My understanding of the broader policy issues benefited from interviews with Koichi Kato, Masahiko Kuroda, Masaru Hayami, Kiichi Miyazawa, Michio Ochi, Larry Summers, and Hakuo Yanagisawa. In addition to this, I am grateful to dozens of other people who helped in various capacities. These include Jonathan Allum, Kenichi Amano, David Asher, David Atkinson, Gawain Barnard, Peter Baron, Simon Boote, Gavin J. Buckley, Kent E. Calder, Orlando Camargo, Bruce Carnegie Brown, Mark Chiba, Jonathan Colby, D. Ronald Daniels, David de Rosa, Robert S. Dohner, Charles D. Ellis, Robert E. Feldman, James Fiorillo, Graham P. Francis, Yoshi Fujisawa, Mitsuhiro Fukao, Eiji Furukawa, Hirofumi Gomi, Matthew Goodman, William W. Grimes, Takayoshi Hatayama, David Hatt, Karen Hawkins, Deborah Hayden, Brett Hemsley, Andrew L. Herz, Akinari Horii, Takatoshi Ito, Sahoko Kaji, Donald P. Kanak, Masaaki Kanno, Anil K. Kashyap, Richard Katz, Yosuke Kawakami, Ross Kerley, Alex Kinmont, Takeshi Kiuchi, Ted Knetzger, Shoichiro Koike, Jesper Koll, Daisuke Kotegawa, Simon Locke, John MacFarlane, Shun Maeda, Anthony E. Malkin, Mark Mason, Masayuki Matsushima, Hajime Matsuura, Eugene Matthews, Sir Deryck Maughan, Peter McKillop, Yoshihiro Mikami, Henry J. Miller III, Arthur Mitchell, Yoshihiko Miyauchi, Mario Mizukami, Allan F. Munro, Sei Nakai, Naoko Nakamae, Yoshiro Nakamatsu, Tomohiko Nishino, Izumi Nizhizaki, Tetsuro Nishizaki, Shigeo Niwa, Marcus Noland, Mark Norbom, Osamu Odawara, Alicia Ogawa, Michael O'Hanlon, Katsuto Ohno, Kazuhiko Oiwa, Ken Okamura, George Olcott, Nana Otsuki, Hugh Patrick, Thierry Porte, Christopher Purvis, Robin Radin, Nick Reid, Jason Rogers, Wilbur Ross, Ross Rowbury, T. Timothy Ryan, Mark Schwartz, Henry Scott-Stokes, John Seivright, Masahiro Sekino, Cliff Shaw, Paul Sheard, Sakura Shiga, Yasuhisa Shiozaki, Tom Skwarek, Andrew Smithers, Tony Sorrenti, Robert Stenram, Atsushi Takahashi, Yo Takeuchi, Gary Talarico, Peter Tasker, Kiyoshi Tsugawa, John S. Wadsworth, J. Brian Waterhouse, Chris Wells, Charles Whitehead, Martin Whitman, Rikuichi Yoshisue, Hiroshi Yoshitsugu, and Kenji Yoshizawa. It should be stressed that none of these people can be held accountable for information in this book and some valuable sources have chosen to remain completely nameless. I often worked through interpreters in conducting the research and I am intensely conscious that it can be treacherous to translate concepts from Japanese to English; the analysis is mine, and any mistakes rest entirely with me.

While I wandered around the world conducting this research, Laurie Adams, Kay Allaire, Lexy and John Nusbaum, Gwen Robinson, and Merryn Somerset Webb provided hospitality, while Nick Reid spotted helpful quotes. My employer, the *Financial Times,* gave me a sabbatical to pursue this project; Mitsuko Matsutani and Nobuko Juji offered logistical support over the years, while Paul Abrahams, Alexandra Harney, Ken Hijino, David Ibison, Michiyo Nakamoto, David Pilling, and Bayan Rahman were stimulating colleagues. Akiko Nakazawa, Atsuko Imai, Ken Takasu, and Yu Wada conducted research for the book; at various stages, Peter and Romaine Tett, Gwen Robinson, George Olcott, Peter Tasker, Ro Fallon, and Merryn Somerset Webb all read chapters and offered comments. Ian Rodger played a particularly crucial role in the last stages. The staff at Gavin Anderson kindly helped to publicize the book in Japan. My agent, Amanda Urban at ICM, was a source of great inspiration in shaping my nebulous early ideas; Marion Maneker, my editor at HarperCollins, did an excellent job in creating structure out of a complex tale, while Edwin Tan steered me through the logistical complexities of publishing.

Lastly, I have a lifelong debt to Sally Muggeridge and Dr. Oon Teik in Singapore: Without their actions in 2001, I would not have been around to write the book at all. But the final thanks must go to Henry, for all his support and love over the years.

INDEX

Abbey National, 293
Abe, Shintaro, 35, 51
ABN Amro, 175, 177, 285
accounting practices, 66–69, 99, 118, 122–23, 158, 251
AIG, 172, 177
Allianz, 287
American Exim Bank, 13
Anzai, Takashi, 70, 116, 129–30, 146–53, 158, 162, 169
Anzen (safety) credit union, xxii, 72–73, 75, 76, 77
Aozora Bank, xxiv, 222–25, 248, 285
Arakawa, Hidehiko, 201
Arnold, Luqman, 92–93, 94, 97–104, 109, 119–20, 175, 293
Arthur D. Little, 140
Asahi (newspaper), 70, 211, 287
Asahi Breweries, 178
Asao, Keiichiro, 216, 242
Ashikaga Bank, 49
Asian financial crisis, xxii–xxv
asset management services, 9, 95, 103, 114, 175, 192
asset price bubble. *See* bubble
AT Kearney, 92
baburu shinshi (bubble gentlemen), 75
bad loans, xxv, 67–69, 79, 100, 106, 131, 277, 281, 283
  definition of, 313–14
  Japanese estimates, 314–15
  Koizumi and, 260–62
  by LTCB, 79, 81–83, 88, 96, 97, 98–103, 107–8, 116, 118, 123, 158, 173, 275
  Ministry of Finance policy, 88, 90, 107–9, 159–60, 266, 268
  Shinsei and, 207, 227–37, 240–41, 246, 252, 276
bailouts, xxii, 104, 105, 110, 113, 153, 154, 159–60, 165, 248, 253, 262
Banco Santander Central Hispano, 175, 178, 284–285
Bankers Trust, 22, 106, 228
Bank for International Settlements, 62, 266
  LTCB ratio, 110, 111
  Shinsei ratio, 251, 252
Bankgesellschaft, 287
Bank of America, 85–86
Bank of Japan, 54, 94, 104, 155, 282
  Anzai at, 147–48
  bank equity purchases, xxiv, 262–65
  credit unions and, 73

Bank of Japan (*continued*)
discount rate, 19–20
Homma and, 221, 222, 223
interest rates and, xxii, 37, 54–56, 58, 83–84
LTCB inspection by, 63–64, 68–69
Shinsei annual results report to, 250–52, 257
Bank of Nova Scotia, 176
Bank of Tokyo Mitsubishi, xxiii, 152, 172, 202, 257, 282
Bank of Yokohama, 113
bankruptcy, 104–6, 106, 219–20, 233–34, 237, 271, 279
bad loan policies, 313–15
government bailouts, xxii, 104, 105, 110, 113, 153, 154, 159–60, 165, 248, 253, 262
LTCB collapse, xxiii, 4, 109–12, 113–21, 123, 129, 157, 161
banks
bad loan policy, 313
consolidation of. *See* megabanks
deregulation proposal, 89–91
history in Japan, xxi–xxv, 7–12, 14, 22, 92
See also specific banks and bank types
Beach-comber group (hotels), 47
Bear, Stearns, 204
Bible study group (Tokyo), 163–64
"Big Bang" reforms (*Bigu Ban*), xxii, 89–90, 91, 95–96, 109
BIS. *See* Bank for International Settlements
Bond, Alan, 47
Bond, John, 38, 41
Bond Center, 47
bond market, 20, 22, 240, 252, 257
Bond University, 47
Boskin, Michael J., 178–79
Botin, Emilio, 178
Bradock, Rick, xviii
Bridgestone, 13
Brinson (company), 102
Brinson, Gary, 54, 102
BSCH. *See* Banco Santander Central Hispano
BTM. *See* Bank of Tokyo Mitsubishi
bubble, xxii, 28–29, 54–69, 75, 209, 264
burst of, 58, 62–63, 94, 248
Burns, Bob, 41–43, 47, 50, 51
LTCB oversight and, 61–62
Regent hotels sale and, 65–66, 291–92
Bush, George H. W., 136, 262
Bush, George W., 260–61
business entertainment, 51–53, 70, 75–76, 242–43
business promotion, 46, 56, 98

cancellation right, 159–60, 235
capital markets, 8, 21–22, 24, 27, 89–91, 253
BIS tightened adequacy standards, 62
cash flow, 40, 313
"category two" loans, 233, 237
Cerberus, 222, 248–49, 285
Changing Fortunes (Volker and Gyohten), 144
Chase Manhattan Bank, 176
Chuo-Mitsui alliance, 153, 161–62, 164–65
Chuo Trust, 153
Citibank, xviii, xx, 85, 140, 185, 189, 191, 193, 287
Citigroup, 155, 168, 177, 199, 244, 284
Citigroup Japan, 140, 189–91
city banks, 9, 10
Clinton, Bill, xvi, 136, 154–55, 163, 179
Clinton, Hillary Rodham, 154–55
CLO (collateralized loan obligation) program, 253
collateral, 253, 313, 314
property as, 40–41, 138
Collins, Timothy C., xv–xx, 146, 180–82, 287–88, 291
background of, xv–xvi, 135–37, 154–55
Flowers and, 142–43
FSA-Shinsei breach and, 241–43
Japanese opportunities and, xvi–xvii, 137–42, 279–80, 284

Shinsei and, 194, 199, 217–19, 283
yakuza risks and, 225–26
See also Ripplewood
Columbia Music, 288
Columbia Pictures, 50
conglomerates, 11
consumer banking. *See* retail banking
corporate families. *See keiretsu*
corporate restructuring, 85
corruption, 75–76
Corzine, Jon, 142
Council of Economic Advisers, U.S., 261
credit control, 46, 228–31
Crédit Foncier, 7
credit risk, 97, 102. *See also* risky loans
Credit Suisse Financial Products, 122
Credit Suisse First Boston, 66, 67, 93, 121–22, 289
FSA raid on, 122–23
credit unions, 72–78
cross shareholding, 8, 173
CSFB. *See* Credit Suisse First Boston
culture clash, 196–207, 231, 238–40, 249
currency swaps, 22

Daiei, 233–34, 254, 271
Dai-Ichi Hotels, 219
Dai-Ichi Housing, 68
Dai-Ichi Kangyo Bank, xxiii, 10, 152, 220, 232
Daiwa Securities, 149
debenture funding, 252–53, 257
deflation, xxiv, xxv, 261, 264, 277, 281, 313–14
Dell, 206
Deloitte and Touche, 168, 169
Democratic Party of Japan, 114, 115, 133, 211, 242
Denon, 288
Deposit Insurance Corporation, 214, 235
deregulation, xxii, 25–28, 63, 89–91, 95–96, 109
Deutsche Bank, 67, 168, 169, 175, 177, 284
diet. See parliament
discount rate, 19–20
DKB. *See* Dai-Ichi Kangyo Bank
Dorchester Hotel (London), 41
DPJ. *See* Democratic Party of Japan
due diligence, 97, 120–21, 158, 168–69, 218
Dvivedi, "Jay," 198–201, 206

EIE, 29–34, 228, 289, 290
debt servicing, 56
hostile takeover of, 33–34
LTCB loans to, 38, 40–42, 49, 57–59, 71–72
LTCB oversight of, 59–62
oil deals, 47–48
real estate and, 30, 35–43, 46–47
subsidiaries, 73
Takahashi scandal and, 70–78, 104
Electronics and Industrial Enterprises. *See* EIE
Empire State Building, 176
Enstar, 287
entertainment. *See* business entertainment
equity market brokers, 9, 27
Esso Sekiyu, 188
Exxon, Yashiro at, 188–89, 287
Exxon building, 49

Federal Reserve System (U.S.), 130, 143, 144
Financial Institutions Group, 142
Financial Reconstruction Commission, 149, 153, 158, 159, 165, 210, 212
abolition of, 232
Financial Services Agency, 232–37, 264, 267
on banking system health, 281
Shinsei breach with, xxiv, 240–48
Shinsei improved relations with, 270–71
Shinsei inspection by, 235–36
short-selling guidelines and, 247–48
Financial Supervisory Agency, xxiii, 121–22, 149, 153, 155, 232
LTCB inspection and, 168, 170–71, 209

Financial Supervisory Agency (*continued*)
 parliamentary investigation of, 212–16
 Sogo collapse and, 210
First Credit (LTCB affiliate), 231, 271
Fitch (credit rating agency), 282
Fite, David, 180–82, 227–31, 234–35, 258, 271–72
Flexcube, 199–200, 206
Flowers, J. Christopher, 141–45, 156–59, 162, 166–67, 191–92, 216, 217–19, 225–26, 269, 271–72, 284, 287–88, 291
 background of, 141–42
 board creation and, 178–79
 Collins and, 142–43
 FSA meeting and, 242–44
 LTCB bid and, 171–75, 177–78
 Shinsei hiring and, 204, 228, 230
Foley, Thomas, 162, 163–64
foreign exchange controls, 36, 90
Foreign Securities House, The (Takasugi), 269
four-and-a-half-*tatami*-mat system, 20
Four Seasons Hotel (N.Y.C.), 30, 61
Four Seasons hotel group, 66, 292
FRC. *See* Financial Reconstruction Commission
FSA. *See* Financial Services Agency; Financial Supervisory Agency
Fuji Bank, xxiii, 164, 232
Fujisawa, Yoshiyuki, 3
Fujitsu, 199, 206
Fukuda, Kazunori, 119

G7. *See* Group of Seven
gaiatsu (foreign pressure), 134, 162–63
gaijin (foreigners), 13, 92, 104, 111, 120, 149, 169, 194, 239, 271–72, 293
Gambe, Hitomi, 122
GE Capital, 165, 177, 216–17
Gekan Gendai (tabloid), 110
Ghosn, Carlos, 194, 239
Gier, Hans de, 92, 94
giri (obligation), 223
Glass-Steagall Act (U.S.), 9
Goekjian, Chris, 67, 122–23
Goh, Yuriko, 33
Goldman Sachs, xxiii, 93, 141–42, 149–51, 153, 156–57, 164–65, 174, 175, 212–16, 257, 284, 314
government aid. *See* public funds
Grand Magnetics, 33
Greenberg, Maurice "Hank," 172
Greenwich Capital, 27, 30, 91
Grondine, Robert, 250
Group of Seven, 36–37, 130, 132, 134, 135
Gyohten, Toyoo, 144

hagetaka fando. *See* vulture fund
Hamaguchi, Iwane, 7
Hashimoto, Ryutaro, xxii, 89, 105
Hashimoto, Toru, 164
Hatoyama, Yukio, 211
Hayami, Masaru, 155–56, 164, 262–65, 268
Hazama, 219, 220
Hemsley, Brett, 282
Hibiya General Development Group (Hibiya Sogo Kaihatsu), 64–65
HIC. *See* Hotel Investment Corp.
Higuchi, Hirotaro, 162, 178
Hirao, Koji, 24, 27, 29–32, 81, 85
Hitachi, Prince, 242–43
Hokkaido Takushoku, xxiii, 7, 10, 104–5, 106
Homma, Michiko, xxiv, 223, 224–25
Homma, Tadayo, xxiv, 221–25
Hong Kong and Shanghai Banking Corp., 38–40, 41
honne (private truth), 63
Horie, Tetsuya, 56, 76–78, 80
Hotel Investment Corp., 66
hougachou ("encouragement" funding), 74, 94
HSBC. *See* Hong Kong and Shanghai Banking Corp.
Hubbard, Glenn, 261–62, 265, 266, 267
Hyatt group, 38, 47

IBJ. *See* Industrial Bank of Japan
Igarashi, Fumihiko, 215
Ikeda, Hayato, xxi, 8–10, 21, 36, 90
Imai, Takashi, 162, 165, 178, 186
Industrial Bank of Japan, xxiii, 3, 7–8, 10, 21, 152, 232
  LTCB rivalry with, 48
  Sogo restructuring by, 208–9, 210
Industrial Revitalization Corporation, xxv, 267
information technology systems, 198–201, 206
interest rates, xxii, 12, 19–20, 37
  deregulation of, 27, 63
  raising of, 54–56, 58, 83–84
interlocking ownership, 8, 173
international capital adequacy standards, 62
International Finance Review, 240
internationalization, 25, 46–47
International Monetary Fund, 233
internet bubble burst, 248
investment banking, 46, 95, 103, 114, 122
  Shinsei, 192, 203–6, 240, 252, 257–58, 277
investment trusts, 66–67
Ishizaki, Bungo, 37–39, 41, 42, 47, 51–53, 55, 60, 73, 291
Isobe, Asahiko, 268
Iwasawa-san (the "strange"), 34

Japan Airlines (JAL), 35
Japan Lease, 65, 83, 99, 213
Japan Telecom, 288
J. C. Flowers and Co., 142, 217–19
Jordan, Vernon E. Jr., 136, 146, 179–82
J. P. Morgan, 22, 149, 152, 153, 156, 159, 160–61
jusen (small mortgage lenders), 68, 79, 81, 83, 104, 159

Kahane, Bill, 50–51, 62
Kaieda, Banri, 208, 218
Kamei, Shizuka, 211
kashi-tampo (cancellation right), 159–60, 235
Kashyap, Anil, 283, 315
Katayama, Satoru, 202
Kato, Koichi, 130
Katsu-chan. *See* Suzuki, Yoshiharu
Kawabata, Yasunari, 41
Kawasaki Steel, 13
Keidanren (business association), 162, 165, 178, 179, 186, 266
keiretsu (corporate families), 9, 11, 12, 71, 111, 149, 172
Kinmont, Alex, 268–69
kisha club (press cartel), 70–71, 250–52, 257
Kishi, Satoru, 152
Kobayashi, Yasuhiro, 81
Kodama, Yoshio, 211
Kofuku, 285
Koizumi, Junichiro, xxiv, 260–62, 265, 282, 286
Koll, Jesper, 253
Konishi, Ryuji, 57, 82, 88, 106–7, 108, 117, 119
Kumagai Gumi, 169, 219, 220

Landmark Hotel (London), 47
Lazard Frères, 136
LDP. *See* Liberal Democratic Party
Lehman Brothers, 204, 222, 284
lending policy
  long-term credit, 9–11, 19–20, 191–92, 253
  of LTCB, 170–71
  real estate market and, 40–41
  of Shinsei, 209–10, 231–37, 243, 246, 252, 272–73
  See also bad loans; risky loans
Liberal Democratic Party, xxii, 27, 35, 63, 75, 105, 114, 115, 130, 133, 155, 158, 159, 186
  Collins and, 242
  Sogo collapse and, 210–11
  strategy paper, 238, 248
  Takenaka reform and, 267
Life (finance company), 216–17, 219, 235, 240–41, 242

LIMCO (LTCB subsidiary), 95
loans. *See* bad loans; lending policy; risky loans
Lonestar, 285
Long Term Capital Management, 133, 293
Long Term Credit Bank, 7–22, 286
accounting practices, 64–66, 68–69, 158
bad loans, 79, 81–83, 88, 96, 97, 98–103, 107–8, 116, 118, 123, 158, 173, 275
Bank of Japan inspection of, 63–64, 68–69
BIS ratio, 110, 111
blackmailing of, 111–12
chronology, xxi–xxv
civil suits against, 289
collapse of, xix–xx, xxiii, 4, 109–12, 113–21, 115, 123, 129–30, 157, 161
credit unions rescue by, 74, 76
criminality at, 274–75
Dai-Ichi Housing and, 68
derivatives and, 114–15, 133, 168
EIE loans made by, 38, 40–42, 57–59, 71–72
EIE oversight by, 59–62
employment culture of, 25, 125–26
Flowers and, 142–45, 171–75, 177–78
FSA inspection of, 168, 170–71, 209
Hirao and, 29–32
IBJ rivalry with, 48
internationalists and, 26, 57, 79, 81
market-based banking transition by, xxii, 21–27, 45–46
Ministry of Finance inspection of, xxii, 98–99
Mizukami reform plan for, 23, 24–26, 79
name change, 185, 281. *See also* Shinsei
nationalization of, xxiii, 115–16, 129, 133–35, 143, 147, 148, 157, 209
Onogi and, 3–7, 14–22, 27, 44–46
Onogi as president of, 70, 78–80, 81–84, 86–89
origins of, 7–9, 10
Phoenix Plan and, 113
police raid on, 118–19
real estate market and, 40–41, 44–46, 168
reform plan (1985), xxii, 23, 24–26, 79, 81, 84
Ripplewood and, xxiii, 129, 130, 140, 150, 151, 153–65, 167–68, 171–78, 194, 209–10, 212, 215, 245
risk management by, 82
SBC alliance, 92–96, 97–104, 106, 109
subsidiaries of, 64–66, 97, 121, 213
Sumitomo Trust alliance with, 113–14, 117, 119–20, 130, 148, 232
Takahashi scandal and, 76–80
traditionalists at, 26–27, 28, 57
triple-A rating of, 30, 98
UBS alliance with, 109, 113, 119–20
long-term credit banks, 9–11, 19–20, 191–92, 253
loss-sharing, 158–59
LTCB. *See* Long Term Credit Bank
LTCB Warburg, 110

macroeconomics, 57–58, 278
Mainichi (newspaper), 113, 269
Makihara, Minoru, 138–39, 171–72, 178
Malkin family, 176
Mano, Atsushi, 186
Manufacturers Hanover, 14
Marantz, 288
Marron, Donald B., 176–77, 178, 284–85
Masakado, Taira no, 12–13, 195
Masuzawa, Takao, 80
Matsuda, Noboru, 214, 215
Matsukata, Masayoshi, 7, 14
Matsushita, 50
Maughan, Deryck, 155, 199
MCA, 50
McDonaugh, William, 130
McGuinn, Martin G., 178
McKinsey Co., 139–40
megabanks, xxiii, xxv, 232, 233, 251, 266, 268, 281
Meiji era banking, 7, 9, 14, 22, 92

Meiji Restoration, xxi, 45
Mellon Bank, 175, 177, 178, 284
merchant banks, 14–15, 21, 27, 83, 89
Merrill Lynch, 67, 253, 258, 283, 284
MHL (British merchant bank), 14–15, 21
Midland Bank (Britain), 14
Ministry of Finance, 12, 13, 46, 59, 63, 94, 113, 152
  administrative guidance by, 87–88
  bad loans policy, 88, 90, 107–9, 159–60, 266, 268
  bond market and, 20, 22
  corruption and, 75
  credit unions and, 73
  deregulation and, 26–28, 90
  inspection of LTCB, xxii, 98–99, 275
  reporting standards and, 67–69
  Takahashi and, 52, 71
  Takenaka policy and, 267
  Volker and, 143–44
Mitsubishi Corporation, xvi–xvii, 11, 49, 138–39, 171–72, 178
  Rockefeller Center purchase, 32, 49–50
Mitsubishi Tokyo Financial Group, 232, 287
Mitsui Trust Bank, xxiii, 11, 49, 153, 161–62, 232
Miyazawa, Kiichi, 133, 135, 144, 146, 155, 162–64, 170, 242
Mizuho, xxiii, xxv, 232, 233, 251, 266, 281
Mizukami, Mario, 23–27, 78–79, 108
  Onogi rivalry, 24, 45
Mizushima, Hiroo, 209, 211
Mochida, Masanori, 213
Moody's rating, 30
Morgan Stanley, 50–51, 62, 65, 67, 94, 149, 244, 257, 281, 288
Mori, Hidebumi, 196
Mori, Shoji, 214–17, 232–34, 237, 256, 270
Morningstar, 85
Mycal, 237

Nakai, Sei, 104, 117
Nakamatsu, Yoshiro, 33–34
Nakanishi, Keisuke, 75, 76
Nakaso, Hiroshi, 115
national debt, 20, 277–78
nationalization, 265, 266, 282
  of LTCB, xix, xxiii, 115–16, 129, 133–35, 143, 147, 148, 157, 209
NCB. *See* Nippon Credit Bank
NED (LTCB subsidiary), 65, 99
nemawashi (consensus process), 200
New LTCB Partners, 178, 217–19
newspaper industry, 70–71
New York Federal Reserve Bank, 130
Nichiryoku, 250, 254–55
Niebuhr, Reinhold, 264
Nihon Building, 219
Nikkei (newspaper), 70
Nikkei 225, xxii, xxiii, xxiv, xxv, 36, 54, 58, 62, 161, 247, 266, 281–82
Nikko Salomon Smith Barney, 149, 155, 177, 268–69, 281
Nikko Securities, 109, 172
Niles Parts (auto supplier), 287, 288
ninjo (human relations), 223
Nippon Columbia, 286
Nippon Credit Bank, xxii, xxiii, xxiv, 10, 94, 104, 121, 213, 215, 221, 222
Nippon Kangyo Bank, xxi, 7–8, 10
Nippon Landic, 65, 99, 213
Nippon Shinpan, 169
Nippon Steel, 178, 186
Nishizaki, Tetsuro, 63, 69
Nissan, xxiii, 154, 194, 239, 254
Nissho Iwai, 263
NKB. *See* Nippon Kangyo Bank
Nomoto, Iwao, 37, 46–47, 49, 60, 291
Nomoto, Takumi, 214
Nomura, 27, 213, 281
nonperforming loans (NPLs). *See* bad loans
no-pan shabu shabu (entertainment place), 52, 70
Nozawa, Shohei, 105
NR (LTCB subsidiary), 64–65
NTT (telecommunications group), 213

Obuchi, Keizo, 154–55, 162
Ochi, Michio, 164, 170, 247, 248–49, 251
Ohmae, Kenichi, 274
oil deals, 47–48
Okana, Michiyuki, 200, 206
Okuda, Hiroshi, 266
omiai (marriage introduction), 92
Onex (Canadian equity fund), 136
Onogi, Katsunobu, xix–xx, 118, 120, 123–25, 220, 259, 289
  arrest and prosecution of, 3–5, 123–26, 274–75
  early career of, 10–14
  education of, 5–7
  at LTCB (England), 14–17
  at LTCB (Tokyo), 18–22, 27, 44–46
  LTCB-SBC alliance and, 92–96, 98–102, 103–4, 106, 109
  Mizukami rivalry, 24, 45
  as president of LTCB, 70, 78–80, 81–84, 86–92, 111–12, 118, 185, 193, 267
  sentencing of, 274–75, 282
  Suzuki and, 57
  view of Shinsei, 275–76
Onogi, Yasuko, 15–16, 123–126
Orix (leasing firm), 152, 222
Ota, Seichi, 35
Otemachi (Tokyo financial district), xxi, 12, 12–13, 44, 195
Ozawa, Ichiro, 35, 76
Ozeki, Koyo, 258–59

Paine Webber, 176, 177, 178, 284
Paribas, 67, 93, 149, 152, 153
parliament
  investigation of Shinsei, xxiv, 212, 214–19, 226, 241
  investigation of Takahashi, 76–78
Paulson, Henry, 213
Peer's, 27
Pei, I. M., 30–31, 43, 61
pension funds, 120
Phoenix Plan, 113
Phoenix Seagaia, 288
"Plaza accord," xxii
prime lending rate, 19–20
Prince, Brian, 204–6, 256, 260, 273, 283
private banking, 95, 103
profitability, xxiv, xxv, 25, 251–52, 283, 284
property prices, 40. *See also* real estate market
Publica (Toyota car), 13
public funds
  for bailouts, xxii, 104, 105, 110, 113, 153, 154, 159–60, 165, 248, 253, 262
  Shinsei IPO and, 244
  Sogo collapse and, 211
  as Takenaka reform policy, 265
"put" (refund right option)
  Goldman Sachs and, 214–16
  LTCB sale and, xxiii, 159–61, 165, 168, 174
  Shinsei and, xxv, 210, 214–16, 227, 235, 240, 241, 243, 244, 246, 252, 258, 270, 276, 277
  "yakuza," 225–26

Quayle, Dan, 222, 284

Rainwater, Richard, 136
Raj, Janak, 198
rate of return, 49
RCC. *See* Resolution and Collection Corporation
real estate market, 28, 30, 35–37, 44–46, 49–51, 209
  as bank loan collateral, 40–41, 44–46, 168
  EIE and, 30, 35–43, 46–47
  NCB and, 222
  price drops, xxii, 62, 73, 81
Reed, John, xviii, 189–91, 193, 227, 238–41, 259, 276–77
refund right option. *See* "put"

Regent Hotel Group
  Burns sale of, 65–66, 289, 291
  LTCB oversight of, 61
  Takahashi and, 39, 41–42, 47, 50
regional banks, 7, 9, 113, 284
Renault, xxiii, 154
Resolution and Collection Corporation, 158, 170, 219–20, 225
Resolution and Trust Corporation (U.S.), 177
Resona Holdings bank, 282, 285
retail banking, 189–91, 201–3, 206–7, 230, 240, 252–53, 257, 277
RHJ. *See* Ripplewood Holdings Japan
Ripplewood, xvii, xix, xxiii, 285, 292
  founding of, xv–xvi, 135, 136–37
  Japanese operations, 137–41
  LTCB sale and, xxiii, 129, 130, 150–66, 167–68, 171–78, 191–92, 194, 209–10, 212, 215, 245, 279
  New LTCB Partners and, 178
  Shinsei and, 196–97, 204, 217–19, 284
  Shinsei IPO and, 243–46, 285, 286
  "*yakuza* put" and, 225–26
  Yashiro and, 191–93
Ripplewood Holdings Japan, 139, 287
risky loans, 68–69, 82, 83, 98–99, 107–8, 109
ritual suicide, 4, 6, 107
Rockefeller, David, 129, 176, 178, 242–44
Rockefeller Center, 32, 49–50
Ross, Wilbur, 149, 285
Rothschild, Jacob, 175–76, 179
Rubin, Robert, 174, 179
Russian debt default, 133
ryotei (traditional restaurant), 51

St. James Place Capital, 175
Saipan Hyatt, 38
Sakai, Mamoru, 18
Sakakibara, Eisuke, 100, 132–33
Salomon Brothers, 22
Salomon Smith Barney, 109
samurai bankers, 5–6, 17, 32, 126
Sanctuary Cove resort, 47, 228
Sanwa Bank, xxiii, 152, 232
Sanyo Securities, xxiii, 105
Savings and Loans collapse (U.S.), 85, 120, 131, 177, 262
SBC. *See* Swiss Bank Corporation
Scandinavia, 69, 131–32
Schwartz, Mark, 212
Seiyo (real estate group), 219
Sengoku, Yoshito, 214–15
seppuku (ritual suicide), 4, 6, 107
7-Eleven, 202
SG Warburgs, 92
Sharpe, Isadore, 292
Sheehy, Robert, 204–5, 253
Shinsei, xxiii, 129, 177, 275
  annual results report, 250–52, 257
  bad loans and, xxiv, 207, 227–37, 240–41, 258–59, 276
  BIS ratio, 251, 252
  clients, 254–55
  CLO program, 253
  corporate planning department, 197–98
  credit control, 228–31
  culture clash at, 196–207, 231, 238–40, 249
  debenture funding, 252–53
  FSA and, 235–36, 240–48, 270–71
  Hayami policy and, 268
  human resources department, 197–98
  Indian executives, 198–201, 249
  information technology systems, 198–201, 206
  lending policy, 209–10, 231–37, 243, 246, 252, 272–73
  loan book turnaround, xxiv, 269–70, 276–77
  loan portfolio in bond market, 240, 252, 257
  logo, 185
  opening of, 185–86
  parliamentary investigation of, xxiv, 212, 214–19, 226, 241

Shinsei (*continued*)
profitability of, xxiv, xxv, 283, 284
"put" option and, xxiii, xxv, 210, 214–16, 227, 235, 240, 241, 243, 244, 246, 252, 258, 270, 276, 277
retail banking, 189–91, 201–3, 206–7, 230, 240, 252–53, 257, 277
Ripplewood IPO for, 243–46, 285, 286
Sogo debt forgiveness and, 208–11
Takenaka policy and, 268
Yashiro strategy for, 192–95, 227–37, 251, 256, 275, 276–77, 281
Shiroyama, Saburo, 125
short-selling guidelines, FSA and, 247–48
Shukan Gendai (tabloid), 75
small mortgage lenders, 68, 79, 81, 83, 104, 159
Softbank, 213, 215, 222, 248, 285
Sogo (retailer), 83, 85, 169
debt forgiveness request by, xxiv, 208–11, 219, 271
sokaiya (blackmailers), 111–12
Son, Masayashi, 248
Sony, 50, 202
specialized banks, 9–10
Standard and Poor's rating, 30, 258
Starbucks, 202, 207
stock market, 21-22, 62, 63. *See also* Nikkei 225
Structural Reform of the Japanese Financial Market; towards the Revival of the Tokyo Market by the Year 2001, 89
subsidiaries
bank provision for, 99–102
of EIE, 73
of LTCB, 64–66, 97, 121, 213
Ministry of Finance bad loan measurement, 107–8
Suda, 123, 124, 274
Sugiura, Binsuke, 23, 38, 79
suicide, 4, 6, 107, 113
of Uehara, 4, 116–17, 119
Sumitomo Electric, 186
Sumitomo-Mitsui, xxiii, 232, 233, 257, 284
Sumitomo Trust, xxiii, 11, 49, 152, 220
alliance with LTCB, 113–14, 117, 119–20, 130, 148, 232
Summers, Lawrence, 130–34, 162, 163
Suzuki, Tsuneo, 71
Suzuki, Yoshiharu, 101, 256
criminal case against, 123
as Onogi ally, 57
Onogi bad loan book and, 79, 80, 82, 84, 88, 98, 107, 118, 123
power of, 56–58
Takahasi loans and, 56–58
trial and sentencing of, 124, 274
Swiss Bank Corporation, 92–96, 97–104, 106, 109, 167–68, 175, 192, 292–93
Sydney Hyatt, 39

Tabayashi, Kozo, 86
tabloids, 70–71, 75, 224
Takagi, Shokichi, 270
Takahashi, Harunori, 29–44, 290, 291
arrest of, 77–78, 289
art deals and, 55
buying spree by, 47–53
entertaining by, 51–53, 70
scandal, 70–78, 104
Suzuki loans to, 56–59
Takahashi, "the older," 33–34
Takasugi, Ryo, 269
Takenaka, Heizo, xxiv, 265–69, 270, 273
Tamiwa, Takei, 196, 197
tatari (curse), 13
tatemae (public reality), 63
Teramura, Hisayoshi, 250, 255
Third Avenue Value Fund, 120–21
Thomas, Sajeeve, 198–99, 202, 203, 206
Tokai Bank, xxiii, 232
Tokio Marine and Fire, 165, 172, 222
tokkin (investment trusts), 66–67
Tokyo Electric Power, 13
Tokyo Kyodo, 74
Tokyo Kyowa, xxii, 72–73, 75, 76, 77

Tokyo Metropolitan Government, 73
Tokyo Sowa, 285
Tokyo Stock Exchange, 9, 21–22, 33, 62, 99, 244
Tokyu, 41
Toray, 13
Toshiba, 13
Toyoda, Tatsuro, 186
Toyota, 13, 14, 16, 19, 186, 266
Treasury, U.S., 241–42
Trump, Donald, 31
trust banks, 9, 113–14
Tsushima, Yuji, 164, 186
Tsutsumi brothers, 35

UBS. *See* Union Bank of Switzerland
Uehara, Takashi, 24, 84–85, 101, 108, 109, 118
 suicide of, 4, 116–17, 119
UFJ (megabank), 232, 266, 284
Union Bank of Switzerland, 67, 222, 292–93
 LTCB alliance, 109, 113, 119–20
 Swiss Bank Corporation merger, 106
Uniqlo, 202

Vietnam oil deal, 47–48
Volcker, Paul, 142–45, 146-48, 155–56, 162, 166, 170, 179, 222, 246–47
Volpi, Vittorio, 92–93, 94, 97–104, 109, 292–93
vulture funds, xvi, 137, 150, 152, 153, 161, 167, 269

wa (group harmony), 24, 45–46, 80
Wall Street Journal, 237
Warner, Ty, 292
Weber, Max, 123
Westpac, 228
Wharf (Hong Kong-based company), 66
Wheat, Allen, 67, 122
Whitman, Martin, 120–21
World Bank, 228

yakuza (gangsters), 26, 71, 75, 111, 211
 Homma's death and, 221–26
"*yakuza* put," 225–26
Yamaguchi, Toshio, 35, 44, 73, 75, 76, 78
Yamaichi Securities, xxiii, 27, 105, 106
Yamamoto, Teruaki, 256–57, 273
Yanagisawa, Hakuo, 155, 165, 170, 232, 242–44, 249, 265, 270
Yashiro, Masamoto, xviii–xx, xxiii, 29, 140–41, 150–51, 155, 157, 162, 165, 166–67, 288–89
 background of, 186–90
 board creation, 178–79
 bodyguard for, 225–26
 at Exxon, 188–89, 287
 fund raising for LTCB bid, 171–78
 Homma and, 223–24, 226
 on Japan's economic future, 277–79
 Mori and, 237
 parliamentary investigation and, xxiv, 212, 216–19, 226, 241
 Reed and, 238–41, 259
 report to Bank of Japan, 250–52, 257, 258
 as Shinsei CEO, xxiii, 185–86, 191–95, 197–203, 275
 Shinsei strategy of, 192–95, 227–37, 251, 270–71, 275, 276–77, 283, 286
 Sogo debt forgiveness and, 208–10, 271
Yasuda Fire and Marine, 50
yo-jo-han-taike system, 20
Yomiuri (newspaper), 70

Za Gaishi (The Foreign Securities House) (Takasugi), 269
zaibatsu (conglomerates), 11
Zeckendorf, William, 42
Zelnick, Strauss, 288

Author photo © Ashley Ashwood / *Financial Times*

Gillian Tett was trained as a social anthropologist but became a journalist while doing field work in Soviet Central Asia during the fall of communism in Russia. Since that time, she has risen through the ranks of the *Financial Times,* holding positions on its economic desk before becoming the bureau chief in Japan. She now lives in London.